THE WAY WE WERE

THE WAY

CARROLL & GRAF PUBLISHERS INC.
NEW YORK

WE WERE

1963
THE YEAR KENNEDY WAS SHOT

EDITED BY ROBERT MacNEIL

Design: ROGERS SEIDMAN DESIGN TEAM
Photo Research: STANLEY P. FRIEDMAN
Research: BILL ADLER, JR.
Interviews: CAROL DANA
Concept: BILL ADLER

Publisher's Note: Most of the interviews quoted here were done for this book and have not before appeared in print. Except where necessary the interviewees are identified as they were in 1963.

Carroll & Graf Publishers, Inc.
260 Fifth Avenue
New York, NY 10001

Library of Congress Cataloging-in-Publication Data

The Way We Were.

1. United States—History—1961-1969.
2. Kennedy, John F. (John Fitzgerald), 1917-1963—
Assassination.   I. MacNeil, Robert, 1931-
E841.W37   1988   973.922   88-18885
ISBN 0-88184-433-0

Type composition by Trufont Typographers, Inc.
Printed and bound by Horowitz/Rae Book Manufacturers, Inc.
Manufactured in the United States of America

CONTENTS

"I was in a Social Studies class at Woodlands High School. . . . In the corridor, I saw Mr. Courtney, the art teacher, sobbing against the wall, and I was astonished that a grown-up, a teacher, would be so openly upset. Kennedy was the first important person in my life to die. . . . Months after he died, I realized one night in bed that I would never hear his voice again, and I sobbed for a long time. I didn't cry when he was shot, but I cried then."

BONNIE STEINBOCK, High School Senior, White Plains, New York

INTRODUCTION

The earth is constantly bombarded by radiation from space—invisible particles of fallout from the nuclear fire on the sun. Some go around us and pass on, while others land on the earth and dissipate. But one particle appears to go through the earth; it penetrates so deeply that, to study it, scientists have to place sensors in the deepest mines.

The news of the Kennedy assassination was like that particle. It seemed to flash not just around the earth, but through it: a particle of news with cosmic penetration. It made John F. Kennedy an instant global myth.

In any other age, the Kennedy story would have been a local legend, told and retold, sifting gradually through the generations. His life and death bore the marks that have always turned heroes into legends and legends into myths—stories so powerful that they flow eventually into the underground river of human consciousness.

But Kennedy's legend flew on wings of modern technology and publicity that make the classical metaphors of power and speed—the sun's chariot, Mercury's winged feet—almost literally true. Technology concentrated the terrible facts of November 22, 1963, into a beam of instant global intelligence. It was probably the first piece of news ever that virtually all people heard and all felt personally. People say: "I remember feeling as if the world had stopped," or "I was scared and homesick." For the first time many children saw adults crying. Twenty-five years later we still weep to be reminded.

A woman I know in her early 50s, a successful writer, always appears cheerful and self-possessed. She is solicitous about the pain in others' lives, but laughs away any hint of pain in hers. She is smart, ironic and controlled.

One evening recently I was describing this book and, as everyone does, she remembered how and where she heard about the assassination.

She said: "It's funny. My mother and father were Republicans. They didn't even like Kennedy very much. But when a memorial service was held at the

Presbyterian church, they felt they had to go. They had to do something." As she said "something," she began to cry at the restaurant table. I had never seen her cry. My wife has known her since childhood and says she cries very seldom. Our friend was astonished to find herself crying in public over the Kennedy assassination.

I was in Dallas on November 22, 1963, a reporter in the motorcade when the shots were fired. It was the biggest story I will ever cover, an indelible day professionally and personally. On reading and editing the interviews in this book, I have repeatedly found my eyes filling with tears.

Why is it so powerful a trigger, so direct a key into our emotions, and why does the mourning persist? Our lives have moved on a whole generation since that day, yet a glance at one of these photographs can dissolve our composure. Why is that?

In this book, we look at the persistent power of that grief through the eyes of many people, some who were very close to Kennedy, many who were not. A psychologist tells us that we are mourning our own unfulfilled promise, that people "may cry at the loss of their own dream and the sadness of time itself." Many others, from all walks of American life, describe the effect of Kennedy's personality and his death on them.

That is one theme. Another is the time itself. The shock of hearing that news made a permanent psychological marker in time, emotionally separating time before the assassination from time after, and perhaps warping our memories of the time before.

The force of myth makes us want to bend that time, to project back onto *time before* the feelings Kennedy inspired and the idealism many felt; to put a morning light on the landscape of 1963.

Irresistibly to some it is a turning point: the moment the first ominous minor chord darkened the music of American life for our generation, bringing its first intimations of vulnerability, the first of a long series of blows to the American psyche and self-esteem.

And that is our main purpose: by re-illuminating those moments, to examine life 25 years ago, to re-create the context that made Kennedy's death so unbelievable.

In its fundamental patterns, perhaps, the way Americans live has changed little; yet in a host of material ways and attitudes, 1963 was a different world. Many of the changes that advertisers and journalists like to call "revolutions" had not happened, or were just about to happen. *Time before* was before the computer revolution, the environmental movement, the health and fitness craze, the black revolution, gay liberation, and the women's liberation movement.

In 1963 American women, including college coeds, still wore stockings with garter belts: pantyhose had not arrived. Many wore girdles and, Betty

Friedan claims, wore them on their minds. That was the year she published *The Feminine Mystique* and lit the fuse of women's liberation. You had not yet come a long way, baby. Virginia Slims and *Ms.* did not exist, and *Cosmopolitan* was a magazine your grandmother could read without shock. Diapers were still cloth, and women took washing them for granted.

For many middle-class women, menopause was considered a serious medical problem, often treated by hysterectomy. It made them feel old and finished at 50. One doctor who treated many such women, says, "It was an epidemic." Since Women's Lib it has largely disappeared.

Other material differences reflected different assumptions. Most striking is the absence of many anxieties that govern our behavior today.

Americans drove big cars that flattered their egos and happily guzzled cheap gas. A station wagon that drank a gallon every eight miles concerned no one, because the gallon cost only 21 cents and a shortage was unimaginable. The oil crisis was a decade away, so there were no EPA fuel consumption standards. There was no EPA until 1970. The small-car era had not arrived, except for British sports cars and VW Beetles, cult vehicles for people who wanted to be conspicuously different. Energy anxiety had not arrived, nor the impetus to insulate and conserve and promote new fuels.

Americans did not have the anxieties about safety that have generated entire industries in response. Safety was not a quality considered in cars. No bells or taped voices nagged drivers about seat belts; no talking crash dummies appeared on TV. The government did not impose crash-resistance specifications. Safety features like radial tires and disk brakes were for fancy European imports. The earthquake Ralph Nader caused in Detroit with *Unsafe at Any Speed* was still three years away. There were no emission controls, because concern for the environment was just dawning with the publication of Rachel Carson's *Silent Spring* in 1962. There was no unleaded gasoline, because the deadly effects of breathed-in lead on human brains was not an issue.

We still innocently installed asbestos in the ceilings of schools. Chemical firms and factories dumped toxic wastes without hindrance, and we generally treated rivers like sewers. PCPs were initials that meant nothing. Farmers prospered with the new range of chemical fertilizers, insecticides, and fungicides, and Vietnam had yet to give defoliation a bad name.

The Surgeon General issued his first tentative report on the harm in smoking, but Americans smoked on without anxiety.

We ate guiltlessly. Beef, heavily marbled with fat, was the ultimate American food, and the dairy industry made the heavy consumption of milk, eggs, and cheese sound like a constitutional duty.

Coronary disease was the number one killer, but cholesterol was not yet a public enemy. Nor had medicine provided the relief from heart disease that it

offers now. My father died at 53 after four heart attacks. Today he might well have been given 20 more years of life through better diagnosis, unclogged arteries, bypass surgery, or even a transplant. All were medically impossible in 1963, like other procedures we now take for granted.

The CATscan, for example, could not be invented because the computer capacity did not exist. In 1963 there were an estimated 4,200 computers in the United States, compared with 5,500,000 today. You practically had to be a Fortune 500 company to afford one of the big primitive machines, because the microchip, which brought the breakthrough in smaller, affordable computers, had not arrived.

Telephones still had dials, a few Touch-Tone pushbuttons began appearing in 1963.

The communications miracles that created the "global village" were similarly just about to happen. Early in 1963 I was present at Plumeur Boudou, France, for the first transatlantic television picture transmission by satellite to Europe. In television news, we still shot 16 mm black-and-white film, which usually took 24 hours of shipping, processing, and editing to reach the screen. Network news was only fifteen minutes long until September 1963. NBC's *Huntley-Brinkley Report* and the *CBS Evening News with Walter Cronkite* were very sober, plain, "talking head" shows. Pictures were scarce, graphics almost nonexistent, and stories without visuals would seem very long today.

The pace of all television was more deliberate, because seconds of network time had yet to become so valuable that they forced commercials to become shorter and shorter, in turn dictating a faster pace for the television entertainment and news programs, even movies. The shortcuts in cinematographic logic necessary to compress the commercials created new standards of visual literacy. Viewed through today's eyes, the programs of 1963 seem slow and, significantly, quieter. It is as though over 25 years we have collectively grown more impatient and hard of hearing. Television was not the visual and audible assault it is now. To get back to the feeling of that time, you would have to unwind the cultural mainspring a little: down from Dan Rather's tension setting to Walter Cronkite's.

Drinking patterns were different. People drank gin, Scotch, bourbon (vodka was still exotic), and beer, but no light beer, and relatively little wine. You did not see Perrier in the U.S.

For the Middle American (a term not yet invented), eating out was a rare event. *Fast food* was an uncoined term, because chains like McDonald's were only beginning, as were all the chains that now dominate the retail landscape—Benetton, Waldenbooks, David's Cookies, and Century/21 Realtors. As a woman in Wisconsin says, the "homogenization of America" had not happened.

There was no exercise anxiety. Americans hated death, denied death, and spent lavishly on funerals; but they had not been gripped by today's frantic illusion that diet and exercise will make death go away. (Did all the killings of the 60s make us deny death more?) There was no jogging and little walking. The suburbs killed walking, because they were built for cars. If you walked, someone would stop and ask what was the matter.

Tennis was a tiny, elite sport, undiscovered by television. Football was played on real grass, not Astroturf, and players got mud and grass stains on their uniforms. There was life without a Superbowl.

What may strike the reader of this book just as forcibly as all these material differences is the spirit of hope and optimism that rings through the feelings Americans had, and retain, about that time—and attribute to Kennedy.

"He seemed to represent the promise of America."

"He gave hope—and a personal connection to hopeful politics."

"What he symbolized was the possibility that we could do anything."

Those are the views of three psychologists whom we quote at length. A woman who knew Kennedy well put the difference between then and now more starkly: "In 1963 we still believed you could fix things."

That was part of the optimism. It was the year in which two fundamental problems, racism and the cold war, began to appear fixable. Each problem gave Americans nightmares, and the country craved release from the anxieties. In that sense, history turned a little better in 1963.

It is a measure of the distance we have travelled to realize that a whole group of American citizens were known by a different name then: Negroes, not blacks.

White America could not ignore the marches and demonstrations, police beatings and jailings, fire hoses and police dogs that marked that spring and summer. Television, just feeling its journalistic power, forced the nation to witness and feel the outrage of the blacks. The sight of a black youth swept across a Birmingham street by the fierce jet of a fire hose made their common humanity inescapable. To many it felt as though America was coming apart. In fact, it was beginning to come together, as the March on Washington showed in August, when hundreds of thousands of blacks and whites joined to hear Martin Luther King, Jr., demand the overdue installments of equality. The vast and peaceful assembly moved the nation to hope. It gave blacks, as one tells us, "a sense of new life," and it lifted some guilt from the shoulders of well-disposed whites.

Kennedy, mindful of his thin credit balance with Congress, was cautious, but eventually he embraced the inevitable, with more fervor than any president since Lincoln. Many believe that it took the shock of his death to

pass the Civil Rights Bill, but in late 1963 a feeling of amelioration was in the air.

There was a similar feeling about the cold war. After two chilling showdowns over Berlin and Cuba, Kennedy and Khrushchev seemed disposed to deal on a new basis. Kennedy proclaimed that war was not inevitable and signed a treaty banning most nuclear tests. For many that was a moment of hope, an opening to new possibilities.

Moves to "fix" the race problem and the risks of the nuclear age also contributed to a feeling (except among Kennedy opponents) that government was competent and trustworthy. George McGovern sees it as a time when "government was the agent, not the enemy."

That feeling was reinforced by Kennedy's ability to make public service seem worthy, almost noble. Arthur Schlesinger, Jr., says Kennedy "sensed there were great reserves of idealism in the American people," and he had the gifts to tap them.

The news media shared the spirit. It was the time Before the Fall, before government appeared as the great deceiver, before the media turned aggressively negative and assumed that government was dishonest until proved otherwise. Despite serious disillusionment over the Bay of Pigs, the press was more disposed to take government on trust than it is today.

There were other reasons for the atmosphere of greater trust that colored relations between government and people. The belief Kennedy encouraged that the world could be changed had not yet run aground in Vietnam. A soldier who was there in 1963 tells us that "Vietnam was still make-believe," a singularly apt metaphor. It is difficult to put ourselves back in the pre-Vietnam mind-set as it would have been for someone in 1888 to imagine the innocence before the Civil War. To understand 1963, you have to undo Vietnam; you have to unimagine 55,000 dead Americans.

Americans had none of the later reasons to question the faith they invested in their institutions, government and private: they believed that lawyers fought for justice, schools educated, doctors healed, ministers saved, and police protected. People felt safer in the streets and in their homes. The great fear of crime was still an infant.

In short, there was enormous faith in the system. The months before Kennedy died may have been the high-water mark of America's faith in itself, its way of life, its ability to help the world, the integrity of its public officials and institutions.

Most of the horrors that cracked that faith—war, riots, assassinations, Watergate—did not happen for several years, but many people still date the nation's discouragement from the shooting in Dallas. They say things like:

"Something died in the American spirit."

"It quashed the illusion that we could do anything."

"It was a very bleak dawn, and it's never been the same."

A century before, in the poem *"Dover Beach,"* Matthew Arnold described the emptiness left by the decline of faith as a tide running out:

> The sea of faith
> Was once, too, at the full . . .
> But now I only hear
> Its melancholy, long, withdrawing roar,
> Retreating, to the breath
> Of the night wind down the vast edges drear
> And naked shingles of the world.

That is how many Americans feel about the depletion of spirit after November 1963. Many others, of course, do not. Nevertheless, the strength of the Kennedy myth is such that many think that, had he lived, the horrors would not have come. They believe, for example, that he would have had the sense to get out of Vietnam earlier. Others believe he was committed to a successful outcome. You will find both arguments here.

What is less dramatic, less exhilarating, to accept is that reality would have imposed some curbs on American confidence, even if Kennedy had lived. The soaring hubris of his inaugural—"we shall pay any price, bear any burden, meet any hardship"—had already been chastened, the capacity to impose a Pax Americana already questioned. Despite the rhetoric, the Berlin Wall had meant compromise, and the American sense of invulnerability had been shaken by the Cuban missile crisis. But many Americans invested so heavily in Kennedy that the later defeats all seemed due to his absence.

Shirley Williams, the President of Britain's Social Democratic Party, told an audience at Harvard's John F. Kennedy School of Government in 1986:

> You are now moving from your youth to your middle age. You find it very hard to accept being middle-aged. Your middle age dates from the war in Vietnam, from discovering that the United States was after all vulnerable, was . . . after all capable of being defeated, was after all—dare I say it to my old friends—just occasionally morally ambivalent like all the rest of us.

Perhaps that is where part of the power of the Kennedy myth lives: in the regret that youth must turn into middle age, with its inevitable acceptance of limitations and of dreams beginning to be foreclosed. Individuals usually shake that off for the compensating clarity of vision and insight that come with maturity. But the emotions this 25th anniversary provoke show that the nation is still living with its regret.

ROBERT MacNEIL

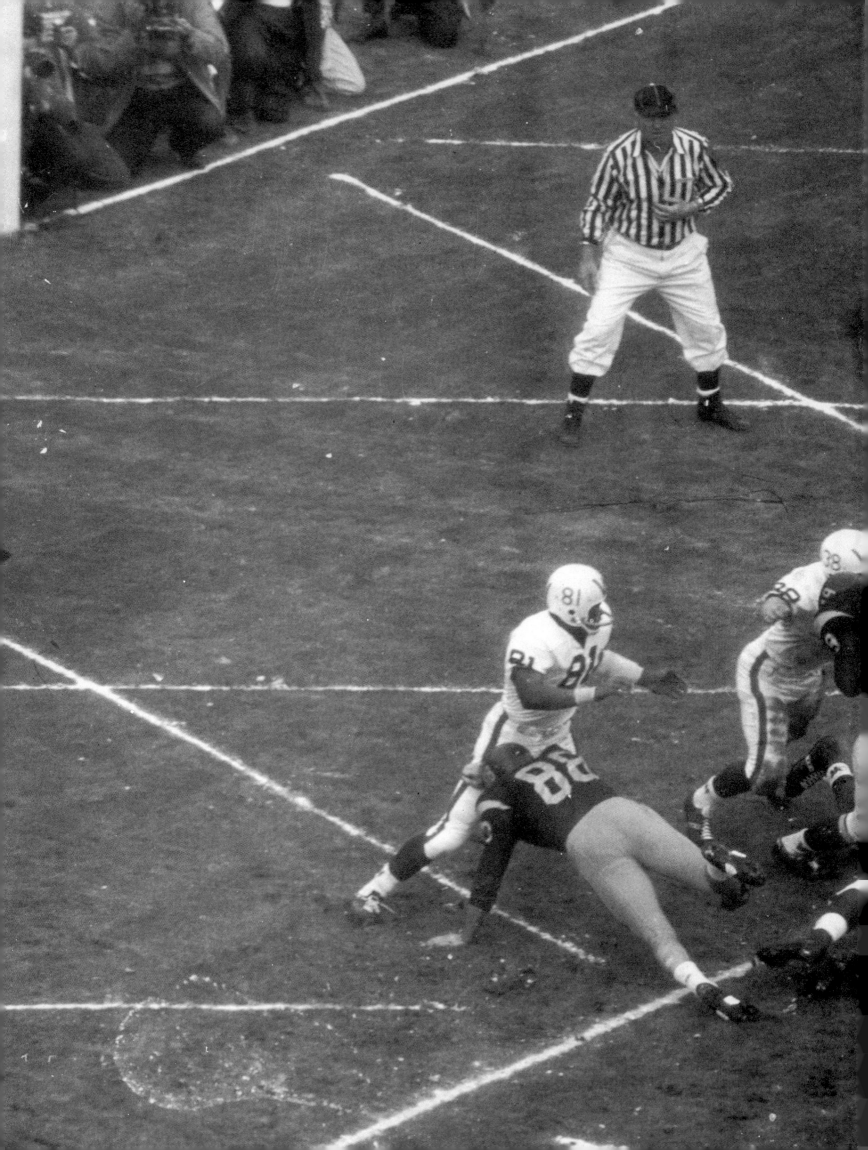

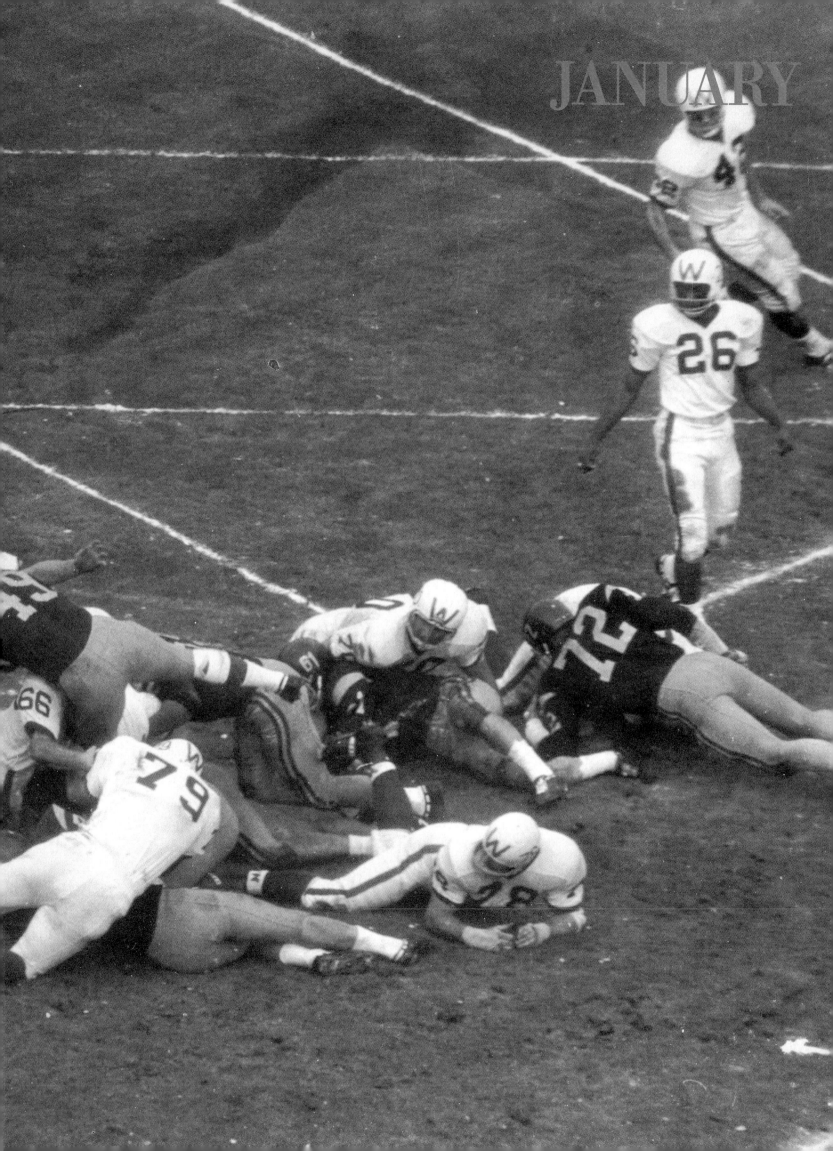

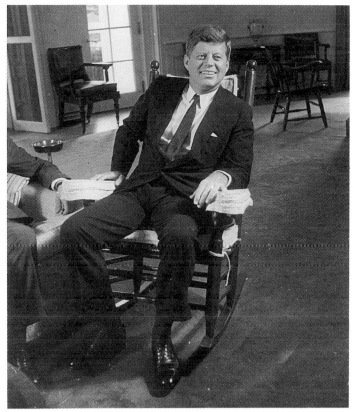

Kennedy used a rocking chair to encourage the image of a relaxed and approachable executive. However, the actual reason for the chair was the relief it offered from his constant back pain.

<P>resident Kennedy could grasp an idea as fast as he could deal with figures—that is to say, he could get an almost instant and permanent grasp on it. He absorbed ideas voraciously—and . . . permanently. One of the few signs of irritation he would ever permit himself was when somebody would try to spell out an idea at great length. If it was new he would get it quickly. If it wasn't new he had long since packed it away. . . . And people plodding away trying to explain something which he already knew would irritate him. Being a well-bred young man, he wouldn't do anything about it but fuss with his hair or something; but if you knew him well you knew that this was a terrible bore. . . .*

**WALT W. ROSTOW, Chairman,
Policy Planning Council, State Department**

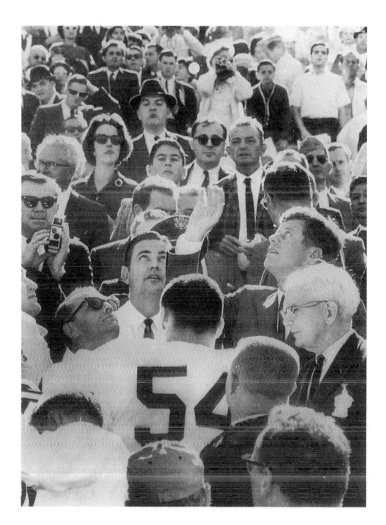

President Kennedy tossed the coin in the Orange Bowl stadium in Miami as Alabama and Oklahoma faced off on January 1. The toss was won by Alabama's All-American center Lee Roy Jordan (54), who elected to receive. Standing to the right of Jordan was Senator Spessard Holland of Florida. Alabama trounced Oklahoma 17–0.

Other January 1 Bowl scores:

Rose Bowl: Southern California 42, Wisconsin 37
Sugar Bowl: Mississippi 17, Arkansas 13
Cotton Bowl: Louisiana State 13, Texas 0.

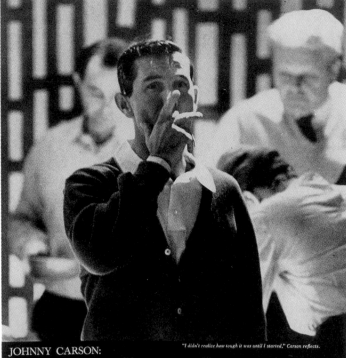

JOHNNY CARSON:
Nighthood's new Prince

"I didn't realize how tough it was until I started," Carson reflects.

Johnny Carson came into his own that year as host of NBC's highly profitable *Tonight Show*. He was no longer viewed as merely Jack Paar's replacement.

Cigarettes were still being advertised on radio and TV in 1963. That year, I did antismoking commercials for the American Cancer Society, which were most effective in getting cigarette commercials off the air. One showed two children dressing up in their parents' clothing. The announcer says, "There are two children up in the attic dressing up in their parents' wedding clothes." Then the commercial shows the children wondering aloud if they looked the way their parents had looked. The announcer says, "Children love to imitate their parents. Do you smoke cigarettes?" Then the Cancer Society logo comes at the end.

The response was phenomenal. Most people say this kind of advertising was responsible for eventually getting cigarette advertising off the air. The tobacco companies didn't want to come up against this kind of thing.

TONY SCHWARTZ, Broadcast Commercial Producer

Every Parliament gives you an extra margin

Tobacco tastes best when the filter's recessed

Parliament keeps its *hi/vi* filter a neat, clean ¼ inch away

A man's world of flavor in a filter cigarette

Marlboro Country

You're on the right side of mildness . . . the rich side of flavor in Marlboro country. You're smoking a finer, richer breed of tobacco—aged for years to suit Marlboro's famous Richmond, Va., recipe. The Selectrate Filter smooths it out, but doesn't tame the taste. Settle back with Marlboro. You get a lot to like.

Ads, without any health warning, encouraging people to smoke cigarettes—to be a manly man, a beautiful woman, a regular guy—were everywhere in 1963. The only public objection was to a tag line that read: "Winston tastes good like a cigarette should." Some educators complained that it fostered bad grammar by using "like" instead of "as."

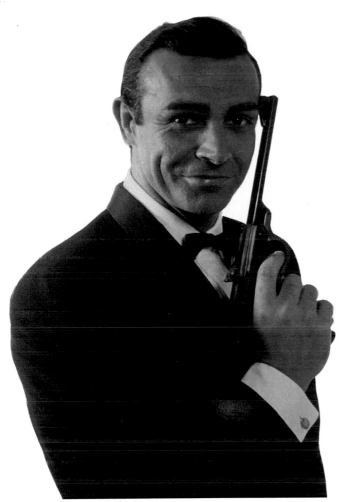

If you recall those early James Bond movies, they were pretty puritanical, in that James Bond always had to do his work first and succeed, and then he got the reward. And the reward was always in a sexual context. It was not in sitting down and having a drink and having a good, intellectual discussion, as he might with a male colleague. Those movies were pretty outrageous in their portrayal of women as items rather than people.

GARY KOERSELMAN,
Student, Northwestern College, Ill.

"Bond. James Bond." Nobody, as Paul McCartney's song later put it, did it better than Sean Connery, pictured here in *Dr. No.* For many fans, he would always remain the only real 007.

John Kennedy fascinated me. I looked at him and Jackie the way I looked at movie stars, only with more interest than I had in any movie star. Their lives appeared so pretty and glamorous. And politically, I was moved by him. I felt like he brought us out of the McCarthy era—out of the backwaters of repression.

So I was very fond of him. I felt emotionally connected to him as a president. As a matter of fact, he was the only president I ever felt emotionally connected to.

LENI WILDFLOWER, Student,
Bennington College

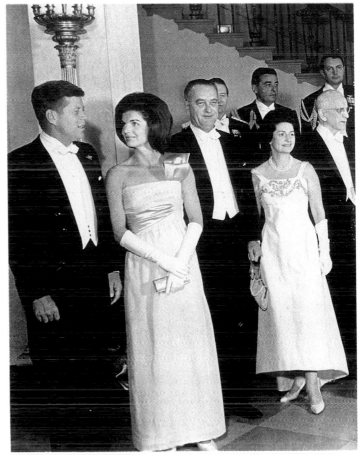

President and Mrs. Kennedy, Vice-President and Mrs. Johnson before a White House dinner saluting ranking officials from the Executive and Judiciary branches of the government.

I was in graduate school in Ohio when Kennedy came through and made a speech to the student body. I'm not positive he was an announced candidate for office yet. It was a typical Kennedy performance. I remember his running down the aisle and bounding up to the platform and making an eloquent call for America's best young people to come into the public service, talking about the nobility of public service. Then he closed the speech with that famous quote from Robert Frost: "For I have promises to keep and miles to go before I sleep." He was applying it to himself and to us— meaning there's so much work to be done, it's a long road and there's miles to go before any of us can sleep. It was very poetic and intoxicating.

It just hit me, who is this person? He's totally different from any political person I've ever known before. Nobody ever talked about public service and there was never any poetry in it before.

I quit a Ph.D. program in English literature and joined the Peace Corps. I was tired of being in school, I'd never been outside the country before, and the idea of getting out into the world was extremely appealing to me. And Kennedy's brand of idealism was very attractive.

My parents were outraged. I didn't know where the hell I was going; it was wildly adventurous. But that's what we wanted— something outside the conventional institutional structure, of elders telling us this is how you do things. I think the people who joined the Peace Corps were forerunners of what became a more widespread phenomenon later.

ROGER LANDRUM, Peace Corps Volunteer

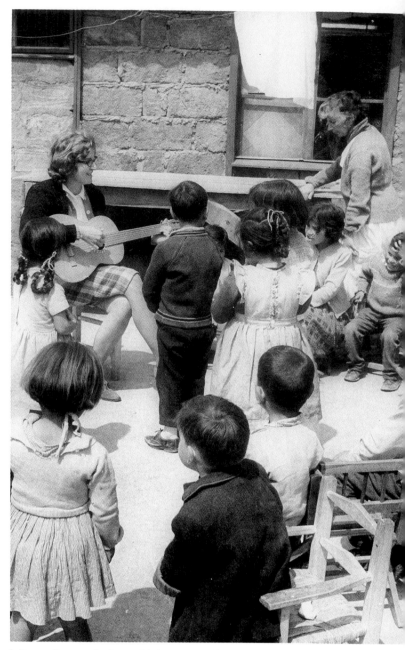

A Peace Corps volunteer with her young charges at a nursery school in Santiago, Chile.

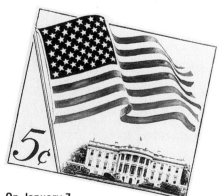

On January 7, first-class postage jumped to 5 cents from 4 cents, the rate since 1959.

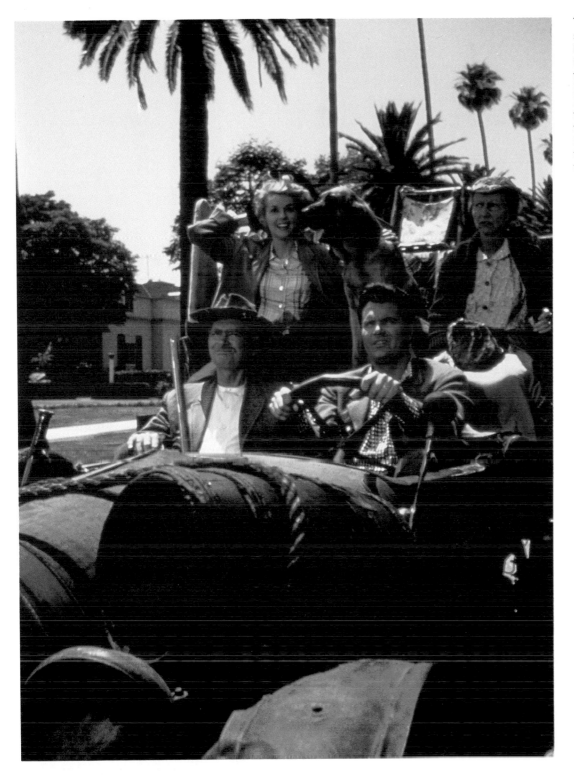

The *Beverly Hillbillies* was in its second year and still a smash hit. The kindly country bumpkins inhabiting a mansion in the title town were played by Buddy Ebsen, Max Baer, Jr., Donna Douglas and Irene Ryan. Situation comedy, a form indigenous to television and the reason for CBS's ratings supremacy during the decade, seemed impervious to social change.

The Beverly Hillbillies *and* Petticoat Junction *were very good programs. They were the equivalent of* All in the Family, *which came later. Paul Henning, who was the principal writer for the* Hillbillies, *was enormously funny. I don't think it would have mattered what the vehicle was. I looked down my nose at the* Beverly Hillbillies *because I thought I should, but on the other hand, whenever I'd watch it, I'd sit there and roar.*

DON WEST, Managing Editor,
Television Magazine

January 1, poet Robert Frost at 88, a photograph taken a month before his death. Frost, who won the Pulitzer Prize for poetry in 1924, 1931, 1937 and 1943, was one of the most admired and widely read American poets. He was best known for his lyric poems about New England life.

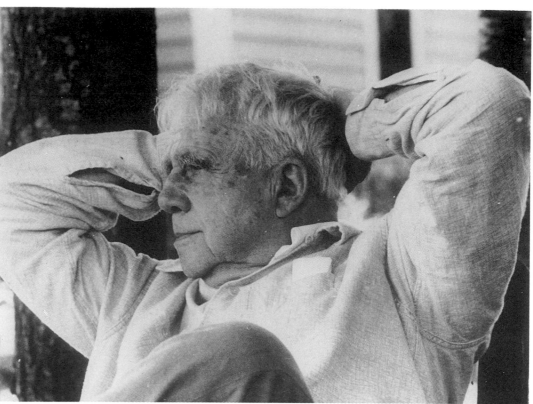

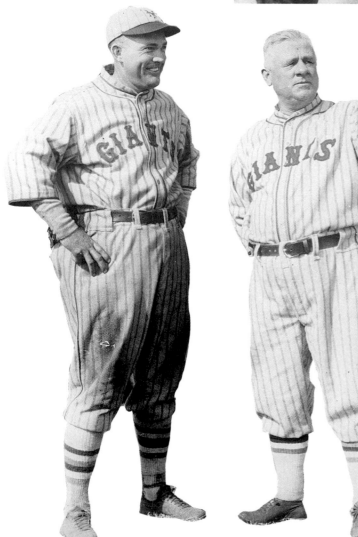

Baseball great Roger Hornsby (left, shown here with legendary manager John McGraw in 1927) died in January.

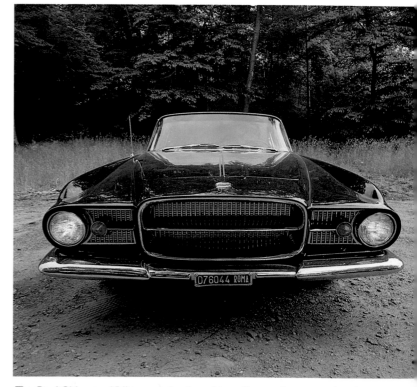

The Dual Ghia was Volkswagen's attempt to sell an underpowered and eccentrically designed "sports" car. Somehow the marketing magic that had made the Beetle the most popular imported car in America did not transfer to this model.

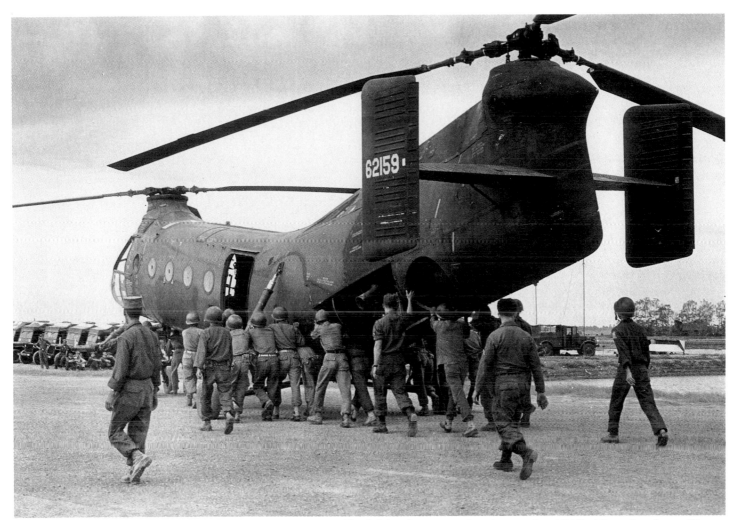

A helicopter damaged in battle near the Vietnam hamlet of Ap Bac. The fighting that occurred on January 2 and 3 killed three American military advisers and 65 South Vietnamese troops, the highest number of casualties in a single action the South Vietnamese had suffered since November 1961.

Initially, in the early sixties, we were using equipment left over from the Korean War. Most of the people who were killed in Vietnam in 1963, in my experience, were killed by faulty equipment or by pushing the limits of the equipment. We had helicopters with blades that flew apart and killed people, and airplanes whose wings fell off. At one time or another, just about every airplane in the unit I was in crash-landed. That was one of the frustrations, but over and above that, what was the purpose? You were not satisfied that you were carrying out a clear purpose, as seemed to have been the case in World War II. We flew around and took people out on missions. And the whole time, it looked as though nothing was being resolved.

JAN BARRY, Private First Class, Vietnam

The bodies of seven Americans killed in Vietnam were sent home. They died on January 11 when their H-21 helicopter crashed on an island in the Mekong River 55 miles southwest of Saigon. By the end of the Kennedy administration, there were 16,000 American "advisers" in South Vietnam. A total of 75 Americans died in the war while Kennedy was president.

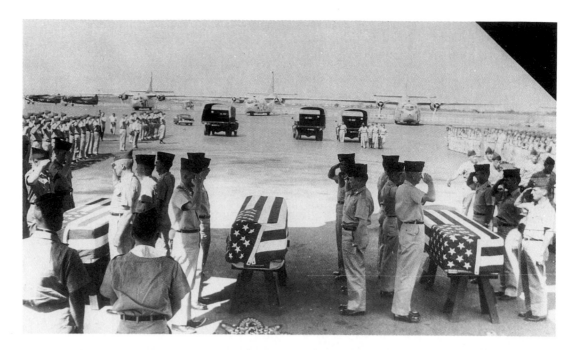

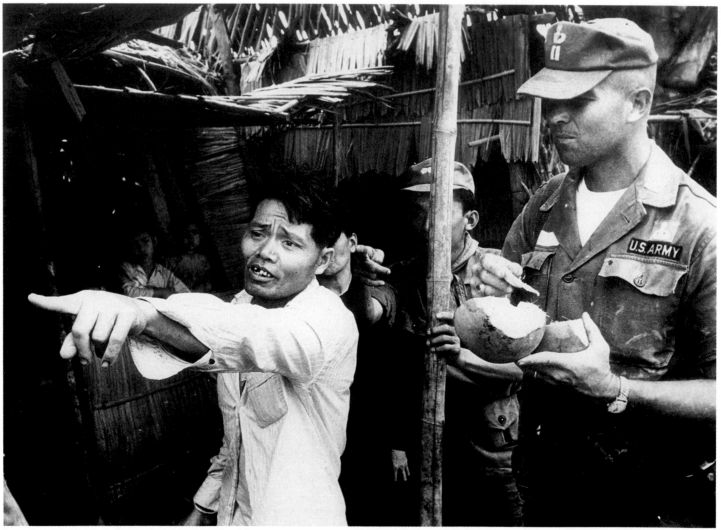

Army Captain Kenneth Good, shown here with a Vietnamese peasant, was later shot by a Vietcong soldier. Good, a 32-year old senior adviser to a South Vietnamese army battalion, was one of the first American casualties of the emerging Vietnam War. He was shot in the shoulder and bled to death on January 2, while assisting his unit in a battle 35 miles southwest of Saigon.

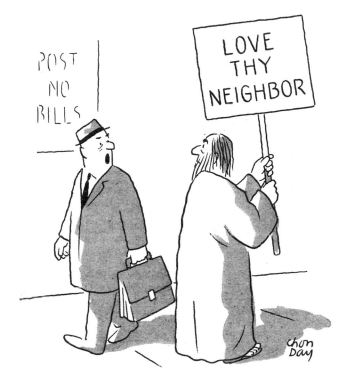

"Even when he plays 'The First Family' over and over and over at peak volume?"

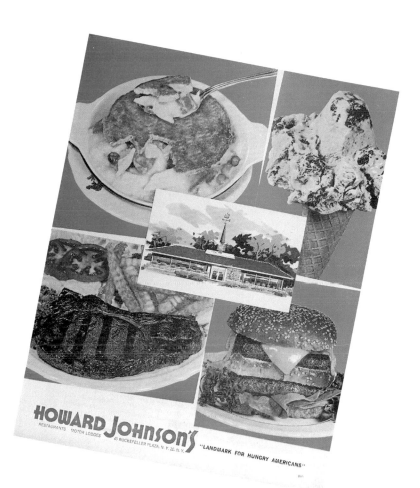

ABOVE: Before Wendy's, Taco Bell, Roy Rogers, The Kentucky Colonel, The King of Burgers, before even McDonald's, there was that familiar and friendly orange roof and the twenty-eight flavors of ice cream.

Rudy Vallee and Robert Morse continued to play the leads in the long-running musical comedy *How to Succeed in Business Without Really Trying*, another play that inherited the vogue for long jocular titles.

The Kennedys wanted to bring American art into the White House, and I was appointed to the White House committee that was focusing on that. One of the points that came up in our committee discussions was how much more effectively France used its culture as a diplomatic instrument. Here we had foreign dignitaries coming to the White House all the time, and this was a place to advertise our culture and American art.

But the effect extended beyond the White House. People saw Jacqueline Kennedy interested in art, and it became more socially acceptable to own American art. People were hearing more about American art, and a lot of people buy with their ears, not with their eyes.

That was also the era of this great expansion of museums around the United States, of little towns having art centers and of exhibitions going on all over.

LAWRENCE FLEISCHMAN, President, Detroit Arts Commission

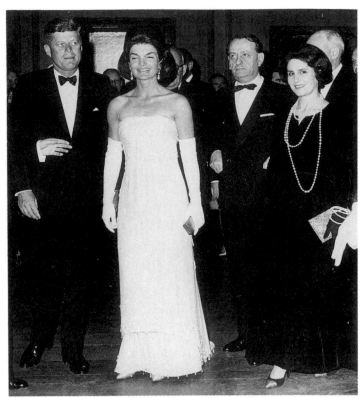

The President and the First Lady, accompanied by French Cultural Minister André Malraux and his wife (right), arrive at the National Gallery to view the *Mona Lisa*. Leonardo da Vinci's painting was on loan from the Louvre museum in Paris.

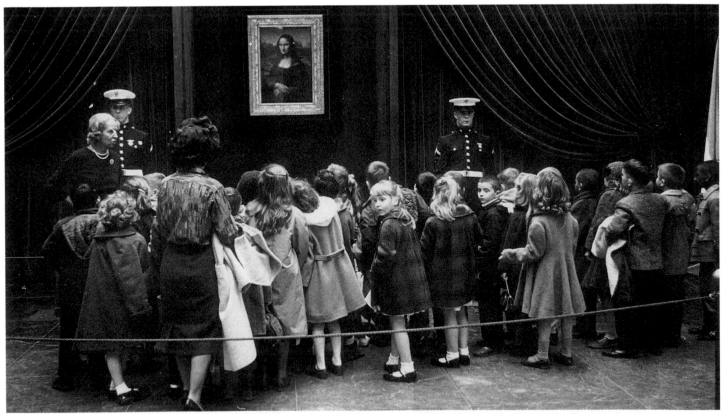

Young visitors to the National Gallery of Art in Washington, D.C., got a glimpse of the *Mona Lisa*'s mysterious smile. The painting drew record crowds in Washington and New York.

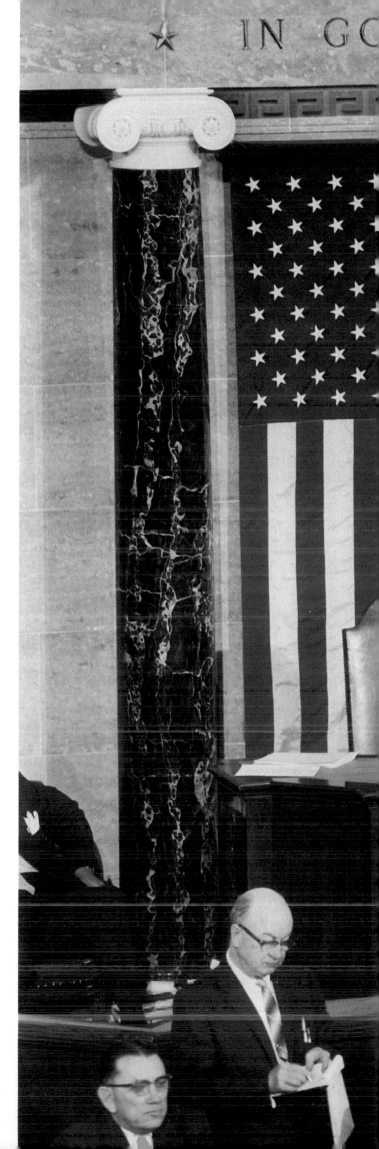

He gave our spirit a booster shot. He called upon us to give, to be generous, to be rededicated to our democracy, to be adventurous as our ancestors were adventurous, to take risks and grow. He initiated our space program, as an example, and had the vision of the great adventure this would ultimately become. Many presidents before him had not discerned the risk-taking need of the American psyche.

I think his appeal was a personality one—his personality. No president in this century quite seemed to be so closely an expression of the buoyant idealism of America as JFK. He was a form of adventurer, and this country loves adventurers. I cannot overstate his physical and personal appeal. He was a handsome and charming Irish devil the likes of whom the Oval Office had never seen. He gave hope and inspiration. He said we all had a role in creating the world, and he seemed to represent the promise of America.

**FRANK FARLEY, Professor of Psychology,
University of Wisconsin**

I think he sensed there were great reserves of idealism in the American people, pent up after eight years with Eisenhower, and he combined that with the skills of a realistic politician.

ARTHUR SCHLESINGER, Jr.

The president closed his State of the Union message with these words: "We are not lulled by the momentary calm of the sea or the somewhat clearer skies above. We know the turbulence that lies below, and the storms that are beyond the horizon this year. But now the winds of change appear to be blowing more strongly than ever, in the world of communism as well as our own. For 175 years we have sailed with those winds at our back, and with the tides of human freedom in our favor. We steer our ship with hope, as Thomas Jefferson said, 'leaving Fear astern.' "

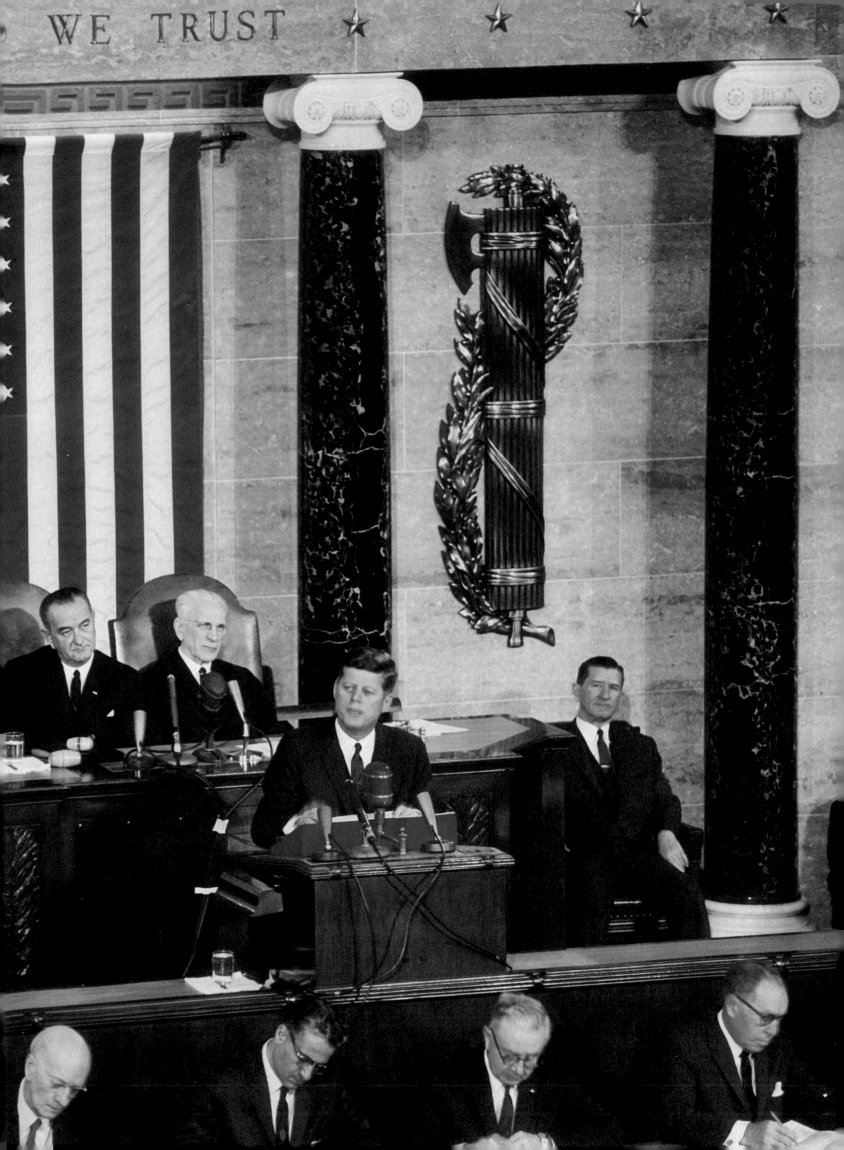

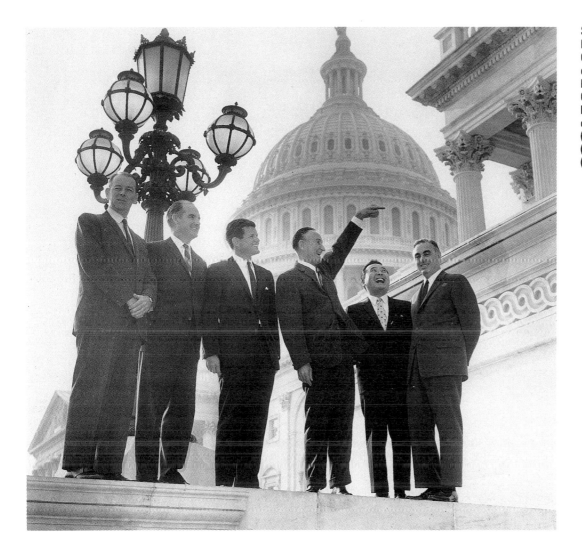

I think in a unique way that hasn't been duplicated since FDR's time, President Kennedy gave people a sense that when you worked for the government, you were serving the national interest rather than enriching yourself. That phrase in his inaugural address, "Ask not what the country can do for you, but what you can do for the country," really said it all. It never occurred to me that I was advancing my own career or enriching myself monetarily. The whole spirit was that you were enlisted to serve the nation.

Another way in which his Administration stood out is in the fact that he saw government not as an enemy of the public, but as an instrument of the public. In the Kennedy years they saw government not as a burden, but as a useful, humanitarian instrument of the people. It wasn't a burden on the people: it was the people.

I think those were the two great contributions of Kennedy: to enlist people in public service and to help them see that government was their agent, rather than their enemy.

GEORGE McGOVERN, US Senator

West German Chancellor Konrad Adenhauer (left) and French President Charles de Gaulle after signing a treaty of cooperation between their countries on January 22. The pact was viewed as an important step in de Gaulle's plan for French leadership of a strengthened European community less dependent on the U.S. Throughout 1963, de Gaulle continued to assert that independence by insisting on developing France's own nuclear force and refusing to cooperate in NATO.

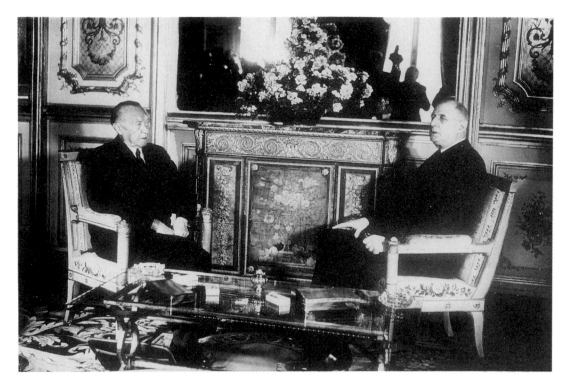

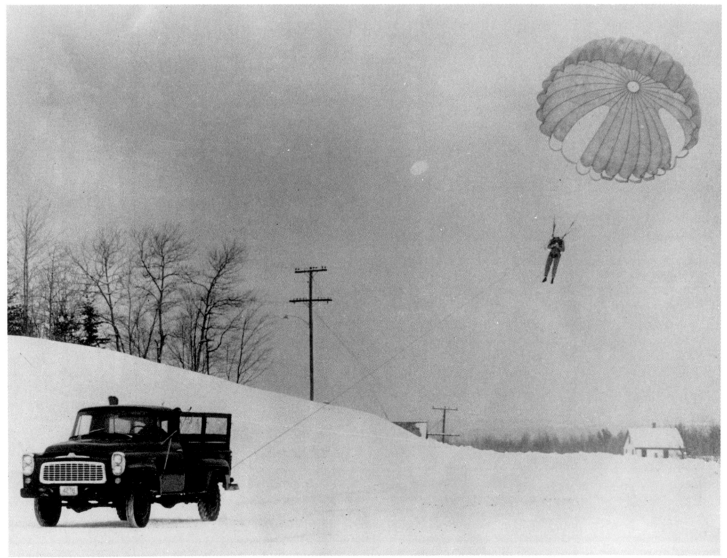

"Car Chuting" had a few months of popularity among New England college students. The idea was to get towed by car or truck until the open parachute could be maneuvered into the air. The rider could reach heights of 50 to 75 feet.

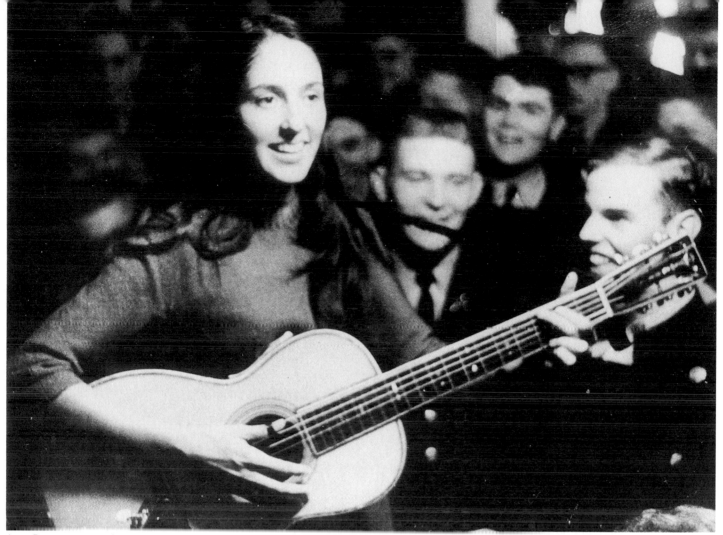

Joan Baez was one of the most popular interpreters of new folk songs. The way she dressed, usually high-necked dark sweaters, and wore her hair, straight and long, had an influence on young college women, who took themselves and the music seriously (very seriously).

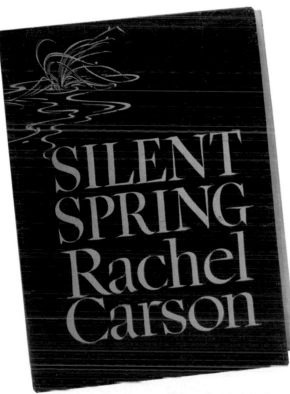

This was one of the first books to alert the public to the pollution of the American landscape. It found a large and receptive audience and would become a cornerstone upon which the ecological movement would be built.

I n 1963 my third album was out and doing well. My audiences had grown from 1,800–3,000-seat town halls to Forest Hills (8,000–10,000) and the Hollywood Bowl (20,000).

I continued to appear in bare feet, usually wearing a simple dress and necklace. My hair was very long now, and straight, and the bangs had grown out completely. The effect was biblical but gloomy. I stood hunched over the guitar, a vocal coach's nightmare, still singing many of the soft ballads, but adding the songs and spirit of the civil rights movement: "Amazing Grace," "Swing Low," "Oh Freedom," and the anthem "We Shall Overcome." I also added the sweet antinuclear song by Malvina Reynolds, "What Have They Done to the Rain?" "Joe Hill" became a favorite, along with the Dylan gems.

JOAN BAEZ, Folk Singer

I was furious with the [Kennedy] Administration's civil rights posture. I thought it was slow, lethargic and unresponsive. Bob Kennedy was in charge of this strategy, and there wasn't a Negro within miles of his office when they sat down to decide what to do with the revolution that Martin Luther King, Jr., and the students and the NAACP and CORE were orchestrating in the South. . . . They were demonstrating against the unfairness and viciousness of the Southern racist system. And white people—[administration civil rights advisors] John Nolan and John Dolan and Byron White and Nicholas deB. Katzenbach and Burke Marshall and John Douglas and John Doar and Ramsey Clark—were the people Robert Kennedy and the president turned to when they decided on what to do about black protest—how to parcel out black rights. They were all white, and the arrogance and the slowness of those people enraged me.

ROGER WILKINS, Attorney, Agency for International Development

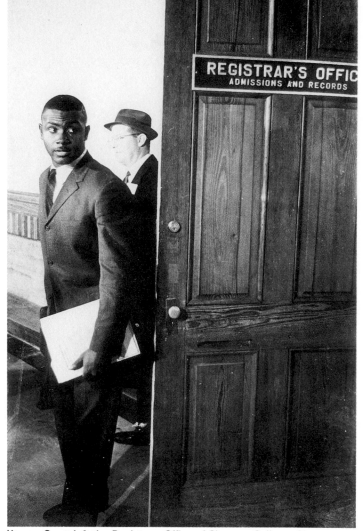

Harvey Gantt left the Registrars Office of Clemson College, Clemson, South Carolina, after enrolling as a student in the previously all-white school.

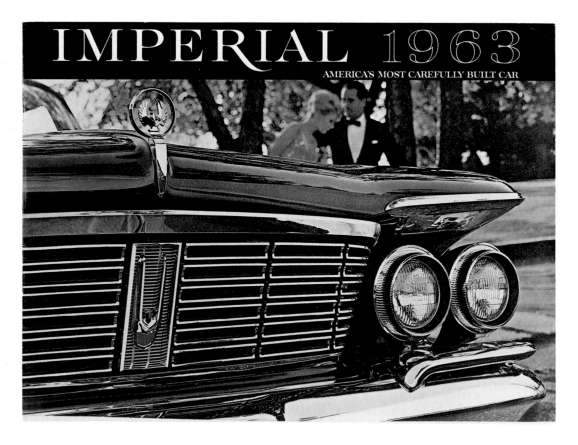

This cover of Chrysler's promotional brochure top-of-the-line *Imperial* emphasized a headlight design that would win no awards and would soon be a memory. The Imperial came in 16 colors (including Mayan Gold) and 178 interior-exterior decor combinations. It offered "TorqueFlite" pushbutton automatic transmission.

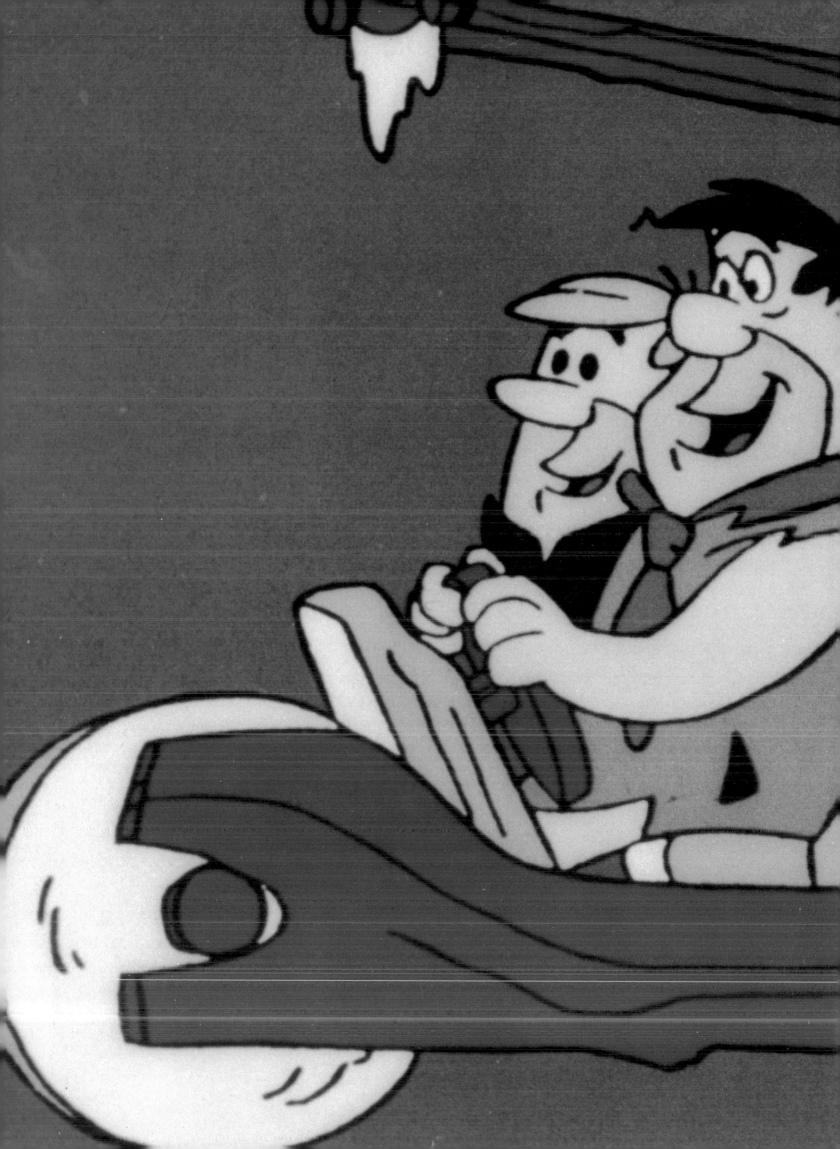

FEBRUARY

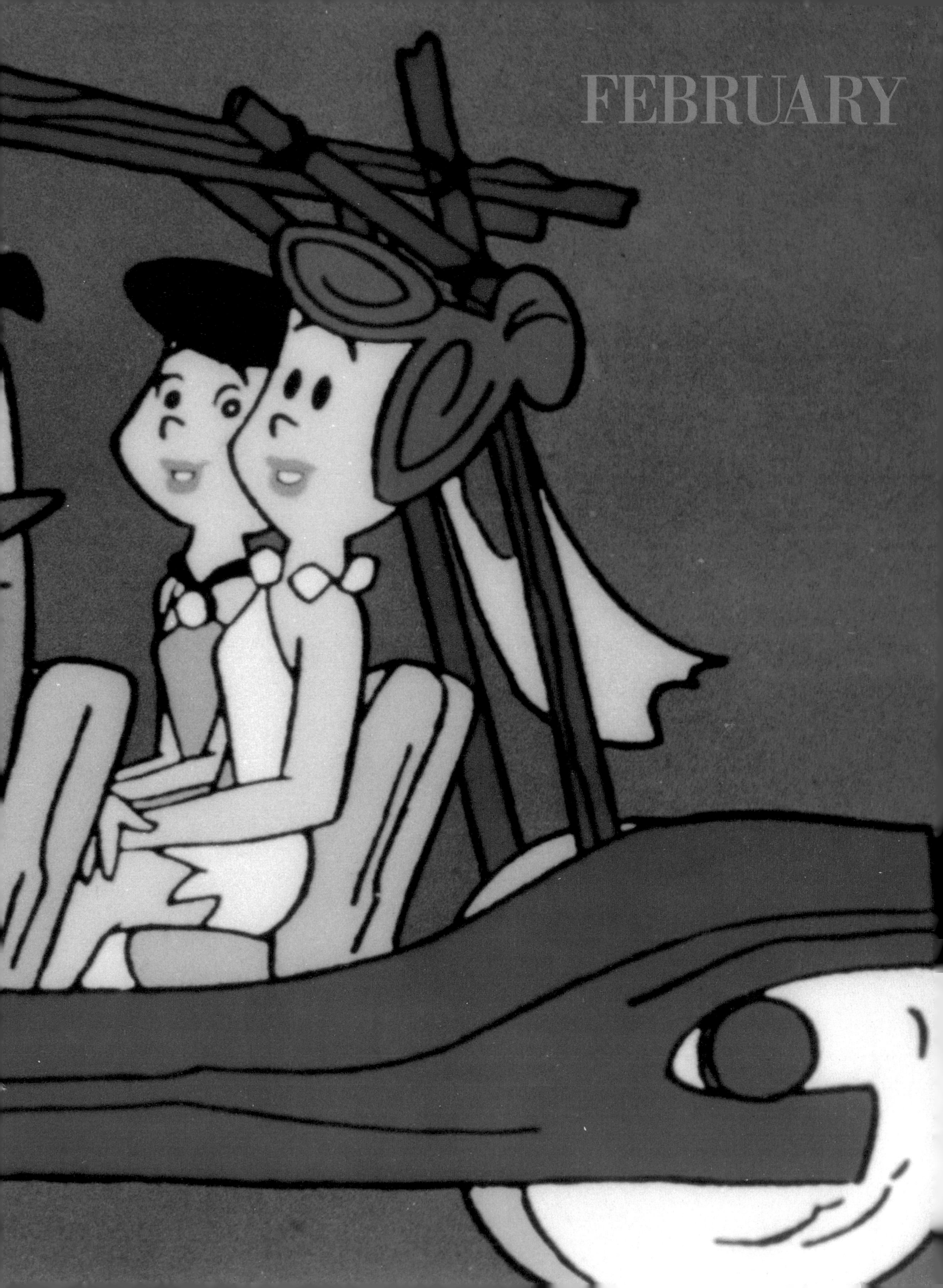

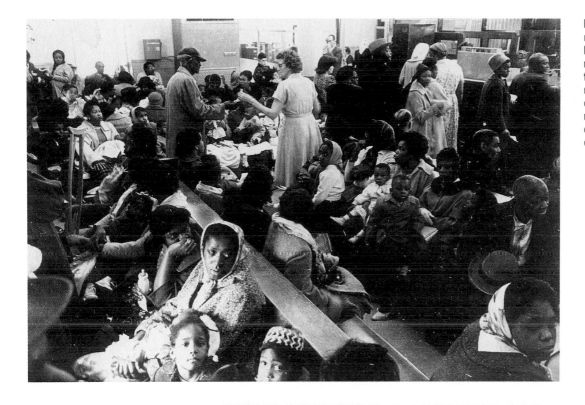

Flu victims crowded the waiting room of the Memphis hospital in February in a scene replayed in many hospitals and clinics as a flu epidemic swept across the nation. More than 40 million doses of flu vaccine were administered; even so, 45,000 deaths were attributed to the epidemic.

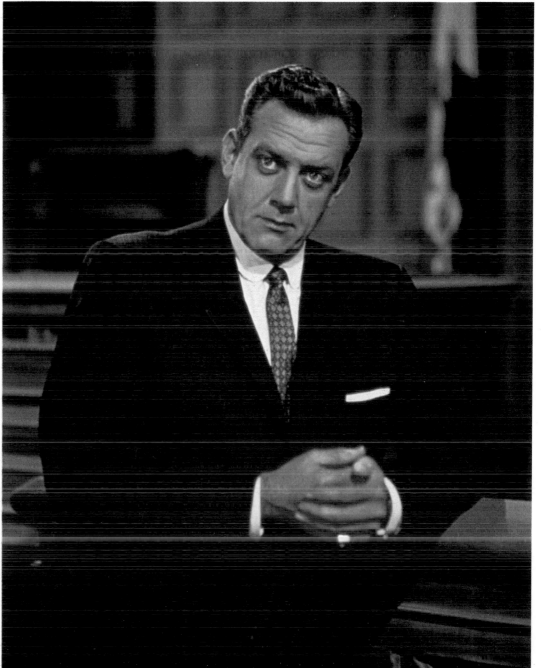

A youngish, slim Raymond Burr starred in the enormously successful *Perry Mason*. Like most of the TV hits carried over from the late fifties, it would not survive the sixties. By 1967, in *Ironside*, Burr had achieved his ambition to act sitting down.

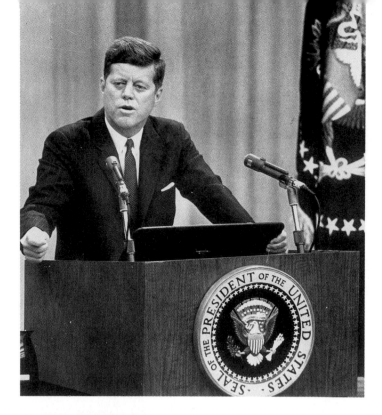

The missile crisis . . . had a dramatic effect on the relationship of [Kennedy and Khrushchev]. Their attitudes toward each other showed evidence of having been somewhat ambivalent before the crisis. That brush with calamity seems to have forged a bond between them. They appeared now to understand each other better, to buttress each other's efforts, to avoid making the other look bad. They began to consult each other more frequently, to work together on problems of common interest.

GLENN SEABORG, Chairman, Atomic Energy Commission

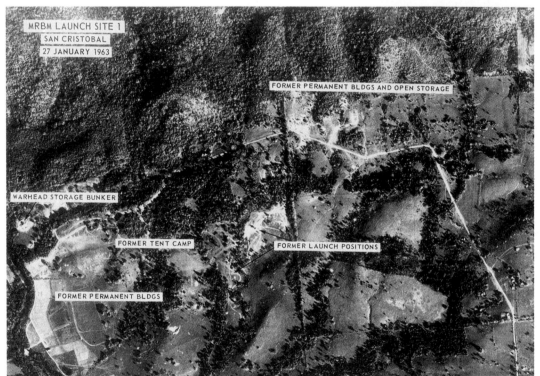

ABOVE: At his February 7 press conference President Kennedy assured Americans that all Soviet missiles were out of Cuba. The president also reiterated his resolve to banish Soviet influence from the Americas. He said that Soviet military strength in Cuba was "of serious concern to this government" even after the reduction in Soviet troops in Cuba following the Cuban missile crisis in October. Despite this rhetoric, the year saw improved relations between the superpowers.

This aerial reconnaissance photograph was made public by the Defense Department in early February to prove that the Soviets had dismantled their ballistic missile sites in Cuba.

With the Cuban missile crisis [behind him] and with the agreement on the test-ban treaty, Kennedy said that he looked forward to his second term as a term when he hoped that Soviet-American relations would be stabilized. He thought he could do business with Khrushchev and that they were both moving in that direction.

Had Kennedy not been killed, I think Kennedy and Khrushchev might have collaborated in further detente-like actions in a way that might have given Khrushchev more prestige in the Soviet Union.

ARTHUR SCHLESINGER, Jr., Special Assistant to the President

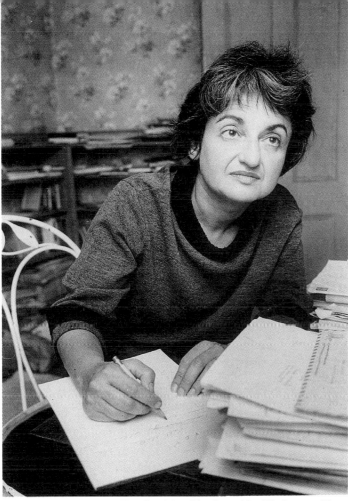

Betty Friedan, author of *The Feminine Mystique*. Ms. Friedan would become one of the key figures in the first stage of "women's liberation," as the feminist movement was then called. Her seminal book would remain an essential social document for two decades.

I ask college students not born in 1963, "How many of you have ever worn a girdle?" They laugh. So then I say: "Well, it used to be, not so long ago, when I was your age, or your mothers were your age, that every woman from about the age of 12 to 92 who left her house in the morning encased her flesh in rigid plastic casing. She wasn't supposed to notice that the girdle would make it difficult for her to breathe or move. She didn't even ask why she wore it. But did it really make her more attractive to men?"

I ask them: "How can you know what it was like to wear a girdle, when you've never worn anything under your blue jeans except a bikini brief? And how can I expect you to know what it felt like when being a woman meant that you wore a girdle over your mind, your eyes, your mouth, your heart, your feelings, your sexuality, as well as the girdle on your belly?"

BETTY FRIEDAN, Author,
The Feminine Mystique

I dreamed I painted the town red in my maidenform bra

SWEET MUSIC with triangle inserts for extra uplift! 2.50

This copy line for Maidenform was one of the most repeated—and presumably successful—of the period. The bra modeled here was called "Sweet Music" (for reasons understood only by the manufacturer) and sold for $2.50.

Van Raalte opens the door to a new world of nice things

Even slim, trim, young women wore girdles. It was considered indecent not to. The garment came equipped with garters, needed to hold up stockings in this pre-pantyhose era.

Fan magazines were not as lurid as they would later become but even the first family was accorded the cavalier gossip treatment usually reserved for movie stars.

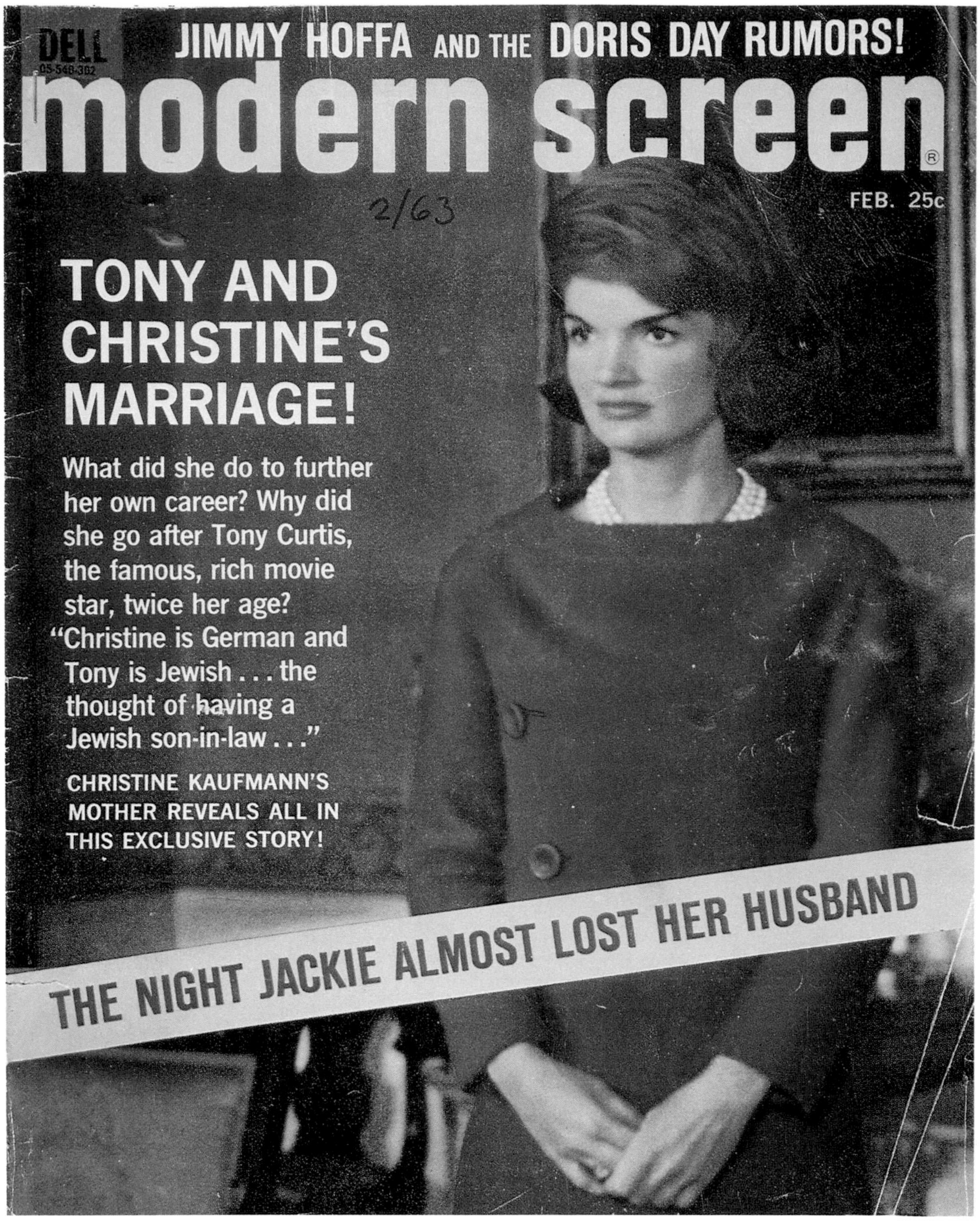
DELL
05-546-302
JIMMY HOFFA AND THE DORIS DAY RUMORS!
modern screen
FEB. 25c
2/63
TONY AND CHRISTINE'S MARRIAGE!
What did she do to further her own career? Why did she go after Tony Curtis, the famous, rich movie star, twice her age?
"Christine is German and Tony is Jewish . . . the thought of having a Jewish son-in-law . . ."
CHRISTINE KAUFMANN'S MOTHER REVEALS ALL IN THIS EXCLUSIVE STORY!
THE NIGHT JACKIE ALMOST LOST HER HUSBAND

I'd often be the only woman in a room and the men would stand up. And I'd say, "Please, don't do that. I'm not going to stand up for you. Don't stand up for me." It was not easy. So many men are not comfortable working with women. I had a lot of trouble with that. But I never had trouble working with Kennedy or any of his people. So it kind of makes me annoyed when they don't talk of Kennedy as one who really furthered the women's cause. He really did.

ESTHER PETERSON, Assistant Secretary of Labor

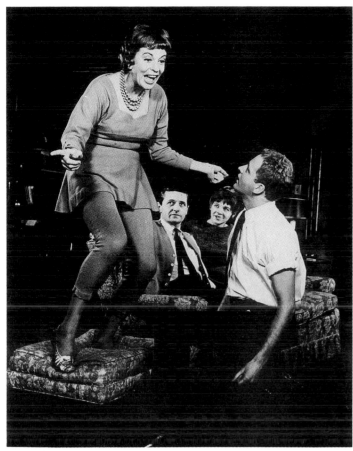

Who's Afraid of Virginia Woolf?, Edward Albee's bombshell of a play, continued its run on Broadway, closing in May 1964 after 600 performances. The principal actors were (from left to right) Uta Hagen, Arthur Hill, Avra Petrides, and Ben Piazza.

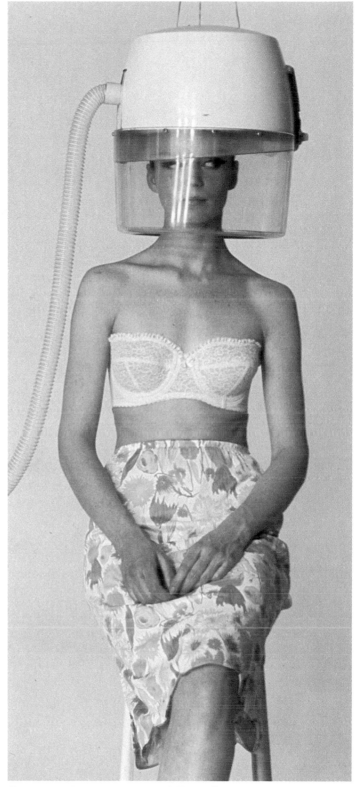

This is how the February issue of *Vogue* illustrated recommendations for undergarments and hairdryers.

T he women's liberation movement really didn't get started until the late sixties, and in 1963, in Kennedy's time, the attitude about the male-female relationship was still very much different. Women and men both, I think, still looked on women as attachments to men. The stereotype was that the woman's success came through her husband's success and status. Sure, there were a minority of women at that time who already saw it differently, and probably more correctly, but for the most part the woman was still trying to please the man. Women were still sex symbols, or style symbols.

GARY KOERSELMAN

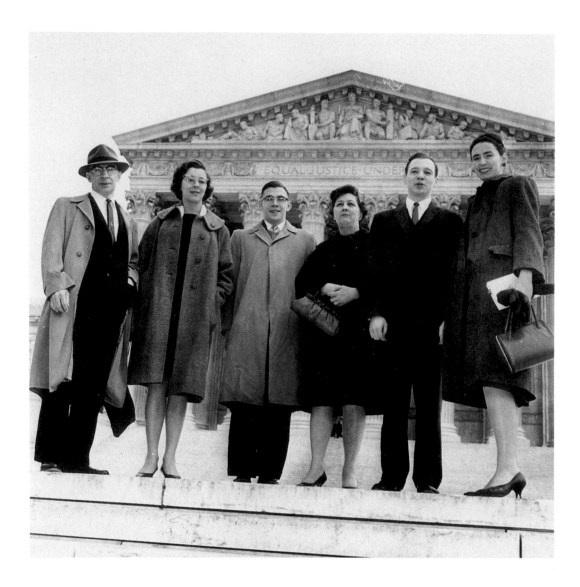

Edward L. Schempp (left) and his wife, Donna (third from right), the Pennsylvania Unitarian couple who challenged a state law requiring the reading of Bible verses in public schools, are shown in front of the U.S. Supreme Court building with other family members. The high court decreed such laws unconstitutional, reaffirming and extending the landmark 1962 ruling outlawing the recitation of prayer in public schools.

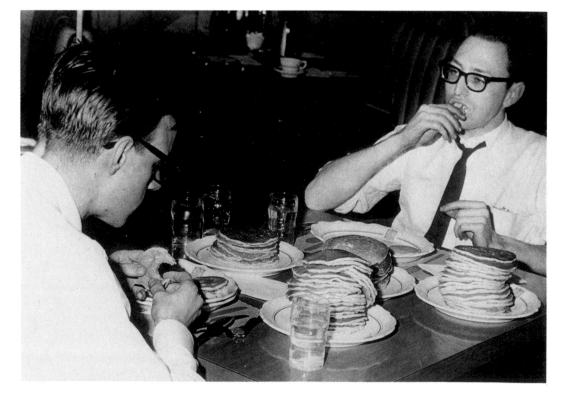

Harvard students attempted to set a pancake-eating record on February 27. The winner of this contest consumed 97.

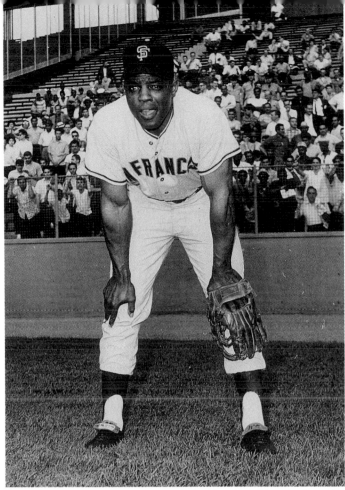

The French Chef *premiered on WGBH-TV in Boston on February 11, 1963. It was something of an experiment. There were no cooking programs on the air at that time.*

We filmed the show in a demonstration kitchen in the Cambridge Electric Light Company. I received $50 per show.

I suppose the program's appeal could be explained by the fact that at that point people were just beginning to go abroad. . . . And the Kennedys were in the White House. They had their wonderful French chef, René Verdon.

Cooking and American tastes in food have changed immensely since then. In 1963, you couldn't have found leeks or shallots in most places. That's all changed.

JULIA CHILD
Host, *The French Chef*

Centerfielder Willie Mays signed with the New York Mets for $100,000, putting him in select company with Joe DiMaggio, Stan Musial, and Ted Williams. Mays earned his salary: in the 1962 season, he led both leagues in home runs with 49, and had 141 RBIs. He hit .304 in 1962. In 1963, May's average was .314 and he hit 38 home runs.

Even Americans who hated to cook tuned in to watch *The French Chef*, an appealingly informal cooking school of the air that instructor Julia Child said was designed to "take the mystery and falderol out of French cooking." With her airy insouciance, Child taught Americans how to wield balloon whisks and cleavers, initiated them into the secrets of roux and puff pastry, and gave them the courage to do battle with "the big, bad artichoke."

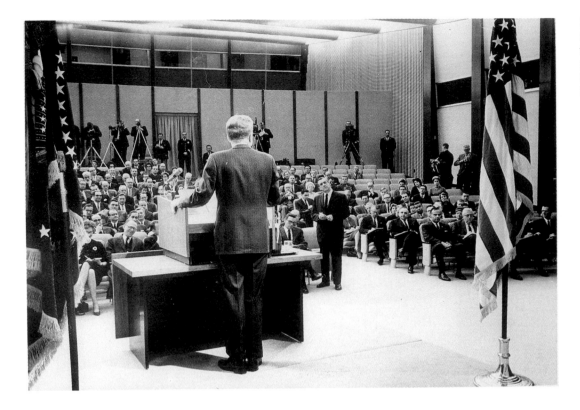

UPI correspondent Merriman Smith asked the final question at the president's February 27 press conference, held in the auditorium of the State Department Building.

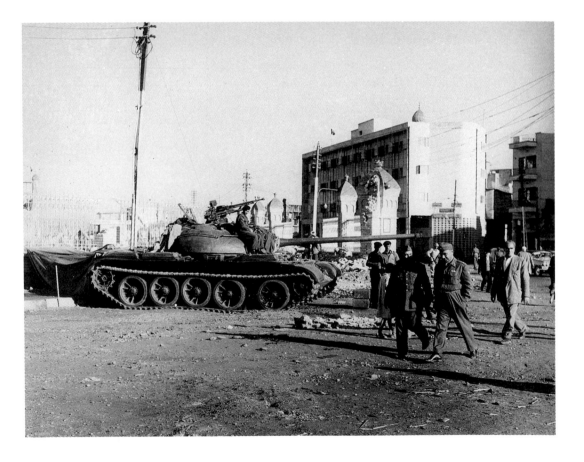

A tank and soldiers of the new Iraqi revolutionary regime that overthrew Premier Kerim Kassen's government in February. In the background is the rubble of the Defense Ministry, where Kassen was slain.

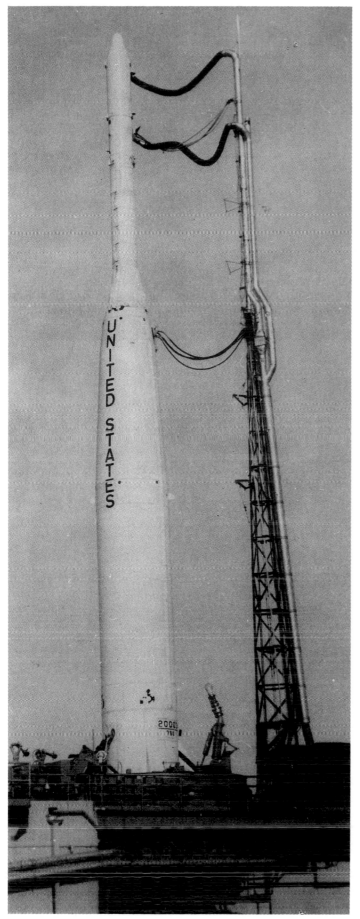

The three-stage Delta rocket ready for launch on February 8. The vehicle would carry a communications satellite into orbit.

O f course, outer space was a big issue in 1963, and I was working out at Convair in San Diego. I was a technical engineer concerned with the rocket engines used in the Centaur rocket. Those booster engines were used to put some of the small pioneer satellites up into outer space. In fact, some of those satellites are still up there. . . .

MARSHALL D. HOLBROOKE,
Aircraft-Industry Engineer

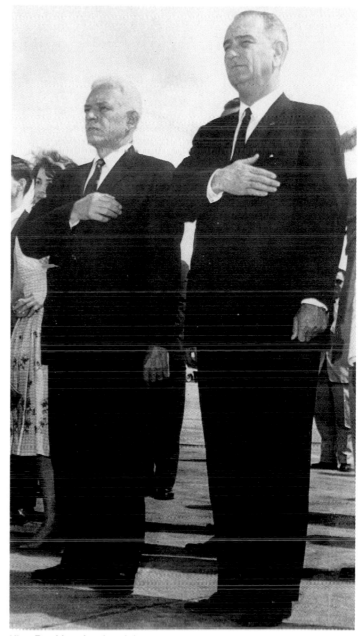

Vice-President Lyndon Johnson attended the inauguration of Juan Bosh, the Dominican Republic's first constitutionally elected president in thirty-four years.

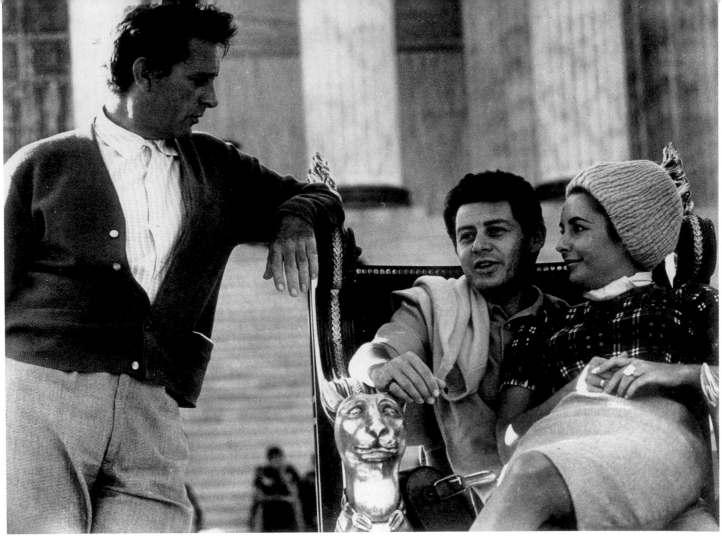

Elizabeth Taylor sat on husband Eddie Fisher's lap while Richard Burton—who may have known something Eddie didn't—looked on. Fisher was in Rome where Taylor (title role) and Burton (Mark Anthony) were making the movie *Cleopatra*.

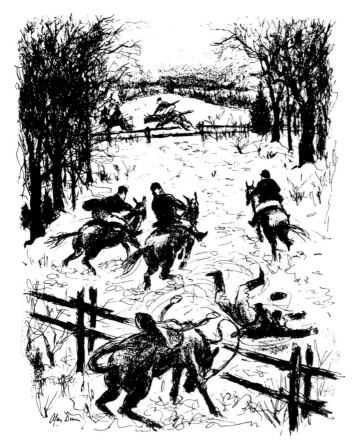

*"Too bad! In all other respects, he's as good a
Secret Service man as she could ask for."*

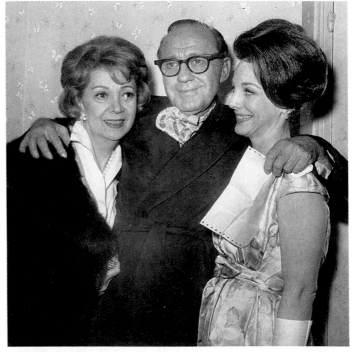

Jack Benny with wife Mary Livingston and daughter Joan backstage at the Ziegfeld Theatre after the entertainer's one-man show opened on Broadway, February 27.

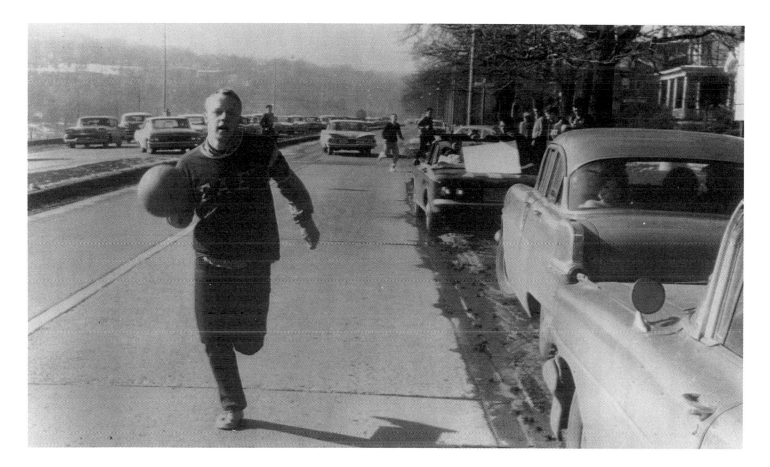

Marshall University students dribbled a basketball 58 miles as part of West Virginia's centennial celebration.

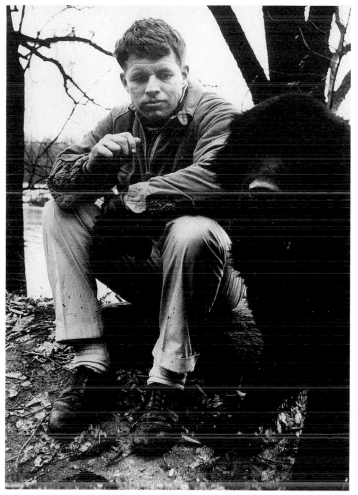

Robert Kennedy and friend took a break during a 50 mile hike undertaken by administration officials to help publicize the president's program for national physical fitness.

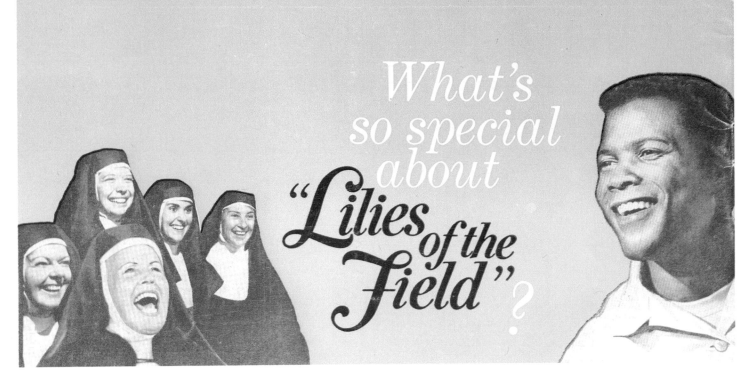

What's so special about "Lilies of the Field"?

nited Artists Corp. *displayed very little faith in* Lilies of the Field. *They offered [Ralph] Nelson and [Fred] Ingels [the producers] a mere $250,000 for the entire production.*

We shot the entire film in 14 days. And indeed, we traveled from California to Tucson, Arizona, made the picture and were back in Los Angeles at the end of two weeks. . . . The picture opened and did remarkably well.

By the end of the year the picture was considered so good that, to my real surprise, I was nominated for the Academy Award. Well, I didn't pay that much mind . . . I was very aware that I was in a field with four other nominees whose performances in their respective pictures made each of them an almost unbeatable competition. There was Albert Finney, whose Tom Jones *was a much bigger success than my picture was—it was just about universally accepted as picture of the year. There was Paul Newman's dynamic performance in* Hud, *there was Rex Harrison's highly praised work in* Cleopatra, *and there was Richard Harris's electric impact in* This Sporting Life.

Annie Bancroft pulled a card from the envelope and said, "The winner is Sidney Poitier." I was about to start the obligatory face-saving applause . . . when it hit me. . . . It's me—it's me!

SIDNEY POITIER, Actor

The most significant element in this story of an itinerant black workman and a group of German nuns in New Mexico was its optimistic attitude that everyone can come to understand everyone else. Sidney Poitier won his Academy Award. The picture was nominated as best of the year. The name of the production company was Rainbow.

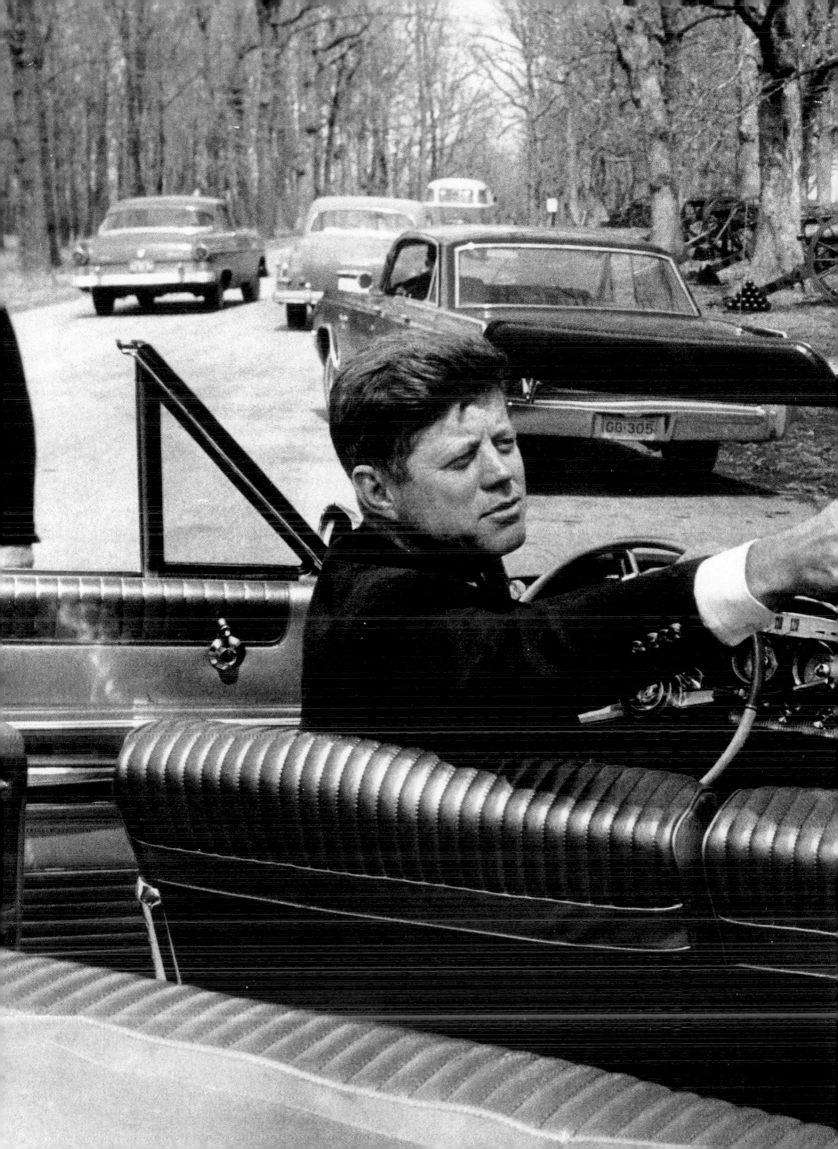

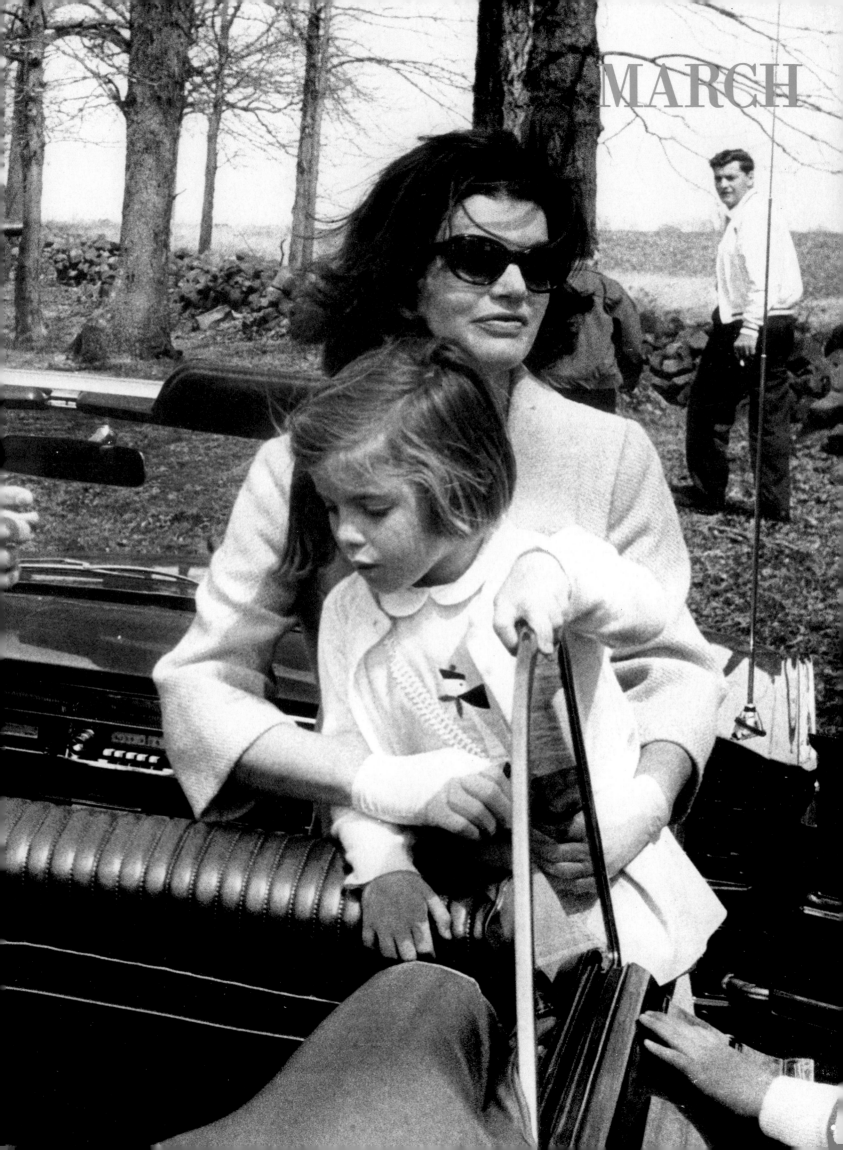

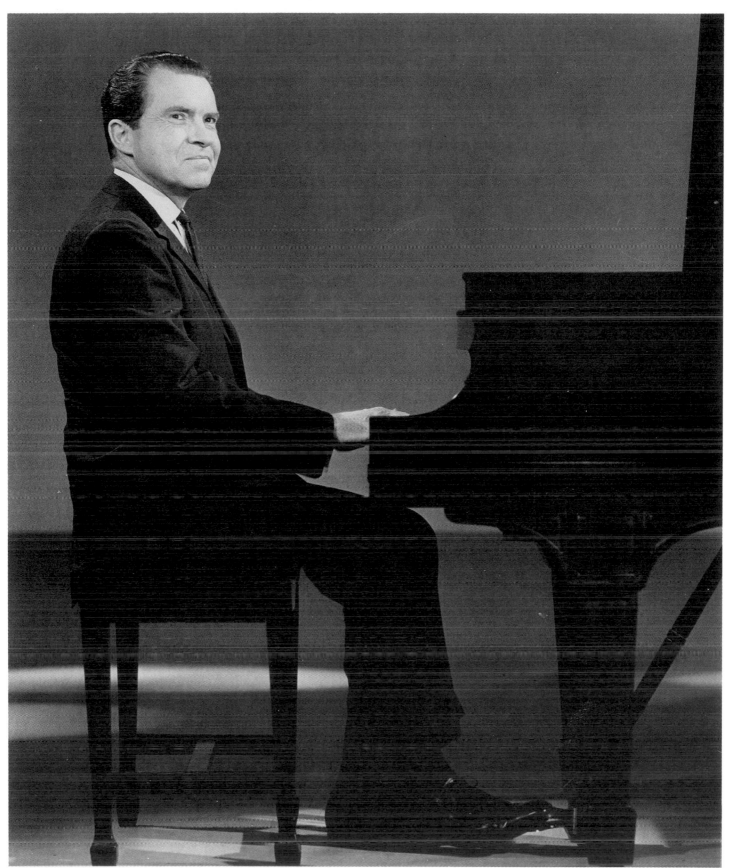

Former Vice-President Richard Nixon played the piano on the *Jack Paar Show* on March 3. During the program Nixon criticized President Kennedy for not providing air cover for the Cuban Bay of Pigs invasion.

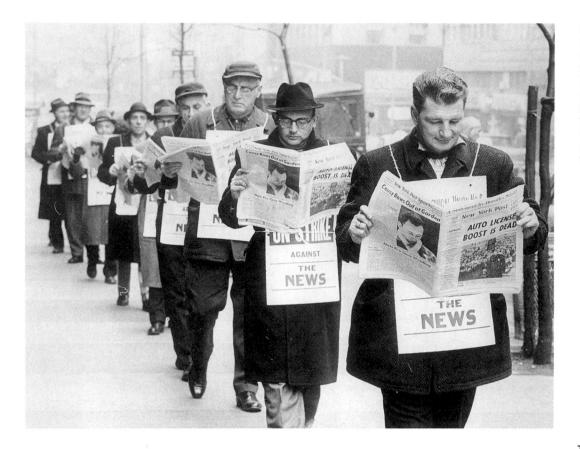

Striking printers picketing the *New York Daily News* read early editions of the *New York Post*, which broke with the other eight New York dailies and resumed publication on March 4. The strike, which was over job protection in an era of increasing automation, began in December and shut down the city's papers for a record 114 days.

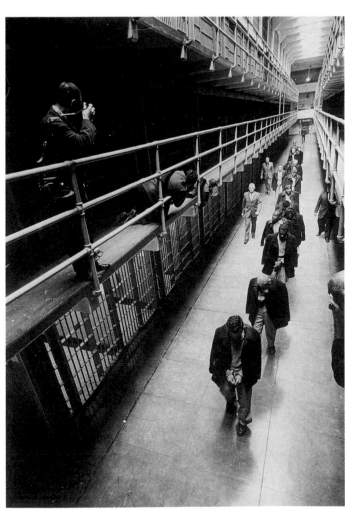

The Chiffons' new album included the cuts "One Fine Day" and "He's So Fine".

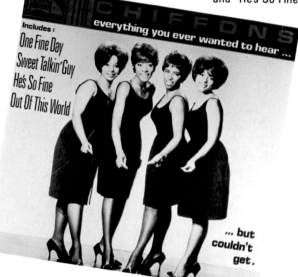

The last of the prisoners to be held at Alcatraz—the federal prison for the nation's toughest criminals—walked in handcuffs down the cellblock during their removal from the deteriorating institution, which was closed in March 1963. The National Park Service later took over the prison, whose gloomy cell blocks and ruined fortifications became a popular tourist attraction.

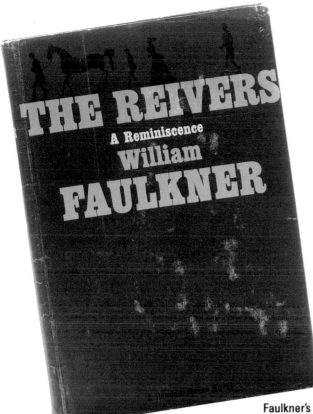

Faulkner's novel was awarded the Pulitzer Prize for fiction in March. The novel was far from the best the Mississippian had ever written, but 25 years after he had done his best, most demanding, and enormously creative work, Faulkner had finally become a Nobel laureate and a safe choice for prizes.

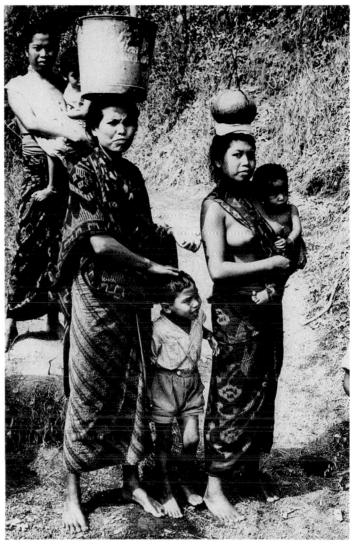

These villagers were among the lucky ones who escaped the volcanic eruptions on Bali, Indonesia, that took 11,000 lives in early April.

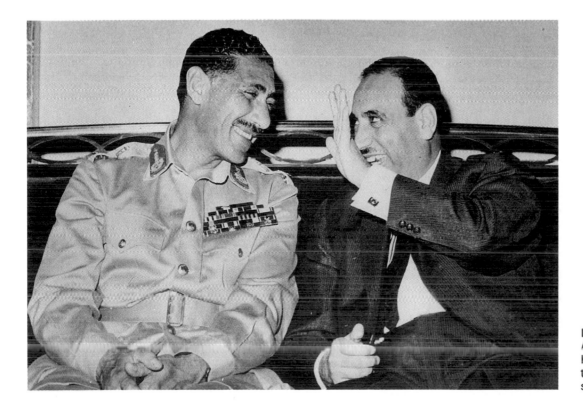

Iraqi's President Abdel Salem Aref (right) met with Abdul Hakim Amer, vice-president of the United Arab Republic, shortly after its creation.

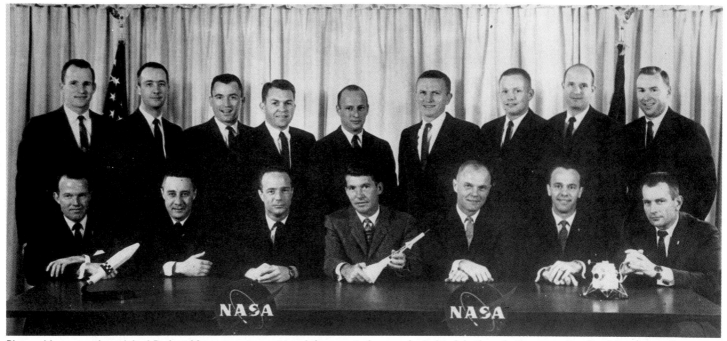

Pictured here are the original Project Mercury astronauts and the new trainees selected to join them in the upcoming Gemini and Appollo projects. Left to right, seated: Gordon Cooper, Virgil Grissom, Scott Carpenter, Walter Schirra, John Glenn, Alan Shepard and Donald Slayton, the original seven. Left to right, standing: Edward White, James McDivitt, John Young, Elliot See, Charles Conrad, Frank Borman, Neil Armstrong, Thomas Stafford and James Lovell.

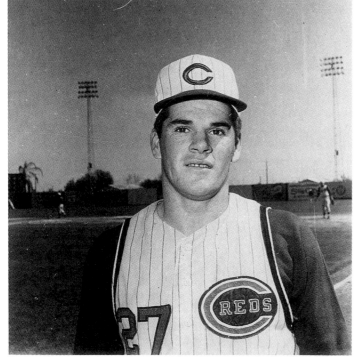

National League second baseman Pete Rose won the Rookie of the Year award. Rose was part of the Cincinnati Reds' 86 wins and 76 losses for the season.

T*hat opening day . . . was one I'll never forget. We were playing the Pittsburgh Pirates, and Earl Francis was pitching for them . . . I was the lead-off batter for the Reds that season, and I had drawn a walk on four straight pitches. I took off for first base like a bird. . . . I didn't walk to first. I didn't stroll. I scooted as if my life depended on it. . . . Well, I stood there on first, and pretty soon Frank Robinson slugged himself a beautiful home run, so I went chugging around the bags ahead of him, and there I was scoring the first round of the season. . . . I'll never forget waiting there at home plate for Frank to come in. It was like being a bit player in the greatest movie ever made.*

**PETER ROSE,
Rookie of the Year**

*F*ast food was just beginning to take over in 1963. The plastic businesses and franchises that have sprung up everywhere hadn't reached into every corner of the country like they have now. There was still a lot of variety, and local ownership of diners and drive-ins. So American culture wasn't quite so homogenized.

Now it seems like everything is tied into a chain—even bookstores. There are very few independent bookstores left. It used to be if you walked into a bookstore, you could expect to find someone there that knew and cared about books. Now it's all B. Dalton, Crown, and Walden. If you go in with a title or an author, they might try to find the book for you by punching it up on a computer screen, but there's no love of books evident in bookstores anymore, and I really miss that.

LEE SMITH, Student,
University of Minnesota

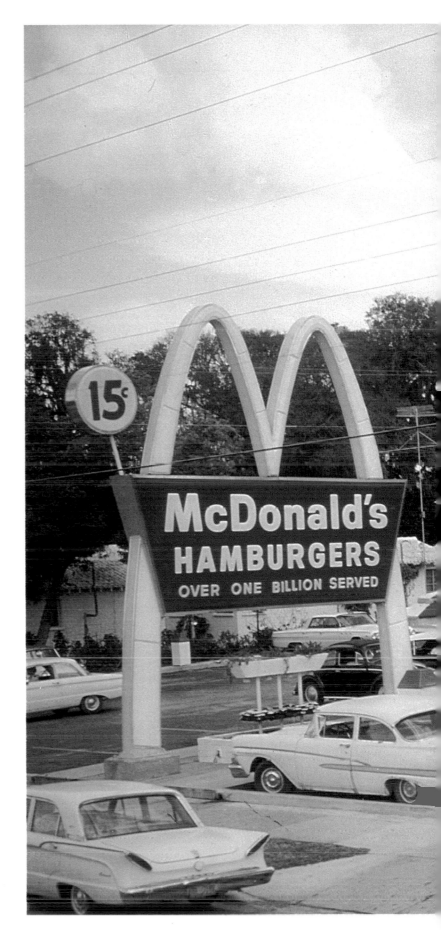

A MacDonald's hamburger cost fifteen cents. The sign on the golden arches advertised the number (to the closest billion or so) of hamburgers that the chain had sold.

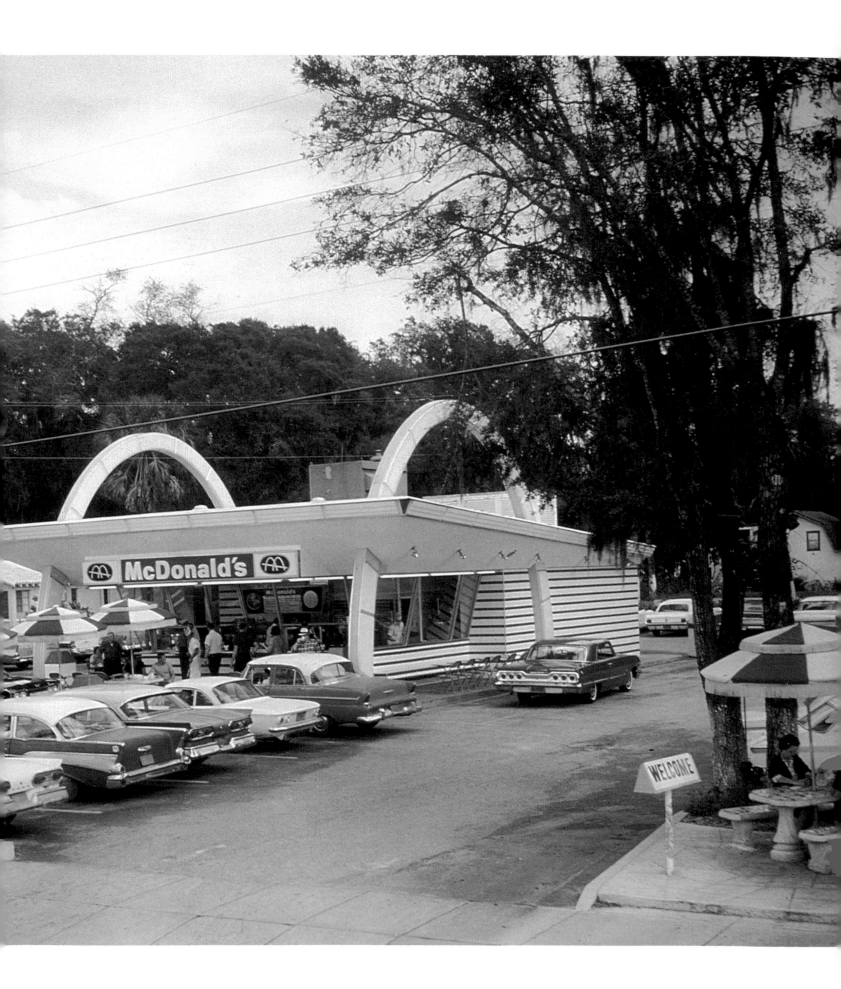

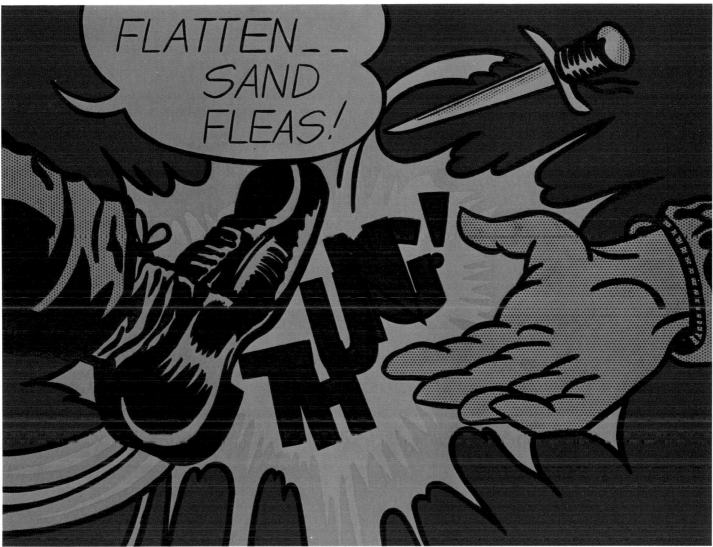

Flatten, Sand Fleas, oil on canvas by Roy Lichtenstein.

Personally, *pop art wasn't my kind of art, but I understood it. I thought pop art was an outcry against all the ads, and it was a natural reflection of our culture.*

I'll tell you how I made sense of it. When I was president of the Detroit Arts Commission, there was a person visiting us from Rome who was involved in modern art. We took him on a drive down Livernois Avenue. At that time, there were a lot of used-car dealers, one after the other, selling cars, and they had flags out and all kinds of colorful signs. All of a sudden this guy says, "Stop the car, I want to take a picture." And suddenly, he's taking all kinds of pictures of Livernois—of all the signs and pennants and so forth used to sell cars. He said, "Now, I understand pop art."

LAWRENCE FLEISCHMAN

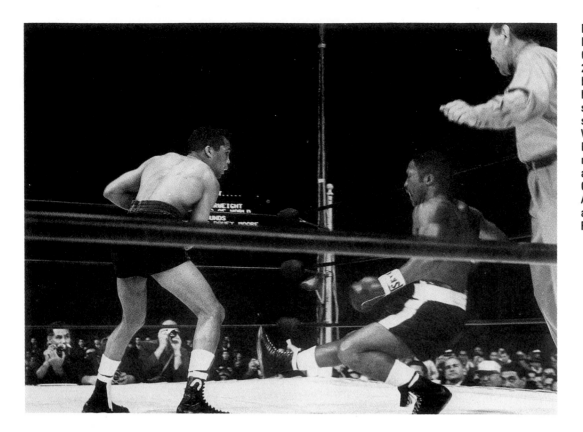

Featherweight champion Davey Moore (right) died while fighting Cuba's Sugar Ramos on March 21. Moore was killed by a fatal blow in the tenth round, when his head hit a rubber-covered steel ring rope. It was the third serious boxing injury in a year. Welterweight champion Benny Paret had died from brain injuries in April 1962, just ten days after he lost the title to Emile Griffith, and heavyweight boxer Alejandro Lavorante was still in a coma after fighting Johnny Riggins in September.

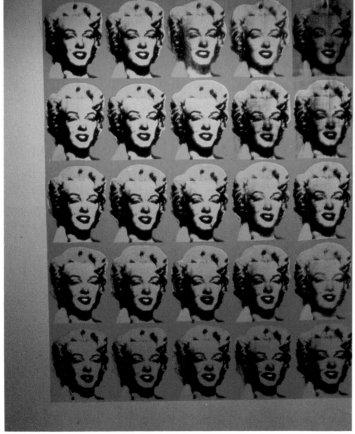

Andy Warhol's *Marilyn Monroe*.

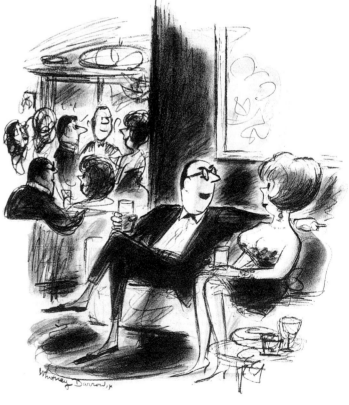

"You're stupid. I like that in a woman."

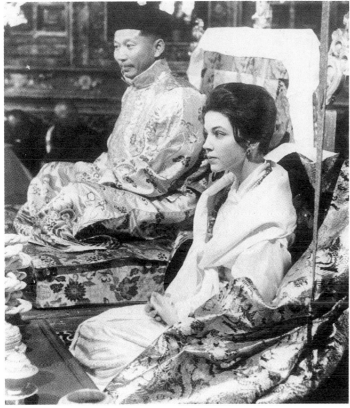

New York socialite, Hope Cooke, 22, wed Palden Thondup Namgyal, 39, the Crown Prince of the Indian protectorate of Sikkim, in a March 20 ceremony held in a Buddhist monastery in the Himalayas.

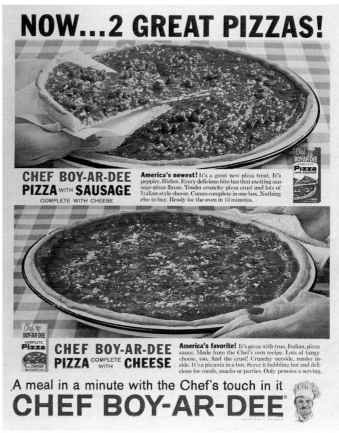

Pizza in a box meant you had to make and bake it using the manufacturer's dough mix, canned sauce and Italian-style cheese. This was adventurous eating for some people at the time.

In 1963, frozen foods were getting more popular, particularly TV dinners. The typical TV dinner was, oh, chicken, potatoes, and peas. Three things. They were never that good, and the entrees were pretty puny, but at least you could have something to eat in 25 or 30 minutes, and it was easy. In 1963, the changing pattern of the working wife had started.

But it was still pretty much a meat-and-potatoes diet in 1963. Meat was a big item in people's diets. My memory is that we were eating about 160 pounds of meat per person per year. We're down to about 90 pounds now. The big things behind the decline were cost—the price went up—and the health interest.

Fresh produce was not very popular in 1963; it was about 6 percent of the store's sales. Today, it's someplace between 12 and 15 percent.

Supermarkets were also much smaller in size. The average store was about a third to a half the size.

The smaller store was the more friendly store. It was a friendlier environment, but totally because of size. You were more apt to know the store manager. You certainly knew your check-out girls. We used to go down to the Grand Union all the time because this very, very nice girl checked us out

CLARENCE G. ADAMY, President,
National Association of Food Chains

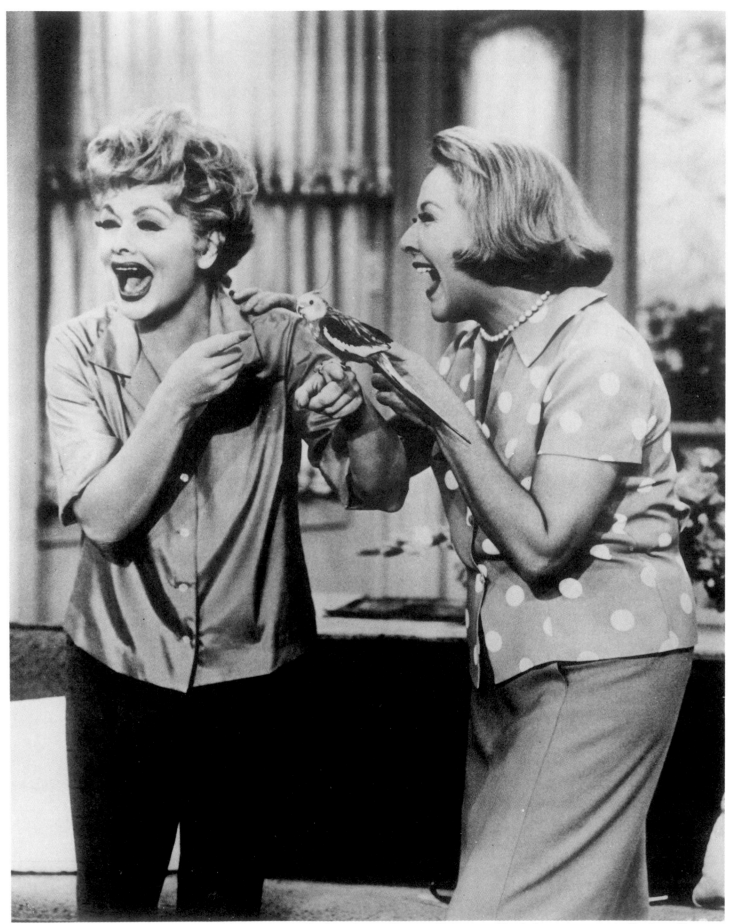

Lucille Ball doubled as president of the production company Desilu and star of her weekly program *Here's Lucy*, successor to *The Lucy Show*. The series featured Gale Gordon and Vivian Vance and included Ball's real-life children, Desi Jr. and Lucie Arnaz. The sitcom played Mondays at 9 P.M., giving CBS dominance of the night through virtually every season (beginning with *I Love Lucy* in 1951) Ball was with the network.

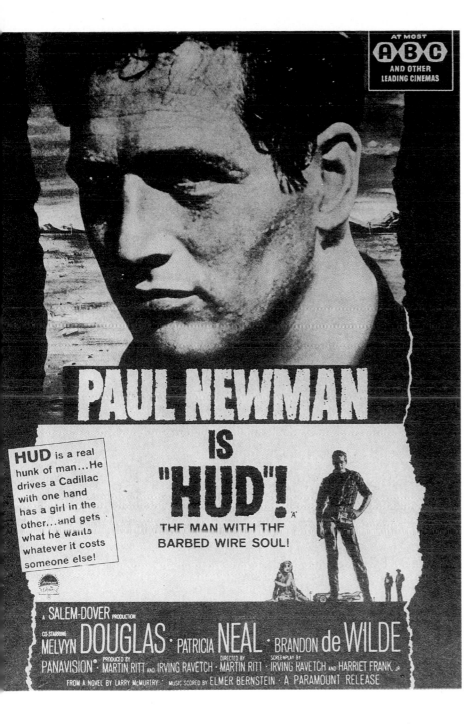

Paul Newman, as the sexually arrogant ne'er-do-well who has a bad influence on everyone, became a certified sex object with this movie based on Larry McMurtry's novel *Horsemen Pass By*. Patricia Neal and Melvyn Douglas (both won Oscars) and Brandon de Wilde—all turned in fine performances. James Wong Howe, the long-venerated cameraman, got an Oscar for his photography. Director Martin Ritt and Newman received Oscar nominations.

I used to ride the bus downtown to go to the movies. Back then, the old movie houses had an entirely different feel. It wasn't like today, where you have small screens and several different movies showing at the same place. You had one huge screen, and hundreds—or even thousands—of people would sit in the same theater. In fact, the old Loew's Grand, where *Gone with the Wind* premiered, was still functioning. It's too bad all of those old theaters have become relics—too bad that they've been lost forever.

MICHAEL RIGGALL,
High School Student, Atlanta

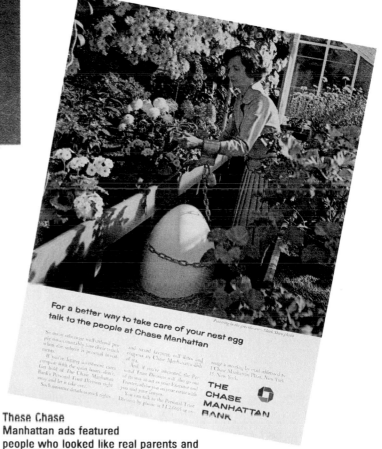

For a better way to take care of your nest egg talk to the people at Chase Manhattan

THE CHASE MANHATTAN BANK

These Chase Manhattan ads featured people who looked like real parents and were always manacled to these gigantic eggs. They ran in magazines like *The New Yorker*. A psychiatrist in Westport, Connecticut, reported a significant incidence of children with recurrent nightmares about being attacked by huge chickens.

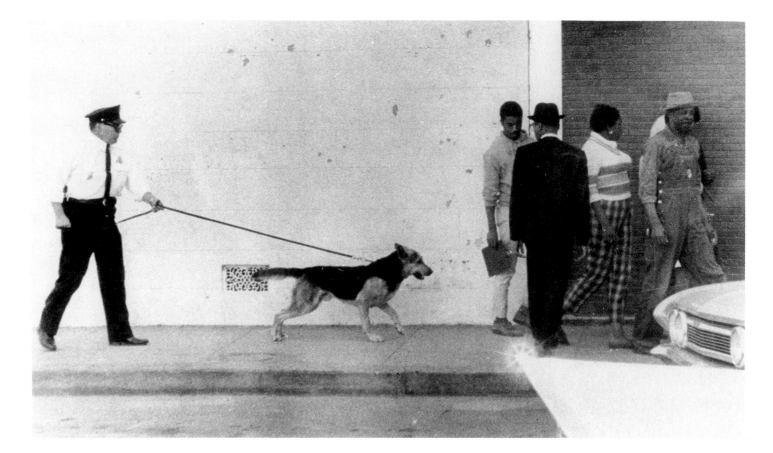

ABOVE: On March 28, Greenwood, Miss., policeman James Switzer held the leash as his police dog, Tiger, growled at a group of blacks who were on their way to register to vote. Although the right to vote was extended to blacks by the Fifteenth Amendment in 1870, barriers such as literacy tests, poll taxes, gerrymandering, white primaries, and other discriminatory registration practices frequently stood in their way.

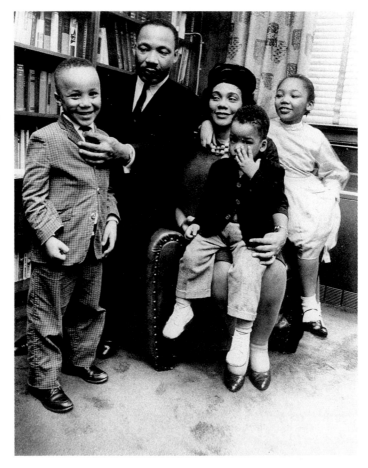

The Reverend Martin Luther King, Jr., and his family on March 17, the day after his son, five-year-old Martin Luther King III, was denied admission to a private school in Atlanta.

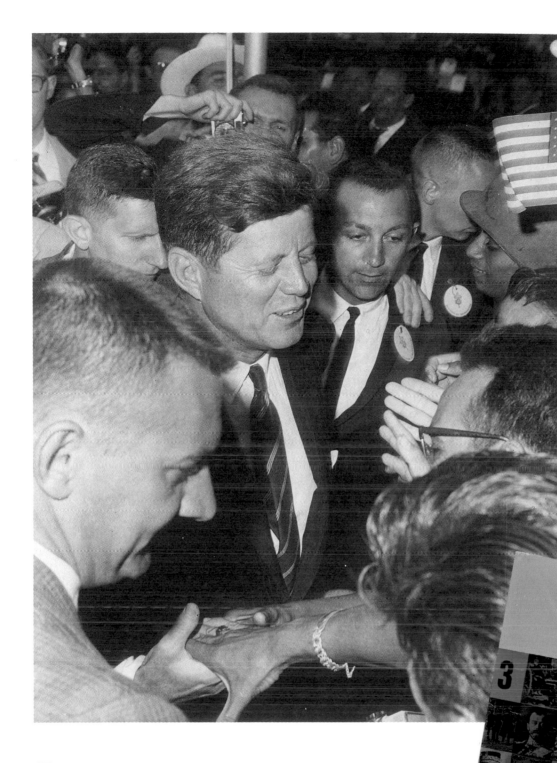

On March 22, President Kennedy was greeted by an enthusiastic crowd in San Jose, Costa Rica, as he toured the El Bosque housing development. The project, built by Costa Ricans with funds from the Alliance for Progress, was designed to shelter 8,000 persons. Kennedy called this ten-year program of inter-American cooperation, launched in 1961, "a plan to transform the 1960s into an historic decade of democratic progress."

I've watched some old tapes of the Kennedy speeches, and it still strikes me that he had a clearer vision of this country's role in the world and a more elegant and more noble and clear perspective on it than any president since. And that's sort of amazing to say. It's been 25 years.

ROGER LANDRUM

THE GUNS OF AUGUST

3   14   19   27

The drama of August, 1914, a month of battle in which war was waged on a scale unsurpassed, and whose results determined the shape of the world in which we live today.

Barbara W. Tuchman

The Pulitzer Prize committee bestowed its nonfiction award on Barbara Tuchman for her account of the beginning of World War I.

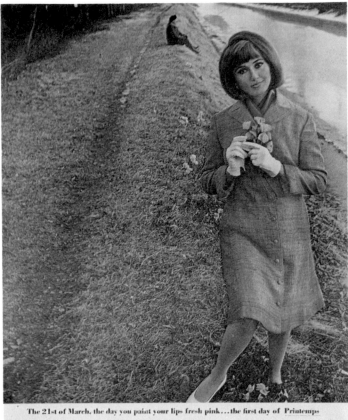

The 21st of March, the day you paint your lips fresh pink...the first day of Printemps

Printemps is Elizabeth Arden's new pet of a color? It's pure pink, poetic pink, Seine at sunset pink. The second you put it on, you smile and say, "Spring is in the atmosphere." Elizabeth Arden created the color in her French Salon, and Miss Arden says, "The sky, the Bois, the River are so incredibly beautiful one cannot help coloring in the manner of the French Impressionists." To create the Printemps look, Miss Arden rounded out her palette and designed a new preparation called Faint Blush, a new hint of a tint of a pink to wear under your foundation. It's the very tooiest of glows. Printemps Click-Change Lipstick 2.00, Printemps Nail Lacquer 1.00, and Faint Blush 5.00. Prices plus tax. Elizabeth Arden preparations are sold at fine stores in America, France and throughout the whole world—and in the Paris Salon, of course, at

Elizabeth Arden
7 Place Vendome

"Printemps" was Elizabeth Arden's name for a new line of cosmetics. Ads described the color thus: "A pet of a color, poetic pink, the color of the Seine at sunset." The lipstick sold for $2, the nail "lacquer" for $1.

Within a year after [Jacqueline Kennedy] moved into the White House, women all over the United States had memorized the high-fashion mathematics of multiplying chic by subtraction. Her little-nothing dresses, her un-adorned cloth coats, her plain pillboxes and pumps had been upper-crust specialties. They became mass fads.

MARILYN BENDER ALTSCHUL, Fashion Reporter, *New York Times*

I n college I drove a '49 Chevy. It was a real clunker, but at least that car had character. The heater didn't work, and it had one of those metal ignition buttons that you had to push to start it. On cold mornings, if I didn't put my gloves on, my thumb would get stuck on the starter button. Baldwin, Kansas, where I was in school, didn't have any pubs or taverns. So, if we wanted to go out for pizza—or go out drinking beer and chasing women—we had to drive 25 miles to Lawrence. In the winter four or five of us would bundle up and drive all that way without any heater, because the '49 Chevy was the only car we had.

GIL MERRITT, Student, Baker University

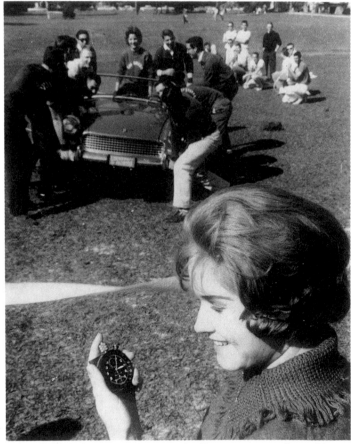

In need of novel amusements to work off excess energy, fraternities at the University of Florida took to races carrying coeds perched on small cars. The Austin Healey Sprite, transported in the fastest time, weighed 1,365 pounds.

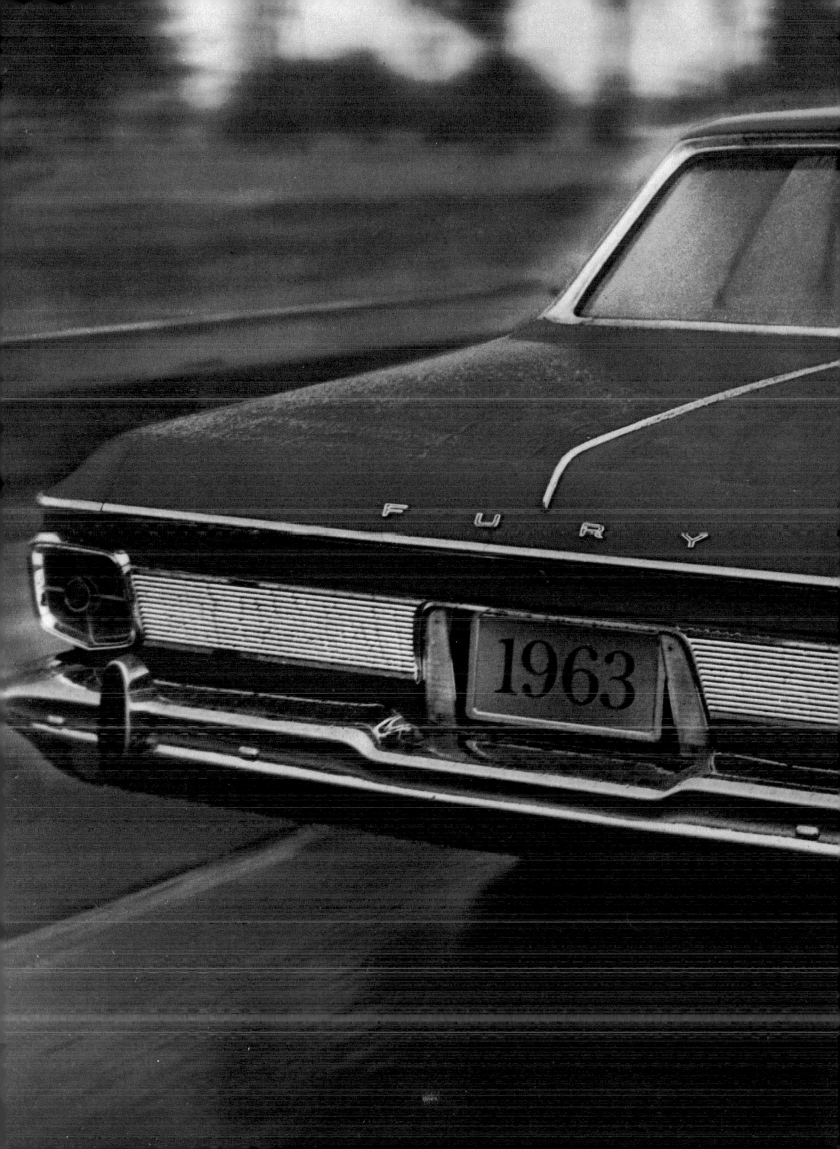

APRIL

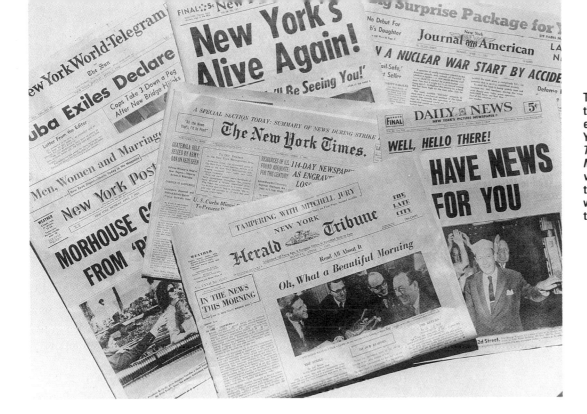

The New York newspaper strike that began December 8, 1962, ended on April 1. Four of New York's seven dailies—the *World-Telegram*, *Journal American*, *Mirror*, and *Herald Tribune*—would never fully recover from the strike and its settlement, and would cease to publish within the next few years.

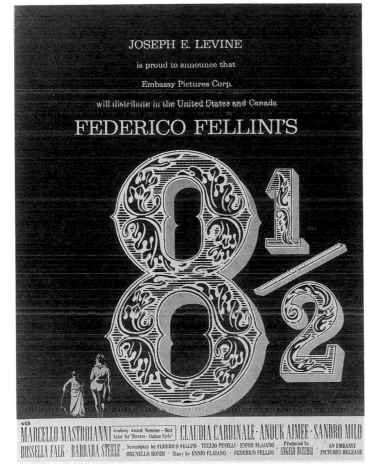

Fellini's *8½* received Academy Award nominations as best foreign film and for its direction and script. In 1963 foreign films, which generally meant European, were beginning to be labeled works of art, as opposed to the commercial craft produced by Hollywood. There were, however, some dissenters. The critic John Simon was not to be fooled. "Fellini's intellectualization is not even like dogs dancing, it is not well done, nor does it surprise us that it is done at all. It merely palls on us, and finally appalls us."

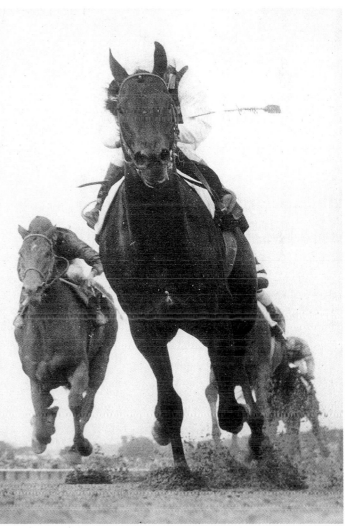

Leading the pack in the homestretch at the 78th running of the $75,000-added Futurity Stakes at Aqueduct Race Track was Captain's Gig, ridden by Willie Shoemaker. Vitriolic, ridden by Braulio Baeza, followed his lead. Captain's Gig won by three lengths, setting a track record of 1:15 for the 6½-furlong race.

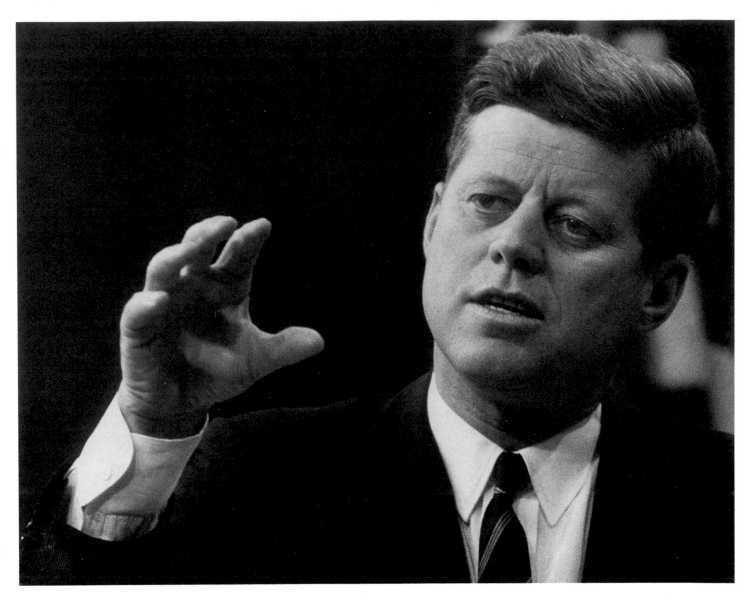

President Kennedy illustrating a point during his April 3 news conference, when he confirmed that 4,000 Soviet troops had left Cuba.

I was very inspired by John Kennedy. When he gave his inaugural address, and showed such skill at those televised news conferences, I thought he was the most wonderful thing I'd ever encountered in my whole life. It wasn't that I hadn't been patriotic before so much that he made me feel differently about patriotism. With him, I really thought this country had a mission.

A lot of it had to do with having lived through eight years of Dwight Eisenhower, who was a lot older and had a lot of really old men around him. Old men like John Foster Dulles. Then Kennedy came in and he brought all these young intellectual people to the White House. He played touch football, and he knew all about art, literature, and music. It was something I hadn't seen in any politician before. He was so eloquent. He was someone you could be really proud of as a representative of this country. I was coming into adulthood with this guy at the helm, and I really thought we were going to make the world a better place.

LEE SMITH

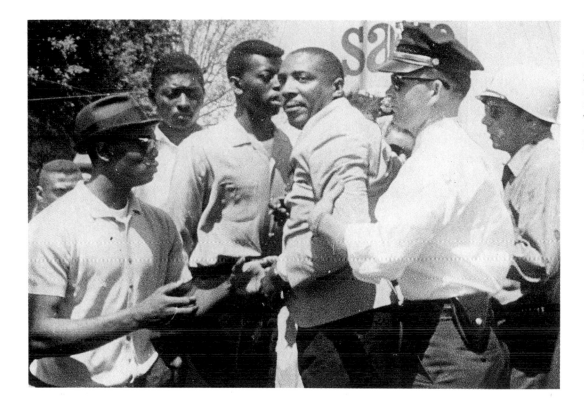

Police in Greenwood, Miss., arrested comedian Dick Gregory and other blacks during a voter registration drive on April 2 and 3. The demonstrations were an attempt to increase the number of black voters in Leflore County, where blacks made up 65 percent of the population but only 2 percent of registered voters.

I was brought downstairs and put in a cell built for 25 people. There must have been 500 of us in there. . . . There was a little boy, maybe four years old, standing in the corner of the cell sucking his thumb. I felt sorry for him. He didn't even have someone his age to play with. I kind of rubbed his head and asked him how he was.

"All right," he said.

"What are you here for?"

"Teedom," he said. Couldn't even say freedom, but he was in jail for it.

DICK GREGORY, Comedian
and Political Activist

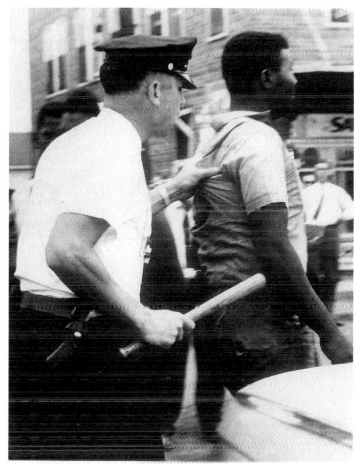

The civil rights movement succeeded because the majority of Americans came to believe it was morally right. Every additional photograph or television image of non-violent activists being arrested or beaten increased the influence of Martin Luther King's philosophy.

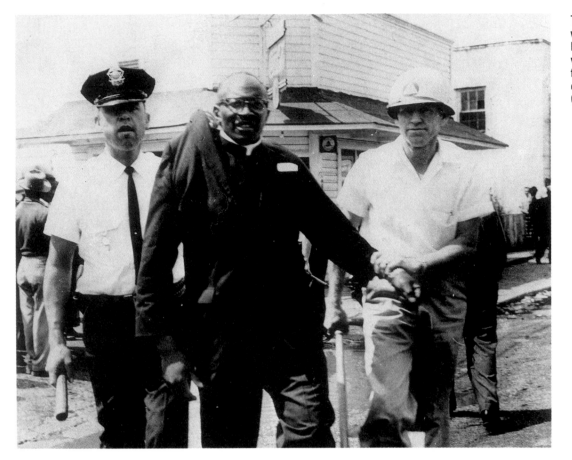

The Reverend Robert Kinlock was arrested in Greenwood, Miss. after he and 19 other voter-registration workers refused to obey police orders to disband their march to the County Court House.

I n Atlanta, I went from elementary school all the way through high school, and there were never any black kids enrolled. The schools were totally white. On the buses going downtown there were signs that said colored people were to be seated from the rear and white people from the front. At the movie theaters, there were colored rest rooms and water fountains, and there were restaurants downtown that wouldn't serve black people. It was the old Jim Crow thing of "separate but equal."

But it didn't work that way the other way around. I used to go to black nightclubs in Atlanta even though I was underage. The best jazz was being performed in the black clubs. There was a place called Pascal's that had entertainers like Miles Davis and Ramsey Lewis, and white people were always accepted. Segregation was strictly a one-way street.

MICHAEL RIGGALL

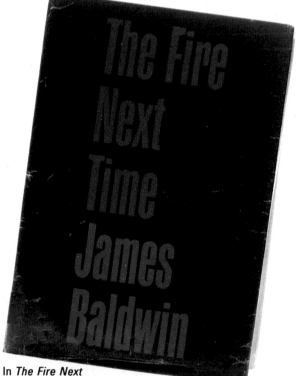

In *The Fire Next Time*, James Baldwin told—actually predicted—a lot of things about race relations in America that most of the population did not want to hear. But since purchasers of hard-cover books as well as book review editors tended to be liberal in 1963, Baldwin's sermon was widely read and praised.

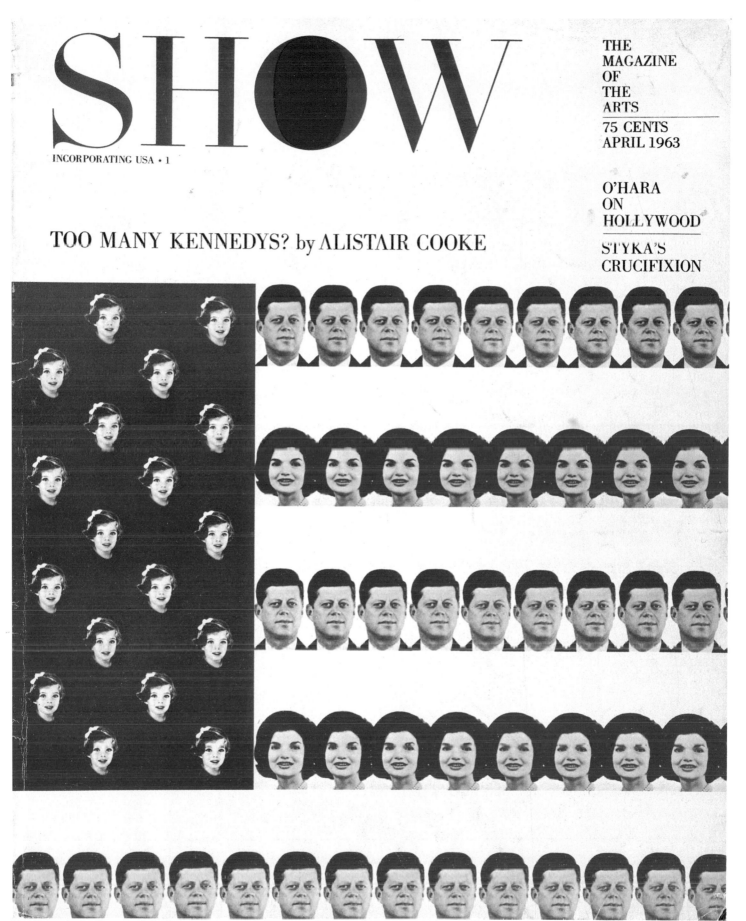

SH○W

INCORPORATING USA • 1

THE
MAGAZINE
OF
THE
ARTS

75 CENTS
APRIL 1963

O'HARA
ON
HOLLYWOOD

STYKA'S
CRUCIFIXION

TOO MANY KENNEDYS? by ALISTAIR COOKE

The Kennedy family, especially Jacqueline, graced the cover of practically every magazine published in 1963. Many of the covers treated the family members as if they were movie or pop stars. This April cover of the estimable *Show* was, by comparison, both clever and restrained. *Show* was published by Huntington Hartford, heir to the Great Atlantic and Pacific Tea Co., better known as the A & P. It was an intelligent, well-edited magazine with good writing and superior graphics. Alistair Cooke's comments (opposite page) appeared in this issue.

*T*he president's determination to mold his public face has set some forces in motion that are now clearly beyond his contrivance or his control. The new publicity has extended the area of permissible public curiosity and therefore invaded the area in which the pulps and scandal sheets usually score their scoops. Respectable magazines seem to be taking over what used to be squatter's territory. Consequently, the scandal sheets, the pulps, the comics and the parodists have expanded their own twilight zone—under the impression that in the Kennedy regime anything goes. Hence, the coloring books, the phonograph record skits, the lurid "unauthorized" biographies and . . . the "intimate" revelations of the fan magazines. . . .

Since the 35th president and his wife are about the most physically attractive couple to have lived in the White House, the urge of the publicists, magazines, networks and photographers to fuse two American dreams and reveal the White House as the ultimate movie set is irresistible. To put it mildly, the president has yielded to this urge and has manipulated it with the no doubt serious purpose of setting a contemporary "style" of public life for the presidency.

ALISTAIR COOKE, Journalist

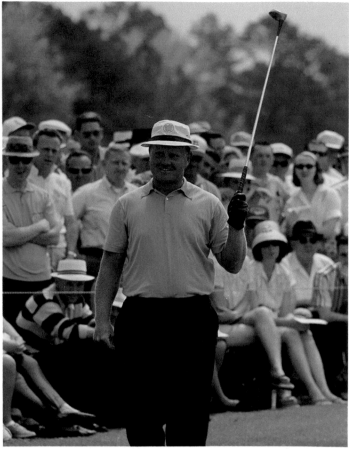

Jack Nicklaus putted out a winner on the 18th hole in the final round of the Masters Golf tournament in Augusta, Ga., on April 7. He shot a 72, for a four-round total of 286. Nicklaus also won the World Series of Golf in Akron and the Tournament of Champions in Las Vegas, which awarded the largest golf prize of the year—$50,000. Arnold Palmer took the Los Angeles Open, Pensacola Open, Thunderbird Classic, and the Cleveland Open. Julius Boros won the United States Open, Deane Beman, the National Amateur, and Anne Q. Welts, the National Women's Amateur.

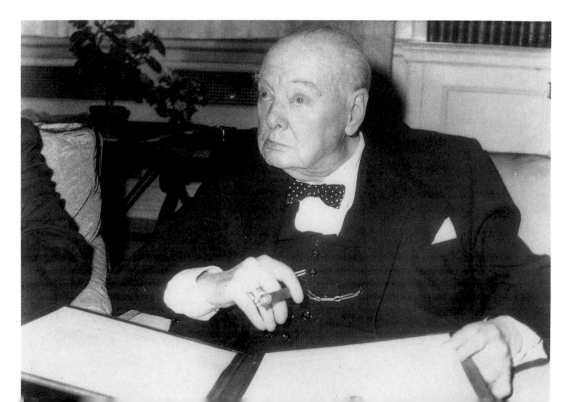

On April 9, Winston Churchill became the first honorary citizen of the United States. Less than a month later, Sir Winston, 88, announced that he would not stand for Parliament again, ending more than 60 years of parliamentary service. He said that a thighbone he fractured in 1962 made it difficult to attend House sessions.

Kennedy threw the ceremonial first pitch to open the major-league baseball season on April 8. Behind the president (left to right) were Senator Hubert Humphrey, Senate Majority Leader Mike Mansfield, and James M. Johnston, Chairman of the Board of the Washington Senators.

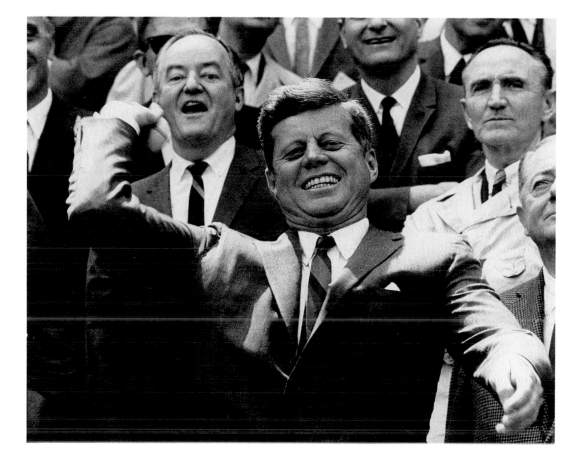

E verybody liked John Kennedy. Even people who were against him politically liked him. You couldn't help but like him. He was a very dramatic, intelligent person. He had an aura of knowing what was happening, and of being in charge. That was very attractive. All of us in Congress tried to copy him in unobtrusive ways. We tried to copy his sense of style, and his bearing. In running for office I certainly did not mind people drawing any connection that maybe a new or younger person was in line with what this country was looking for.

**CHARLES WELTNER,
Congressman, Atlanta**

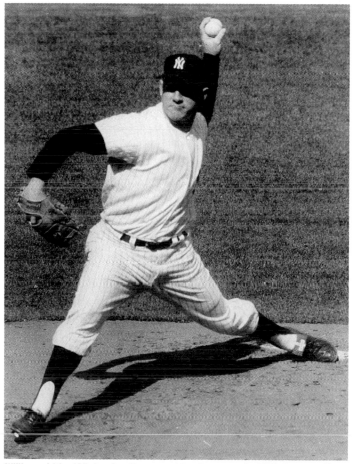

1963 would be Whitey Ford's second best season. In 1961, he won 25 games and lost only four. This year his 24 and 7 record would again be the best winning percentage in the American league. And the New York Yankees would, for the fourth consecutive year, win the pennant.

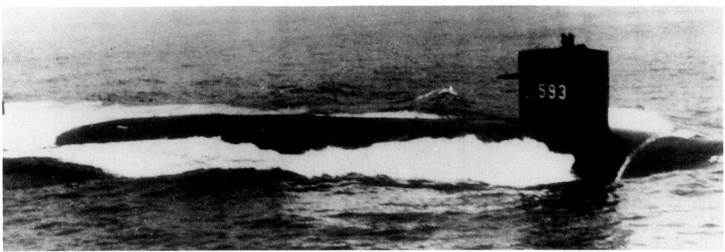

On April 10 the nuclear submarine *Thresher* disappeared 200 miles off Boston while on post-overhaul testing in the Atlantic. One hundred twenty-nine men, including 17 civilian technicians, died in what was the worst submarine disaster in U.S. history.

The president and I took a long walk one weekend. . . . It was a beautiful spring day. It was the last year of his life. And we walked all over, first around the White House, and then he had . . . the car take us down to the Mall. We walked down that long reflecting pool toward Lincoln's monument. . . . Then we got into the car, and we drove over to Arlington Cemetery. It really was rather amazing, because we wandered all through that, where those stones are at the top of the hill. We didn't go down to the part of the hill where he was [later] buried. . . .

And we discussed that day where he was going to be buried. He said, "I guess I'll have to go back to Boston." And I remember arguing for the National Cemetery. But we left it sort of up in the air.

But this trip was very much in my mind the night he was killed, when Bob McNamara . . . [suggested] to the family where the president should be buried. But Bob McNamara had urged that he be buried at Arlington. And as soon as I heard Bob say this, why, then I . . . jumped in . . . and I did say that it is such a beautiful place, and it was something that he loved and was part of the heritage he loved.

CHARLES BARTLETT, Journalist and Friend of the President

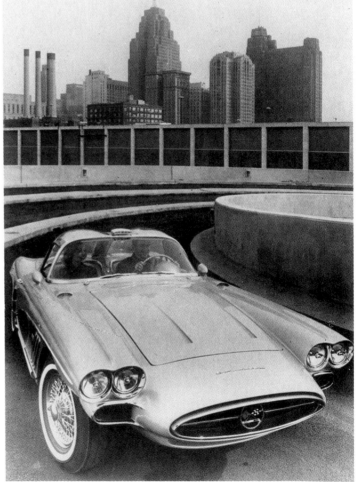

The experimental Chevrolet XP-700 Corvette was unveiled in Detroit on April 9.

Billboard

TOP LP's

★ STAR performer—LP's on chart 9 weeks or less registering greatest proportionate upward progress this week.

Record Industry Association of America seal of certification as million dollar LP's.

This Week	Last Week	Title, Artist, Label	Wks. on Chart
1	1	MY SON, THE NUT — Allan Sherman, Warner Bros. W 1501 (M); WS 1501 (S)	9
2	3	INGREDIENTS IN A RECIPE FOR SOUL — Ray Charles, ABC-Paramount ABC 465 (M); ABCS 465 (S)	7
3	5	TRINI LOPEZ AT PJ's — Reprise R 6093 (M); R9-6093 (S)	13
4	2	BYE BYE BIRDIE — Sound Track, RCA Victor LOC 1081 (M); LSO 1081 (S)	25
5	4	PETER, PAUL & MARY — Warner Bros. W 1449 (M); WS 1449 (S)	77
6	7	THE JAMES BROWN SHOW — King 826 (M); S 826 (S)	16
7	6	MOVING — Peter, Paul & Mary, Warner Bros. W 1473 (M); WS 1473 (S)	39
8	11	SHUT DOWN — Various Artists, Capitol T 1918 (M); ST 1918 (S)	14
★9	12	ELVIS' GOLDEN RECORDS, VOL. 3 — Elvis Presley, RCA Victor LPM 2765 (M); LSP 2765 (S)	5
10	8	WEST SIDE STORY — Sound Track, Columbia OL 5670 (M); OS 2070 (S)	103
★11	14	THE SECOND BARBRA STREISAND ALBUM — Columbia CL 2054 (M); CS 8854 (S)	5
12	10	DAYS OF WINE AND ROSES — Andy Williams, Columbia CL 2015 (M); CS 8815 (S)	26
13	16	BLUE VELVET — Bobby Vinton, Epic LN 24068 (M); BN 26068 (S)	10
14	13	HOLLYWOOD—MY WAY — Nancy Wilson, Capitol T 1934 (M); ST 1934 (S)	10
15	17	RAMBLIN' — New Christy Minstrels, Columbia CL 2055 (M); CS 8855 (S)	8
16	9	SUNNY SIDE! — Kingston Trio, Capitol T 1935 (M); ST 1935 (S)	9
★17	28	GOLDEN HITS OF THE 4 SEASONS — Vee Jay LP 1065 (M); SR 1065 (S)	6
18	19	THE BARBRA STREISAND ALBUM — Columbia CL 2007 (M); CS 8807 (S)	27
19	15	JOAN BAEZ IN CONCERT — Vanguard VRS 9112 (M); VSD 2122 (S)	51
20	21	JOHNNY — Johnny Mathis, Columbia CL 2044 (M); CS 8844 (S)	8
21	26	I LEFT MY HEART IN SAN FRANCISCO — Tony Bennett, Columbia CL 1869 (M); CS 8669 (S)	67
22	29	SO MUCH IN LOVE — Tymes, Parkway P 7032 (M); (no Stereo)	11
23	20	WIPE OUT — Surfaris, Dot DLP 3535 (M); DLP 25535 (S)	10
24	24	SURFIN' U. S. A. — Beach Boys, Capitol T 1890 (M); ST 1890 (S)	24
25	31	LAWRENCE OF ARABIA — Sound Track, Colpix CP 514 (M); SCP 514 (S)	33
26	27	RING OF FIRE—THE BEST OF JOHNNY CASH — Columbia CL 2053 (M); CS 8853 (S)	12
27	25	JOAN BAEZ, VOL. I — Vanguard VRS 9078 (M); VSD 2077 (S)	85
28	22	THE FREEWHEELIN' BOB DYLAN — Columbia CL 1986 (M); CS 8786 (S)	6
29	32	CHUCK BERRY ON STAGE — Chess LP 1480 (M); (no Stereo)	8
★30	46	LET'S GO — Ventures, Dolton BLP 2024 (M); BST 8024 (S)	7
31	39	MONDO CANE — Sound Track, United Artists UAL 4105 (M); UAS 5105 (S)	13
32	33	THINK ETHNIC — Smothers Brothers, Mercury MG 20777 (M); SR 60777 (S)	28
33	34	SCARLETT O'HARA — Lawrence Welk, Dot DLP 3528 (M); DLP 25528 (S)	10
34	23	HOW THE WEST WAS WON — Sound Track, MGM 1E5 (M); 1SE5 (S)	26
35	18	LITTLE STEVIE WONDER THE 12 YEAR OLD GENIUS — Tamla 240 (M); (no Stereo)	14
36	41	JOHNNY'S GREATEST HITS — Johnny Mathis, Columbia CL 1133 (M); CS 8634 (S)	284
37	43	BROADWAY—MY WAY — Nancy Wilson, Capitol T 1828 (M); ST 1828 (S)	28
38	38	SURF CITY & OTHER SWINGIN' CITIES — Jan & Dean, Liberty LRP 3314 (M); LST 7314 (S)	10
39	42	THE BEST OF THE KINGSTON TRIO — Capitol T 1705 (M); ST 1705 (S)	71
40	47	JOAN BAEZ, VOL. II — Vanguard VRS 9094 (M); VSD 2097 (S)	98
41	63	CALL ON ME — Bobby Bland, Duke DLP 77 (M); (no Stereo)	14
42	30	MOON RIVER & OTHER GREAT MOVIE THEMES — Andy Williams, Columbia CL 1809 (M); CS 8609 (S)	75
43	50	RAMBLIN' ROSE — Nat King Cole, Capitol T 1793 (M); ST 1793 (S)	56
44	45	FRANK FONTAINE SINGS LIKE CRAZY — ABC-Paramount ABC 460 (M); ABCS 460 (S)	8
45	40	I LOVE YOU BECAUSE — Al Martino, Capitol T 1914 (M); ST 1914 (S)	18
46	44	CLEOPATRA — Sound Track, 20th Century-Fox FXG 5008 (M); SXG 5008 (S)	17
47	52	THOSE LAZY-HAZY-CRAZY DAYS OF SUMMER — Nat King Cole, Capitol T 1932 (M); ST 1932 (S)	15
48	58	UNIQUELY MANCINI — Henry Mancini, RCA Victor LPM 2692 (M); LSP 2692 (S)	16
★49	54	IN DREAMS — Roy Orbison, Monument MLP 8003 (M); SLP 18003 (S)	9
50	59	WEST SIDE STORY — Original Cast, Columbia OL 5230 (M); OS 2001 (S)	157
51	64	TWO SIDES OF THE SMOTHERS BROTHERS — Mercury MG 20675 (M); SR 60675 (S)	43
★52	69	SEPTEMBER SONG — Jimmy Durante, Warner Bros. W 1506 (M); WS 1506 (S)	4
53	61	MODERN SOUNDS IN COUNTRY & WESTERN MUSIC — Ray Charles, ABC-Paramount ABC 410 (M); ABCS 410 (S)	78
54	49	THEMES FOR YOUNG LOVERS — Percy Faith & Ork, Columbia CL 2023 (M); CS 8823 (S)	17
55	56	THE LANGUAGE OF LOVE — Jerry Vale, Columbia CL 2043 (M); CS 8843 (S)	6
56	37	OLDIES BUT GOODIES, VOL. V — Various Artists, Original Sound 5007 (M); 8855 (S)	20
57	51	THE NEW CHRISTY MINSTRELS TELL TALL TALES! — Columbia CL 2017 (M); CS 8817 (S)	21
58	65	SINATRA—BASIE — Frank Sinatra & Count Basie, Reprise R 1008 (M); R9-1008 (S)	37
59	60	THE SMOTHERS BROTHERS AT THE PURPLE ONION — Mercury MG 20611 (M); SR 60611 (S)	14
60	53	CAMELOT — Original Cast, Columbia KOL 5620 (M); KOS 2031 (S)	142
61	71	I WANNA BE AROUND — Tony Bennett, Columbia CL 2000 (M); CS 8800 (S)	28
62	70	NIGHT BEAT — Sam Cooke, RCA Victor LPM 2709 (M); LSP 2709 (S)	5
63	48	ROY ORBISON'S GREATEST HITS — Monument MLP 8000 (M); (no Stereo)	59
★64	76	PETER NERO IN PERSON — RCA Victor LPM 2710 (M); LSP 2710 (S)	6
65	85	PAUL ANKA'S 21 GOLDEN HITS — RCA Victor LPM 2691 (M); LSP 2691 (S)	15
66	73	STREETS I HAVE WALKED — Harry Belafonte, RCA Victor LPM 2695 (M); LSP 2695 (S)	17
★67	108	SINATRA'S SINATRA — Frank Sinatra, Reprise R 1010 (M); R9-1010 (S)	2
68	72	MY BOYFRIEND'S BACK — Angels, Smash MGS 27039 (M); SRS 67039 (S)	3
69	116	JOHNNY'S NEWEST HITS — Johnny Mathis, Columbia CL 2016 (M); CS 8816 (S)	26
70	35	THIS IS ALL I ASK — Tony Bennett, Columbia CL 2056 (M); CS 8856 (S)	8
71	36	OLIVER — Original Cast, RCA Victor LOCD 2004 (M); LSOD 2004 (S)	50
72	78	THE IMPRESSIONS — ABC-Paramount ABC 450 (M); ABCS 450 (S)	7
73	75	THE SOUND OF MUSIC — Original Cast, Columbia KOL 5450 (M); KOS 2020 (S)	199
74	84	MY SON, THE CELEBRITY — Allan Sherman, Warner Bros. W 1487 (M); WS 1487 (S)	39
75	57	THE CONCERT SINATRA — Frank Sinatra, Reprise R 1009 (M); R9-1009 (S)	17
76	79	SHIRELLES GREATEST HITS — Scepter 507 (M); (no Stereo)	38
★77	95	THE BEST OF THE CHAD MITCHELL TRIO — Kapp KL 1334 (M); KS 3334 (S)	3
78	55	I'LL CRY IF I WANT TO — Lesley Gore, Mercury MG 20805 (M); SR 60805 (S)	14
79	93	MODERN SOUNDS IN COUNTRY & WESTERN MUSIC, VOL. II — Ray Charles, ABC-Paramount ABC 435 (M); ABCS 435 (S)	30
80	107	STILL — Bill Anderson, Decca DL 4427 (M); DL 74427 (S)	15
81	89	LITTLE TOWN FLIRT — Del Shannon, Big Top 1308 (M); LPS 1308 (S)	17
82	87	SONGS I SING ON THE JACKIE GLEASON SHOW — Frank Fontaine, ABC-Paramount ABC 442 (M); ABCS 442 (S)	36
83	90	HOOTENANNY WITH THE HIGHWAYMEN — United Artists UAL 3294 (M); UAS 6294 (S)	6
84	92	WONDERFUL WORLD OF LOVE — Robert Goulet, Columbia CL 1993 (M); CS 8793 (S)	25
85	81	TIME OUT — Dave Brubeck, Columbia CL 1397 (M); CS 8192 (S)	143
86	77	WHERE CAN YOU GO FOR A BROKEN HEART — George Maharis, Epic LN 24064 (M); BN 26064 (S)	5
★87	113	FOURTEEN 14K FOLK SONGS — Limeliters, RCA Victor LPM 2671 (M); LSP 2671 (S)	3
★88	101	IRMA LA DOUCE — Sound Track, United Artists UAL 4109 (M); UAS 5109 (S)	5
★89	111	ABILENE — George Hamilton IV, RCA Victor LPM 2778 (M); LSP 2778 (S)	2
90	103	KNOCKERS UP — Rusty Warren, Jubilee JLP 2029 (M); (no Stereo)	153
91	96	BUDDY HOLLY STORY — Coral CRL 57279 (M); (no Stereo)	144
★92	129	ODETTA SINGS FOLK SONGS — RCA Victor LPM 2643 (M); LSP 2643 (S)	3
93	102	TEEN SCENE — Chet Atkins, RCA Victor LPM 2719 (M); LSP 2719 (S)	4
94	00	SAY WONDERFUL THINGS — Patti Page, Columbia CL 2049 (M); CS 8849 (S)	1
95	62	SEVEN STEPS TO HEAVEN — Miles Davis, Columbia CL 2051 (M); CS 8851 (S)	5
96	100	PRISONER OF LOVE — James Brown, King 851 (M); (No Stereo)	3
97	106	THIS TIME BY BASIE: HITS OF THE 50's AND 60's — Count Basie, Reprise R 6070 (M); R9-6070 (S)	13
★98	126	THE LETTERMEN IN CONCERT — Capitol T 1936 (M); ST 1936 (S)	7
99	68	BRITTEN: WAR REQUIEM — Various Artists, London A 4255 (M); OSA 1255 (S)	6
100	67	MORE (Soul Surfin') — Kai Winding, Verve V 8551 (M); V6-8551 (S)	10
101	99	THE SONGS I LOVE — Perry Como, RCA Victor LPM 2708 (M); LSP 2708 (S)	4
102	124	ANDY WILLIAMS MILLION SELLER SONGS — Cadence CLP 3061 (M); CLP 25061 (S)	40
103	66	GENE PITNEY SINGS WORLD-WIDE WINNERS — Musicor MM 2005 (M); MS 3005 (S)	11
104	91	HEAVENLY — Johnny Mathis, Columbia CL 1351 (M); CS 8152 (S)	112
105	86	SURFIN' SAFARI — Beach Boys, Capitol T 1808 (M); ST 1808 (S)	34
106	121	SURFING — Ventures, Dolton BLP 2022 (M); BST 8022 (S)	24
107	105	JUST KIDDIN' AROUND — Ray Conniff & Billy Butterfield, Columbia CL 2022 (M); CS 8822 (S)	5
★108	145	THE PATSY CLINE STORY — Decca DXB 176 (M); DXSB 7176 (S)	7
109	120	TWANGIN' UP A STORM — Duane Eddy, RCA Victor LPM 2700 (M); LSP 2700 (S)	2
110	104	HONEY IN THE HORN — Al Hirt, RCA Victor LPM 2733 (M); LSP 2733 (S)	4
111	98	THE NEW CHRISTY MINSTRELS — Columbia CL 1872 (M); CS 8672 (S)	46
112	88	BYE BYE BIRDIE — Original Cast, Columbia OL 5510 (M); OS 2025 (S)	53
113	125	THE MONKEY TIME — Major Lance, Okeh OKM 12105 (M); OKS 14105 (S)	2
114	112	SURFIN' WITH THE ASTRONAUTS — RCA Victor LPM 2760 (M); LSP 2760 (S)	11
115	119	THE FIRST FAMILY — Vaughn Meader, Cadence CLP 3060 (M); CLP 25060 (S)	44
116	109	MY SON, THE FOLK SINGER — Allan Sherman, Warner Bros. W 1475 (M); WS 1475 (S)	50
117	118	STOP THE WORLD—I WANT TO GET OFF — Original Cast, London AM 58001 (M); AMS 88001 (S)	47
★118	—	GOLDEN FOLK SONG HITS, VOL. II — Johnny Mann Singers, Liberty LRP 3304 (M); LST 7304 (S)	1
119	82	HOBO FLATS — Jimmy Smith, Verve V 8544 (M); V6-8544 (S)	22
120	131	1963's EARLY HITS — Lawrence Welk, Dot DLP 3510 (M); DLP 25510 (S)	28
★121	—	FOR YOU — Roger Williams, Kapp KL 1336 (M); KS 3336 (S)	1
★122	—	IN PERSON — Chubby Checker, Parkway P 7026 (M); (no Stereo)	1
123	127	THE GREAT ESCAPE — Sound Track, United Artists UAL 4107 (M); UAS 5107 (S)	4
★124	—	I AM THE GREATEST — Cassius Clay, Columbia CL 2093 (M); CS 8893 (S)	1
★125	—	SURFER GIRL — Beach Boys, Capitol T 1981 (M); ST 1981 (S)	1
126	136	SINCERELY YOURS — Robert Goulet, Columbia CL 1931 (M); CS 8731 (S)	41
127	130	I GOT SOMETHING TO TELL YOU — Moms Mabley, Chess LP 1479 (M); (no Stereo)	16
128	134	JAZZ SAMBA — Stan Getz & Charlie Byrd, Verve V 8432 (M); V6-8432 (S)	57
129	137	GREAT SCENES FROM GERSHWIN'S PORGY & BESS — Leontyne Price & William Warfield, RCA Victor LM 2679 (M); LSC 2679 (S)	2
130	135	OUR MAN IN HOLLYWOOD — Henry Mancini, RCA Victor LPM 2604 (M); LSP 2604 (S)	35
★131	147	HERE COMES FATS DOMINO — ABC-Paramount ABC 455 (M); ABCS 455 (S)	2
132	133	12 STRING GUITAR — Various Artists, World Pacific WP 1812 (M); ST 1812 (S)	3
133	94	GLORIA, MARTY & STRINGS — Gloria Lynne, Everest BR 5220 (M); SDBR 1220 (S)	4
★134	—	DANKE SCHOEN — Wayne Newton, Capitol T 1973 (M); ST 1973 (S)	1
135	140	GREATEST AMERICAN WALTZES — Connie Francis, MGM E 4145 (M); SE 4145 (S)	2
136	142	FLATT & SCRUGGS AT CARNEGIE HALL — Lester Flatt & Earl Scruggs, Columbia CL 2045 (M); CS 8845 (S)	3
137	—	HATARI! — Henry Mancini, RCA Victor LPM 2559 (M); LSP 2559 (S)	47
138	132	TELL HER YOU LOVE HER — Frank Sinatra, Capitol T 1919 (M); DT 1919 (S)	3
139	141	THE MIRACLES ON STAGE — Tamla 241 (M); (no Stereo)	2
★140	—	PAINTED, TAINTED ROSE — Al Martino, Capitol T 1975 (M); ST 1975 (S)	1
141	149	IT HAPPENED AT THE WORLD'S FAIR — Elvis Presley, RCA Victor LPM 2697 (M); LSP 2697 (S)	26
142	110	SOUTH RAMPART STREET PARADE — Pete Fountain & His Mardi Gras Strutters, Coral CRL 57440 (M); CRL 757440 (S)	6
143	139	FOUR STRONG WINDS — Ian & Sylvia, Vanguard VRS 9133 (M); VSD 2149	3
144	123	SEVERAL SHADES OF JADE — Cal Tjader, Verve V 8507 (M); V6-8507 (S)	7
145	148	FOR YOUR SWEET LOVE — Rick Nelson, Decca DL 4419 (M); DL 74419 (S)	19
146	—	BIG FOLK HITS — Brothers Four, Columbia CL 2033 (M); CS 8833 (S)	1
147	115	KINGSTON TRIO #16 — Capitol T 1871 (M); ST 1871 (S)	29
148	146	BLOWIN' IN THE WIND — Chad Mitchell Trio, Kapp KL 1313 (M); KS 3313 (S)	22
149	80	PUCCINI: TOSCA — Various Artists, RCA Victor LD 7022 (M); LDS 7022 (S)	6
150	74	SHE LOVES ME — Original Cast, MGM E 4118 (M); SE 4118 (S)	17

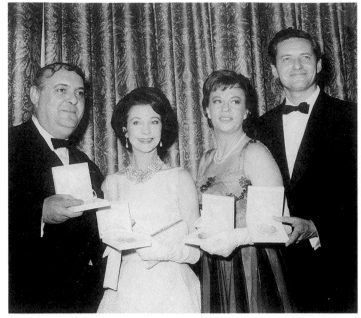

On April 28, Tony awards were given to (left to right) Zero Mostel for his role in the musical *A Funny Thing Happened on the Way to the Forum*, Vivien Leigh for her leading part in the musical *Tovarich*, and Uta Hagen and Arthur Hill for their performances in the drama *Who's Afraid of Virginia Woolf?*

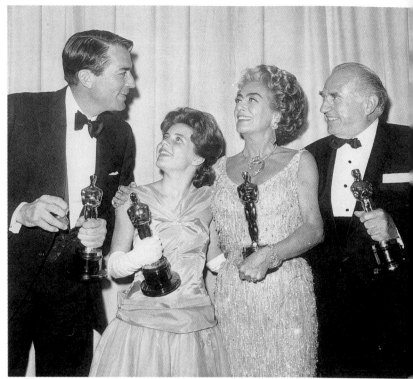

Hollywood's Oscars were something to smile about. From left, Gregory Peck, best actor (*To Kill a Mockingbird*); Patty Duke, best supporting actress (*The Miracle Worker*); Joan Crawford, accepting for Anne Bancroft, best actress (*The Miracle Worker*); and Ed Begley, best supporting actor (*Sweet Bird of Youth*).

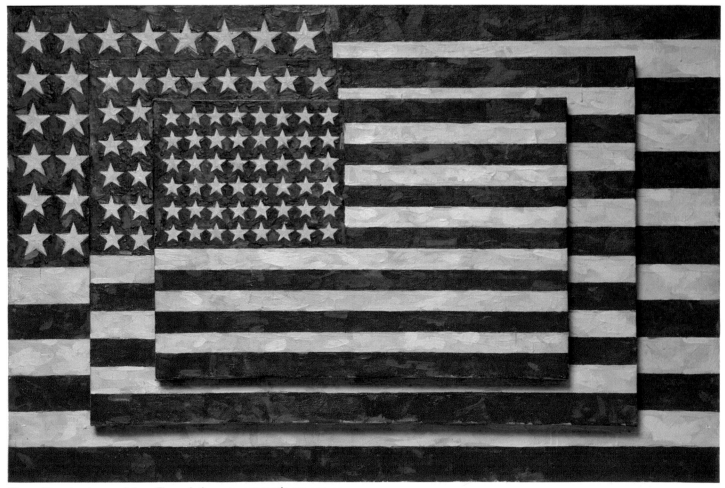

Three Flags by Jasper Johns. The painting was encaustic on canvas.

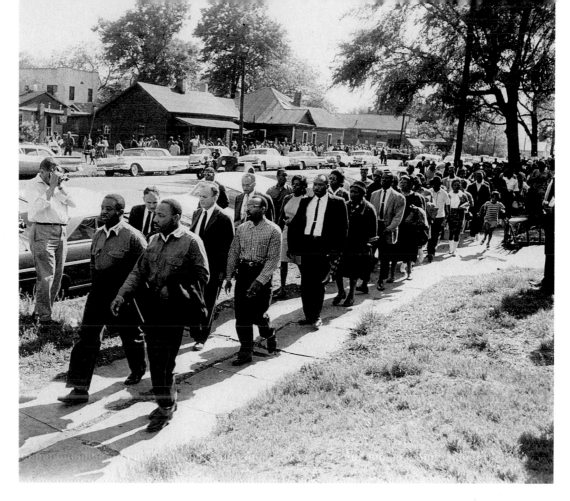

With ministers Ralph Abernathy (left) and Martin Luther King, Jr., in the lead, about 1,000 black demonstrators marched through downtown Birmingham on April 12, as part of a major campaign to attack discrimination in shops, restaurants, and employment. King called Birmingham "the most thoroughly segregated big city in the U.S."

Coming from the background that he came from, John F. Kennedy was isolated from the problems of race—from the problems of racial discrimination that so many Southern politicians knew about but failed to address. There was something about the philosophy of the movement and the leadership of Martin Luther King that inspired and educated him. He had to admire the physical courage and the discipline. This, after all, was the man who wrote Profiles in Courage, and when he saw people standing up and facing police dogs and fire hoses, he was moved. He did respond.

JOHN LEWIS,
Civil Rights Leader

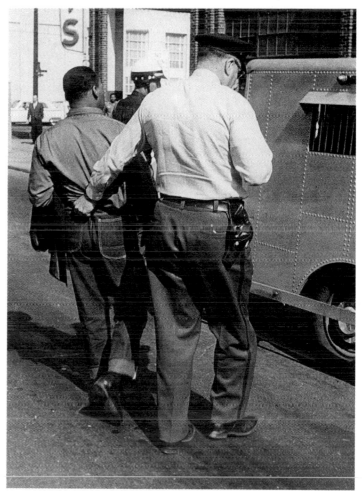

King was led into a paddy wagon following the April 12 demonstration. He, Abernathy, and about 60 others were jailed for defying an injunction, obtained by Police Commissioner Eugene ("Bull") Connor, that barred demonstrations.

The rights we were seeking to establish in the 1960s seem like such basic things today. We were talking about desegregating public accommodations—so that it would be possible for black citizens to buy a hot dog in a public restaurant or for black citizens to check into a hotel. These seem like such simple things, but these were rights that needed to be spelled out.

JAMES FARMER
National Director,
Congress of Racial Equality

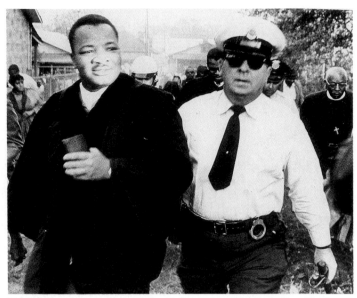

The Reverend A. D. King of Birmingham, Ala., Martin Luther King's brother, was taken away by police on April 14. He led more than 1500 blacks in an antisegregation march toward downtown Birmingham.

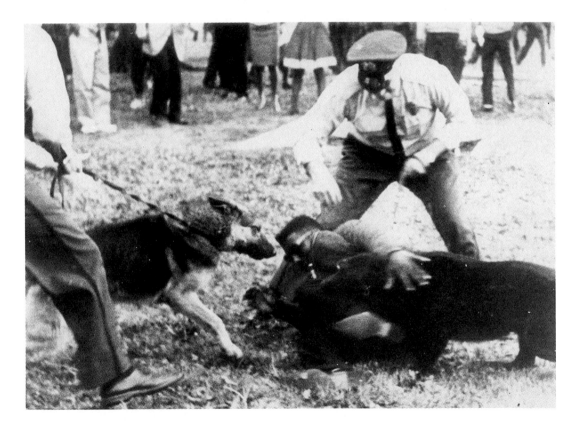

Pictures such as this aroused sympathy for civil rights demonstrators and rallied public opinion against segregation policies.

I guess the beginning of the civil rights movement was the most exciting thing about 1963. We really felt that society was changing, and that we could effect that change. I planned to live in an integrated neighborhood, or even to move into a black neighborhood to integrate it.

I miss that idealism. The young people I teach in college today don't seem to have the sense that the world can be changed, or that it is up to them to try and right injustice.

BONNIE STEINBOCK

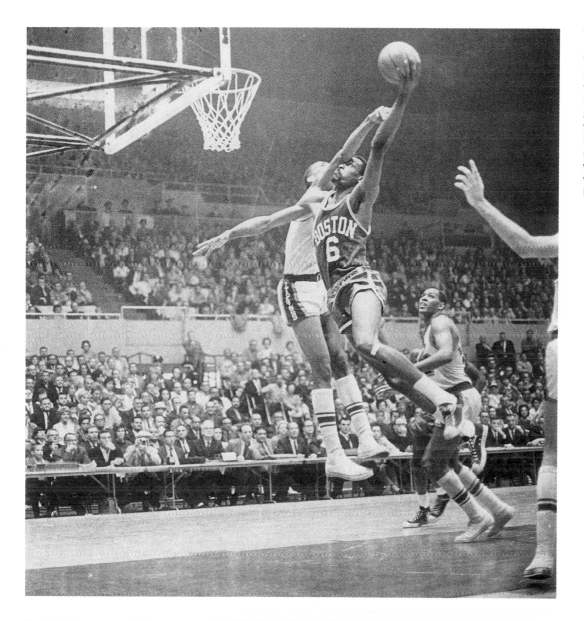

The Boston Celtics' Bill Russell received an elbow from Gene Wiley of the Los Angeles Lakers as Russell went for a basket in the final period of the NBA champion play-off on April 19. Although Russell did not make the basket, the Celtics beat the Lakers 108–105 in the fourth game of the play-offs. Boston won the NBA crown for the fifth year in a row after defeating the Lakers four games to two.

Twilight Zone expanded from a half hour to an hour in January 1963. CBS, realizing its error, returned it to the half-hour format that fall. The anthology series, telling tales of the supernatural, turned its playwright-creator, Rod Serling, who served as the host-narrator, into a television star. The stories were invariably morality yarns that seemed to caution viewers not to overstep themselves.

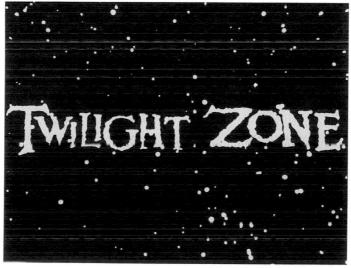

Two English actresses (and twins) ornamented the hood of an MG sports sedan at the International Automobile show in New York's Coliseum in April. The British MG and Triumph were among the best-selling imported sports cars in 1963. The most popular U.S.-made sports models that year were the Chevy Monza, Pontiac Grand Prix, Oldsmobile Starfire, Buick Riviera, and Ford Thunderbird.

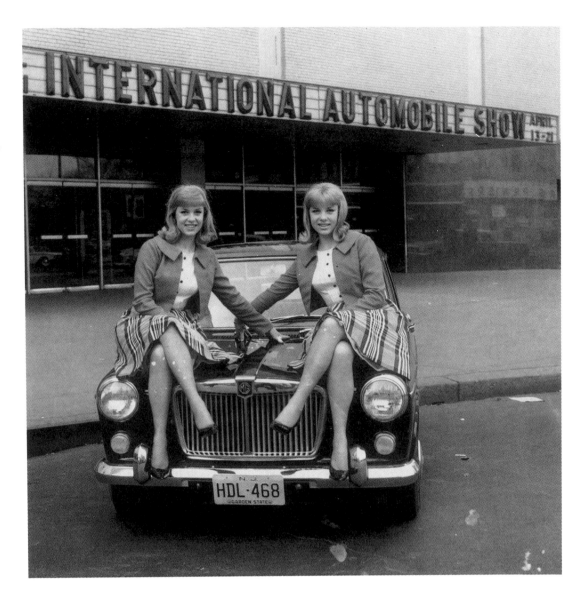

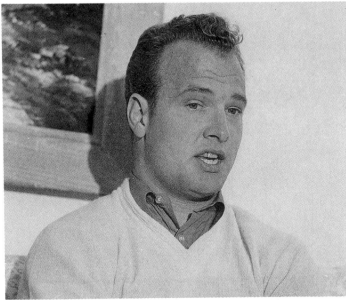

Green Bay Packer's halfback, Paul Hornung, (above) and Detroit Lion lineman, Alex Karras, were suspended indefinitely April 17 by the National Football League for betting on games. Hornung accepted the suspension and said he would "just have to stay with it." Karras said: "I haven't done anything I am ashamed of, and I am guilty of nothing." Green Bay ended the year in the number two position in the Western Conference; Detroit placed fifth.

A lot of advertising in those days had the beautiful woman with the car, with the indirect suggestion that with the car would come the woman. It hasn't all changed, but have you noticed how much advertising of cars today is directed at women? It's a sign of change.
GARY KOERSELMAN

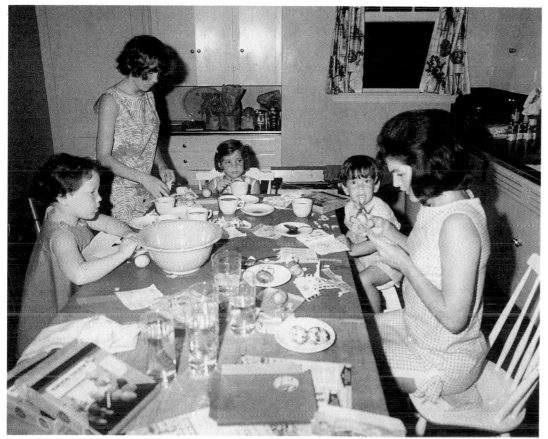

Jacqueline Kennedy, her children and two friends, decorated Easter eggs in the kitchen at Joseph Kennedy's Palm Beach home.

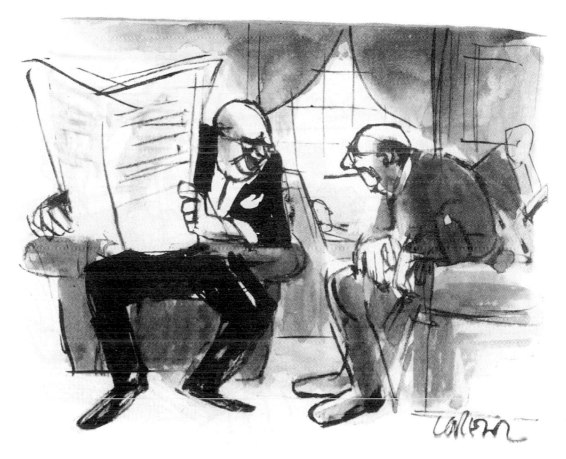

"I notice friend Jack isn't yukking it up the way he used to."

New York Yankee catcher Elston Howard would win the American League's Most Valuable Player Award for 1963. Howard was one of the very few blacks to play for the Yankees.

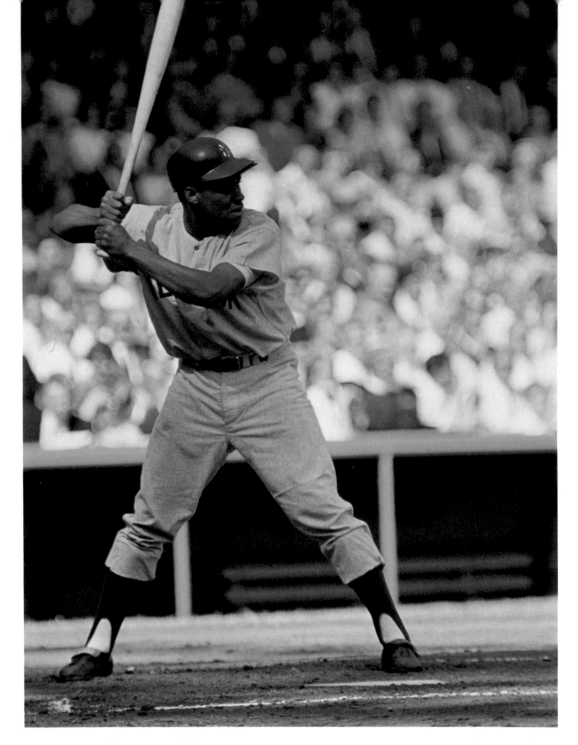

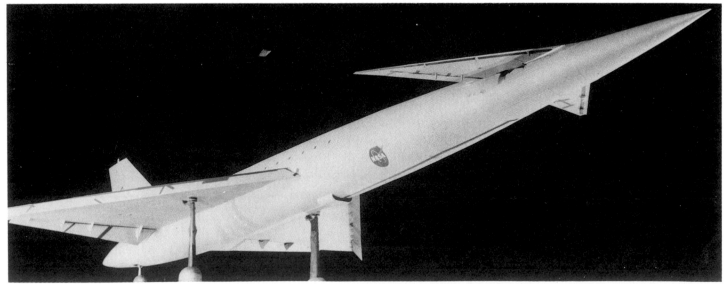

Model for the Boeing Supersonic Commercial Air Transport plane being developed for NASA. The US would later abandon pursuit of a 2,000 mph passenger aircraft, leaving the field to the British-French consortium that would build and fly the Concorde.

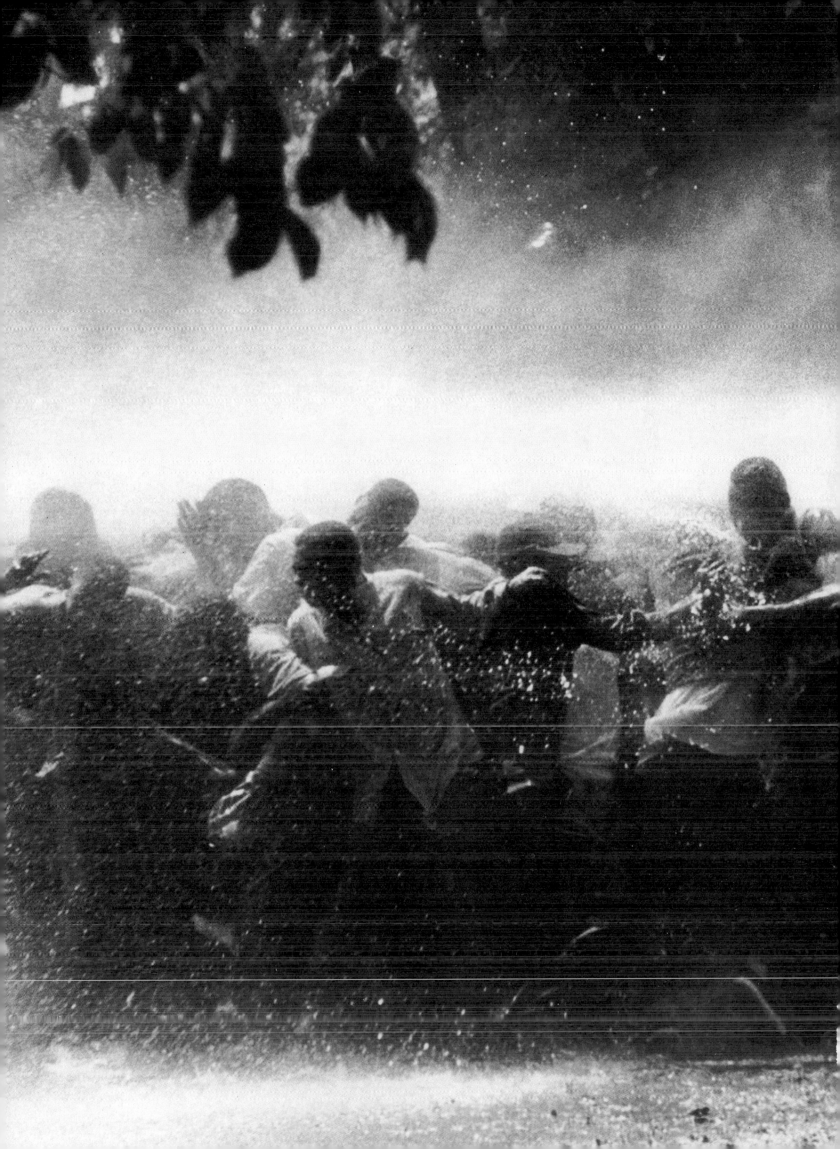

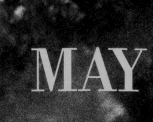

MAY

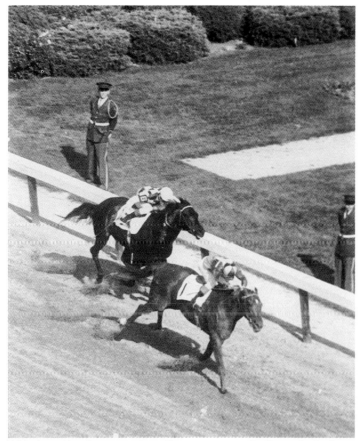

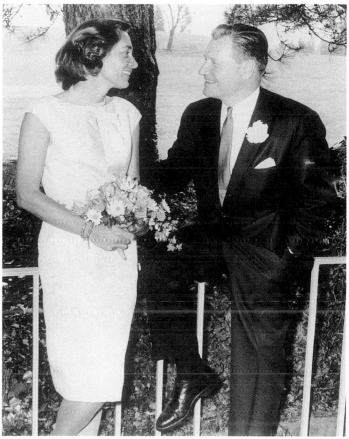

With the odds of 9 to 1 against, Chateaugay was the Kentucky Derby long shot. Candy Spots, 3 to 2, was the favorite; second-place bets went to No Robbery, 5 to 2; and the close third choice was Never Bend, 3 to 1. But 1¼ miles later, Chateaugay beat Never Bend by a significant 1¼ lengths, bringing his owner, John Galbreath, $108,900 in prize money.

New York Governor Nelson Rockefeller and the former Mrs. Margarita Fitler Murphy were married on May 4 at the home of the Governor's brother, Laurance. Three months earlier Rockefeller had divorced his wife of 31 years, Mary Todhunter Clark. Some Republicans thought the divorce and remarriage scandalous and damaging to Rockefeller's presidential aspirations.

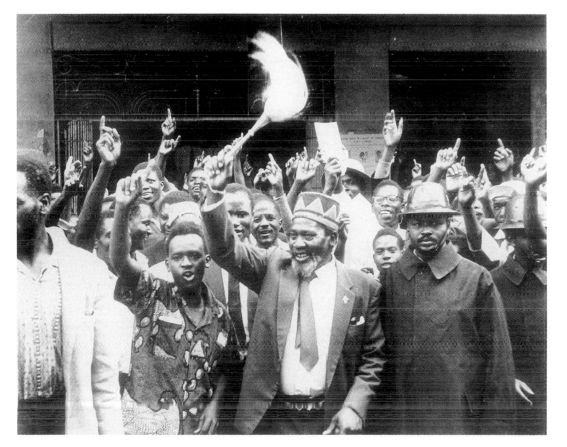

Waving his fly whisk, the leader of the Kenya African National Union (KANU), Jomo Kenyatta smiled to the cheers of his followers as the general election got under way on May 5. Kenyatta had served seven years in jail as the convicted "manager" of the Mau-Mau, a terrorist group. Three years earlier, he had been denounced by the previous British governor as "the leader to darkness and death." Kenyatta won the election, and became Kenya's first president. The former colony was granted internal self-rule on June 1 and full independence on December 31.

The Beach Boys—Brian Wilson, Dennis Wilson, Mike Love, Al Jardine, and Carl Wilson—rose to the top of the charts in the summer of 1963 with their high-harmonied, melodic album *Surfin' USA*. "Wet rock and roll" was the way one reviewer described surf music by the Beach Boys, Jan and Dean, and others. It celebrated endless California beaches, blond "surfer girls" and "catching the big wave."

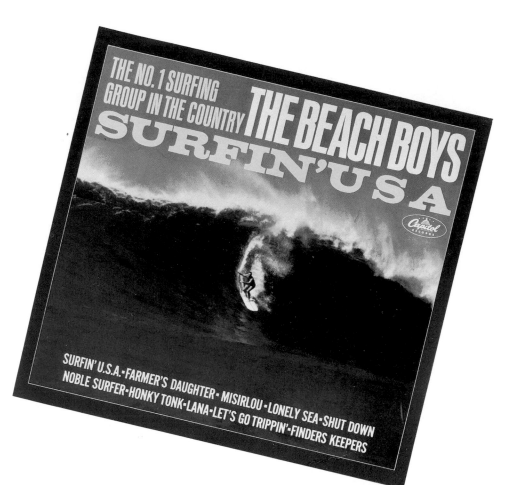

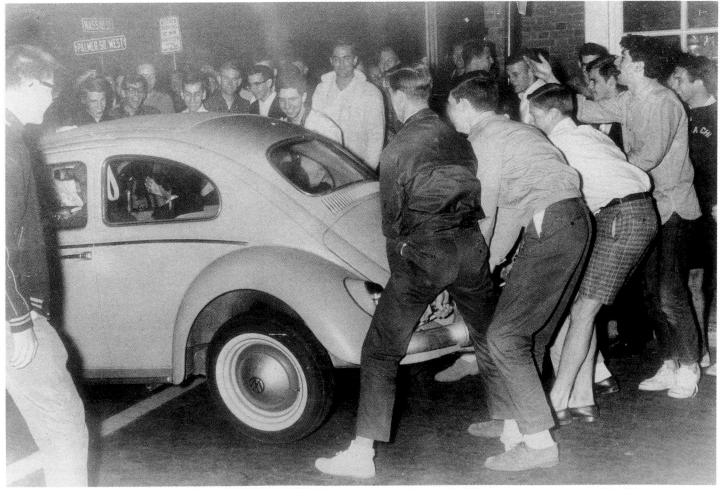

When college students rioted in 1963, it was called "spring fever" and was deemed a normal, if somewhat destructive, activity. Fifteen hundred undergraduates took part in the May 7 disturbance at Princeton University.

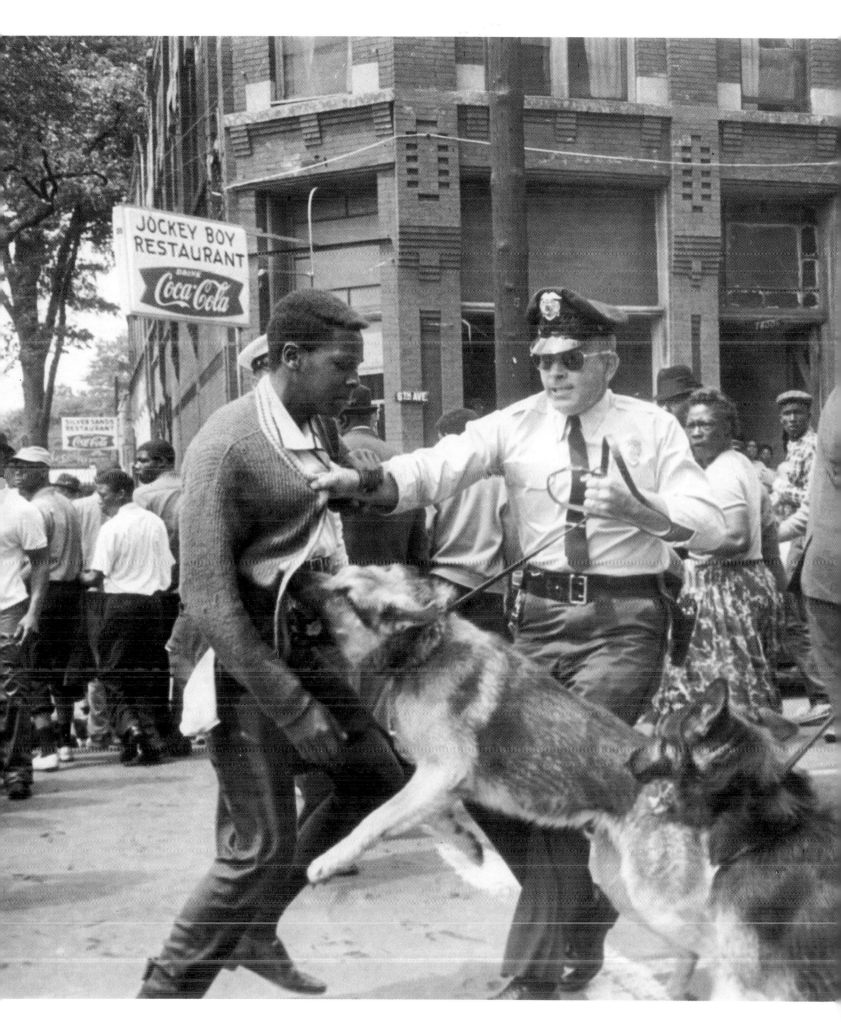

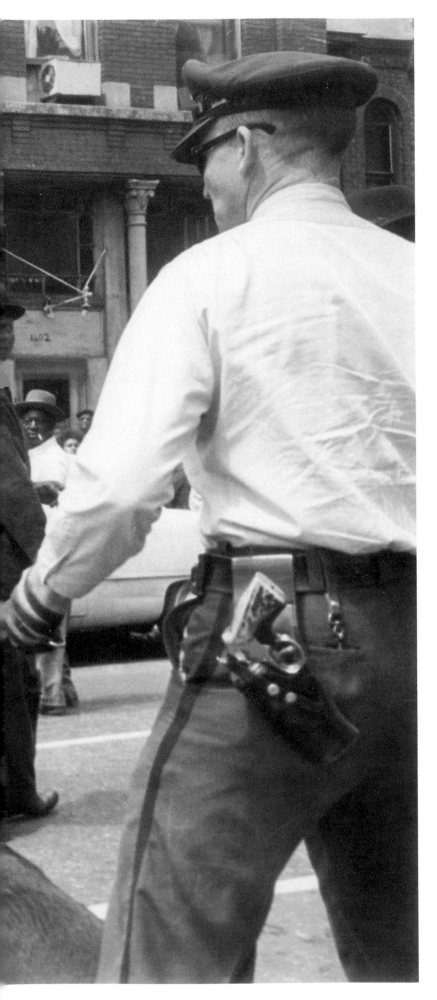

Kennedy, like most white politicians, underestimated the moral passion behind the civil rights movement.

But Kennedy was soon educated by events; and his brother, as attorney general with direct responsibility, was educated even faster.

But for a long time, civil rights legislation was simply not feasible. In 1962, Kennedy had trouble in getting a new Department of Housing and Urban Development because legislators were afraid he was going to appoint Robert C. Weaver, a black economist, and they didn't want a black Cabinet member. That suggests the primitive state we were still in in the early sixties. What changed the balance of opinion were the outrages of 1962 and 1963, beginning with the University of Mississippi and then particularly Bull Connor and his police dogs in Birmingham.

The Kennedys finally threw themselves, belatedly in a moral sense, realistically in the sense of getting Congressional legislation, into the civil rights fight. It was one of the president's less popular acts. In January 1963, his approval rating was 76 to 13 percent, which is an astonishing figure when you think of the presidents in recent times. By November, mainly as a result of the civil rights fight, it was down to 59 approval, 28 percent disapproval. This is still good enough by contemporary standards but suggests the political cost of the civil rights battle.

ARTHUR SCHLESINGER, JR.

The Birmingham demonstrations against segregation were a turning point in the quest for civil rights.

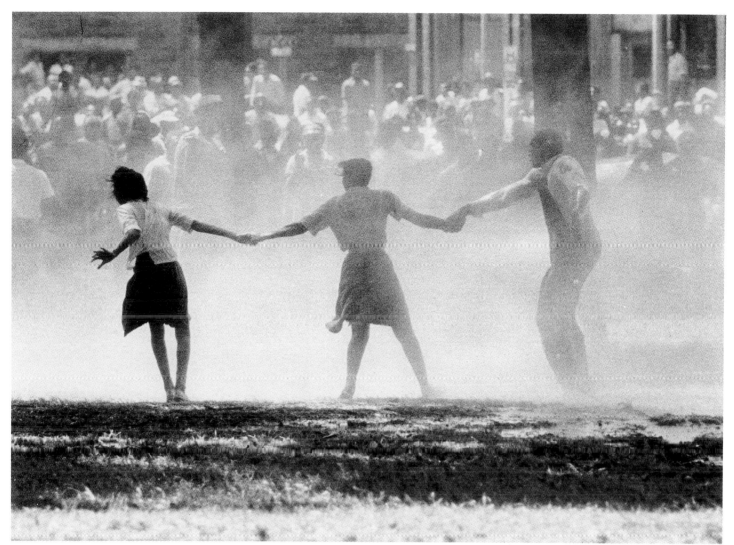

Demonstrators linked hands to remain on their feet in the face of high-pressure fire hoses used to break up a rally of 3,000 protesters.

I think [Kennedy] was probably the first one to put all this [civil rights] on a moral basis.

How he felt about it and what he thought he could accomplish politically about it were two different things. . . . His political priority was to get that tariff business through, and to get it through he needed Southern votes, and he knew he wouldn't get the Southern votes if he got them angry about civil rights legislation initially. I think he, in his own mind, said, "I'm going to get this thing done, but first I've got to get this other thing done, and this looks more important at the moment. . . ."

I had the impression that . . . you look at a job as a four-year span, possibly an eight-year span. You don't have to do everything tomorrow morning, and you have to establish some priorities.

REVEREND THEODORE HESBURGH,
Member, U.S. Civil Rights Commission

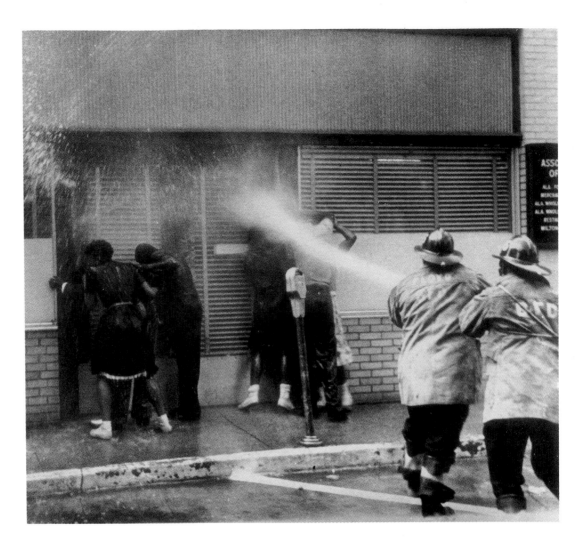

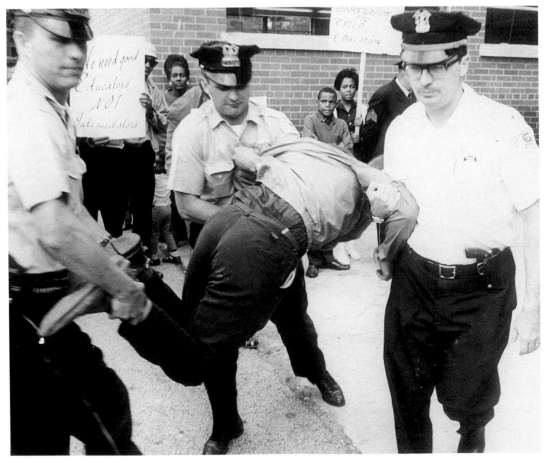

Events in Birmingham, Ala. dramatically awakened the nation to the civil rights struggle. Martin Luther King, Jr., with his brother, the Reverend A. D. King, led marches demanding access to restaurants and motels and jobs. Police arrested hundreds for "parading without a permit." More marchers came, and police chief Bull Connor met them with dogs and fire hoses. The nation watched on television and was shocked by the brutality.

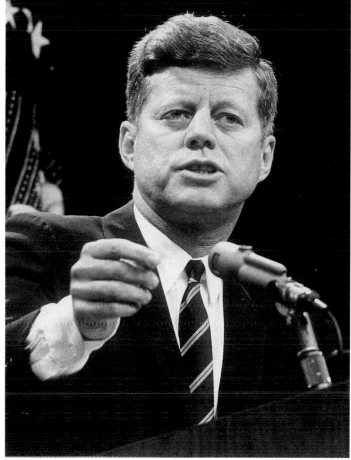

President Kennedy threatened to send federal troops to restore order. Alabama Governor George Wallace challenged him, but the Supreme Court rejected the challenge. Troops were never sent and tensions gradually eased, but Birmingham convinced Kennedy of the need for federal civil rights legislation.

I'm a native Southerner, born in Georgia and raised here. I was very aware of what was going on in Birmingham in the summer of 1963. One had to be aware of the civil rights struggle. I was horrified by the pictures of the police dogs and Bull Connor. Absolutely horrified that this was going on in a part of the country that I loved.

I fondly remember the tremendous speech John Kennedy made on television in response to the Birmingham events, where he said that in confronting the issue of civil rights, we were confronting an issue "as old as the Scriptures and as clear as the Constitution." The force of his presence and the power of that speech affected me greatly. Looking back at where the country was . . . then, I don't know how he could have been more forceful.

CHARLES JACKSON,
Student, Georgia State University, Atlanta

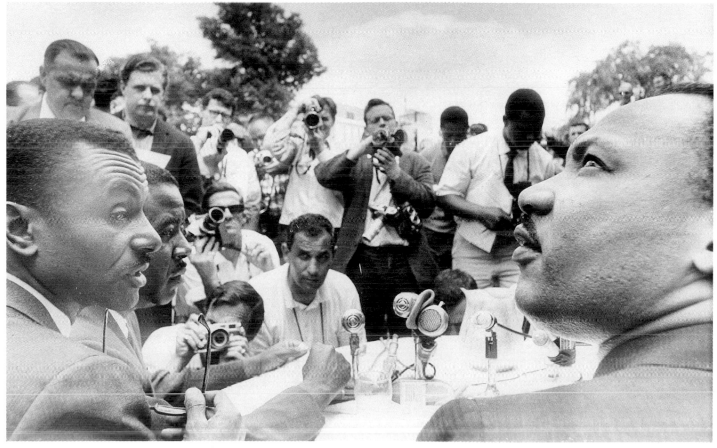

The violence led to negotiations, and on May 10, Martin Luther King, Jr. (far right), and other black leaders announced an agreement to end segregation in 90 days. That night King's motel room and his brother's home were bombed, and blacks responded by setting fires.

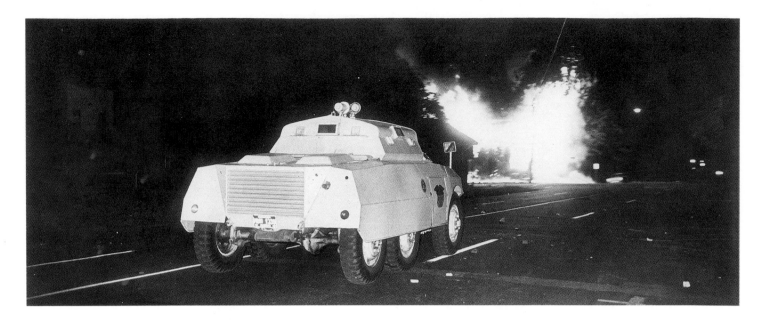

An armored police truck was used to disperse rioters who set fires in retaliation for the bombing of Reverend A. D. King's home.

Kennedy was the first president to really put his office, and its weight and dignity, at the front of the civil rights effort, not only by sending legislation to Congress and by appealing to the nation on television, but by a series of meetings with national leaders—leaders of the bar, leaders of business, leaders of academia—in order to enlist their efforts.

It's true, he was slow in coming to it. But there was a reason for it. He never for a moment expressed any prejudice of his own, but he felt hamstrung by the narrow majority that he had in Congress. But he never failed to meet his obligations, and his support for civil rights continued to pick up pace as the issue picked up pace.

THEODORE C. SORENSEN,
Special Counsel to the President

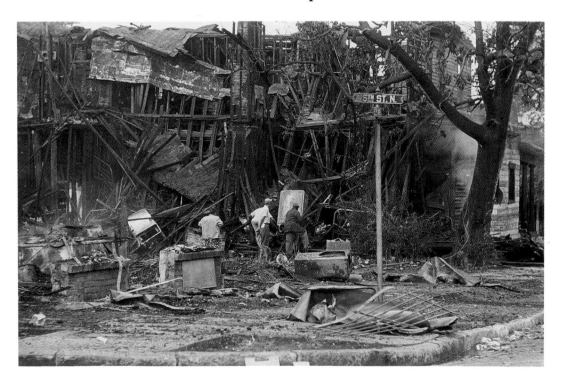

The remains of one of the homes set fire by the rioters.

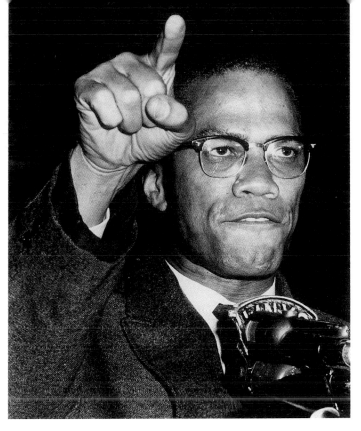

Malcolm X addressed a Harlem rally in support of the integration efforts in Birmingham.

Both President Kennedy and his brother, Robert, had told civil rights leaders, including me, that they did not favor new civil rights legislation. They did not feel it was either necessary or feasible—until after the Birmingham demonstrations. Their reasons appear to be that they felt the push for civil rights legislation would have angered the South and they might have lost the election. They changed their minds after the Birmingham demonstrations. People had seen the scenes from Birmingham on TV. They had seen Bull Connor's policemen beating people over the head, the fire hoses rolling women down the street, police dogs biting little children. It changed public opinion, and it changed Kennedy's attitude toward civil rights legislation.

JAMES FARMER

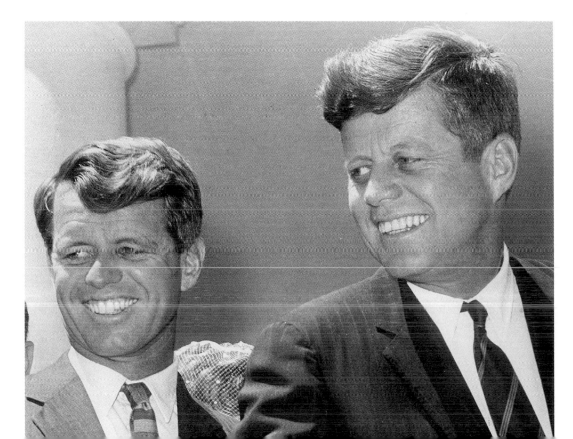

The famous Kennedy smile belied the pressure on the president and Attorney General to act decisively on Civil Rights issues in light of the on-going crisis in Birmingham.

This curious work, which begins as light comedy and ends as apocalyptic allegory, did not become an instant classic. Most of the opening reviews were negative or worse. But then, in 1963 Hitchcock was considered a maker of commercial thrillers, not, as he was later to be dubbed, *the master*. Evan Hunter wrote the screenplay, from the novel by Daphne du Maurier. With Rod Taylor, Tippi Hedren, Jessica Tandy, and Suzanne Pleshette—all mere pawns on the director's chessboard.

NOTHING YOU HAVE EVER WITNESSED BEFORE HAS PREPARED YOU FOR SUCH SHEER STABBING SHOCK!

ALFRED HITCHCOCK'S "The Birds"

TECHNICOLOR

"It could be the most terrifying motion picture I have ever made!" –ALFRED HITCHCOCK

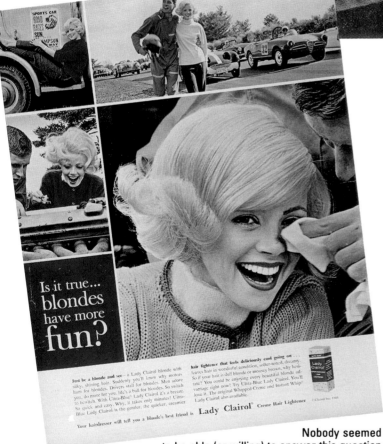

Is it true... blondes have more fun?

Just be a blonde and see—a Lady Clairol blonde with silky, shining hair. Suddenly you'll know why motors hum for blondes. Drivers stall for blondes. Men adore you, do more for you, life's a ball for blondes. So switch to bewitch. With Ultra-Blue® Lady Clairol it's a breeze. So quick and easy. Why, it takes only minutes! Ultra-Blue Lady Clairol is the gentler, the quicker, creamier hair lightener that feels deliciously cool going on ... leaves hair in wonderful condition, softer-toned, dreamy. So if your hair is dull blonde or mousey brown, why hesitate? You could be enjoying every beautiful blonde advantage right now! Try Ultra-Blue Lady Clairol. You'll love it. The original Whipped Creme and Instant Whip® Lady Clairol also available.

Your hairdresser will tell you a blonde's best friend is **Lady Clairol** Creme Hair Lightener

Nobody seemed to be able (or willing) to answer this question about hair color, so Clairol kept asking it for years. At some point, the sheer repetition of this catch line supplied its own answer. Like De Beer's "Diamonds are forever," the Clairol ads created their own reality. People came to believe that blond *was* better, or, as the ad read: "Motors hum for blonds. Drivers stall for blonds. Life's a ball for blonds."

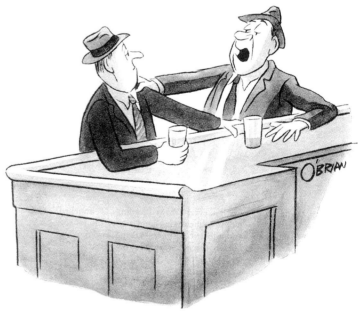

"Mind you, I haven't anything against Caroline personally."

91

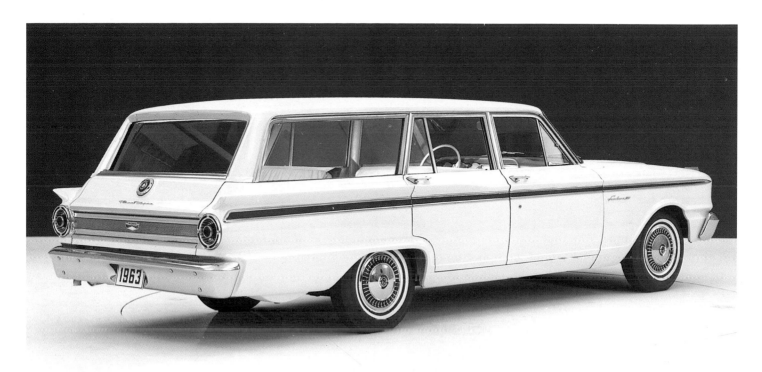

The 1963 Ford Fairlane 500 station wagon made up in utility what it lacked in appeal to the imagination.

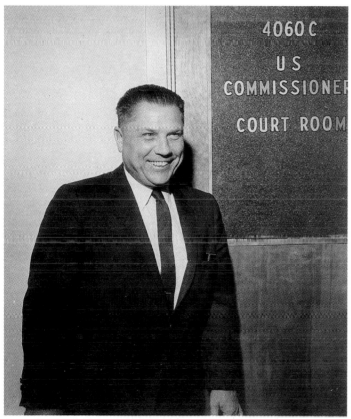

James Hoffa, president of the Teamsters Union, was released on $10,000 bail to ensure his appearance before a Nashville grand jury investigating jury tampering and misuse of union funds.

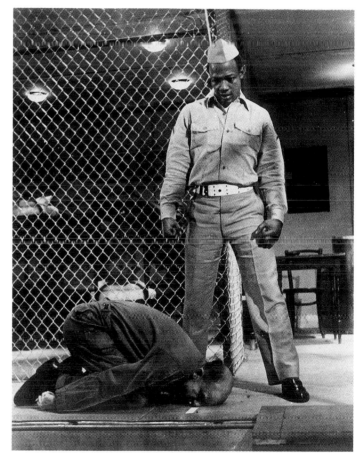

Ken Brown's powerful drama of the peacetime U.S. Army in Japan, *The Brig*, was perhaps the most important new play of the year. Although it ran fewer than 200 performances, it earned its author a Pulitzer Prize nomination and an international reputation. The alternative theatrical group known as The Living Theatre, which mounted the play, assumed a leading position in the American dramatic avant-garde.

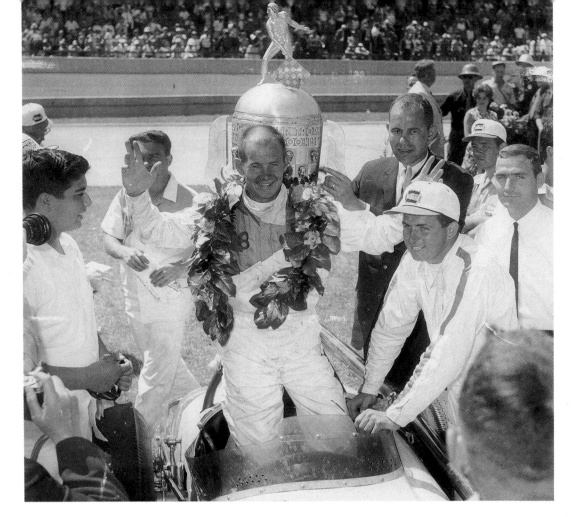

On May 30, Parnelli Jones smiled after he won the 500-mile race at the Indianapolis Speedway. He captured the 47th running of the event with the winning speed of 143.137 and time of 3:29:35.40. Jones' car was the Agajanian-Williard Battery Special. In other events, the 12-hour World Championship Endurance Race held in Sebring, Fla., was won by Ludovico Scarifiotti of Italy and John Surtees of Britain in a Ferrari. The distance was 1,804 miles and their speed averaged 90.391 mph. Graham Hill of England won the Grand Prix de Monaco and the Grand Prix of the United States. Bobby Unser won the Pikes Peak Hill Climb in a Chevrolet Special.

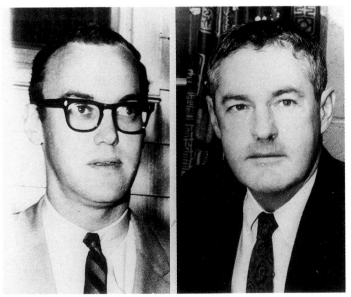

Their experiments with the "consciousness expanding" drug LSD attracted notoriety for Harvard faculty members Richard Alpert (left) and Timothy Leary and earned them dismissal from the university in May. Leary, who was convinced LSD trips were religious experiences, founded a drug-oriented spiritual league, but later wound up in jail on drug possession charges. Alpert changed his name to Baba Ram Dass and developed a cult following in the 70s.

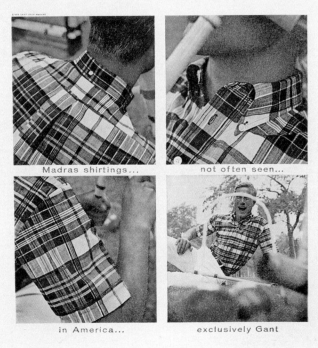

Madras shirtings... not often seen... in America... exclusively Gant

Madras—rare multi-colorings, not-often-seen patterns. All hand picked and imported from India; London finished. Like all Gant shirts, they have elan in a gentlemanly manner. About $9 at discerning stores. For one nearest you, write Gant Shirtmakers, New Haven, Connecticut.

GANT
SHIRTMAKERS

At Yale that year only those who had spent spring vacation in Bermuda were allowed to wear madras.

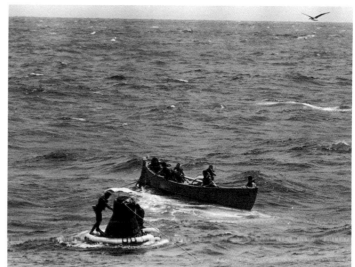

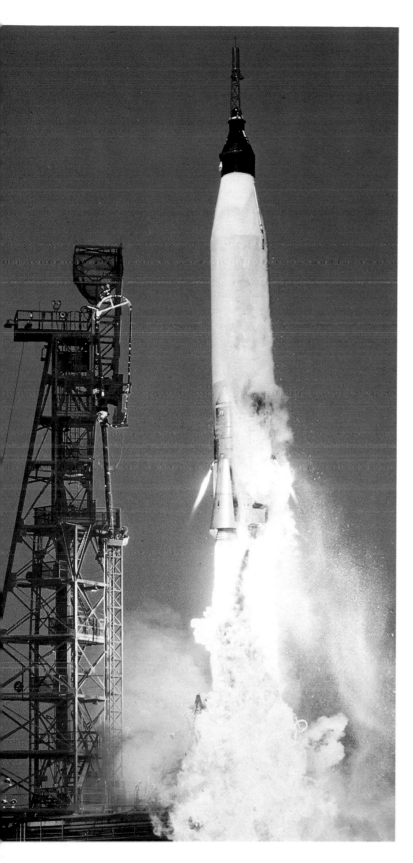

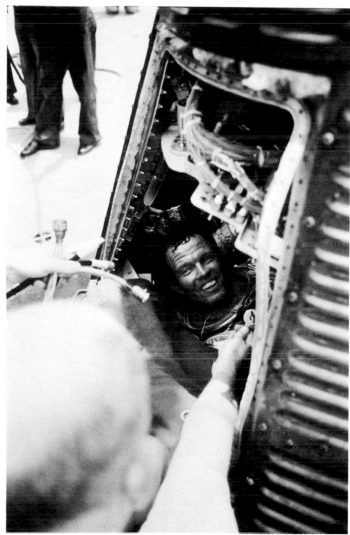

On May 16, astronaut Gordon Cooper thrilled the nation with the longest space flight (34 hours 20 minutes) to date and a hair-raising ending. After 22 earth orbits, when he was due to reenter the atmosphere, a power failure shut down the automatic controls. Guided verbally by fellow astronaut John Glenn, with a tense world watching, Cooper brought the *Faith 7* capsule to splash-down in the Pacific only four miles from the recovery ship. Cooper's flight was one of many steps to build confidence and experience for the flight to the moon that Kennedy had promised within the decade.

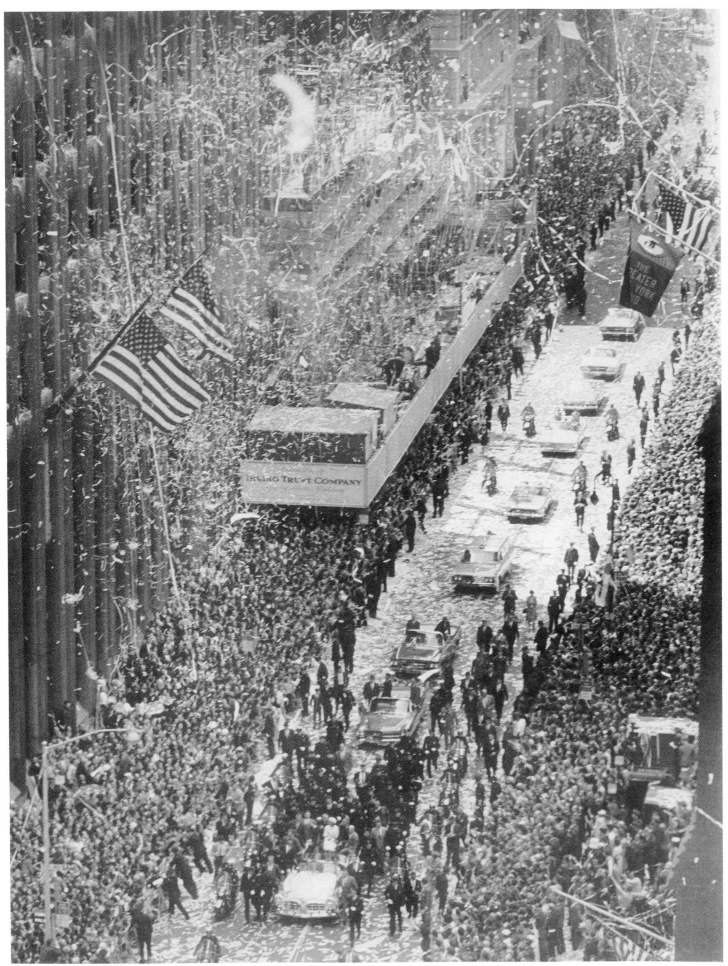

Gordon Cooper received a hero's welcome with the traditional New York "ticker tape" parade up Broadway from the financial district to City Hall.

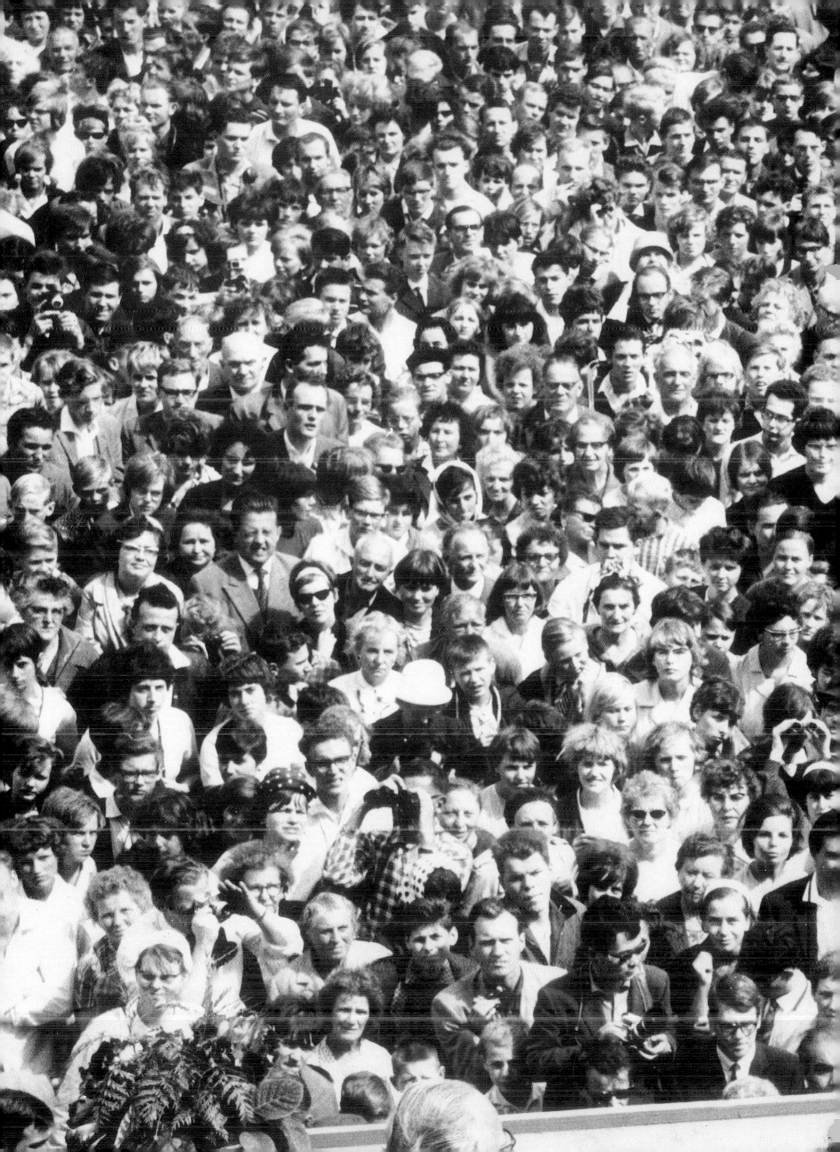

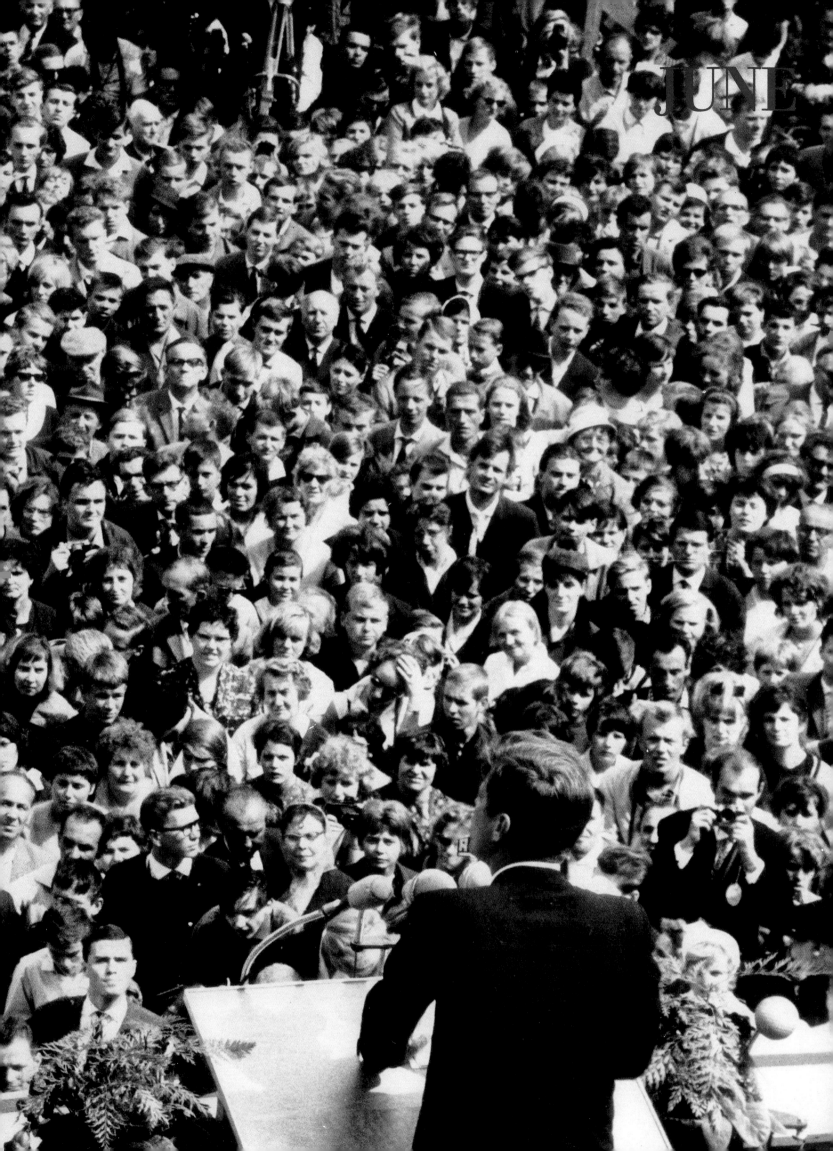

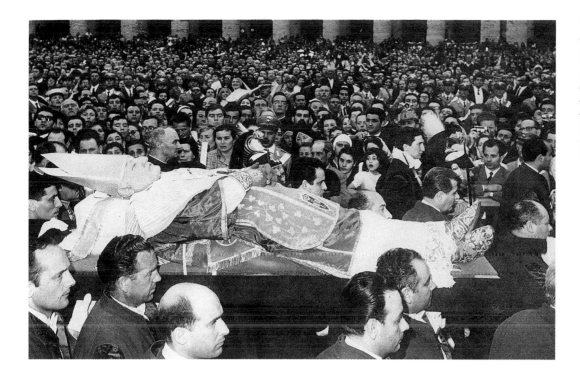

Pope John XXIII, who died on June 3 during the fifth year of his reign, had led efforts for Christian unity and urged the Roman Catholic Church to devote its attention to achieving world peace. He also convened the second Vatican Ecumenical Council, which took steps to modernize the Roman Catholic Church.

E ven though women made up something like 30 percent of the work force in the early sixties, we were pretty well left out. We did not have equal pay. We were not covered under the Fair Labor Standards Act.

The Equal Pay Act [signed on June 10, 1963] was one of the first victories that we had. It was definitely one of the landmark equal rights measures.

But you see the trouble nowadays is that the rate for the job is the same, but women don't get the jobs. That's why the discrepancy continues between the earnings of women and men. We haven't gone very far.

ESTHER PETERSON

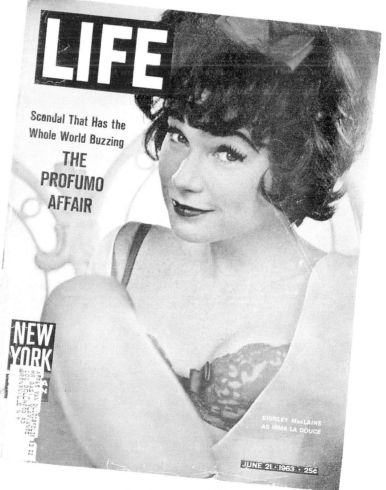

The June cover of *Life*.

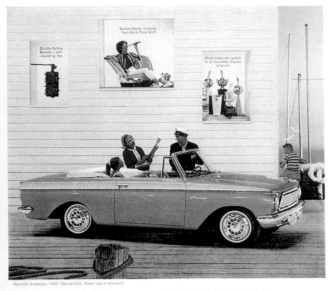

GO FOR FUN – SAVE A BUNDLE
(it's the Economy King with brand-new zing!)

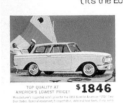

$1846

TOP QUALITY AT AMERICA'S LOWEST PRICE!

RAMBLER '63 *MOTOR TREND AWARD* CAR OF THE YEAR

This Rambler came with "Twin-Stick Floor Shift" and "Instant Overtake." *Motor Trend* magazine named it Car of the Year for 1963.

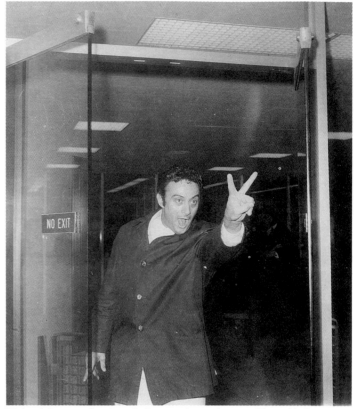

Night club comedian Lennie Bruce, shown here making a V sign after U.S. authorities failed to turn up drugs during a search at New York's Idlewild Airport in April, was declared a narcotics addict by a Los Angeles Superior Court Judge in June and ordered confined to a California rehabilitation center.

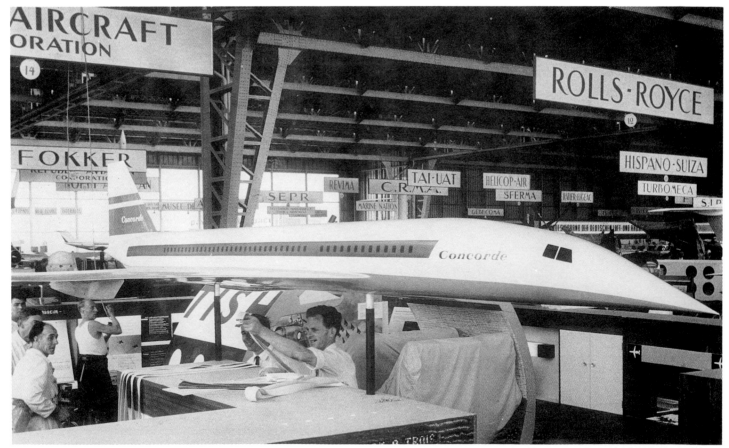

The International Air Show in Paris the week of June 7 featured a scale model of the Concorde, the Anglo-French supersonic airliner. A prototype was expected to fly in 1966 with commercial service beginning in 1970.

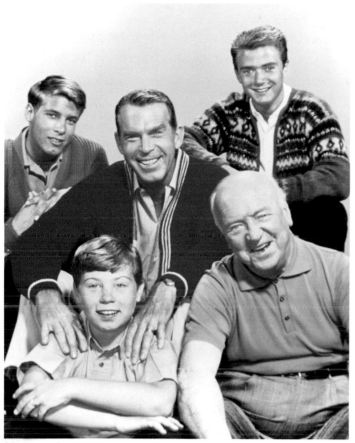

My Three Sons was a highly successful sitcom for film star Fred MacMurray. That certain elements in the show, particularly the ages, disposition, and whereabouts of the sons, made increasingly less sense as the years rolled by, seemed not to have bothered the audience. MacMurray was ably supported by William Frawley (late of *I Love Lucy*) as a housekeeping grandfather.

T he program content was enormously different. You would never have anything on the air about homosexuality, you would never see a show about a rape. Now you see these subjects portrayed quite frequently. So there has been a sea change in the content of television, in those terms. Programs today deal with presumably adult topics, but for the most part, it's exploitative. That would not have been permitted in 1963. They would have run you off the air.

DON WEST

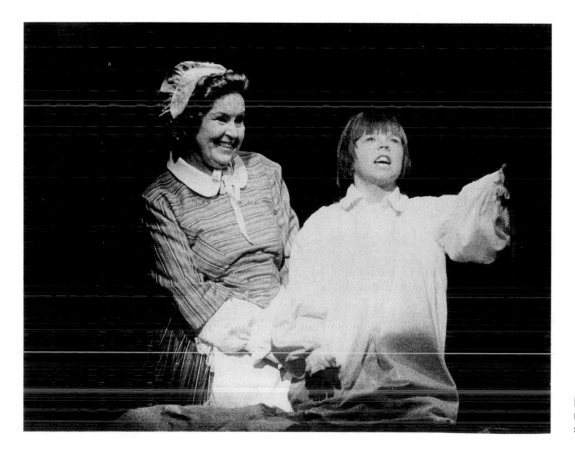

Lionel Bart's *Oliver* was the musical hit of the Broadway season.

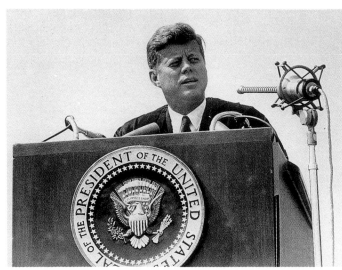

T he speech Kennedy gave [on June 10, 1963] at American University, on reexamining the meaning of peace and our relations with the Soviet Union, was a threshold talk on changing attitudes about the cold war. It led to the Limited Nuclear Test Ban Treaty.

THEODORE C. SORENSEN

In a major policy address on June 10 at American University in Washington, D.C., the president announced that the U.S. would not hold any further nuclear tests in the atmosphere as long as the other nuclear powers agreed to honor such a ban.

K ennedy left us with two countervailing legacies. The Vietnamese war escalated, and that's what people tend to pin on him. Whether he in fact was going to do something different—was going to pull the troops out, we don't know. On the other hand, he cut that deal with the Soviet Union— the Limited Nuclear Test Ban Treaty—which is one of the most important things his Administration did. I've reread his speech at American University—that the U.S. and Soviet Union have to change the way we behave toward each other. It's one of the best speeches he ever made.

JAN BARRY

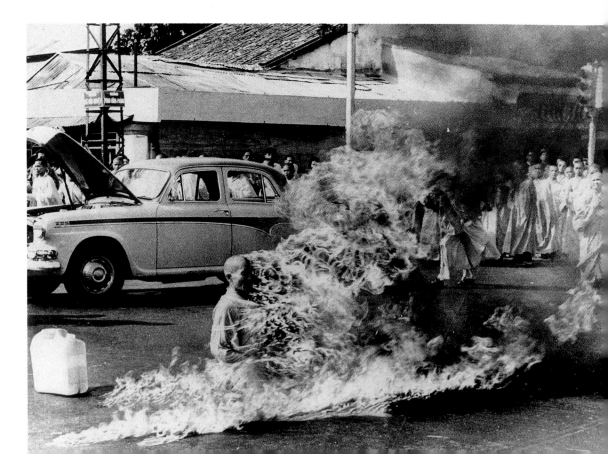

Flames devoured Quang Doc, a Buddhist monk who burned to death in Saigon on June 11 after putting a match to his gasoline-soaked robes. In 1963, a series of suicides by monks protesting the Diem regime's persecution of Buddhists—and a cruel reference to the Buddhist "barbecue show" made by Diem's sister-in-law, Madame Nhu—raised questions about continued U.S. support for this repressive and unpopular dictatorship.

Alabama Governor George Wallace tried to stop black registration at the University of Alabama, defying Deputy U.S. Attorney General Nicholas Katzenbach. Wallace backed down when Katzenbach read a proclamation by President Kennedy putting the Alabama National Guard under federal control. Under their protection Vivian Malone became the first black to register.

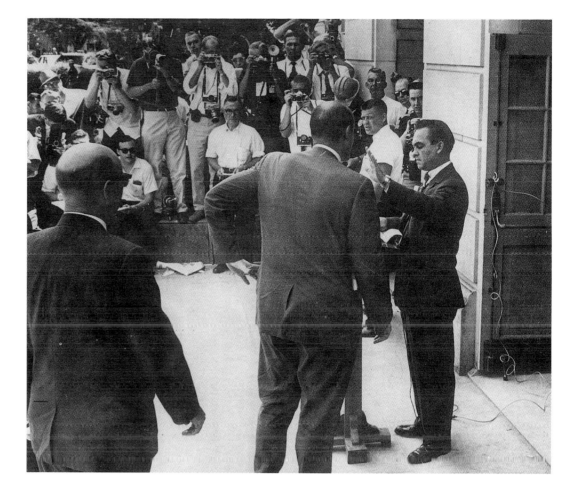

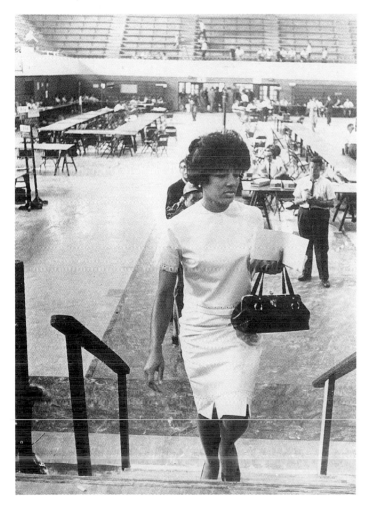

I was present [on June 22] when Kennedy met with Martin Luther King and other black leaders. Someone mentioned [Police Commissioner Eugene] Bull Connor, and Kennedy said, "We shouldn't be too tough on Bull Connor." This caused a stunned reaction. Kennedy continued, "After all, Bull Connor has done more for civil rights than any of us." This was true because the photographs of Bull Connor's police dogs lunging at the marchers in Birmingham did as much as anything to transform the national mood and make legislation not just necessary, which it had long been, but possible.

ARTHUR SCHLESINGER, Jr.

Vivian Malone left the Foster Auditorium on June 11, after registering at the University of Alabama.

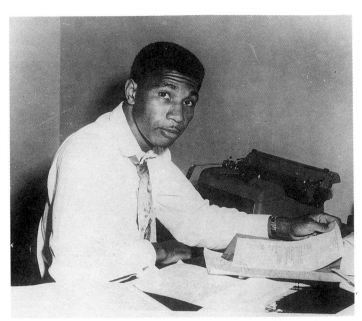

June 11. Medgar Evers, leader of the Mississippi NAACP, was shot outside his home in Jackson, Miss. He tried to crawl into the house but died of his wounds.

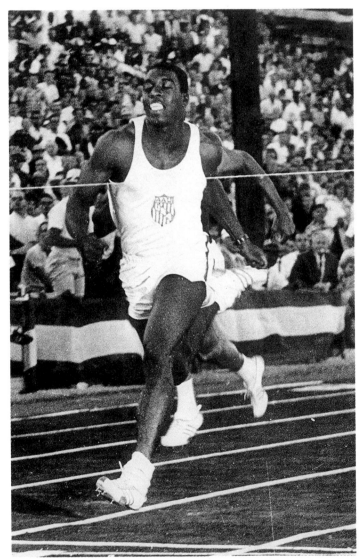

Bob Hayes set a world record of 9.1 seconds for the 100-yard dash at the AAU international competition in June.

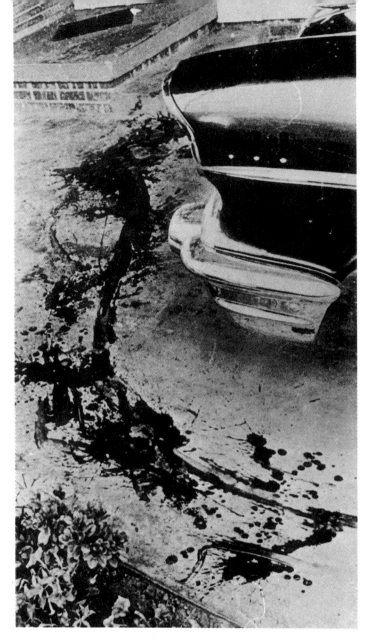

When we walked behind the body of Medgar Evers through the streets of Jackson, the line stretched so far back it looked like ants in a parade, old folks, young folks, black and white folks, nappy hair and pressed hair and blown hair. Thom McAnn and Buster Brown and barefoot, they walked and walked. It looked like we had enough folks to march on God that day. We turned a corner, and the same white policemen who had fought Medgar so hard were directing traffic at his funeral procession. . . .

DICK GREGORY

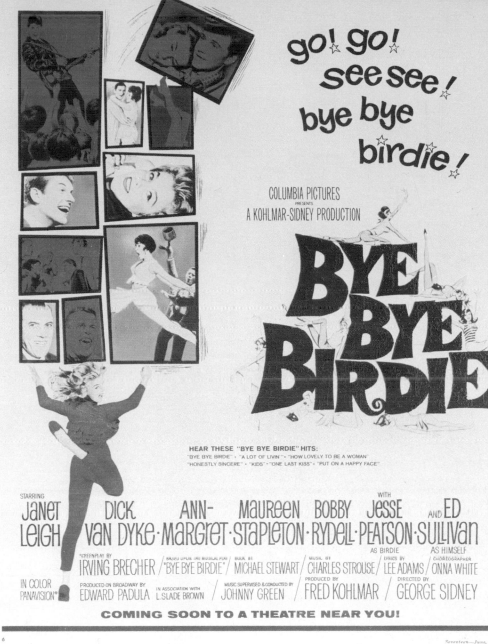

The movie was even sillier than the Broadway show, but both were box office successes. The whole mess, which probably wanted to have something to do with Elvis Presley, was an affront to current pop music, which was on the verge of embarking on the most explosively creative period in rock and roll history.

The scandal that titillated the world and rocked the British government: War Minister John Profumo confessed to having lied about an affair with a ravishing model, Christine Keeler. But Keeler was having a simultaneous affair with Captain Yevgeni Ivanov, a Soviet agent. Profumo claimed he had not compromised British security; but he had compromised the government and he left in disgrace.

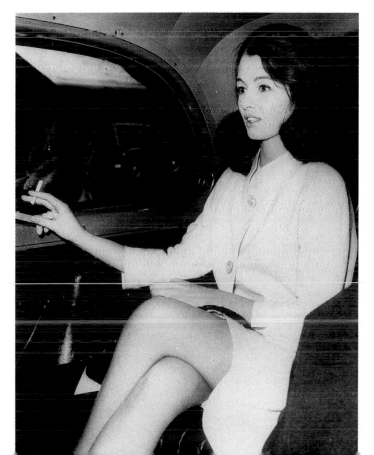

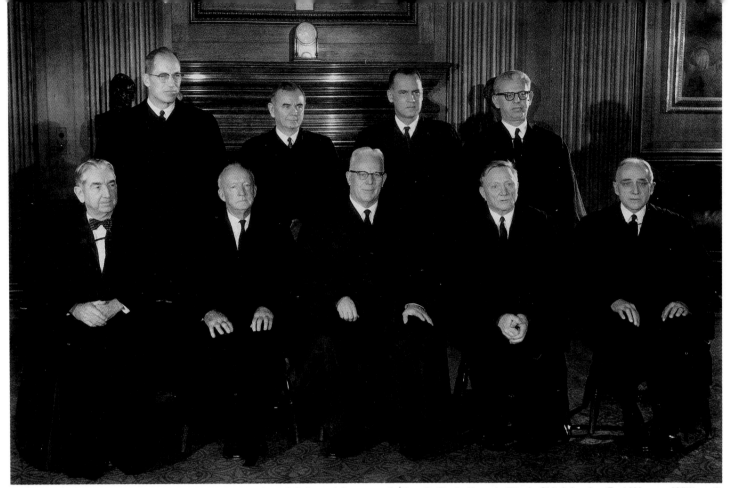

Members of the U.S, Supreme Court—the "Warren Court" (left to right, seated): Tom C. Clark, Hugo L. Black, Chief Justice Earl Warren, William O. Douglas, John M. Harlan; (standing): Byron R. White, William J. Brennan, Jr., Potter Stewart, and Arthur J. Goldberg. White and Goldberg were appointed by President Kennedy.

I remember hearing about the Supreme Court ruling [outlawing prayer in public schools], and I remember being very pleased by it. In Brooklyn, I can remember occasions when the teacher had asked us to pray silently. I don't remember ever having been asked to articulate the Lord's Prayer in class, but when the teacher was Christian, it made all the Jewish kids in the class uneasy because we knew that her silent prayer was going to be to Christ. I resented being told that I had to pray, because Jews go to synagogue and they pray—out loud in Hebrew. They don't do this silent devotional stuff. Even as a young child I knew that. So any time I was asked to pray in school, even if it was a silent prayer, it turned my stomach a little. Because I knew for Mrs. McCue, it was a Christian prayer. So I remember the ruling, and I remember being glad about it.

BARRY HOBERMAN,
Junior High School Student, Brooklyn

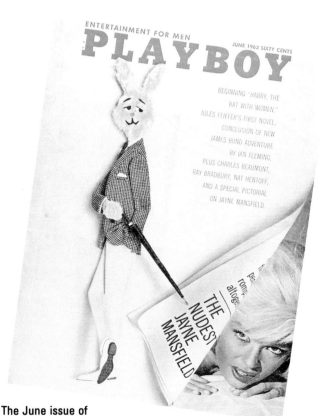

The June issue of *Playboy* featured a photo spread on Jayne Mansfield. Several of the photos showed her nude above the waist. This caused something of a sensation and led to the magazine being charged with obscenity. By way of contrast, the *Playboy* Playmate of the Month was almost demure. None of her pictures included any above-the-waist nudity.

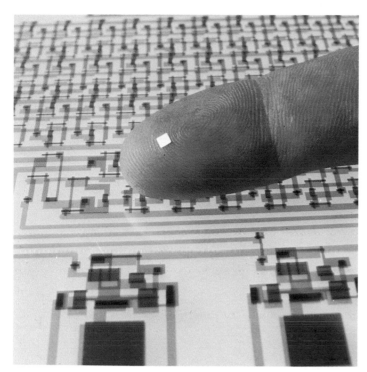

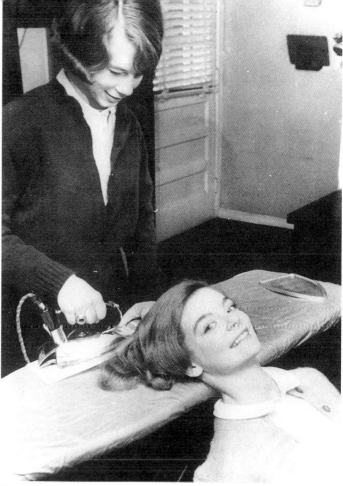

This year saw the experimental development of the miniature integrated circuit, or chip, that would make possible the third generation of computers. The tiny device would lead the way to explosive growth in the use and ownership of computers by business and individuals. In 1963 there were only about 4,200 computers in the U.S. All were large "main frames."

Each month—sometimes it seemed like each week—brought a new fad . . .

T̲hat summer, Peter, Paul and Mary [had] a hit with [Bob Dylan's] "Blowin' in the Wind." Eventually something like 60 people [recorded] that song—not just Peter, Paul and Mary . . . but such unlikely people as Sam Cooke, Marlene Dietrich, Duke Ellington, Percy Faith and the New Christy Minstrels.

LILLIAN ROXON, Rock Critic

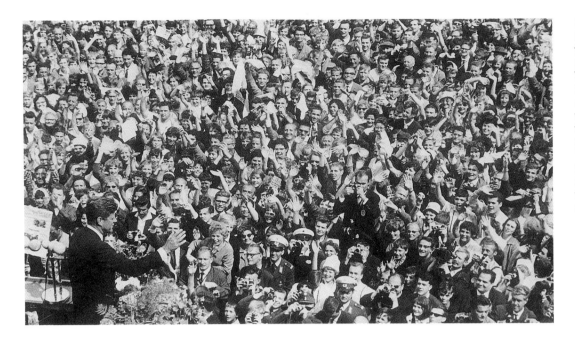

President Kennedy was greeted by a huge and ecstatic crowd in front of the West Berlin city hall on June 26. Berlin was a Cold War flashpoint throughout his Presidency. In 1961, the Soviets and East Germans erected a wall sealing off East Berlin from the West. Kennedy boosted morale by telling West Berliners: "All free men, wherever they may live, are citizens of Berlin. And therefore, as a free man, I take pride in the words 'Ich bin ein Berliner.' "

K ennedy's trip to Western Europe and his dramatic commitment to the people of West Berlin—expressed in his "Ich bin ein Berliner" speech—were extremely important in holding the Western alliance together at a very crucial time. And they made possible the recognition on both sides of the Iron Curtain, on both sides of the Wall, that Western unity would continue, and that made East-West trade and cooperation that much more possible.

THEODORE C. SORENSEN

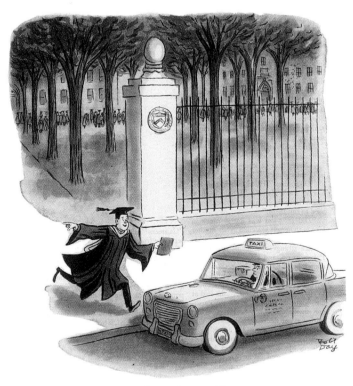

"Madison Avenue!"

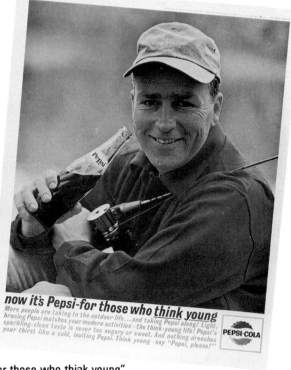

now it's Pepsi-for those who **think young**

More people are taking to the outdoor life...and taking Pepsi along! Light, bracing Pepsi matches your modern activities—the think-young life! Pepsi's sparkling-clean taste is never too sugary or sweet. And nothing drenches your thirst like a cold, inviting Pepsi. Think young—say "Pepsi, please!"

PEPSI-COLA

"For those who think young"
was the key line around which all Pepsi ads were built.
Print ads also encouraged the reader to "say Pepsi please."

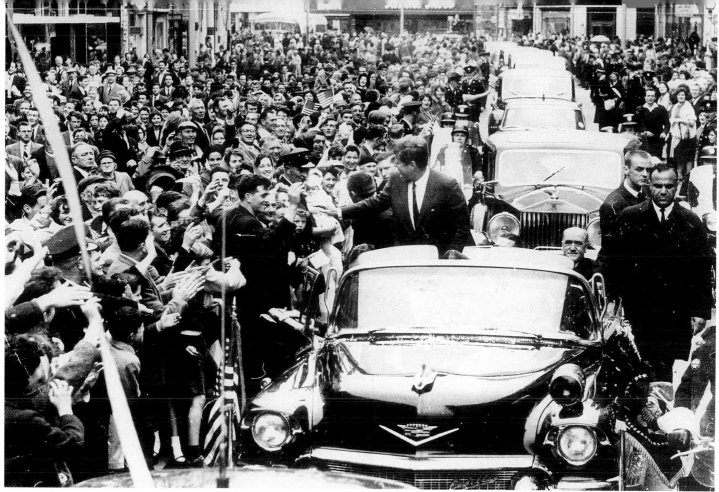

President Kennedy rode through the streets of Cork, Ireland, on June 28, during his two-day visit. Kennedy addressed a joint session of the two houses of the Irish Parliament, and was made an honorary freeman of Dublin, Cork, Limerick, Wexford, and Galway. The president also saw the home of his ancestors at Dunganstown. Ireland's prime minister reciprocated by visiting the United States in October.

I t mustn't be forgotten that this was a romantic Irish-American politician—a very gifted politician. Somewhere in him he had the mysterious gift for communicating with masses of people: absorbing within himself the pressures and impulses that came from a whole political body of people; of communicating back; and of finding the right balances. A politician is a communicating instrument both ways. He receives and he sends communications, words, images, actions. Kennedy was awfully good at it. . . . This was a fellow who had walked out and moved a million people . . . in order to get himself elected in very tricky circumstances, because he was a great politician. He would just do it.

WALT W. ROSTOW

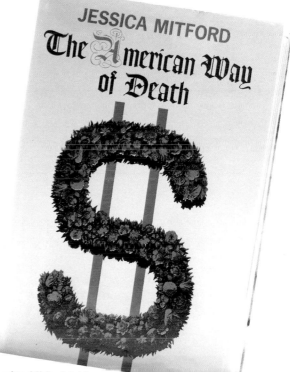

Jessica Mitford told the public about all the untoward things that went on in funeral homes and why it cost so much to bury someone. The funeral directors of America were not happy.

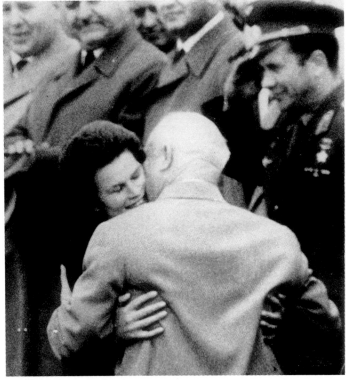

Soviet Premier Nikita Khrushchev greeted Valentina Tereshkova, the first woman in space, at a Red Square ceremony.

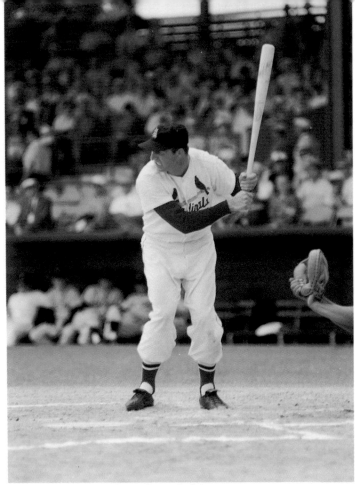

Stan Musial would retire at the end of the season.

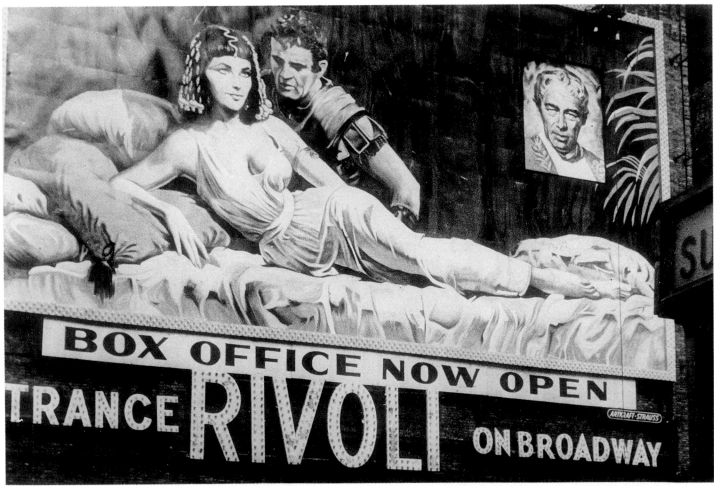

Cleopatra, starring offstage lovers Elizabeth Taylor (in the title role) and Richard Burton (as Antony), premiered at New York City's Rivoli theater in June. Although the poster had originally included only Taylor and Burton, the film's third star, Rex Harrison, (Caesar) demanded to have his picture (upper right) included in the promotion. Despite a $37 million budget—the largest ever for a film as of that date—and massive publicity, the film got mixed reviews and was a disappointment at the box office.

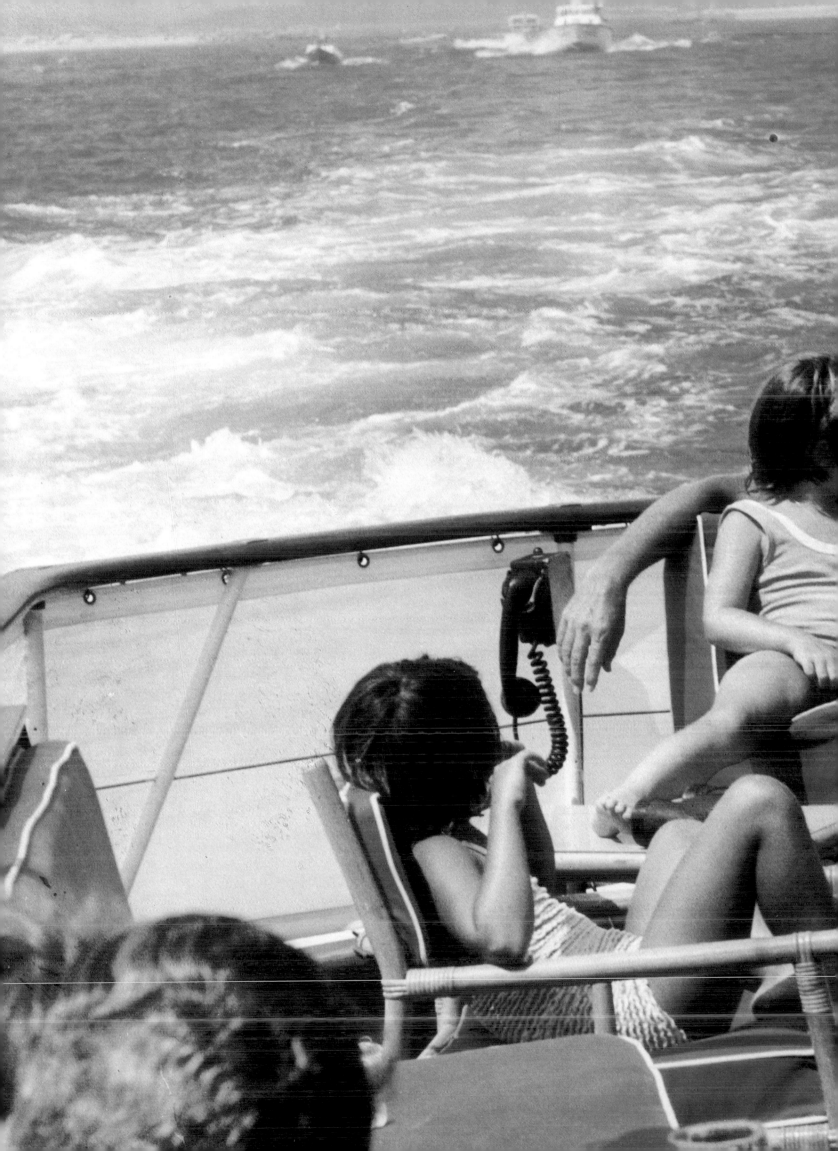

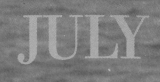

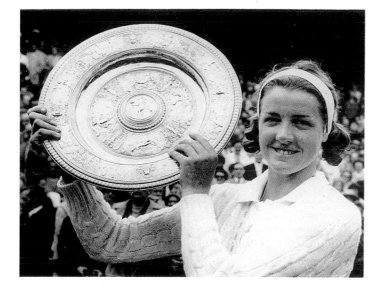

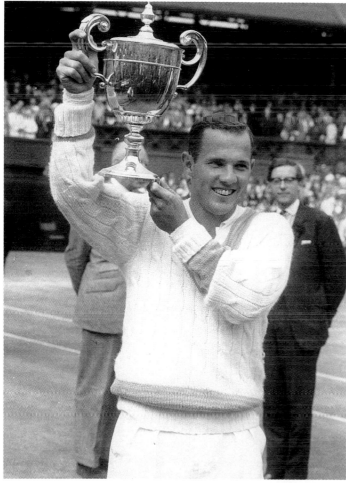

Chuck McKinley of San Antonio defeated Fred Stolle of Australia 9–7, 6–1, 6–4 at the men's singles tennis championship at Wimbledon on July 5. He became the first American to win Wimbledon in eight years. Roy Emerson—the number-one seed—lost in the semi-final round to Wilhelm Burgert. Margaret Smith won the women's title.

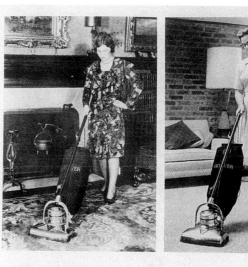

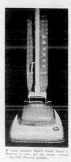
For many people the name Hoover was synonymous with vacuum cleaners, and the latest model did not actually look that different from the traditional one.

There were fewer consumer choices than there are today, although I feel so often now that we've sacrificed a lot in quality. I can't, for example, find an ironing board as sturdy as our 1963 wedding gift ironing board.

There were no malls to speak of. Most of our purchases were bought with money, not plastic. Since my husband was finishing his master's degree and working and I was a new mother, our income was tight. We owned a VW Beetle, rented an apartment, went to the movies for a night out, and made our own entertainment with friends.

We bought blankets, not comforters; records, not compact discs; a reel-to-reel tape recorder to send talking letters to a brother-in-law in Japan. Baby diapers were still made of cloth. Maternity clothes were still pretty disastrous; I designed and made most of mine to avoid the limitations.

JUDITH HOOVER,
Housewife, Racine, Wis.

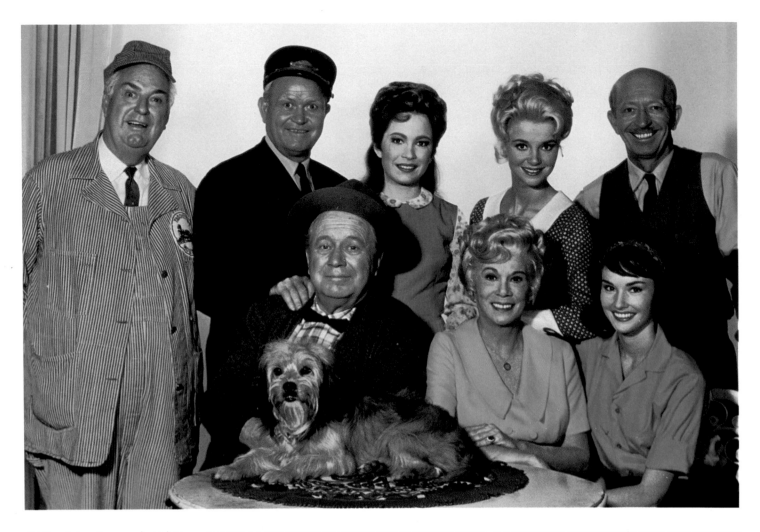

Petticoat Junction was based on the premise that stupidity was both virtuous and rewarding. Three exceptionally well endowed young women helped their mother (played by Bea Benadaret) run a small, rural hotel. The show premiered in 1963. By 1970 it had become too sappy even for CBS, which, despite good ratings, cancelled it in a general house-cleaning designed to upgrade the network's image.

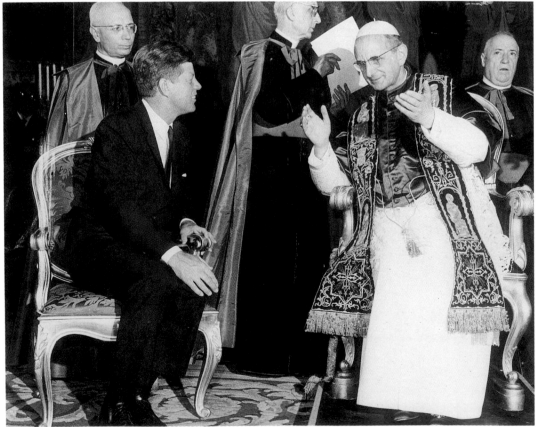

Newly crowned Pope Paul VI and America's first Catholic president during a meeting on July 2. Kennedy's Vatican visit was the last stop on his triumphant Berlin-Ireland-Rome swing that summer.

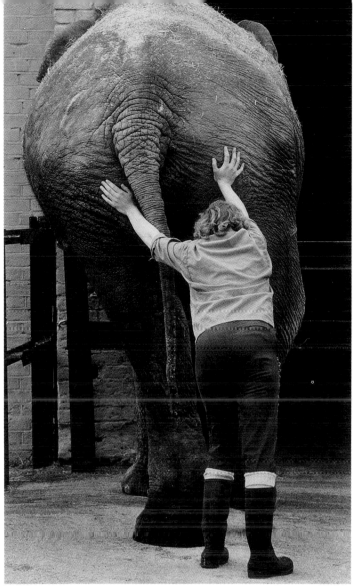

"How do you tell if there's an elephant in your refrigerator?" "By the footprints in the pudding." In July elephant jokes were big.

Socially, it was a different world back then. I was a freshman at the University of Minnesota, and we had some really primitive dress codes. For people who lived in dormitories, there was a total double standard in the treatment of men and women. The men had freedom to stay out all night if they wanted, but the women had to check in by a certain hour. And to go eat dinner in the dormitory cafeteria, the girls had to wear nylons.

I knew this one girl, Judy Barnes, who was black, and the lady who checked to make sure the girls were wearing nylons claimed she couldn't tell whether Judy had nylons on because she was black. So she would reach down and pinch her legs to make sure she had her nylons on. Judy hated that.

LEE SMITH

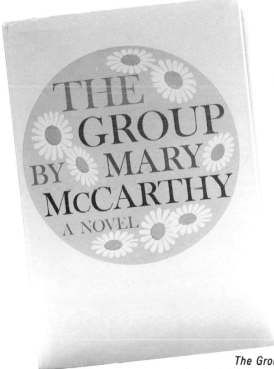

The Group was about what happened to a bunch of young women who attended Vassar together. The story benefited greatly from Miss McCarthy's wit and command of the language.

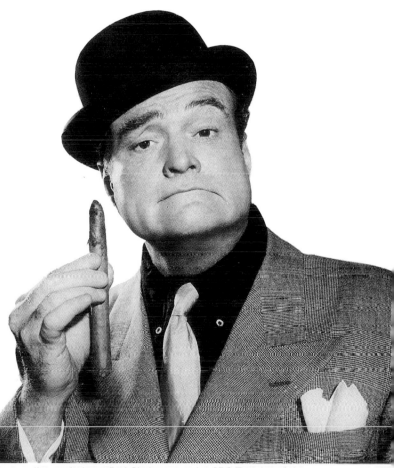

The comedian and clown Red Skelton was the CBS Tuesday-night mainstay, a position he first occupied in 1953 and maintained until 1970.

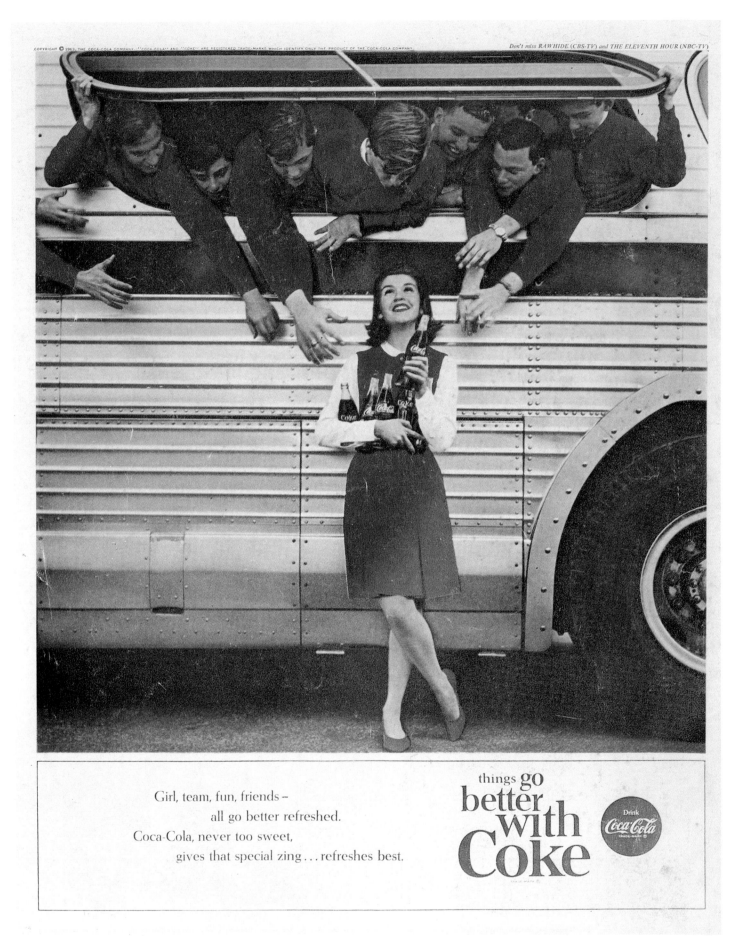

Don't miss RAWHIDE (CBS-TV) and THE ELEVENTH HOUR (NBC-TV)

Girl, team, fun, friends –
all go better refreshed.
Coca-Cola, never too sweet,
gives that special zing... refreshes best.

things **go**
better
with
Coke

Drink
Coca-Cola
TRADE-MARK ®

Coke still came in that oddly shaped bottle made of glass. Plastic and aluminum cans—to say nothing of littering the landscape—were only a twinkle in a marketing executive's eyes. In 1963, more people drank Coca Cola for breakfast than they did fruit juice.

ZIP (Zone Improvement Program) codes, which allowed mail to be scanned and routed electronically, helped speed up mail delivery. The Postal Service called the codes the greatest development in moving mail since the pony express.

The need for some improvement [in the mail system] was apparent to all. The United States Post Office handles more than half the world's mail. . . . Anybody could see that a machine could comprehend the meaning of 70631 easier than it can locate and direct a letter to . . . Anaktuvuk Pass, Alaska. Immediately, seers prophesied . . . the end of such American Place names as Lost Mule Flat, Deadwood, Painted Post, Wounded Knee, Truth or Consequences, and so on, which were sure to be replaced by the five colorless digits of ZIP. . . .

After thorough . . . testing to be sure the system would work, we started off ZIP with a zing. Ethel Merman recorded a special version of "Zip-A-Dee Doo-Dah" which was used around the country on thousands of radio and television promotional spots. . . . [And] when people realized that they weren't going to become anonymous ciphers, they were ready to accept the ZIP code.

J. EDWARD DAY, Postmaster General

Some people thought the Nash Metropolitan cute. Others thought it an affront to the car culture. This practical car, surprisingly well designed, would soon go the way of the Packard and the Kaiser.

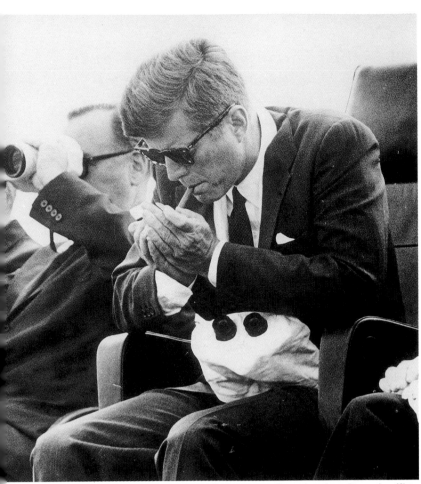

The president watched naval maneuvers from the aircraft carrier *Kitty Hawk*. He did not wish to be shown smoking his cigars, and his aides were usually successful in preventing such photos from appearing.

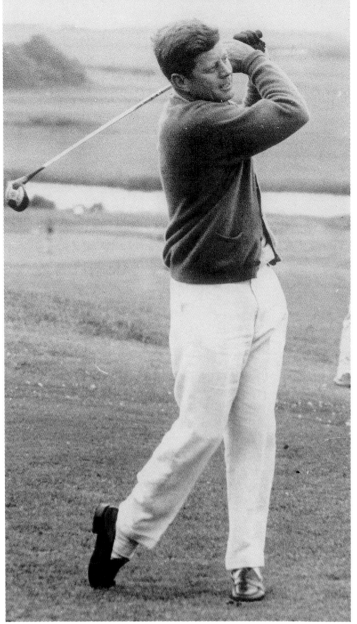

The president played a round of golf at the Hyannis Port Club on July 20.

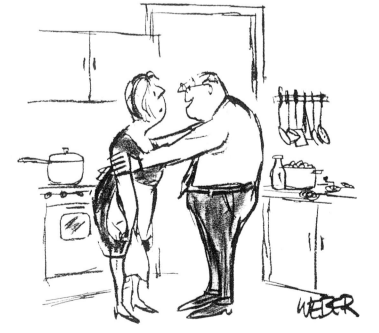

"You say you're only a housewife, and I say what do you mean, 'only'?"

I'll never forget going into one of the agencies . . . and hearing someone say that his boss was looking for a man for a particular job. And I said, "I'm terribly sorry, but you can't say that anymore; it's against the law." And he said to his boss, "We've got the Assistant Secretary of Labor here, and she says we can't specify that we want a man." And his boss said, "For heaven's sakes, then send me a good woman."

ESTHER PETERSON

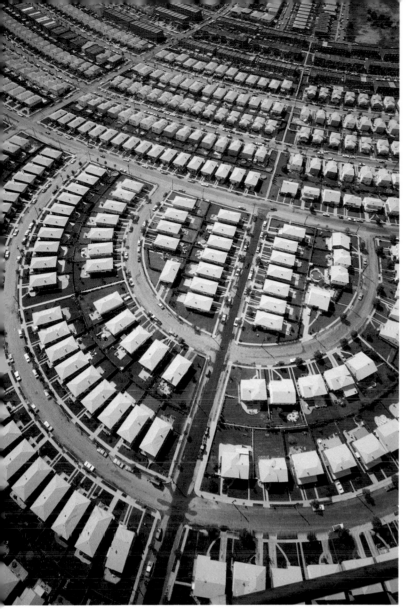

The pattern of a suburban development as seen from the air.

I remember 1963, because it was the year we moved. My father was 31 and my mother was 25. That year my father got a job with a law firm in New York, and they bought a new home—typical American dream. They had two young kids, and bought this brand-new house in the suburbs, within walking distance of the train station so my father could commute. I guess they paid something like $15,000 for it and when they sold it in 1983, the house was worth $170,000.

The house was very boring. It didn't have any of the character of an older house. It was typical sixties: plywood construction, linoleum everywhere.

MERYL MANEKER,
Student, Larchmont, N.Y.

The downtown area was alive and well, although there were shopping centers at the edge of town. The big-name stores were still downtown, and the crowds still went there to shop. There were two large theaters operating on Main Street, often showing good movies for children and family.

The streets were absolutely safe at all times. I could and did walk around the shopping areas and my home area at any time of the day or night without a thought of violence. I never had to worry about any of the children being kidnapped or abused.

CHARLOTTE COTE,
Housewife, Racine, Wis.

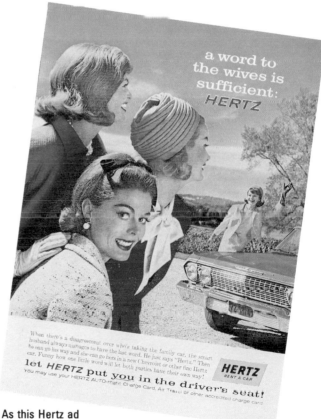

As this Hertz ad demonstrates, clothing was more formal in 1963. Many women felt underdressed in public without hats, gloves and stockings.

President Kennedy and his cabinet. From left, clockwise, were: Postmaster General J. Edward Day; Vice-President Lyndon Johnson; Secretary of Defense Robert McNamara; Undersecretary of Agriculture Charles Murphy; Secretary of Labor W. Willard Wirtz; Secretary of Welfare Anthony Celebrazze; Secretary of Commerce Luther Hodges; John Douglas of the Department of Justice; Secretary of State Dean Rusk; Kennedy; Secretary of Treasury L. Douglas Dillon and Secretary of Interior Stewart Udall.

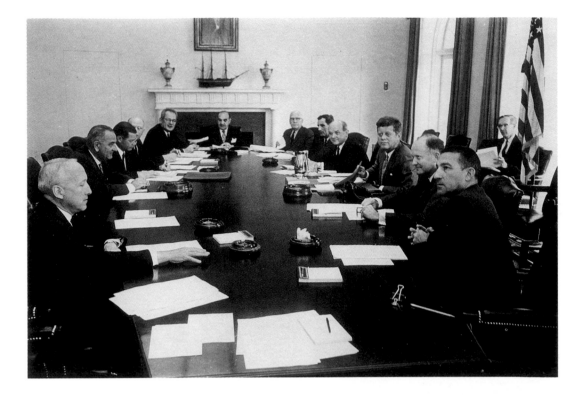

T*he expansion of network news to a half hour was part of the coming of age of news. News had been a throwaway, something stations were obliged to offer in order to keep their FCC licenses. It was done grudgingly and sparingly. But somewhere in that period, they suddenly discovered that there was an audience for it and that they could make money with it—news is a lot cheaper to produce than entertainment programming. Now news is one of the most profitable time slots on television.*

DON WEST

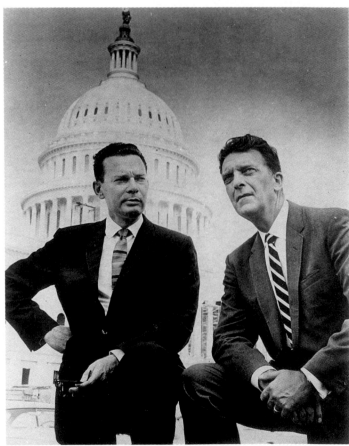

David Brinkley and Chet Huntley were coanchormen on NBC's *The Huntley-Brinkley Report*. Huntley played straight man to the drily witty Brinkley. The news seemed a bit more important and perhaps even more accurate because they reported it. This personalized style would become the extra dimension that all succeeding TV newscasters would strive to capture. With the notable exception of Walter Cronkite on CBS, few would be as successful.

*If you were 20 or 21 years old, Jack Kennedy
and the early sixties went wonderfully
together. We had a hero in the White House, and
our lives were changing. It was the beginning of
NASA and space exploration. Astronauts were
orbiting the earth. Musically, it was the beginning of the British invasion, with the appearance
of great British bands like the Dave Clark Five,
Herman's Hermits, Gerry and the Pacemakers,
and the Beatles. Even rock and roll was
changing. The music was happy and upbeat. For
me, it was a very exciting, optimistic time.*

CHARLES JACKSON

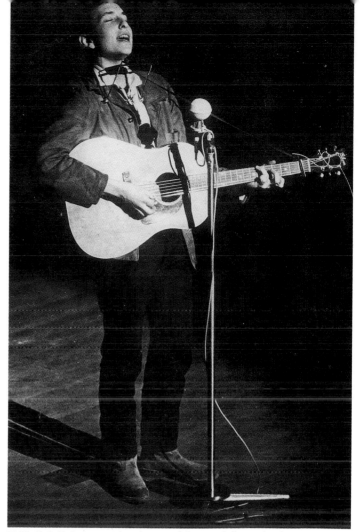

At 22, Bob Dylan was already one of the top folk music singer-composers in 1963. In July, he made a headline appearance—with Joan Baez, Pete Seeger, and Phil Ochs—at the Newport Folk Festival.

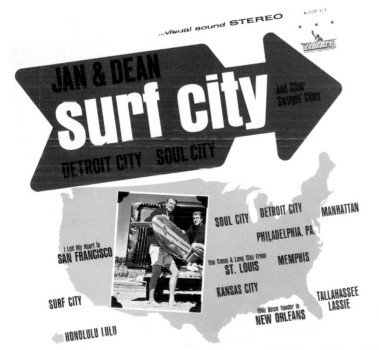

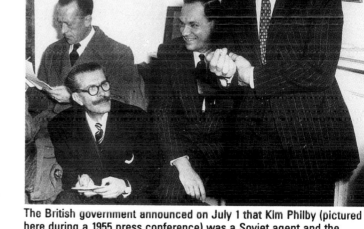

The British government announced on July 1 that Kim Philby (pictured here during a 1955 press conference) was a Soviet agent and the "third man" in the Burgess-Maclean spy case.

That Jan and Dean did not progress beyond the short-lived surfer music vogue, as did the Beach Boys, may have had something to do with their selection of tunes. For reasons known only to their A & R (Artists and Repertoire) man at Liberty Records, this album, which spent over 20 weeks on the charts, included such chestnuts as "I Left My Heart in San Francisco," "You Came a Long Way from St. Louis," and "Way Down Yonder in New Orleans."

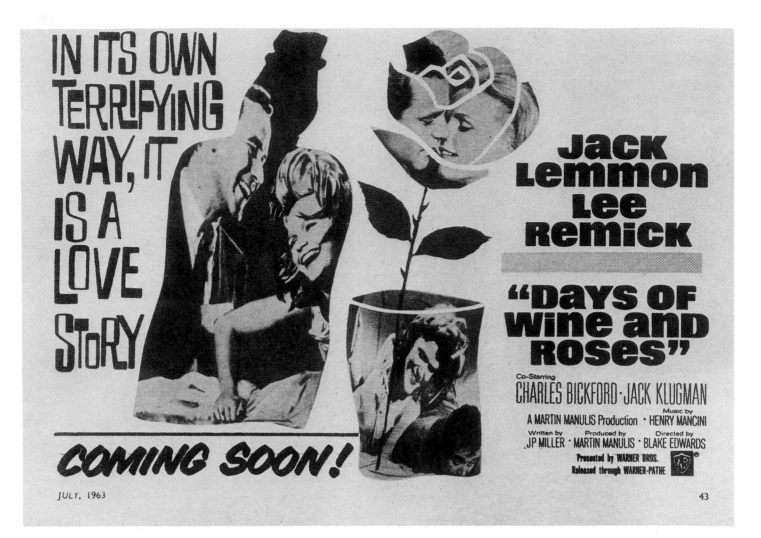

IN ITS OWN TERRIFYING WAY, IT IS A LOVE STORY

COMING SOON!

JULY, 1963

JACK Lemmon Lee Remick

"DAYS OF WINE AND ROSES"

Co-Starring
CHARLES BICKFORD · JACK KLUGMAN

A MARTIN MANULIS Production · Music by HENRY MANCINI

Written by JP MILLER · Produced by MARTIN MANULIS · Directed by BLAKE EDWARDS

Presented by WARNER BROS.
Released through WARNER-PATHE

43

The title song for *Days of Wine and Roses* was almost as popular as the movie. This tale of a young businessman who becomes an alcoholic and leads his wife into the same misery had a powerful effect on audiences. If the movie did not intend to make a direct connection between climbing the corporate ladder and the ravages of alcoholism, many others were anxious to do just that. Newspaper editorials, Sunday sermons, and magazine articles used the movie to warn against this danger of the fast-paced modern world.

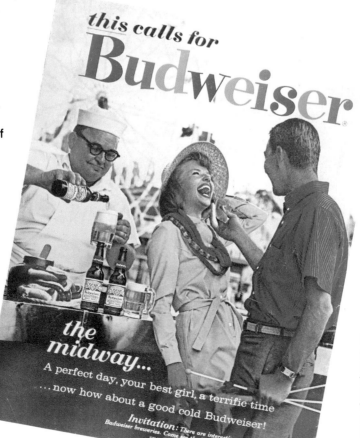

this calls for Budweiser

the midway...
A perfect day, your best girl, a terrific time
...now how about a good cold Budweiser!

Invitation: There are interesting guided tours through all Budweiser breweries. Come see the 7 Golden Keys to brewing Budweiser.

Budweiser, like other nationally distributed beers, was considered a "premium" brew. It would take a step down in class, if not popularity, some years later when imports arrived from the distilleries of Germany and Holland.

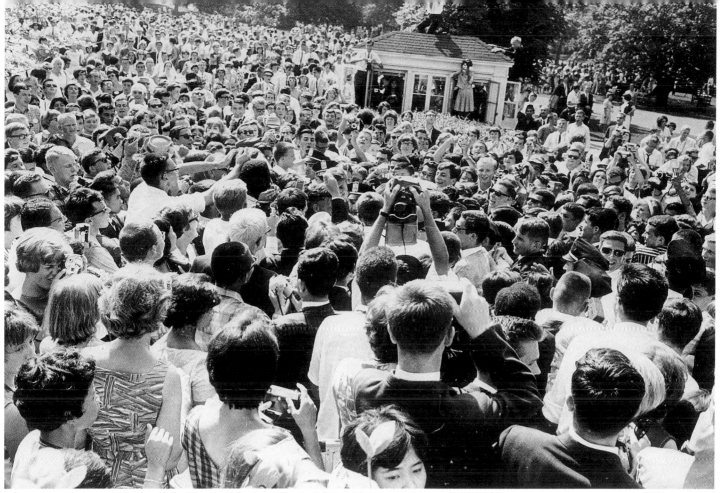

This mob scene was evidence of the Kennedy charisma. Some 2,500 visiting foreign high-school students all wanted to get close to JFK when he greeted them on the White House lawn in July.

F or a vacation, we took a trip down the Mississippi in our VW Beetle, having figured out a way to convert it into a double bed for the night. My parents provided us with a camping cook kit; we bought a one-burner stove; and we were self-sufficient, traveling without a preconceived schedule or absolute route.

JUDITH HOOVER

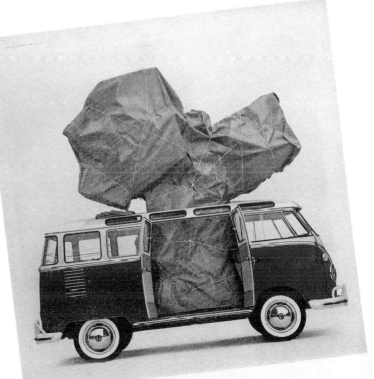

Volkswagen was far and away the best-selling import. The Beetle reigned supreme, so the VW people began pushing something they insisted upon calling a station wagon. Everyone else referred to it as a "bus."

The 1960s was the decade in which the arts became truly popular. More people had more time for art, and they had more money.

Faced with a superabundance of consumer goods, artists in the 1960s turned their attention to food—in supermarkets and restaurants and on dining-room tables, as well as in advertising—as nourishment of their art. The patronage of modern art had changed critically in this decade: New patrons entered the art market, and many of them did not want to be perturbed by complex works of art that made great demands on them.

**PETER SELZ, Curator,
Museum of Modern Art, New York**

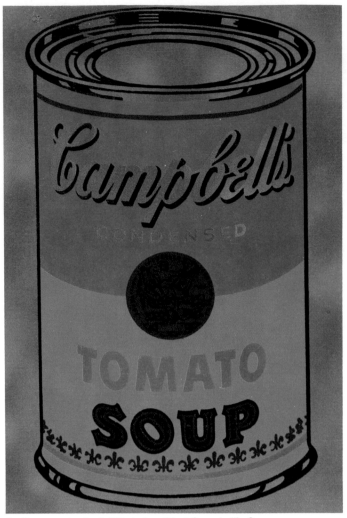

A silkscreen by Andy Warhol entitled *Campbell's Soup*.

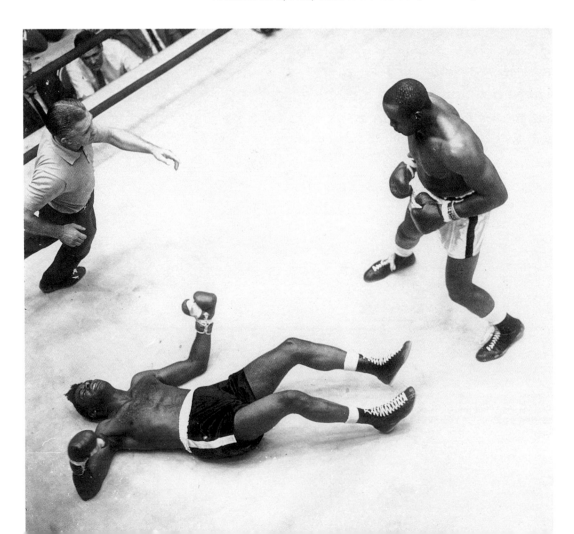

On July 22 heavyweight champion Sonny Liston clobbered Floyd Patterson, knocking him out two minutes and six seconds into the first round. About his relentless pounding of Patterson, Liston said, "It was something I had to do." For his victory, Liston, an ex-convict, received $300,000 of the $1,600,000 gate. The fight was held in Las Vegas.

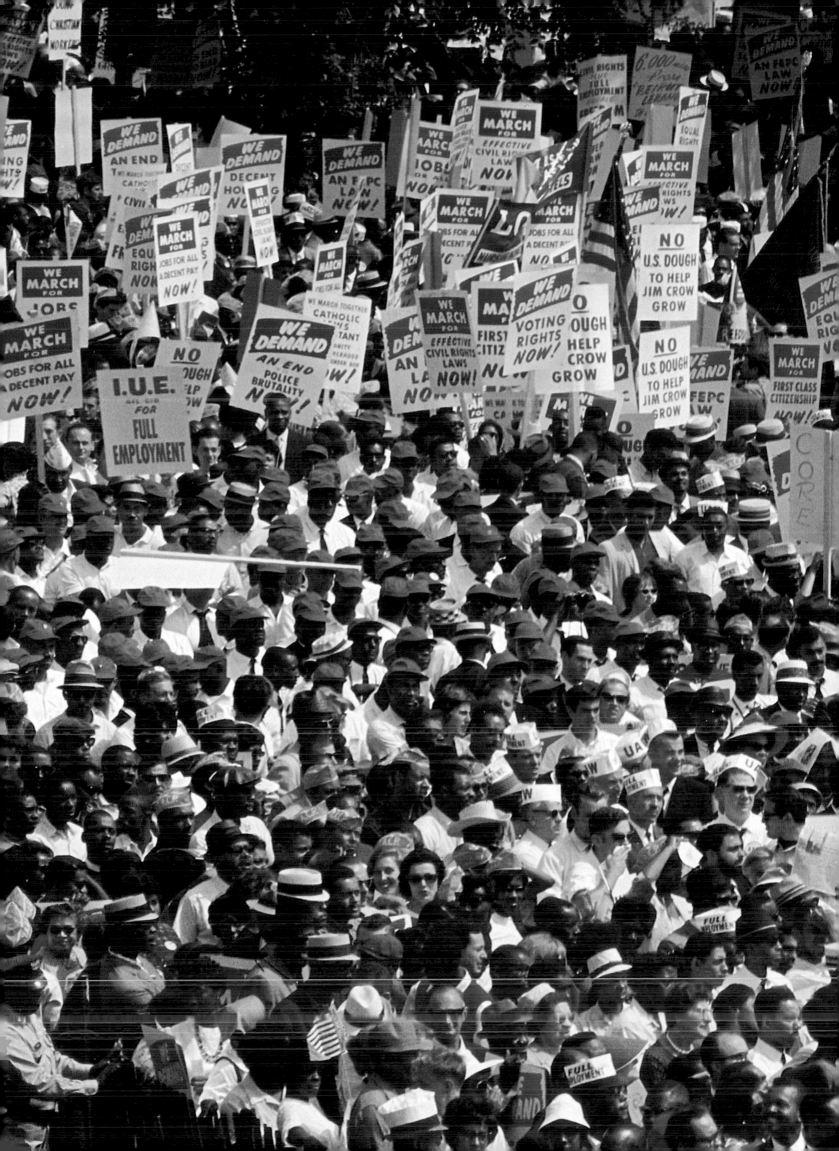

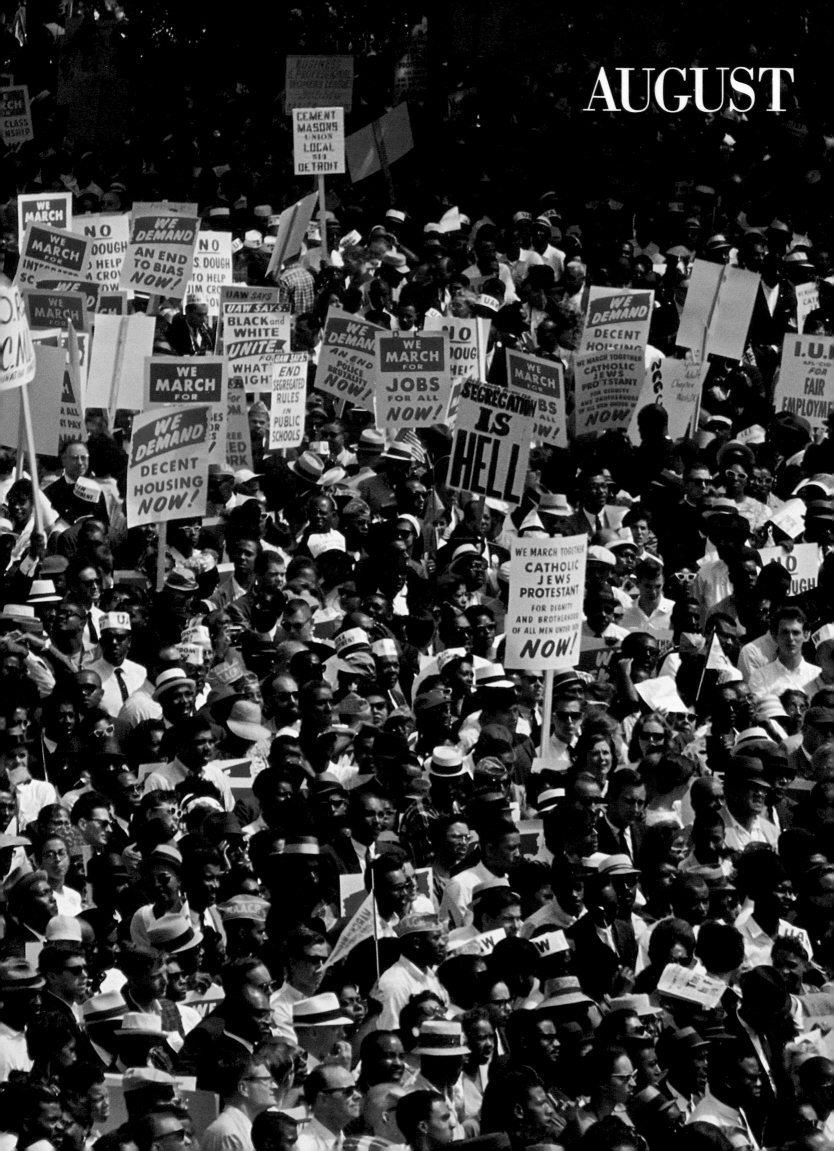

AUGUST

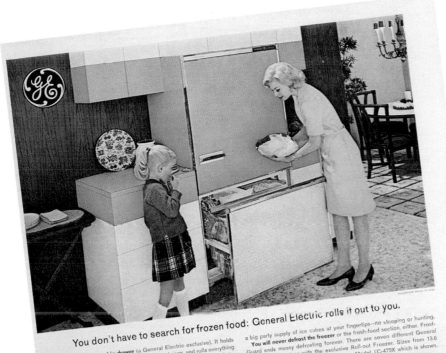

You don't have to search for frozen food: General Electric rolls it out to you.

The freezer section is a big drawer (a General Electric exclusive). It holds up to 5.8 cu. ft. of frozen food, including bulky packages, and rolls everything out in plain sight, within easy reach. Has juice can rack; two sliding baskets. **You will never refill another ice tray.** The tray refills all by itself, when you close the drawer. No more spilly trips from faucet to freezer. You can store

a big party supply of ice cubes at your fingertips—no stooping or hunting. **You will never defrost the freezer** or the fresh-food section, either. Frost-Guard ends messy defrosting forever. There are seven different General Electric refrigerators with the exclusive Roll-out Freezer. Sizes from 13.6 cubic feet to the 18.8-cu. ft. Spacemaker. Model TC-479X which is shown.

Household appliances were made in America and bore familiar names like General Electric, Westinghouse, Philco. Few US homes contained anything whose brand name would not have been recognized by the grandparents of the occupants. Foreign products were considered either shoddy imitations or exotic luxury items like bone china, vintage wine, or hybrid flower bulbs.

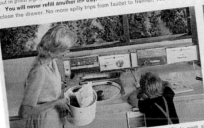

12-lb.-capacity washer has a separate washer—the MINI-BASKET*—to wash all the things you now do by hand: delicate things, last-minute loads, leftover loads. It's two washers in one: 12-pounder and MINI-BASKET. Filter-Flo® System works for both. Shown, Model WA-1050X.

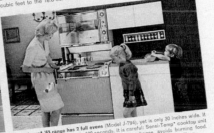

Americana* '63 range has 2 full ovens (Model J-794), yet is only 30 inches wide. It is fast: boils a pint of water in 130 seconds. It is careful: Sensi-Temp* cooktop unit holds the temperature you choose, avoids burning food. Easy to clean: oven door lifts off, cooking units tilt up.

GENERAL ELECTRIC

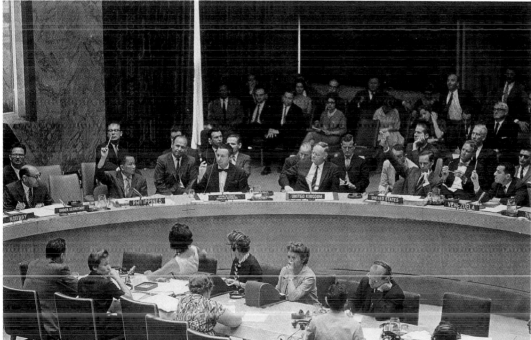

On August 7 the UN Security Council voted an embargo of all arms and military equipment to South Africa because of that country's racial segregation policies. Charles Yost represented the U.S.

126

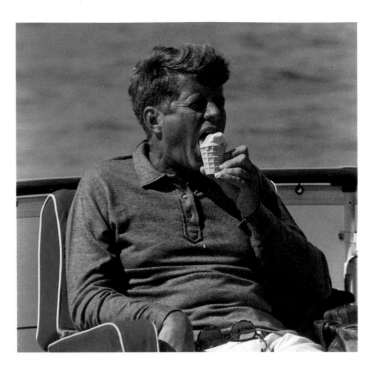

Millions of . . . Americans soon began to emulate the youthful president. The slick, two-button suit, the swirling splash of hair over the forehead, narrow ties and pointed shoes—all became fashionable for an entire generation of young Kennedy admirers.

GARY KOERSELMAN

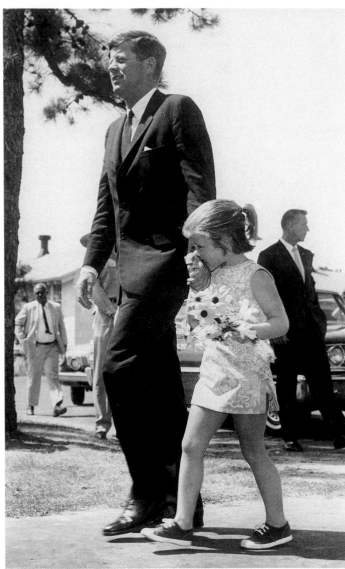

Caroline Kennedy scratched an itchy nose with her father's hand on the way to visit Mrs. Kennedy in the Massachusetts hospital where the first lady was recovering.

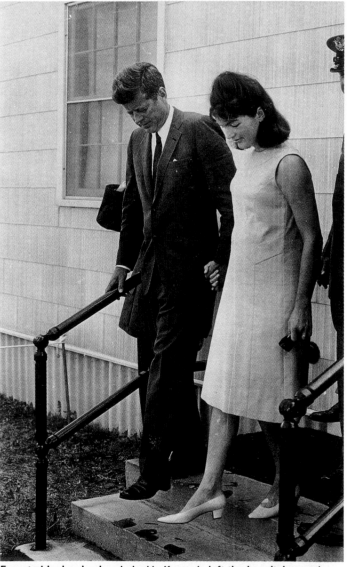

Escorted by her husband, Jackie Kennedy left the hospital a week after the premature birth of Patrick Bouvier on August 7. He lived only two days.

The limited Nuclear Test Ban Treaty was a small but useful step. And the Russian wheat deal and the hot line. Those things were steps in the right direction. It's ironic that it took Nixon to open up China and negotiate and get ratified the Salt I treaty with the Russians. I think that had he lived, Kennedy would have been in favor of initiatives like that—probably in his second term. He was a little bit fearful of that in the first term. I've always thought that Kennedy would have been a better second-term president than he was in the first term, because he was painfully aware of the cliff-hanger margin by which he was elected in the first term.

GEORGE McGOVERN

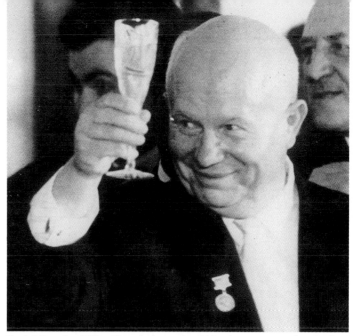

Soviet Premier Nikita Khrushchev raised his glass to toast the signing of the limited Test Ban Treaty between the United States, the Soviet Union, and Great Britain in Moscow on August 5. President Kennedy called the signing "an important first step—a step toward peace, a step toward reason, a step away from war."

Kennedy threw himself into the ratification process with every resource available to him. He did so out of a sense of conviction which he probably felt for no other measure sponsored by his Administration. Indeed, he confided to his associates that he "would gladly forfeit his re-election, if necessary, for the sake of the Test Ban Treaty."

GLENN SEABORG

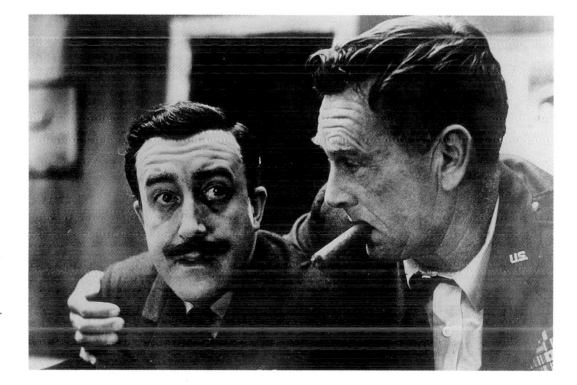

Dr. Strangelove: Or How I Learned to Stop Worrying and Love the Bomb was, historically, the most important movie of the year. The picture, the director (Stanley Kubrick), and the principal actor (Peter Sellers, who played three parts, including the title role) were all nominated for Academy Awards. In addition to Sellers and Sterling Hayden (pictured here), the movie featured George C. Scott, Slim Pickens, and James Earl Jones. Terry Southern wrote the screenplay with Kubrick and Peter George.

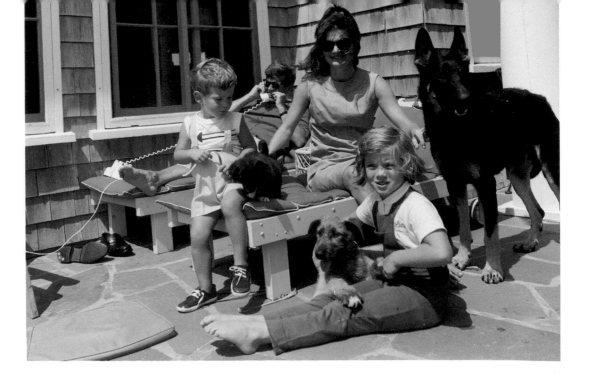

The first family photograph after Mrs. Kennedy returned from Otis Air Force Base hospital.

He's the only president I can remember who had children while he was president, had babies while he was president—certainly one of the most emotionally evocative events in one's life—and the American people shared all of that. He lost a child, a tragedy that happens to people, and everybody is part of that. He had an older brother lost in the service, his own family links and ties to his brothers and to his parents were very public; so that in a sense, he was able to bring the public into the orbit of a tight family life and all the emotions that go along with a family relationship. Of course, his own sexual behavior wasn't public at that time, so that the image that was given was that of quite a strong family, and I don't think other presidents have been able to capitalize on that. Certainly Reagan hasn't, even Roosevelt—although he had a lot of sons, they were all older, grown. It's different having small children running around your office, showing up at reviews of soldiers and things like that.

DAVID SEARS, Professor of Psychology
and Political Science, UCLA

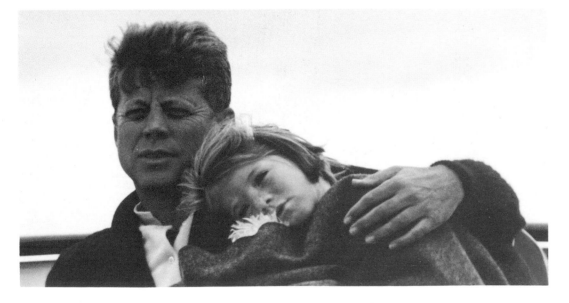

The president and his daughter aboard a yacht off Cape Cod.

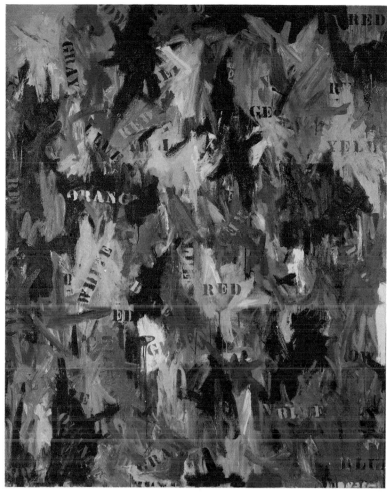

False Start painted by Jasper Johns.

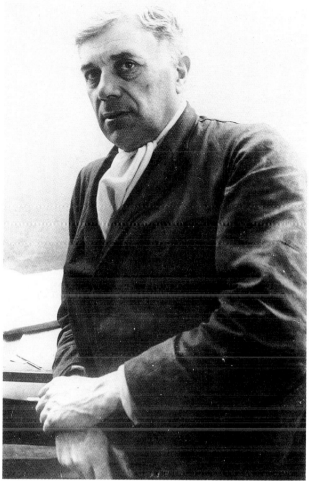

Another era ended on August 31 with the death of French painter Georges Braque in Paris. Together with Pablo Picasso, he had founded the cubist movement, which altered the development of 20th-century art. Braque's death came in the house on the Left Bank where he had lived and worked since the 1920s.

One Flew Over the Cuckoo's Nest, based on Ken Kesey's novel of the same title, opened to poor reviews. It lasted for eighty-two performances. The show's star, Kirk Douglas, would later turn the property over to his son Michael who would produce a much more successful film version starring Jack Nicholson.

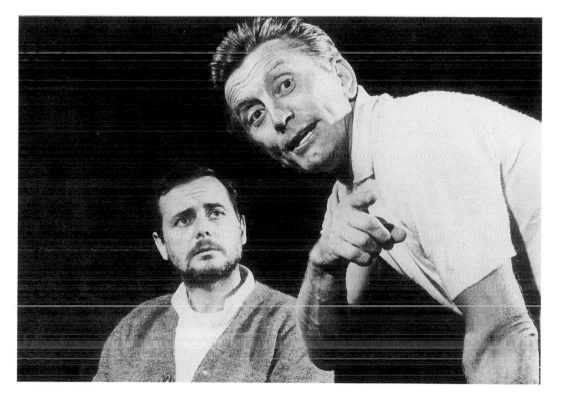

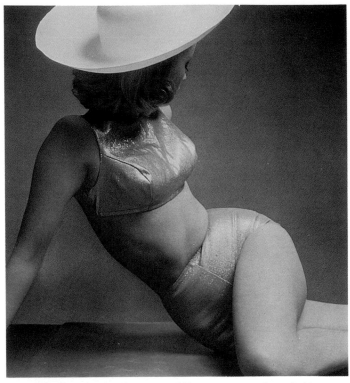

If this bathing suit from the pages of *Vogue* was ever intended to actually enter the water, it was unlikely that the event would have been observed at the public beach or local swimming pool.

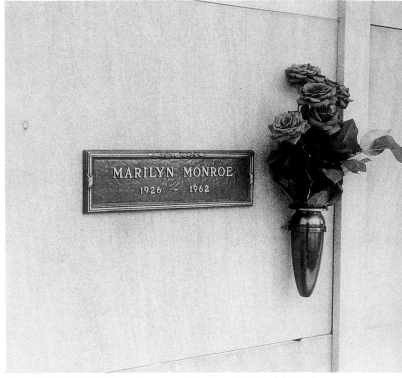

August 5, 1963, the first anniversary of actress Marilyn Monroe's death, was marked by a bouquet of red roses from Joe DiMaggio. Monroe's 1954 marriage to the baseball star had lasted only nine months.

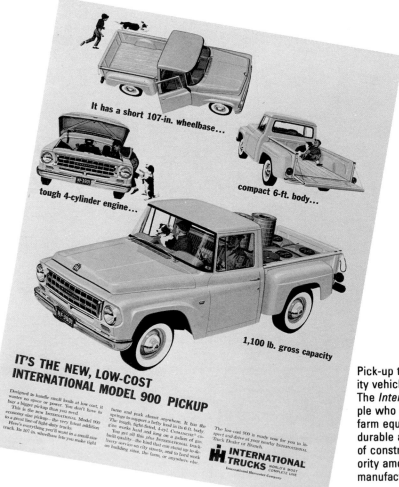

It has a short 107-in. wheelbase...

tough 4-cylinder engine...

compact 6-ft. body...

1,100 lb. gross capacity

IT'S THE NEW, LOW-COST INTERNATIONAL MODEL 900 PICKUP

Designed to handle small loads at low cost, it buy a bigger pickup than you need.
This is the new International Model 900 economy size pickup—the very latest addition to a great line of light-duty trucks.
Here's everything you'll want in a small size truck. Its 107-in. wheelbase lets you make tight turns and park almost anywhere. It has the springs to support a hefty load in its 6 ft. body.
The tough, tight-fisted, 4-cyl. Comanche™ engine works hard and long on a gallon of gas.
You get all this plus International truck-built quality—the kind that can stand up to delivery service on city streets, and to hard work on building sites, the farm, or anywhere else.
The low-cost 900 is ready now for you to inspect and drive at your nearby International Truck Dealer or Branch.

INTERNATIONAL TRUCKS WORLD'S MOST COMPLETE LINE
International Harvester Company

Pick-up trucks were strictly utility vehicles bought to do a job. The *International*, made by people who specialize in things like farm equipment, was sturdy and durable at a time when quality of construction was not a priority among the 'big three' car manufacturers.

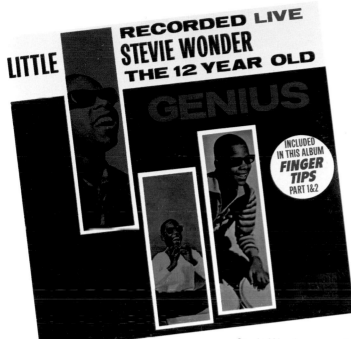

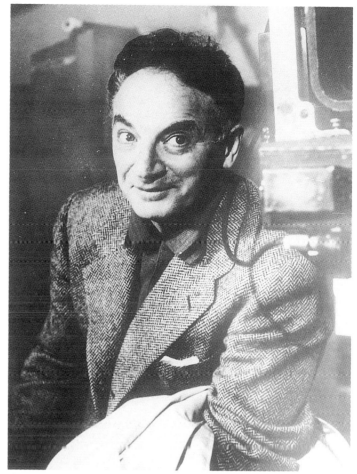

Stevie Wonder was only 12 in 1963 and the term "little" always preceded his name. This Motown album was produced by Berry Gordy, Jr. The liner notes warned the listener to be careful or you might find yourself tempted to dance or sing along. In addition to *Fingertips*, the big number here was *Hallelujah I Just Love Her So* composed by Ray Charles.

Playwright Clifford Odets died of cancer at the age of 57 on August 14. During the Great Depression, Odets' plays, such as *Awake and Sing* and *Waiting for Lefty*, criticized society and politics. He later went on to write movie scripts, including *The Sweet Smell of Success*.

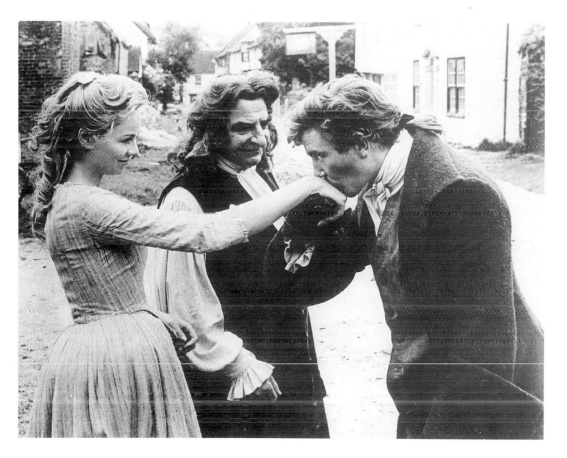

The winsome Susannah York, Hugh Griffith and a young talented Albert Finney in a scene from *Tom Jones*. Finney's career was to be the big winner from this movie hit. He has been a major stage and film star ever since.

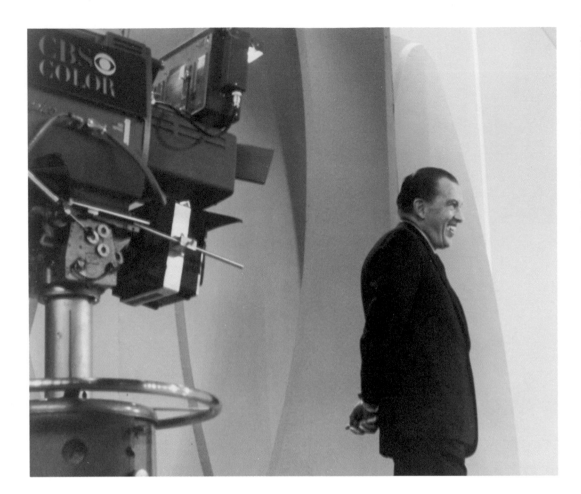

The Ed Sullivan Show (originally titled Toast of the Town) was a Sunday-night habit in millions of homes. Sullivan was certainly no performer; what he brought to the medium was a news-paperman's flair for identifying the right moment to exploit a topical act. No one ever suggested that he had refined taste—trained dogs in tutus would follow a violin solo that had been preceded by a ventriloquist whose dummy spoke better English than he did—but Sullivan's timing was exquisite. He was the first to present the Beatles in the U.S. and he gave Elvis his first network exposure.

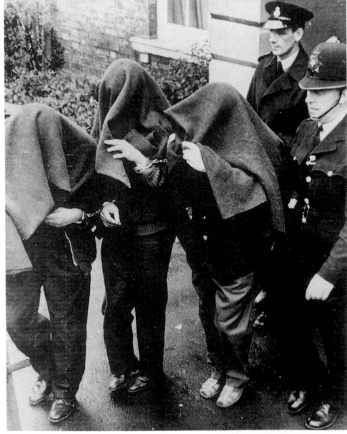

In Linslade, England, on August 16, these men were photographed leaving court after being charged with complicity in what came to be called the Great Mail Train Robbery. In all, charges were filed against nine people. Of the $7 million stolen, only $500,000 was ever recovered.

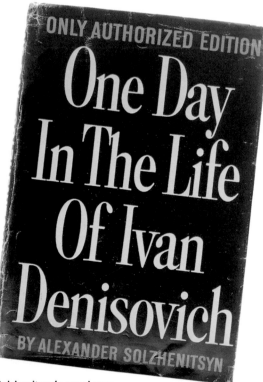

Solzhenitsyn's novel was the first piece of Soviet literature by an outright dissident to achieve best-selling status in the West.

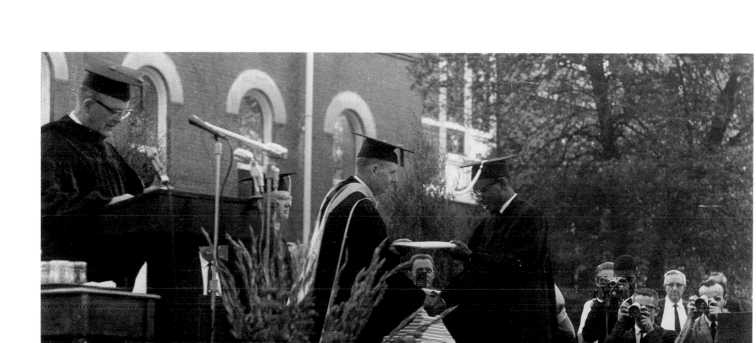

The last day of classes at the University of Mississippi I wore the same clothes that I had worn the day I enrolled—dark suit, white shirt, red necktie and black shoes. There was one notable difference. I put on upside down one of the NEVER, NEVER buttons that [Governor Ross] Barnett had made so popular during the first few weeks after I enrolled.

On September 30, 1962, I had flown into the university airport with the U.S. marshals from Tennessee. That day, two men were killed and several hundred were wounded in the fighting between the United States and Mississippi. The next day I was enrolled as a student.

On August 18, 1963, I drove out of Mississippi with the U.S. marshals to Tennessee, after receiving [my] degree. . . . A serious question kept plaguing my mind: Did this constitute the privilege of attending the school of my choice?

We drove at top speed down the four-lane highway that led to Memphis. But this was still not fast enough for my friend and great freedom fighter, Robert L.T. Smith Jr., who rode with me. Everyone was silent. Finally, looking at the marshals' cars in front and in back of us, Robert asked, "J., was it like this all of the time?" Without waiting for a reply, he continued, "Man, I don't see how you stood it! I just don't see how you could take it."

JAMES MEREDITH, Student, University of Mississippi

James Meredith, the first black to graduate from the University of Mississippi, accepted his diploma from the university's chancellor on August 18. The previous fall, when Governor Ross Barnett threatened to defy a Supreme Court ruling ordering Meredith's admission, President Kennedy ordered Federal troops to the campus. Two people were killed in the ensuing rioting, but Barnett backed down, and the resolution of the conflict became another landmark in the struggle for equal rights.

James Meredith [is] a man who gave dignity to every Negro in the country, who put every Negro in college, who played one of the biggest parts in setting up the revolution in the history of the American Negro struggle. Negroes looked a little different and acted a little different when James Meredith was graduated because they all graduated with him, graduated from the derogatory stigma that all Negroes are ignorant, that all Negroes are lazy, that all Negroes stink.

DICK GREGORY

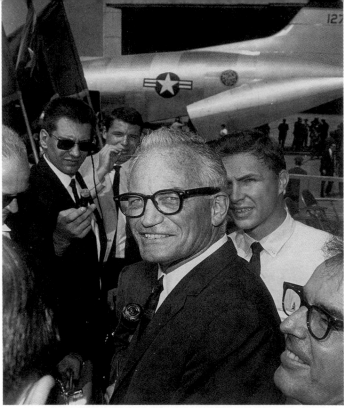

Senator Barry Goldwater attended the unveiling of the new Lockheed C141 Starlifter in Marietta, Georgia, on August 22. He looked forward to contesting the presidency with Kennedy in 1964.

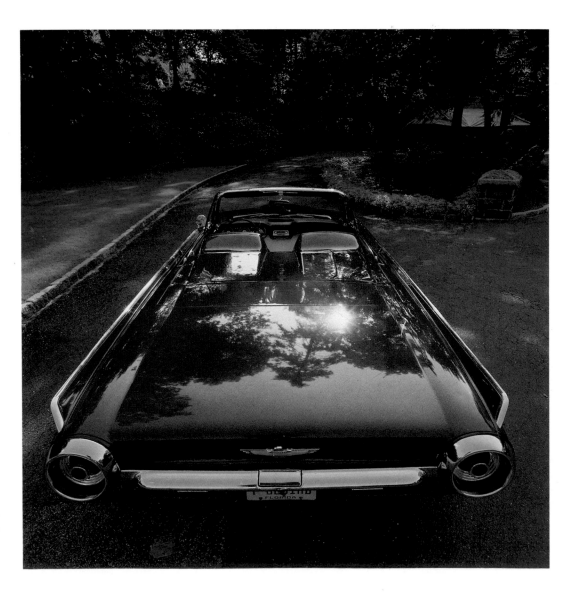

The Thunderbird, while not the classic design of the late fifties, was still a symbol of America's muscular road culture: powerful, enormously wasteful of gasoline, overweight, and overpowered— but still a machine of no small wonder.

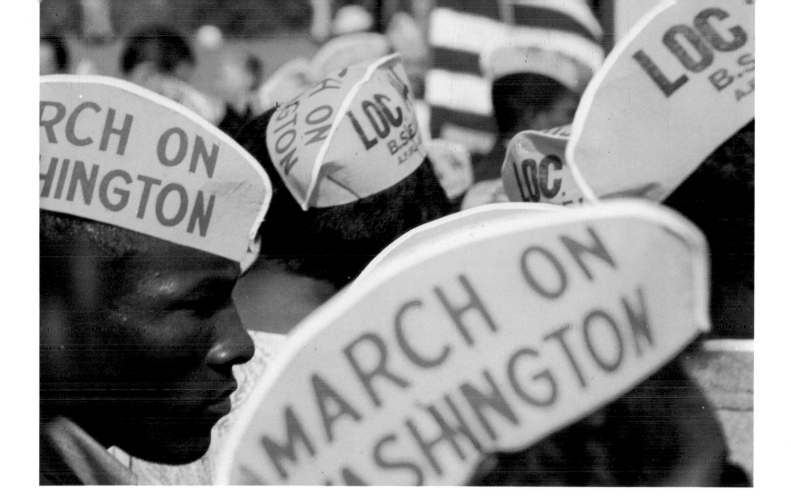

I have never seen such a crowd of people as there were there that day. There was a special feeling of closeness. I have never felt so small and yet part of something so immense, wonderful and grand.

I had a feeling of pride for my race and for the whites who thought enough to come. And there was a sense of triumph. We had proved by being orderly, nonviolent, and determined that we were not the kind of people our enemies said we were.

All around, in the faces of everyone, there was this sense of hope for the future—the belief that this march was the big step in the right direction. It could be heard in the voices of the people singing and seen in the way they walked. It poured out into smiles.

EMILY ROCK, Student, Woodland High School, New York

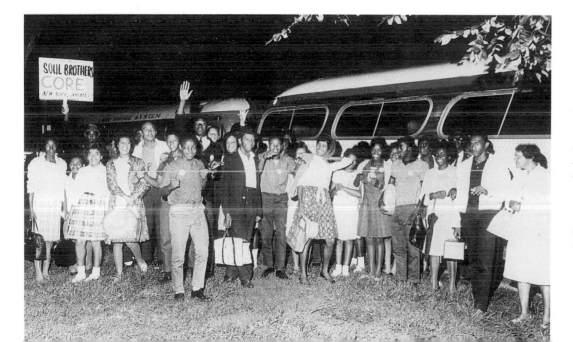

More than 200,000 people marched for civil rights in the largest demonstration ever held in Washington, D.C. Thousands of whites joined the mostly black marchers. "We want our freedom—and we want it NOW!" was a banner seen frequently. People came from around the country to march from the Washington Monument, where they signed a pledge of dedication to the civil rights struggle, down Constitution and Independence Avenues to the Lincoln Memorial. Along the way the marchers sang "We Shall Overcome."

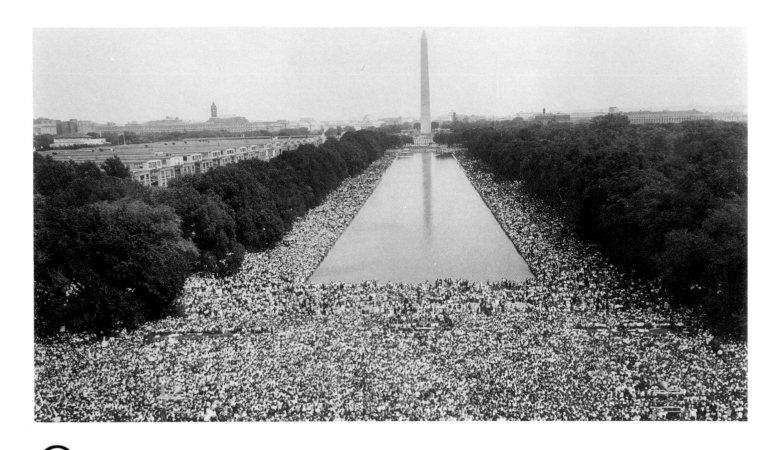

Oh, baby, to stand on top of the Lincoln Memorial and look down, it was like everyone in the world was standing there, smiling in the sunshine and singing. Saw Negroes and whites in their best clothes, with their best manners, on their best behavior. And the Negroes . . . demonstrated to the world that day that we're more first-class than a lot of whites.

The climax of that beautiful day was Martin Luther King's speech, "I have a dream." Never have so many people cried, whether they wanted to or not. When it was all over, I just stood there because I didn't know which way to go. Thought of a million and one things, oh, how my mind wandered that glorious day. That day I felt like the Negro had been given his equal rights.

I felt that way right into September, right into the Sunday morning when the forest turned pitch-black cold again. Someone threw a bomb in a Negro church in Birmingham. Four kids were dead.

DICK GREGORY

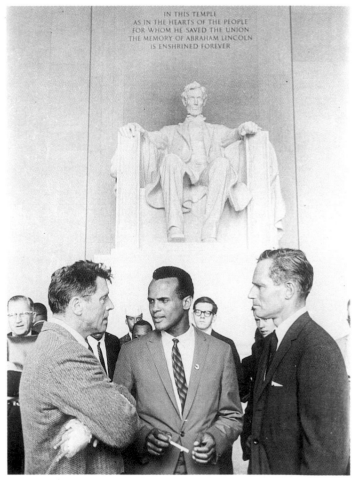

Chatting together inside the Lincoln Memorial as they waited to speak to the large crowd were Burt Lancaster, Harry Belafonte, and Charlton Heston.

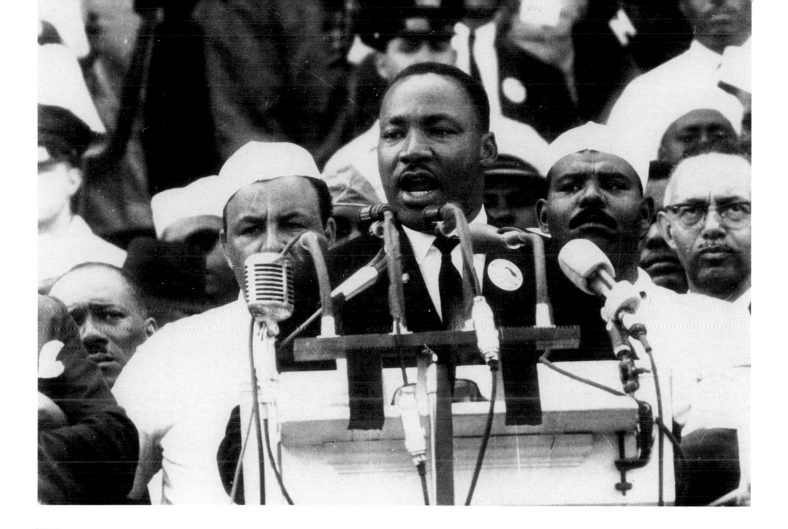

I have a dream that one day on the red hills of Georgia, sons of former slaves and sons of former slave owners will be able to sit down together at the table of brotherhood.

I have a dream that one day, even the State of Mississippi, a state sweltering with the heat of oppression, will be transformed into an oasis of freedom and justice.

I have a dream that my four little children will one day live in a nation where they will not be judged by the color of their skin but by the content of their character. I have a dream today!

I have a dream that one day, down in Alabama, with its vicious racists, with its Governor having his lips dripping with the words of interposition and nullification, that one day, right there in Alabama, little black boys and black girls will be able to join hands with little white boys and white girls as sisters and brothers. I have a dream today!

I have a dream that one day every valley shall be exalted, every hill and mountain shall be made low, the rough places shall be made plain and the crooked places shall be made straight, and the glory of the Lord will be revealed and all flesh shall see it together.

This is our hope. This is the faith that I go back to the South with.

MARTIN LUTHER KING, Jr.,
Southern Christian Leadership Conference

Martin Luther King told the throng gathered in front of the Lincoln Memorial of his dreams for all America's people.

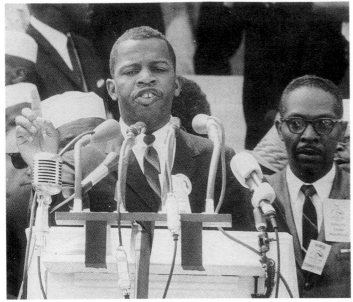

John Lewis, chairman of the Student Non-Violent Coordinating Committee, spoke at the Lincoln Memorial.

I became Chairman of the Student Non-Violent Coordinating Committee on June 14, 1963. Seven days later, I was invited to Washington to meet with President Kennedy. Along with other black leaders, I sat in the East Room of the White House and listened to A. Philip Randolph—in his baritone voice—tell the President, "The masses are restless. We must do something." He referred to what had taken place in Birmingham, to the fight Medgar Evers had made in Mississippi, and the fact that Evers had been shot and killed. He kept saying, "We have to do something. We're going to march on Washington."

President Kennedy responded by saying, "How can you handle a march on Washington? There will be violence and chaos. The end result will be that we'll never get any civil rights legislation passed."

Mr. Randolph came back and said, "Mr. President, this will be an orderly, peaceful, non-violent protest. We are going to march on Washington."

JOHN LEWIS

The president conferred with the March leaders after the rally had ended.

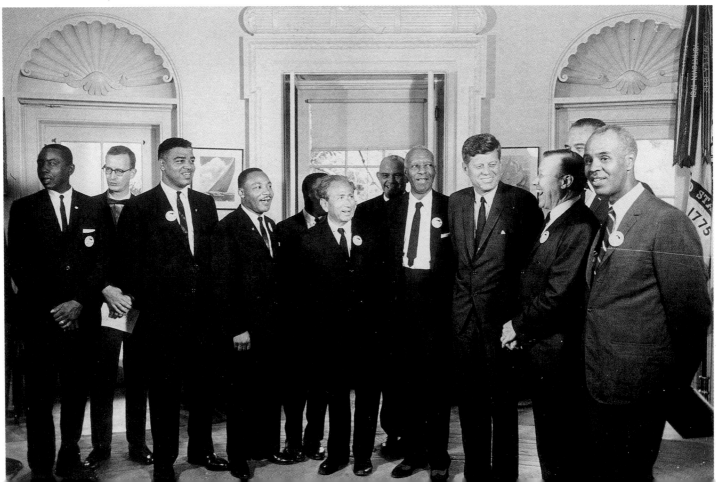

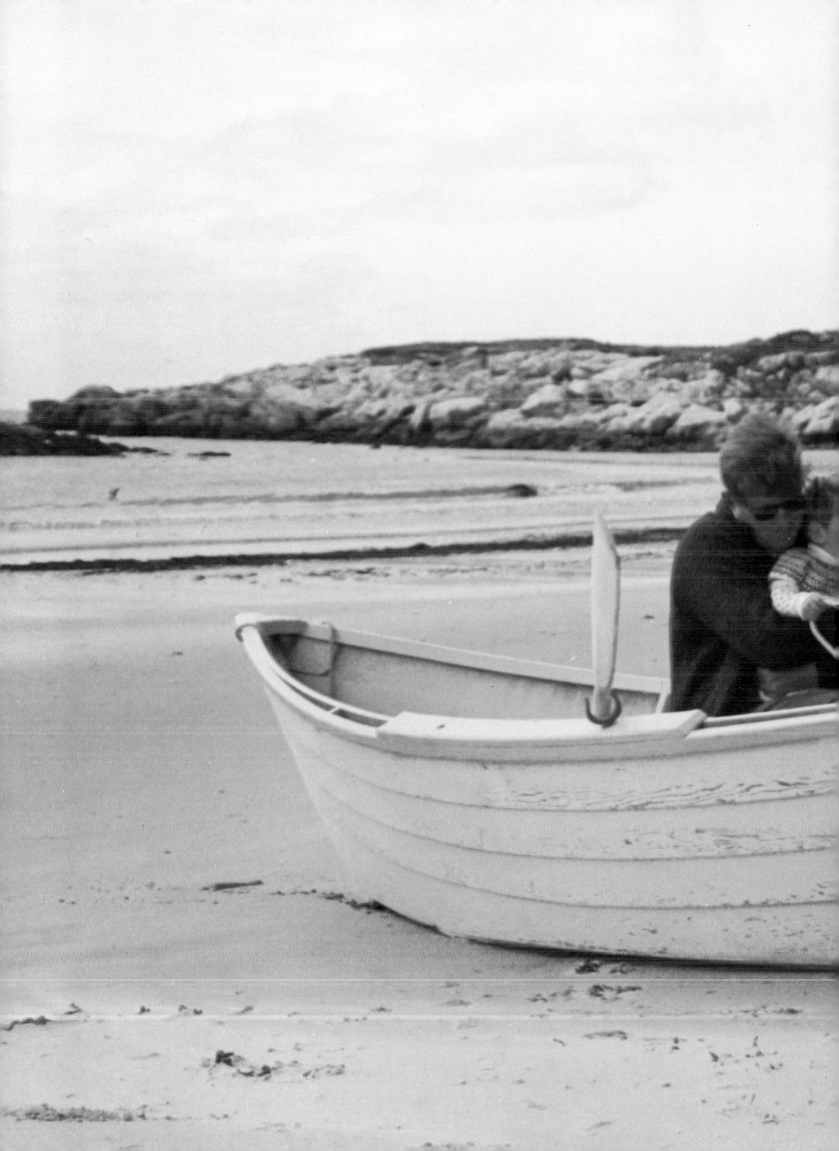

SEPTEMBER

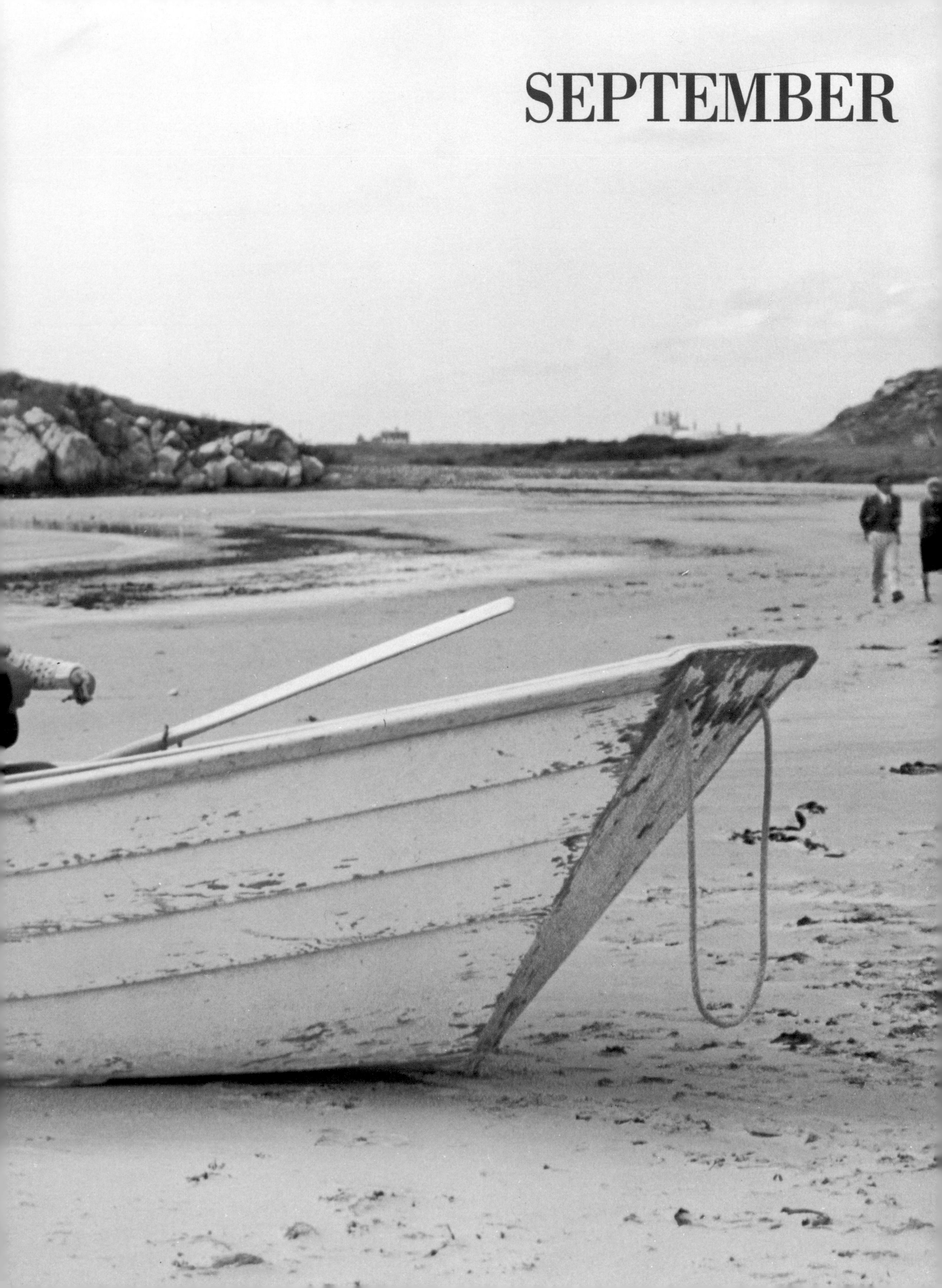

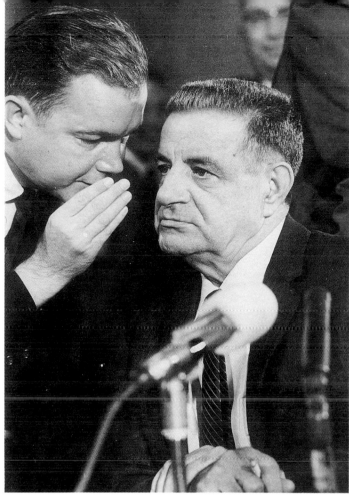

In colorful mob language, Joseph Valachi, a convicted Mafia killer, gave Senate investigators lurid details about the workings of the Vito Genovese branch of the Cosa Nostra. It was the fullest account ever heard in public of the killing, extortion and intimidation practiced by the Mafia.

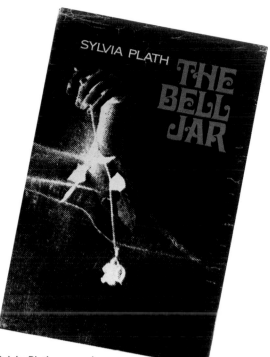

Sylvia Plath was only a cult figure and not yet a legend when *The Bell Jar* appeared. The elevation of her reputation would have to wait until feminists required patron saints.

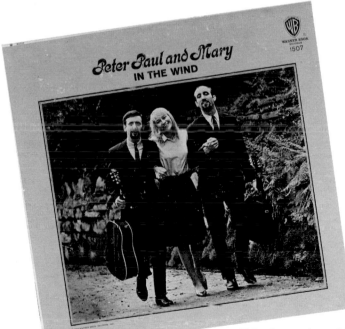

This album, released in early fall, would reach the number two position on the charts, right behind *The Singing Nun*. Along with *Peter, Paul and Mary* from the previous year, it was the group's major recording success. The liner notes, written in free verse by Bob Dylan, were a lament for the good old days in Greenwich Village.

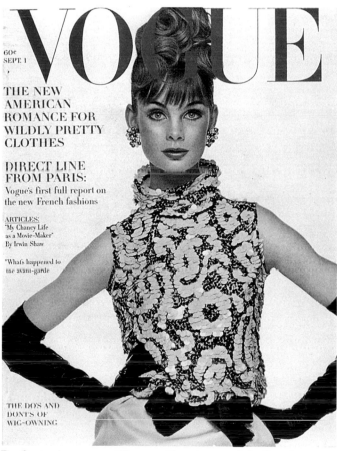

The September cover of *Vogue*, with a photograph by Bert Stern.

The night of September 1, 1963, in the town of Plaquemine, Louisiana, I was confronted with what, in fact, was a lynch mob. It was composed of members of the state police, with their name plates and badge numbers taped over, and others deputized for the occasion.

It was a manhunt, and they were looking for me. Policemen had been heard in the streets, beating up marchers, saying "We'll let you go, nigger, if you let us know where Farmer is." Two young CORE members hiding under the steps of the church heard a state trooper say to others, "When we catch that nigger Farmer, we're going to kill him."

I sent a young person crawling through tall grass to a neighboring funeral home to ask if we could hide there for refuge. We crawled in twos, threes, and fours to get there.

It didn't take the troopers long to figure out where we were. One of the troopers kicked open the back door looking for me. But those who were in there wouldn't let me go out, saying it was a lynch mob. Finally, the funeral director, a woman, made her way to the door, and asked him if he had a search warrant to come into her place of business, saying he could not come into her place of business without a search warrant.

The troopers went away for a time. But we knew they'd be back, and my life wouldn't be worth a nickel if they got a warrant. So we finally worked out an escape plan. We had heard that there were roadblocks set up all around the town. We sent out one hearse to draw troopers away from the roadblock. They pursued that hearse, thinking I was in it. And I was put in the second hearse, and then sped through the unmanned roadblock, and sped down back roads in the dead of night to New Orleans.

JAMES FARMER

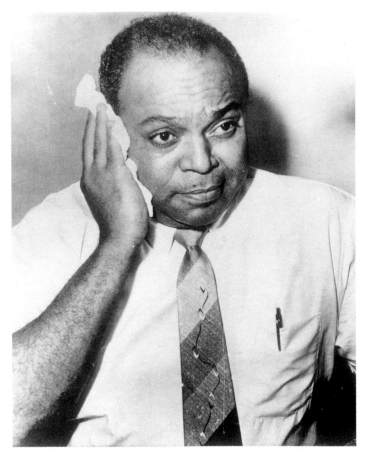

James Farmer, national director of the Congress of Racial Equality, after desegregation demonstrations in Plaquemine, Louisiana.

I think there were fewer poor people in '63, and we felt there were solutions to it. There was still hope that you would reach the child in the ghetto. You could solve the minority housing crisis. With goodwill, you could solve a lot of the social problems. You thought that the race problem was on its way to being solved. The great leap forward was in civil rights. In many ways we lived in a better land.

MARIE RIDDER, Washington Editor,
Glamour, Vogue

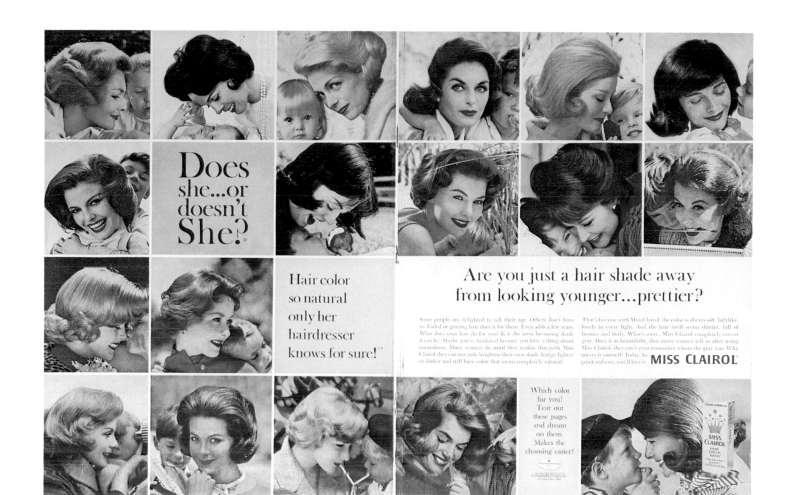

Does she...or doesn't She?®

Hair color so natural only her hairdresser knows for sure!™

Are you just a hair shade away from looking younger...prettier?

Some people are delighted to tell their age. Others don't have to. Faded or graying hair does it for them. Even adds a few years. What does your hair do for you? Is it the most becoming shade it can be? Maybe you've hesitated because you have a thing about naturalness. Many women do until they realize that with Miss Clairol they can not only brighten their own shade but go lighter or darker and still have color that seems completely natural.

That's because with Miss Clairol the color is always soft, ladylike, lovely in every light. And the hair itself seems shinier, full of bounce and body. What's more, Miss Clairol completely covers gray. Does it so beautifully, that many women tell us after using Miss Clairol, they can't even remember where the gray was. Why not try it yourself? Today. So quick and easy, you'll love it. **MISS CLAIROL**

Which color for you? Tear out these pages and dream on them. Makes the choosing easier!

MISS CLAIROL HAIR COLOR BATH

ABOVE: Another great (i.e., commercially successful) ad line, widely misinterpreted—to the amazement of the ad agency.

I n 1963, we did not have a very strong Federal Trade Commission. We did not have very good food laws. We didn't have a lot of the antitrust things. We didn't have redress. We didn't have any labeling or anything on packaging. There was a complete dearth of a lot of the basic consumer protections that came forward. We didn't even have a big national organization, a consumer federation.

ESTHER PETERSON

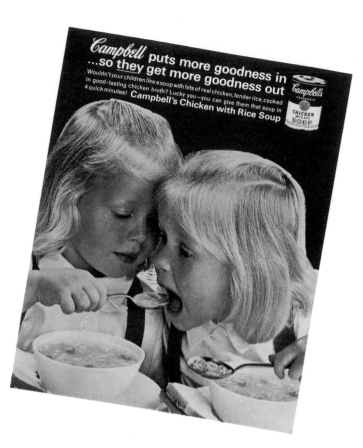

If you were brought up on soup for lunch—most likely Campbell's—it didn't matter whether you became a 'yippie' or a 'yuppie,' the taste, smell and sense of security stayed with you forever.

The Kennedy and Fitzgerald clans gathered at the Hyannis compound in early September to celebrate the seventy-fifth birthday of patriarch Joseph P. Kennedy.

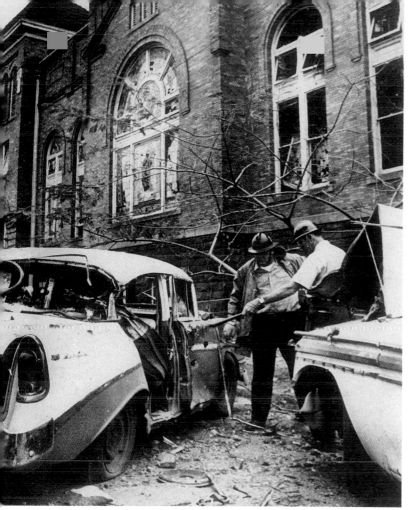

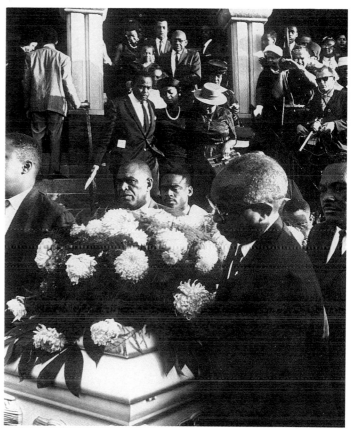

At 10 A.M. on September 15, Sunday school classes were just ending at the 16th Street Baptist Church when a bomb exploded with the force of 12 sticks of dynamite. In the rubble, rescue workers discovered the bodies of four girls: Denise McNair, 11; Carole Robertson, 14; Cynthia Wesley, 14; and Addie Mae Collins, 14.

The casket carrying one of the four girls was taken for burial on September 18.

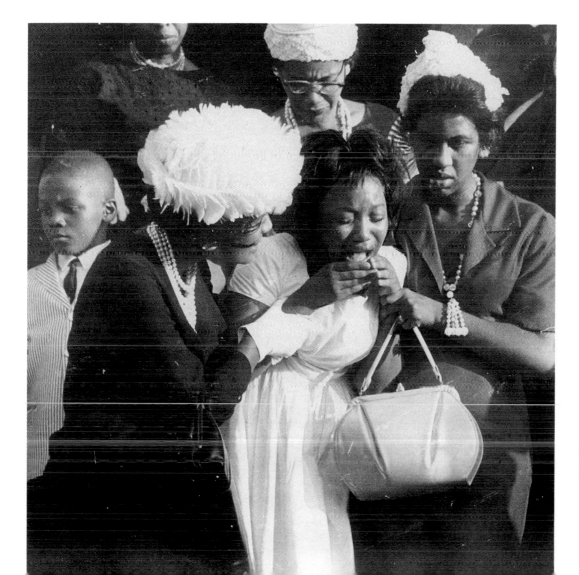

Relatives of one of the girls killed in the Birmingham church bombing.

Having no faith in Alabama's ability to squelch escalating racial violence in Birmingham, the Reverend Martin Luther King said that the U.S. Army ought to "take over this city and run it." King took his case to the White House.

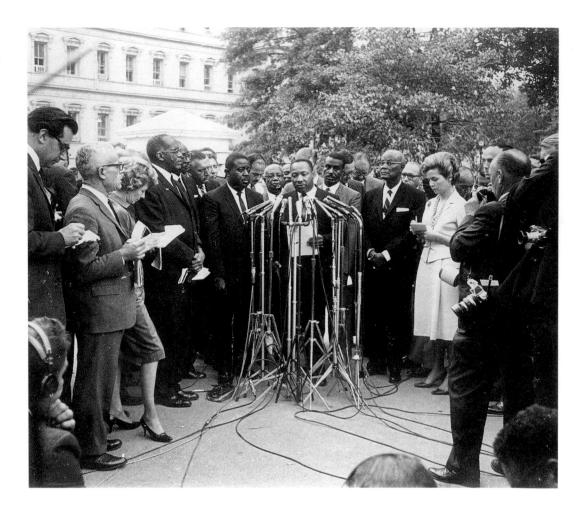

I guess the greatest lesson of that Birmingham bombing was for the Negro who thought that civil rights didn't pertain to him—the principal, the teacher, the doctor, the preacher, the lawyer. Those were his kids in that church, and whether he wanted to demonstrate or not, whether he thought we were going too fast or not, he found out that as long as your skin was black. . . .

After awhile, [my wife] Lil and I walked over to the church that had been bombed. We saw a strange and terrible thing. All the windows but one had been completely blown out. The stained glass window of Christ was almost intact. Only Christ's eyes and the top of his head were blown out. And it frightened me because I wondered what it meant. . . .

But it wasn't the only frightening symbol I saw in Birmingham that day. I saw a state policeman with a tommy gun cradled in his arm, a smile on his face, leaning against a mailbox across the street from the church. The mailbox was painted red, white and blue.

DICK GREGORY

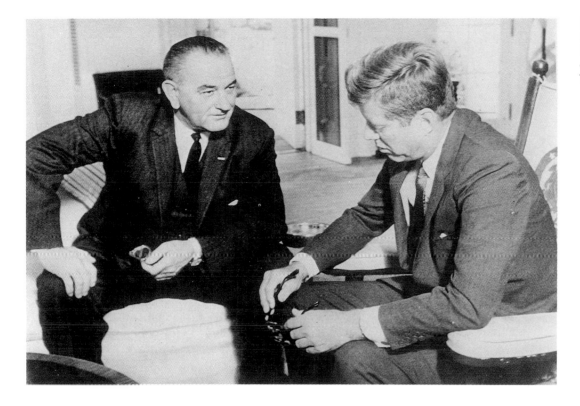

On September 17 the president and Vice-President Johnson met in the Oval Office to discuss Johnson's five-nation goodwill tour of Europe.

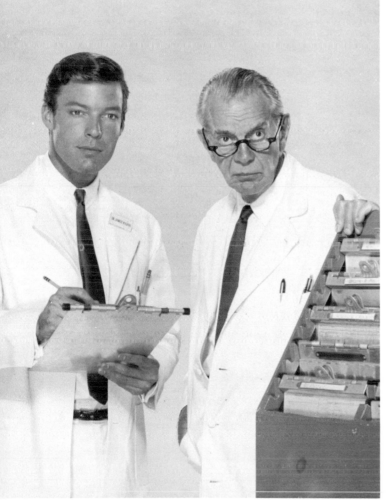

In 1963 Richard Chamberlain was one of the early television personalities (as opposed to trained actors like Raymond Massey). Re-created in 1961 by NBC from the MGM movie series of two decades earlier, *Doctor Kildare* was intended to counter ABC's hit doctor series *Ben Casey*. It succeeded.

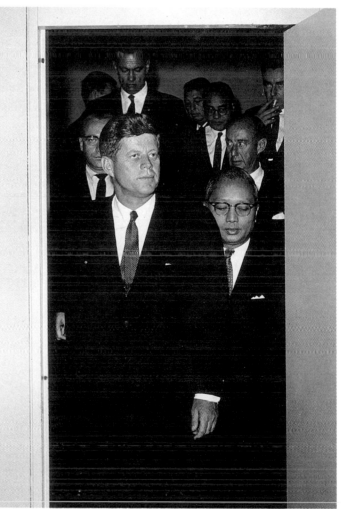

President Kennedy (followed by UN Secretary General U Thant) leaving the UN after his speech calling for joint US-Soviet space operations to eliminate the immense expenditure of duplicate projects.

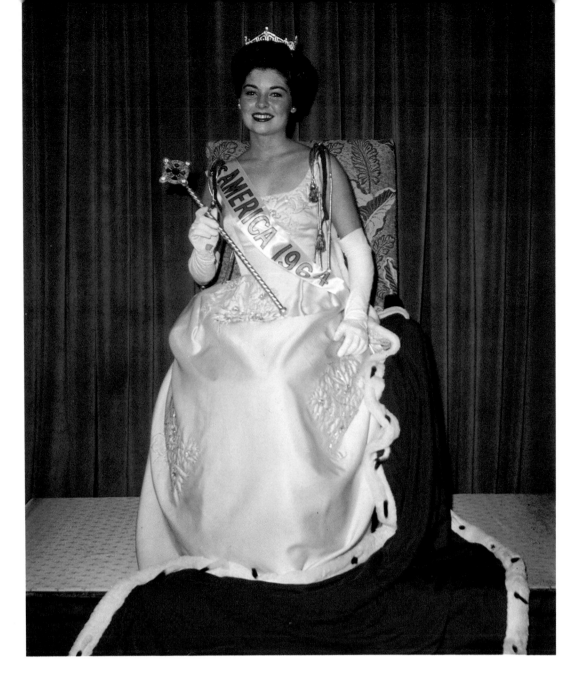

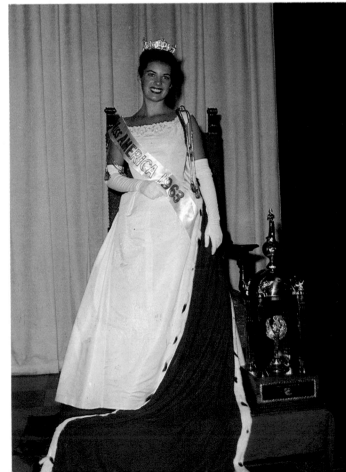

At the annual pageant Donna Axum of Arkansas was crowned Miss America for 1964. The 1963 reigning Miss was Jacquelyn Jeanne Mayer of Ohio.

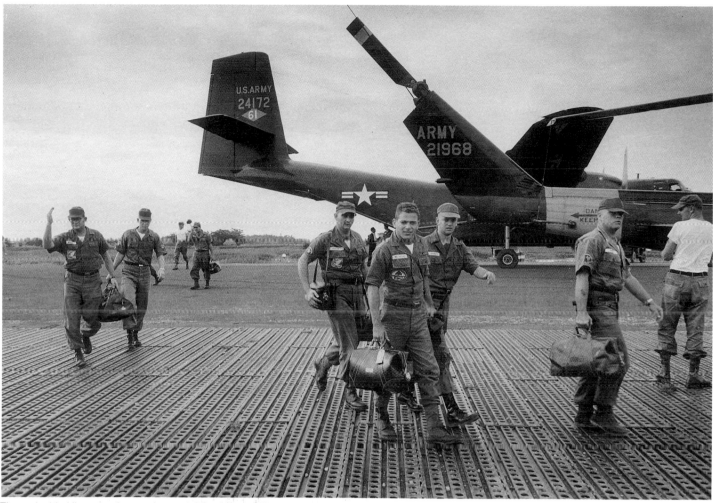

The arrival in Vietnam of a contingent of American military advisers.

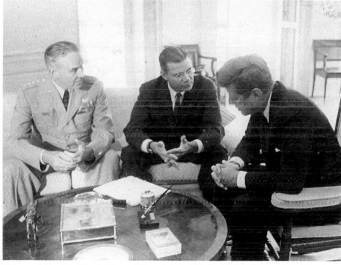

Maxwell Taylor, Chairman of the Joint Chiefs of Staff, and Defense Secretary Robert McNamara, met with President Kennedy on September 23, before leaving on a fact-finding tour of South Vietnam.

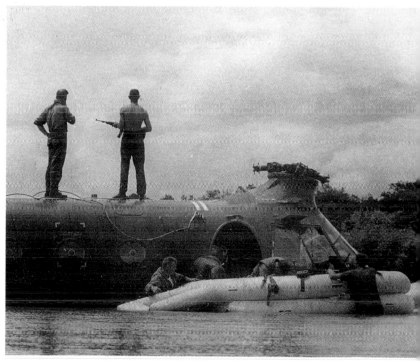

Two U.S. soldiers guarded a downed H-21 army helicopter while others inflated a life raft in a flooded rice paddy on the Ben Cat area northwest of Saigon, Vietnam. The area was saturated with Vietcong guerillas. American aid to the government of South Vietnam had been increasing throughout 1963, as had the U.S. resolve to defeat the North Vietnamese attempt to conquer the South.

It is unlikely that *PT 109* would have ever seen the silver screen had it not been based on the true-life adventures of President-to-be, John Kennedy, while he was in the Navy during World War II. Cliff Robertson played Kennedy. As one critic noted, "at 140 minutes, it was an extraordinarily protracted and very dull action story which seems to have been overawed by its subject." The great Robert Surtees filmed it.

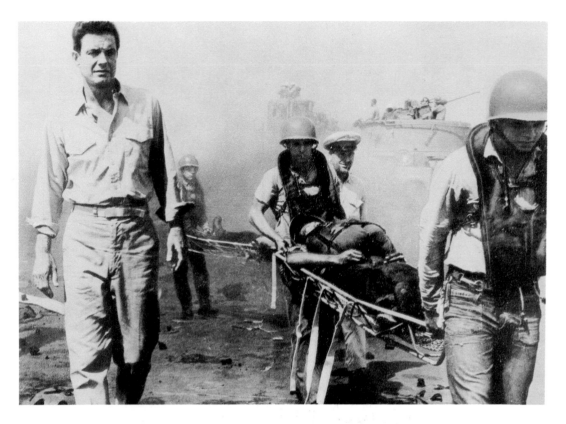

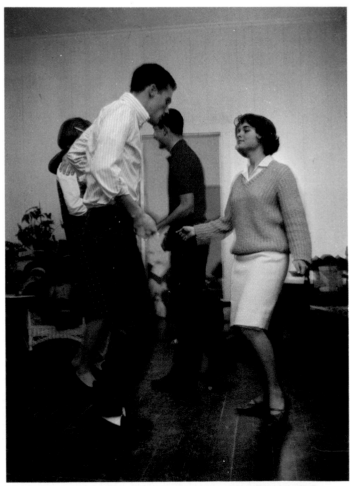

Many private universities did not become co-educational until the early 1970s and those that were had strict rules about fraternizing with the opposite sex.

I was a sophomore at Bennington College in Vermont. Even though Bennington was very progressive in terms of arts and education, it was very traditional in terms of the way men and women related. We had these big football weekends where we would go to Harvard or Dartmouth. On Friday nights, there would be a huge bonfire with freshman tugs and other kinds of Animal House-*type* activities, and everybody got drunk.

These were not the serious-minded, dedicated college students that kids became a couple of years later. There was just a lot of getting smashed, totally drunk. I remember at Dartmouth, all the nice girls stayed in this one boardinghouse where we stayed in little rooms under the eaves with flowered wallpaper and chintz curtains. I think there was probably less sex taking place than there is among college students today. Certainly, there was a lot more pretense. Good girls were supposed to slap the boy away when he tried to kiss you.

LENI WILDFLOWER

151

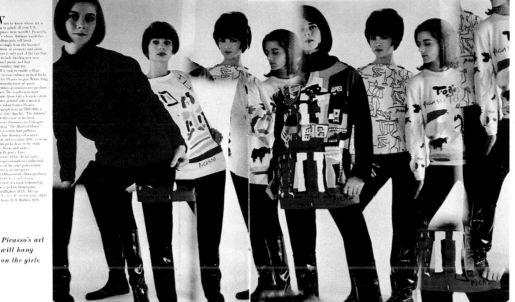

Fall fashion forecasters pre-dicted that Pablo Picasso's art would find favor with college girls, that is, if it could be worn. They also suggested new fash-ion uses for vinyl plastic and "that old stand-by, fake fur." The sweaters retailed for about $45, the stretch pants for $14 and the rubber boots for $10.

LEFT: As written by Eugene Burdick and William J. Lederer, *The Ugly American* was a book that despite (or perhaps because of) its melodramatic and simplistic message was the kind of best seller people thought better of themselves for having read. But even Marlon Brando could not save the movie, which had the distinction in 1962–1963 of making anti-communism boring.

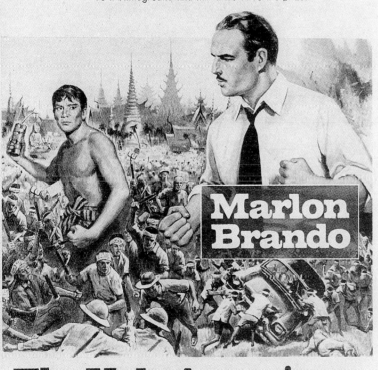
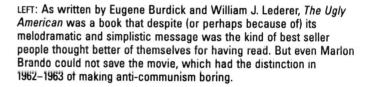

J. D. Salinger's novel was a best seller, as were *The Shoes of the Fisherman* by Morris West, *Caravans* by James Michener, *Elizabeth Appleton* by John O'Hara, *Godmother and the Priests* by Taylor Caldwell, *The Glass Blowers* by Daphne du Maurier, and *The Sand Pebbles* by Richard McKenna.

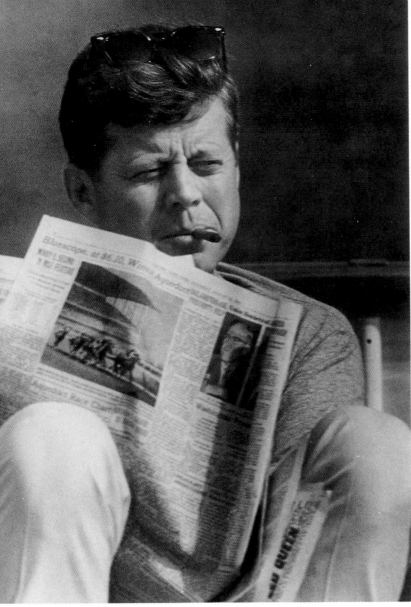

ABOVE: The president in a pensive mood. BELOW: The president and an unidentified partner enjoy a round of golf in spite of the ever constant presence of the Secret Service.

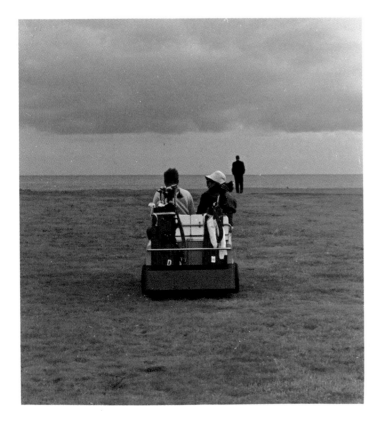

I suppose any president would [think about his death], because it's obviously one of the hazards [with] which he lives. But we had a talk about it in September, before he was shot, I remember, up on the boat off Hyannis Port. It just was interesting that we would discuss it at some length.

But of course he had that kind of mind that he always [was] talking about all the eventualities. I mean, on that same afternoon we talked about what he was going to do when he got out of the presidency. He thought how he'd like to be ambassador to Italy if a friendly regime was put in. He thought that would be a good place because Jackie would like it, because he would be out of the country, and therefore the man who took the presidency wouldn't be in his way. . . .

I think he used to worry about . . . what it was going to be like. I think he loved the presidency. And he never made any bones about how much he loved the comforts of it. He loved the people that were around him.

But the best line I always like was [on] one Sunday [when] Jackie brought it up, and she was sort of being very funny about it. She said, "What are you going to do, Jack?" She said, "I don't want to be the wife of a headmaster of a girl's school." And the whole conversation was rather annoying to him for some reason. It was a gloomy Sunday. I remember he said, "Well now, let's not worry, Jackie." He said, "Something will turn up. . . ."

CHARLES BARTLETT

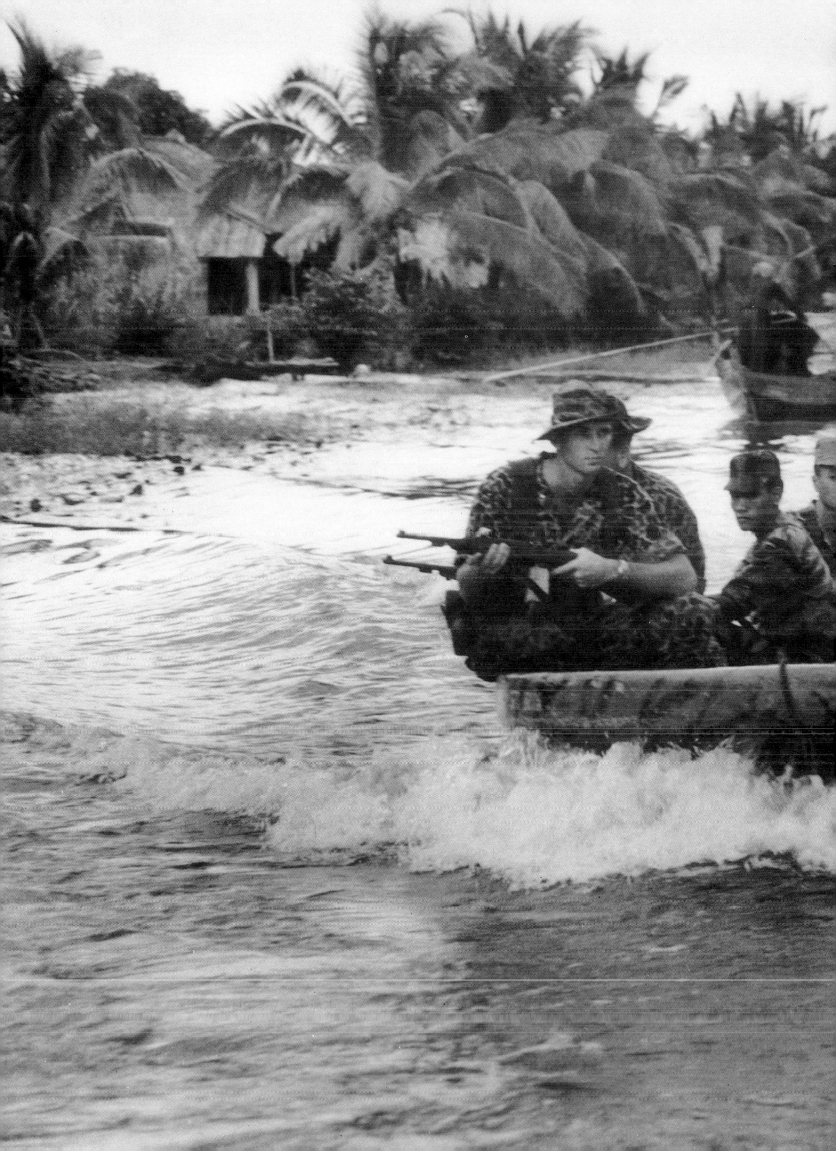

OCTOBER

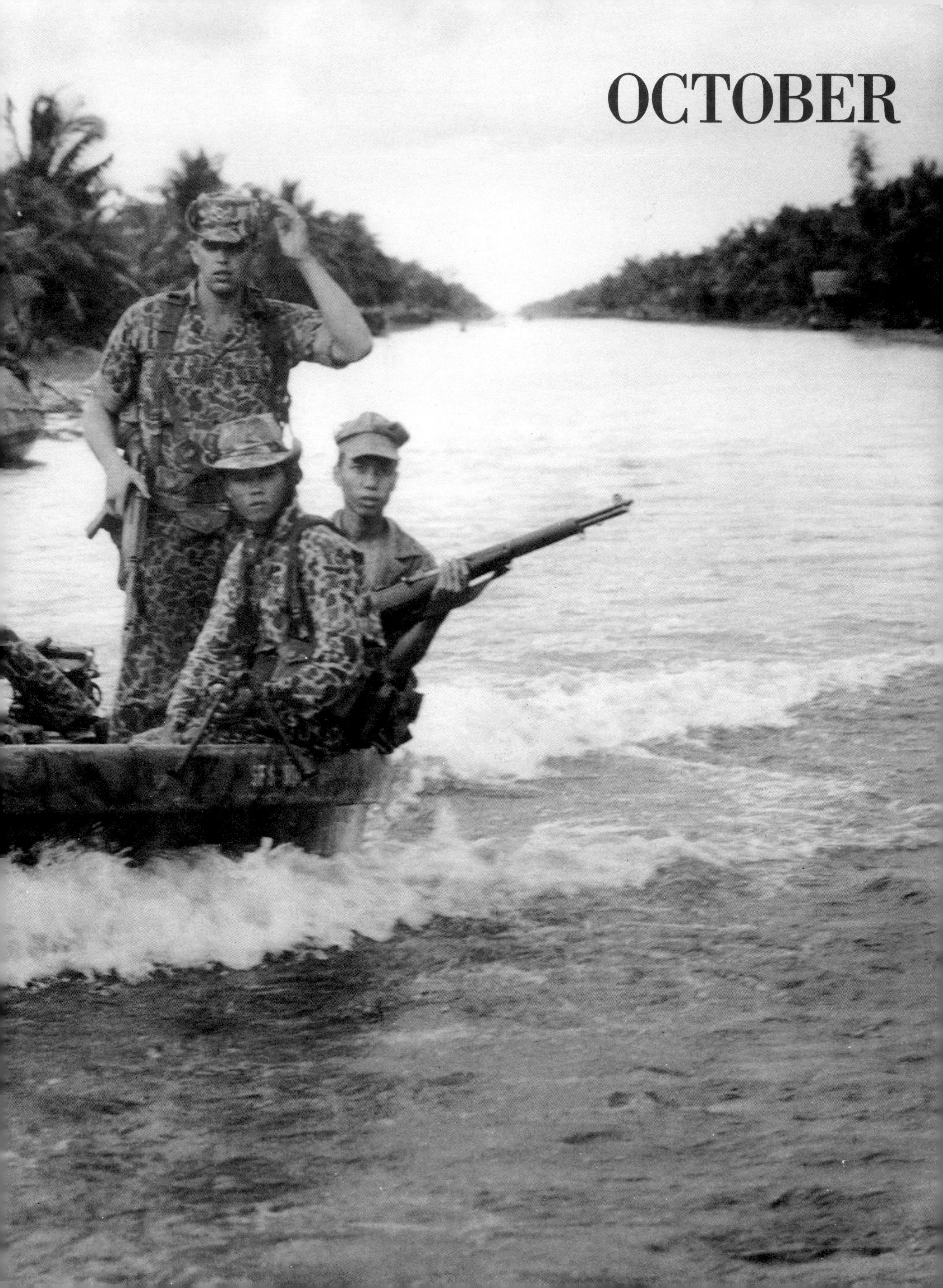

I paid close attention to the World Series that year. I loved seeing the Dodgers beat the Yankees four straight. That was the first hint in my entire life that the Yankees were not invincible. It was the first hint that this dynasty could be slaughtered.

**BILL THOMAS, Student,
University of Maryland**

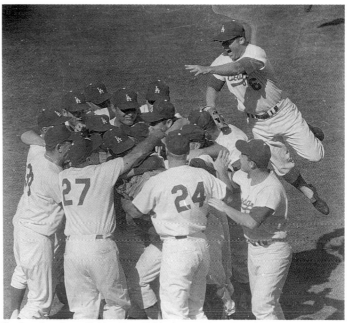

On October 6, outfielder Ron Fairly leaped into the air after the Dodgers won the World Series by beating the New York Yankees in four straight games. The Series was the eighth time the Dodgers and Yankees had met since 1953—seven out of eight times the Dodgers lost.

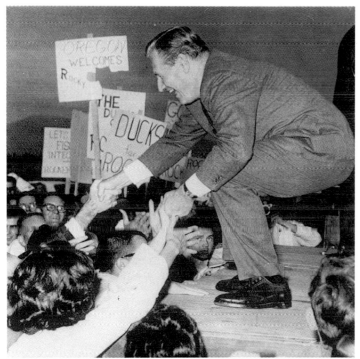

A crowd of Oregonians greeted Governor Nelson Rockefeller on October 11 as he arrived to speak at a Western Republican conference, also attended by Arizona Senator Barry Goldwater. President Kennedy had confided that he relished the chance to run against either of the prospective Republican nominees in 1964. Though Rockefeller had the capacity to attract more Democratic votes away from Kennedy than did the more conservative Goldwater, the New Yorker had been weakened by his divorce and quick remarriage. Kennedy felt that he could have won against Goldwater by a solid margin and gained a powerful mandate for a second term.

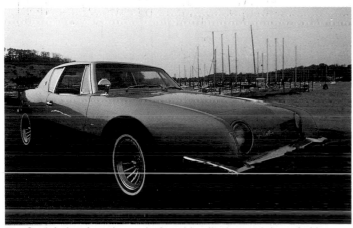

The Studebaker Avanti was designed by Jim Lowry. It is probably more appreciated for its style now than it was in 1963.

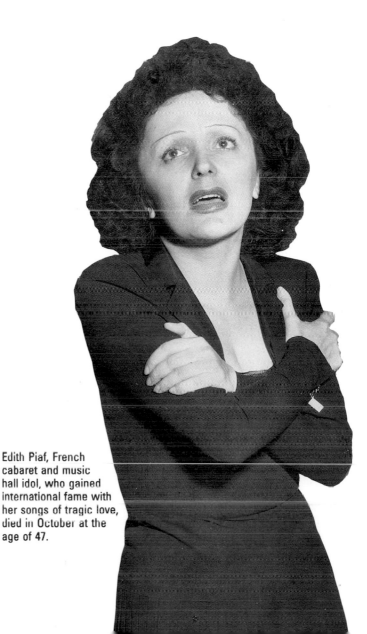

Edith Piaf, French cabaret and music hall idol, who gained international fame with her songs of tragic love, died in October at the age of 47.

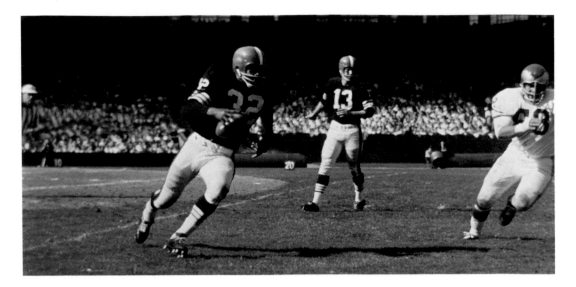

Jim Brown of the Cleveland Browns on a Fall Sunday. For the 1963 season Brown would gain 1,863 yards rushing, a record that might still stand if professional football had not increased the number of games played during the season. Many people who saw Jim Brown play in 1963 believed they were watching the greatest runner the modern professional game had ever seen.

Everything revolved around sports. We played touch football constantly. And that was the year the Chicago Bears won the NFL title. I loved the Bears. Bill Wade was the quarterback, and Mike Ditka was the tight end. They didn't throw the ball very much. They ground it out, and were not very exciting, but they had a tremendous defensive team. They played football in an old-fashioned sort of way. They were fearsome. When I played football on the sandlots, I thought that was the way to be—fearsome and ferocious.

Of course, they played on real grass. No astroturf. And they played in all kinds of bad weather. The uniforms would get muddy and dirty, and that was all part of the game.

BARRY HOBERMAN

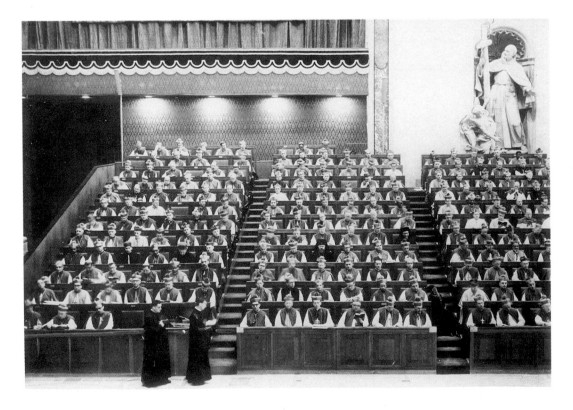

The second Vatican Ecumenical Council convened by Pope John XXIII in 1962, continued to meet in the fall of 1963. In working sessions in Saint Peter's Basilica, the council continued the move to liberalize the Catholic Church, reviewing doctrines to strip away dogma and outdated rituals. One of the major changes was allowing local bishops the discretion to substitute the vernacular for Latin in the mass. The council also explored further steps towards unity with non-Catholic churches.

I remember particularly the optimism I felt during 1963 that change was going to come. It was really based on the Limited Nuclear Test Ban Treaty with the Russians, the wheat deal, and the development of the hot line. I felt we were taking a series of steps toward a change in the cold war, and the great disappointment to me came over the deepening involvement in Vietnam. I saw that jeopardizing everything else we were doing. It was just beginning to come to a head at the time he was assassinated. I felt we were on a very slippery course in Vietnam. I made my first major speech on it in September of 1963, and that was where I first warned that the trap we were getting into in Vietnam would haunt our total policy in the world. But, of course, I was a brand-new senator in 1963, and not in a position to really influence the Kennedy administration.

GEORGE McGOVERN

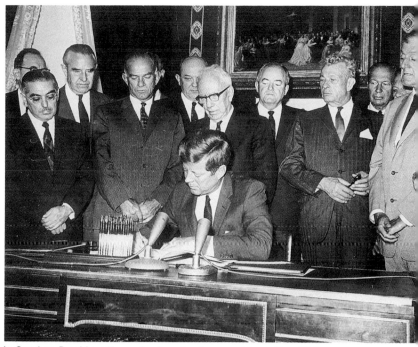

In October, President Kennedy signed a document formally ratifying a nuclear test ban treaty with Britain and the Soviet Union. Looking on were, from left, Senator John Pastore; W. Averell Harriman, Assistant Secretary of State; Senator J. W. Fulbright; Secretary of State Dean Rusk; Senator George Aiken; Senator Hubert Humphrey; Senator Everett Dirksen; William C. Foster, head of the Arms Control and Disarmament Agency; Senator Howard Cannon; Senator Leverett Saltonstall

I think Kennedy would be dumbstruck by the fact that what he called the first step—the Limited Nuclear Test Ban Treaty— was not followed up by a lot more steps, and that 25 years later we still do not have a comprehensive test ban treaty, when we were so close to achieving that in 1963. Meanwhile, the number of weapons and their destructive power have increased, and now we are extending that war to space.

THEODORE C. SORENSEN

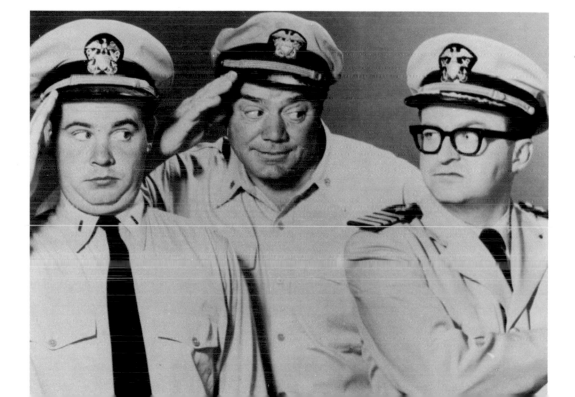

Ernest Borgnine, Joe Flynn, and Tim Conway starred in *McHale's Navy*, one of the more potent items in the military-comedy vogue of the early to mid-sixties. The program ran on ABC from 1962 to 1965 before going into syndication.

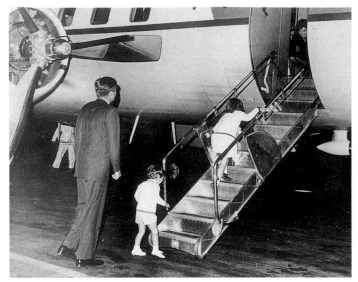

First lady Jacqueline Kennedy got a big welcome from her husband and children when she flew home on October 17 from a Mediterranean vacation aboard the yacht of Aristotle Onassis. She kneeled as Caroline, five, rushed to greet her. John Jr., two, and President Kennedy took a more sedate approach.

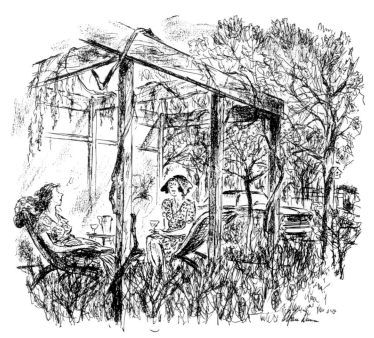

"You understand, it isn't that I have any objection to Kennedys as such."

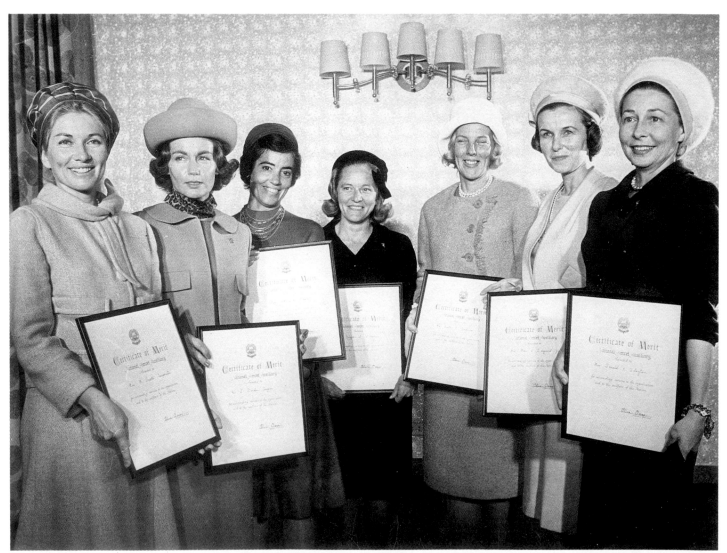

Space was high on everyone's agenda. Honored by the Ladies' Auxiliary of AMVETS, astronauts' wives modeled the "right stuff" for Fall '63. From the left: Mrs. Scott Carpenter, Mrs. Gordon Cooper, Mrs. John Glenn, Mrs. Virgil Grissom, Mrs. Walter Schirra, Mrs. Alan Shepard, and Mrs. Donald Slayton.

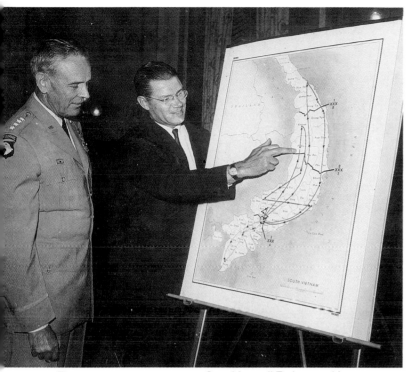

There were no easy answers. Gen. Maxwell Taylor stood by as Defense Secretary Robert McNamara pointed to a map of South Vietnam. McNamara used it to brief Senate members about a fact-finding trip he made.

I arrived in Vietnam just before Christmas of '62 and left in October 1963. I was in an army aviation unit that resupplied Special Forces units. So I had enough of an overview to know that we were up to things that people did not want to acknowledge. There were secret missions into North Vietnam, Laos, and Cambodia; meanwhile, the South Vietnamese government was losing all credibility with the people that we were supposedly protecting.

Everything was crazy. It was not a war in the terms that we are used to. There was no sense of urgency. The war stopped for us at five o'clock; it stopped on Saturday at noon; it stopped on Sundays and holidays. It was still so low-level that nobody really got very concerned about it.

JAN BARRY

I believe Kennedy had every intention of getting out of Vietnam in 1965. He had a plan for the withdrawal of all American advisers in 1965—which he had directed the Pentagon to prepare in the autumn of 1962, and which was completed and accepted in the spring of 1963— which can be found in the Pentagon Papers. Under that plan, the first 1,000 advisers were to be withdrawn by his order in October 1963. It was actually carried out in December, after his death. But they were quickly replaced, and then in the spring of 1964 Johnson canceled the withdrawal plan.

Had he lived, I do believe, we would have gotten out of Vietnam in 1965. I think we all remembered the election of 1952, in which the Republicans made a big issue of who lost China. Kennedy didn't want to go through an election on the question of who lost Indochina. So he was prepared to give Saigon a run for its money, but I think his intention was quite firm.

ARTHUR SCHLESINGER, Jr.

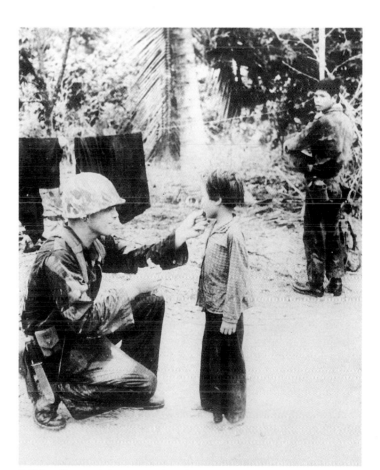

A U.S. military adviser gave chocolate to a little girl in a village in South Vietnam's Mekong Delta. The adviser was with South Vietnamese troops who entered the village because it was being used by Communist Vietcong guerrillas.

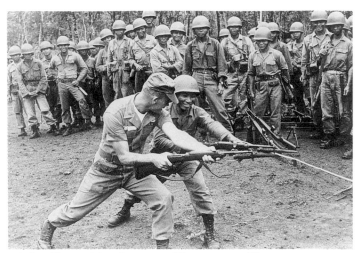

A U.S. military adviser instructs a Vietnamese soldier.

*T*he predominant view by May of 1963 was very optimistic. . . . Indeed, the reporting was sufficiently upbeat at that point for the President to accept Secretary McNamara's recommendation that we should now start planning, or set up a plan, for the progressive withdrawal of the American advisers, trying to get them out by the end of 1965 or before if that were possible.

[But] the question arises whether the President was truly implying an unconditional intent to withdraw. . . . I do not believe that, not at all. . . .

In other words, I believe that the suggestion that Kennedy really thought we should withdraw come what might *is simply not historically the correct assessment of his views. And I would fortify that conclusion by referring particularly to what he said in early September 1963 about the danger that China would become dominant in the area, his belief in the domino theory and other fundamental points that had always lain behind American policy in Vietnam. . . .*

In the three weeks between the coup [which ousted President Diem on November 2] and [Kennedy's] assassination, it became clear that the underlying situation was, in fact, very much worse than had been estimated by the McNamara [Maxwell] Taylor group as recently as late September. And at another meeting, just before the assassination, this was brought out, so that, had Kennedy lived, he would have had to come face-to-face with this deterioration and how to respond to it. As it was, he never had a chance to come to grips with the new situation, and it is, in my judgement, wholly speculative to try to judge how he would have dealt with the decisions that confronted President Johnson from late 1963 right through to early and mid-1965 and thereafter.

WILLIAM P. BUNDY,
Deputy Assistant Secretary of Defense
for International Security Affairs

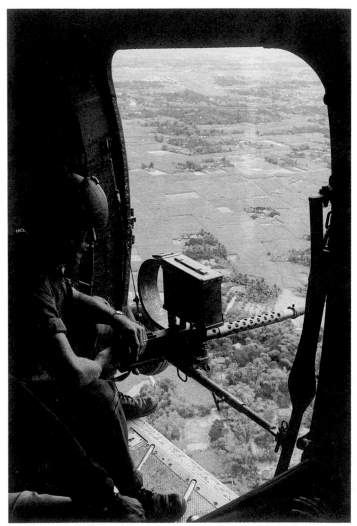

An American soldier keeps armed watch from an airborne helicopter carrying South Vietnamese troops into battle 300 miles south of Saigon.

Kennedy's greatest error on Vietnam was not giving it more attention. It was getting some attention, obviously in the Defense Department and the State Department, but it was never a high priority in the White House. The worst thing, perhaps, was that he didn't pay more attention. But the best thing is that he didn't do what he was urged to do in 1963 and earlier, which was to send in combat troop divisions and to bomb the North.

THEODORE C. SORENSEN

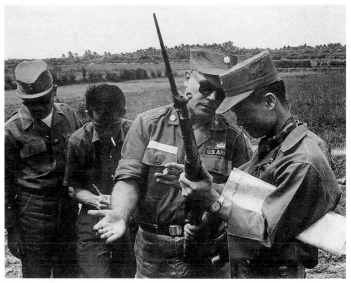

A U.S. military adviser and a South Vietnamese officer inspected a rifle captured from Vietcong troops in Quan Lung area fighting. It was reported that some Russian-model carbines were captured from the Communists, but there was no indication of how the guerrillas obtained them.

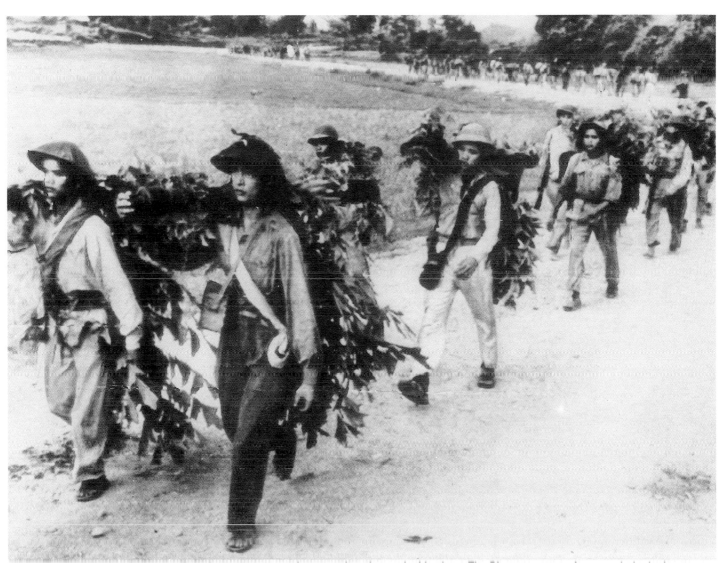

Vietcong guerrillas, carrying camouflaged weapons, were shown on the advance in this photo. The Diem government's unpopularity in the countryside had handicapped antiguerrilla efforts. U.S. officials hoped that the new government would have more success prosecuting the war, but through the end of the year both the South Vietnamese and the Vietcong simultaneously proclaimed successes.

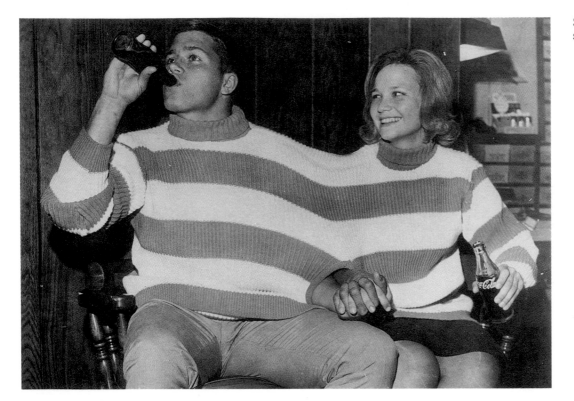

Sweaters built for two were a short-lived fad.

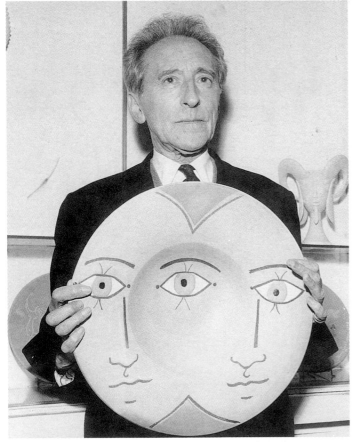

The multi-talented French writer, artist, and film-maker Jean Cocteau—shown here in 1958 displaying a piece from a pottery collection he designed—died in October at the age of 74. He was perhaps best known for the poetry, novels and plays he produced as a leading Surrealist in the 1920s and 1930s.

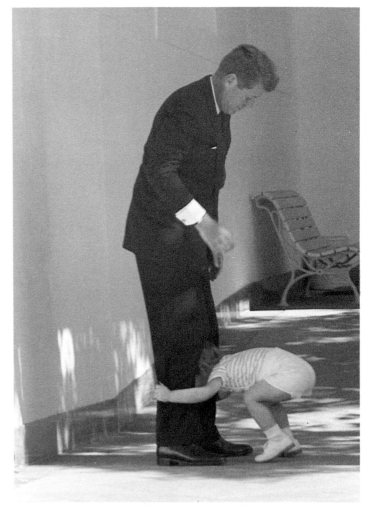

The most famous family in America was also the most photogenic. By the president's third year in office he and his wife were written about in movie fan magazines as often as were Hollywood stars. Here, in an unguarded moment, the president and his 3-year-old son play together as fathers and little boys often do.

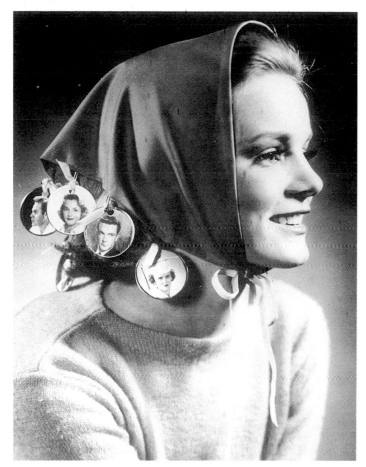

The fashion of attaching wallet photographs to a head scarf came and went in October.

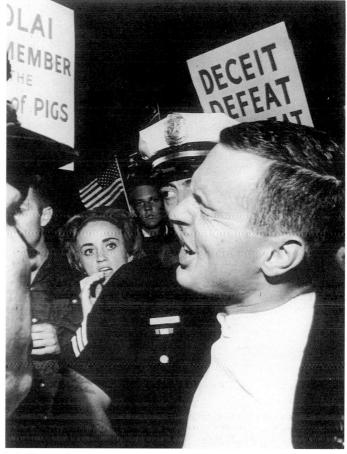

In Dallas on October 27, UN Ambassador Adlai Stevenson was rudely heckled while giving a speech and then spat upon and hit with a sign as he left the auditorium. The demonstrators were strongly opposed to U.S. membership in the international organization. Because of this incident, President Kennedy would be warned not to travel to Dallas.

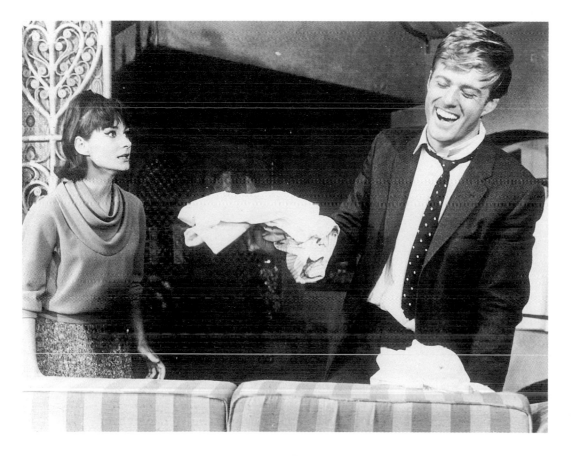

Robert Redford and Elizabeth Ashley starred in Neil Simon's comedy *Barefoot in the Park*. The play opened on Broadway on October 23. It ran for 532 performances.

RIGHT: These disparate magazines—mass circulation ones like *Look* and *The Saturday Evening Post* or radical and literary ones like *Ramparts* and *Evergreen Review* all shared the same fate: they went out of business.

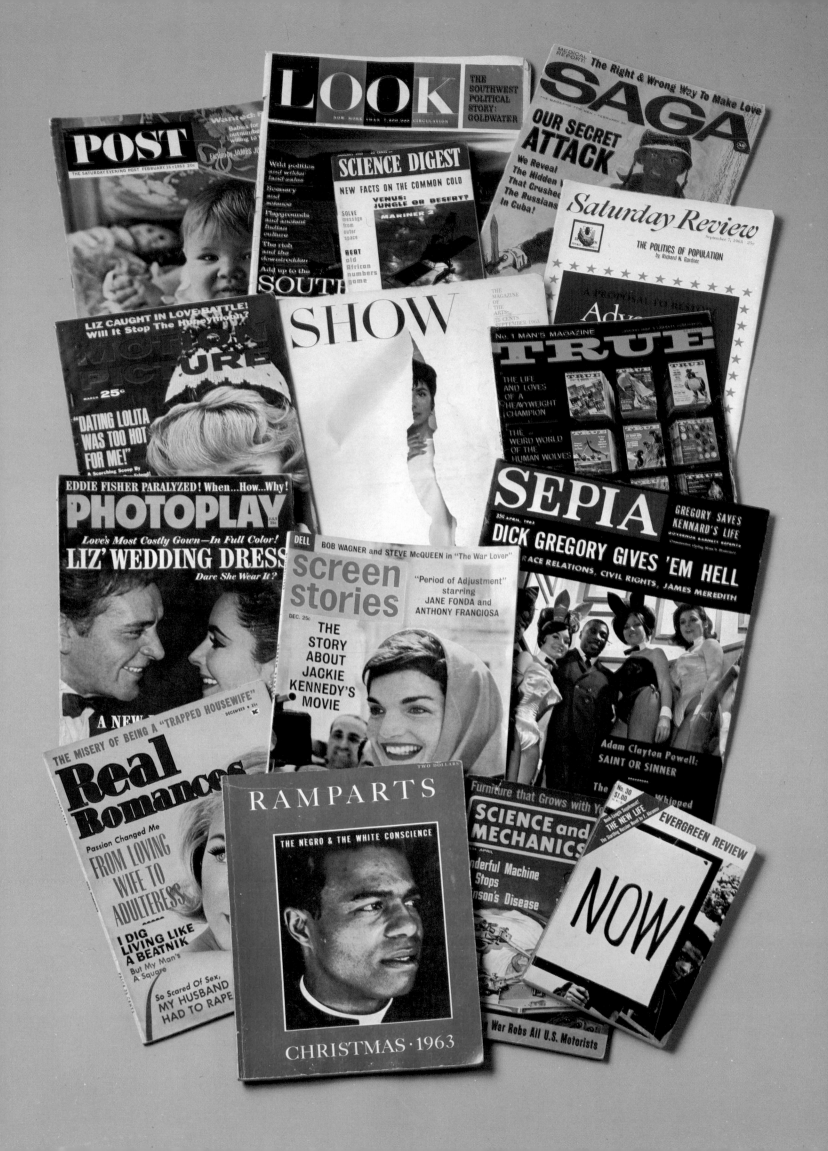

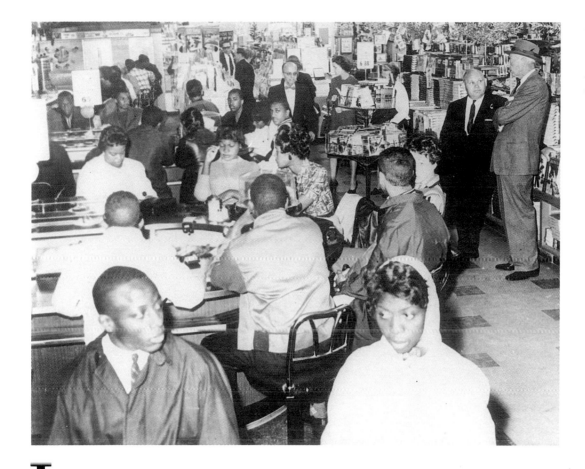

I waited all those years to be admitted to the Woolworth lunch counter, and now I find I don't like anything on their menu! . . .

The waitress said to me, "Sorry, we don't serve colored people here." I said to her, "that's all right, I don't want to eat any. Bring me a chicken."

DICK GREGORY

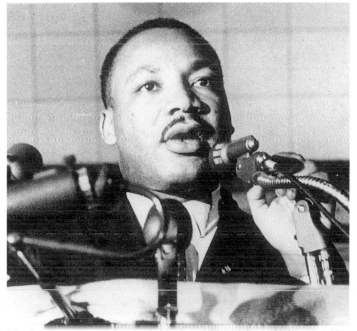

Martin Luther King threatened the city of Birmingham, Alabama, with the largest demonstration in history if it did not accede to desegregation demands.

I remember feeling that life was good. My children, aged 10 and 12, were happy and healthy; we had no money problems, and we were living in a pleasant and friendly environment, and I felt socially useful. So I look back on that period with affection and nostalgia. But the thing about nostalgia is that you wouldn't go back, even if you could.

FLORENCE ISBELL,
Atlanta Civil Rights Worker in 1963

D iscount stores were coming into vogue in 1963, and we found that we could buy name brands at reduced prices. We bought black-and-white television sets, hi-fi record players, electric mixers, battery-operated portable am-fm radios. The groceries we bought were not pre-packaged meals or frozen dinners. We bought a lot of fresh fruits and vegetables, as well as canned vegetables. We seldom bought soft drinks. We bought milk in glass gallon jugs. We drove a 1961 Ambassador station wagon with a push-button shift.

CHARLOTTE COTE

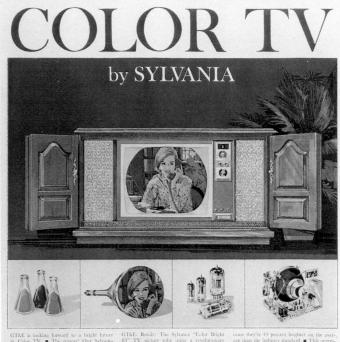

Only about 10 percent of households with television had it in color. And those households tended to think of their set as a piece of fine furniture. Consoles, as they were called, could include a radio and a hi-fi set along with the TV.

The funny things that greed does to people was the running gag that propelled three hours of frantic chases and violent slapstick of *It's a Mad Mad Mad Mad World*. In spite of its seriously overcooked quality, many of the set pieces were well done and genuinely humorous. With Jimmy Durante, Mickey Rooney, Sid Caesar (pictured here), Spencer Tracy, Milton Berle, Ethel Merman, Buddy Hackett, Dick Shawn, Phil Silvers, Terry Thomas, Jonathan Winters, Edie Adams, Peter Falk, Leo Gorcey, Buster Keaton, Joe E. Brown, Carl Reiner, the Three Stooges, Jack Benny, and Jerry Lewis. Director Stanley Kramer refereed.

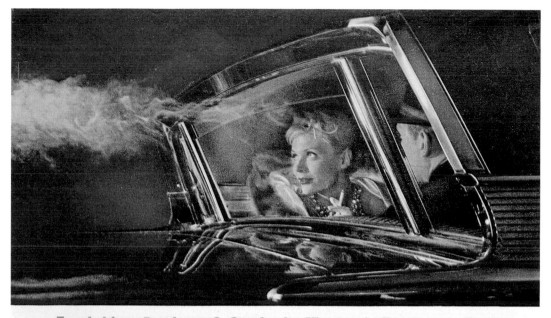

Fresh idea, fresh roof, fresh air: Mercury's Breezeway Design

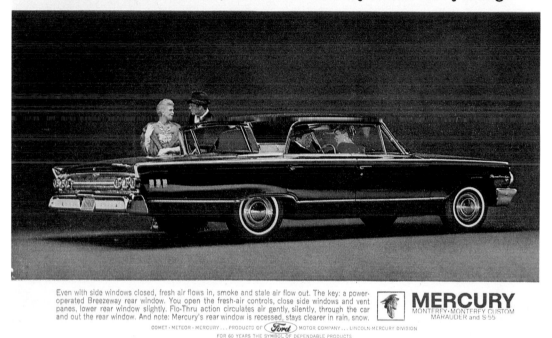

Even with side windows closed, fresh air flows in, smoke and stale air flow out. The key: a power-operated Breezeway rear window. You open the fresh-air controls, close side windows and vent panes, lower rear window slightly. Flo-Thru action circulates air gently, silently, through the car and out the rear window. And note: Mercury's rear window is recessed, stays clearer in rain, snow.

MERCURY
MONTEREY·MONTEREY CUSTOM
MARAUDER and S-55

COMET · METEOR · MERCURY . . . PRODUCTS OF (Ford) MOTOR COMPANY . . . LINCOLN-MERCURY DIVISION
FOR 60 YEARS THE SYMBOL OF DEPENDABLE PRODUCTS

Mercury built an advertising campaign—not to mention an automobile—around the dubious notion that there was something irresistible about a power-operated rear window that slanted in rather than out. They called this "recessed" window a "breezeway," and claimed that it would stay clear in rain or snow—which was probably true if the car never left the garage.

You could see that if Americans had the resources, they would buy into the automobile because of the feeling of freedom they had when they could travel.

The sixties was also the decade of the camper trailer, which caught on because of the American preference for mobility and the growth in the highway system. But there was a ridiculous side to it. How silly to leave your home in a camper trailer, drive several hours on a Friday night in order to park by some polluted lake somewhere two feet away from all the other campers—and think you're free.

GARY KOERSELMAN

I t must have been around the 20th of October.
. . . The Irish prime minister had come to
this country. . . . And the president wanted to put
on a great show for him because he had been
entertained so royally when he had been in
Ireland in the spring. As a matter of fact, the
president told me . . . that he thought the two
happiest days of his entire life were those days
which he spent in Ireland. . . .

After the formal dinner was over, he invited
me to go upstairs to his quarters, along with
some of his other friends there, and to sit around
and . . . talk. The prime minister was there . . .
and Teddy Kennedy was there with his wife, and
they brought up the Irish bagpipers. . . .

But the president was just overcome by it all.
In fact, I think one of the most vivid recollections
of him as I look back is how he looked that
night. . . . You know, the Irish have their very
happy songs, and they also have their very sad
and plaintive melodies, and they played some of
the favorite songs of the president, "The Boys of
Wexford," or whatever it is, and a couple of
others. During the course of their singing these
songs, the president had the sweetest and saddest
kind of look on his face. He was standing by
himself, leaning against the doorway there, and
just sort of transported into a world of imagination. . . .

**JAMES A. REED, Assistant Secretary of
the Treasury and Friend of the President**

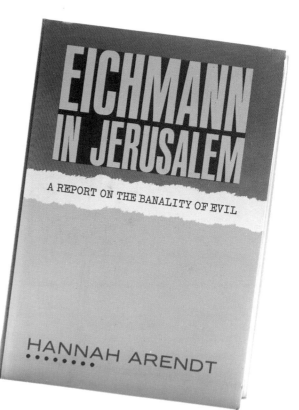

The president would take time out
from his duties to play with his son.

Hannah Arendt's *Eichmann in Jerusalem* was an important book, even
if few seemed to know exactly what it was supposed to mean. Other
nonfiction books of the year that would have a more lasting value
included *The Feminine Mystique* by Betty Friedan and *Beyond the
Melting Pot* by Nathan Glazer and Daniel P. Moynihan.

Billboard
HOT 100

★ STAR performer—Sides registering greatest proportionate upward progress this week.

This Wk	2 Wks	3 Wks	TITLE — Artist, Label & Number	Wks on Chart
★ 1	4	19	65 SUGAR SHACK — Jimmy Gilmer and the Fireballs, Dot 16487	4
2	3	3	12 BE MY BABY — Ronettes, Philles 116	7
3	1	1	1 BLUE VELVET — Bobby Vinton, Epic 9614	10
4	5	9	10 CRY BABY — Garnet Mimms & the Enchanters, United Artists 629	9
5	2	2	5 SALLY, GO 'ROUND THE ROSES — Jaynetts, Tuff 369	7
★ 6	9	13	23 BUSTED — Ray Charles, ABC-Paramount 10481	6
7	6	5	2 MY BOYFRIEND'S BACK — Angels, Smash 1834	11
★ 8	16	32	50 MEAN WOMAN BLUES — Roy Orbison, Monument 824	6
9	8	4	4 HEAT WAVE — Martha & the Vandellas, Gordy 7022	11
★ 10	17	33	52 DONNA THE PRIMA DONNA — Dion Di Muci, Columbia 42852	5
11	13	20	27 HONOLULU LULU — Jan & Dean, Liberty 55613	
12	7	7	11 WONDERFUL! WONDERFUL! — Tymes, Parkway 884	9
13	28	35	53 THAT SUNDAY, THAT SUMMER — Nat King Cole, Capitol 5027	7
★ 14	21	34	51 DON'T THINK TWICE IT'S ALL RIGHT — Peter, Paul & Mary, Warner Bros. 5385	5
15	14	11	7 SURFER GIRL — Beach Boys, Capitol 5009	11
16	10	6	6 THEN HE KISSED ME — Crystals, Philles 115	9
17	11	8	8 MICKEY'S MONKEY — Miracles, Tamla 54083	9
★ 18	23	29	40 I CAN'T STAY MAD AT YOU — Skeeter Davis, RCA Victor 8219	6
19	19	24	26 PART TIME LOVE — Little Johnny Taylor, Galaxy 722	9
★ 20	33	58	74 DEEP PURPLE — Nino Tempo & April Stevens, Atco 6273	5
★ 21	26	31	57 TALK TO ME — Sunny and the Sunglows, Tear Drop 3014	6
22	12	12	14 A WALKIN' MIRACLE — Essex, Roulette 4515	8
23	38	69	100 WASHINGTON SQUARE — Village Stompers, Epic 9617	4
24	18	16	19 MARTIAN HOP — Ran-Dells, Chairman 4403	11
25	27	30	41 BUST OUT — Busters, Arlen 735	6
★ 26	34	46	64 FOOLS RUSH IN — Rick Nelson, Decca 31533	5
27	15	10	3 IF I HAD A HAMMER — Trini Lopez, Reprise 20198	12
28	31	38	48 HELLO HEARTACHE, GOODBYE LOVE — Little Peggy March, RCA Victor 8221	6
29	32	41	55 I'LL TAKE YOU HOME — Drifters, Atlantic 2201	6
30	20	15	22 LITTLE DEUCE COUPE — Beach Boys, Capitol 5009	9
★ 31	41	45	70 BLUE BAYOU — Roy Orbison, Monument 824	5
★ 32	54	66	99 MARIA ELENA — Los Indios Tabajaras, RCA Victor 8216	4
33	22	14	13 THE MONKEY TIME — Major Lance, Okeh 7175	14
34	36	47	56 TWO TICKETS TO PARADISE — Brook Benton, Mercury 72177	6
★ 35	58	86	— IT'S ALL RIGHT — Impressions, ABC-Paramount 10487	3
★ 36	46	74	— THE GRASS IS GREENER — Brenda Lee, Decca 31539	3
37	25	25	35 ONLY IN AMERICA — Jay & the Americans, United Artists 625	9
38	29	17	21 THE KIND OF BOY YOU CAN'T FORGET — Raindrops, Jubilee 5455	10
★ 39	50	70	— YOU LOST THE SWEETEST BOY — Mary Wells, Motown 1048	3
40	24	26	32 WHAM — Lonnie Mack, Fraternity 912	8
41	30	21	15 PAINTED, TAINTED ROSE — Al Martino, Capitol 5000	12
42	48	59	75 A LOVE SO FINE — Chiffons, Laurie 3195	6
43	37	23	18 YOU CAN NEVER STOP ME LOVING YOU — Johnny Tillotson, Cadence 1437	10
44	42	42	45 MORE — Vic Dana, Dolton 81	10
★ 45	56	82	— CROSSFIRE! — Orlons, Cameo 273	3
★ 46	59	81	— SHE'S A FOOL — Lesley Gore, Mercury 72180	3
47	35	22	16 HEY GIRL — Freddie Scott, Colpix 692	12
48	40	43	44 BIRTHDAY PARTY — Pixies Three, Mercury 72130	9
★ 49	63	—	— WORKOUT STEVIE, WORKOUT — Little Stevie Wonder, Tamla 54086	2
50	51	53	60 BETTY IN BERMUDAS — Dovells, Parkway 882	7
51	39	28	17 MOCKINGBIRD — Inez Foxx, Symbol 919	17
52	43	44	46 TREAT MY BABY GOOD — Bobby Darin, Capitol 5019	8
★ 53	65	73	82 RED SAILS IN THE SUNSET — Fats Domino, ABC-Paramount 10484	4
54	62	71	79 SEPTEMBER SONG — Jimmy Durante, Warner Bros. 5382	6
55	53	55	59 WHAT DOES A GIRL DO — Shirelles, Scepter 1259	6
★ 56	69	—	— MISTY — Lloyd Price, Double L 722	2
57	61	80	92 CRY TO ME — Betty Harris, Jubilee 4456	4
58	60	67	78 I'M CONFESSIN' — Frank Ifield, Capitol 5032	6
59	66	—	— MONKEY-SHINE — Bill Black & His Combo, Hi 2069	2
60	57	48	34 MORE — Kai Winding, Verve 10295	14
61	73	87	90 BABY GET IT (And Don't Quit It) — Jackie Wilson, Brunswick 55250	4
62	67	72	77 HE'S MINE — Alice Wonder Land, Bardell 774	5
63	74	—	— TWO SIDES (To Every Story) — Etta James, Argo 5452	2
64	68	75	76 ELEPHANT WALK — Donald Jenkins & the Daylighters, Cortland 109	5
★ 65	89	—	— I'M LEAVING IT UP TO YOU — Dale & Grace, Montel-Michele 921	2
66	78	83	91 DOWN THE AISLE — Patty LaBelle & the Blue Belles, Newtown 5777	5
67	70	76	81 ENAMORADO — Keith Colley, Unical 3006	
★ 68	—	—	— EVERYBODY — Tommy Roe, ABC-Paramount 10478	
69	80	—	— WALKING THE DOG — Rufus Thomas, Stax 140	
★ 70	79	—	— FIRST DAY BACK AT SCHOOL — Paul & Paula, Philips 40142	
★ 71	96	—	— 500 MILES AWAY FROM HOME — Bobby Bare, RCA Victor 8238	
72	85	93	— NIGHT LIFE — Rusty Draper, Monument 822	
73	82	90	— (Down at) PAPA JOE'S — Dixiebelles, Sound Stage 7 2507	3
74	87	99	— POINT PANIC — Surfaris, Decca 31538	
75	76	78	87 MY BABE — Righteous Brothers, Moonglow 223	6
76	72	84	88 CINDY'S GONNA CRY — Johnny Crawford, Del-Fi 4221	3
77	83	97	— LITTLE EEEFIN ANNIE — Joe Perkins, Sound Stage 7 2511	3
78	81	91	— BLUE GUITAR — Richard Chamberlain, MGM 13170	2
★ 79	94	—	— NEW MEXICAN ROSE — 4 Seasons, Vee Jay 562	2
80	91	96	— SWEET IMPOSSIBLE YOU — Brenda Lee, Decca 31539	
81	—	—	— SPEED BALL — Ray Stevens, Mercury 72189	
82	84	89	— STRANGE FEELING — Billy Stewart, Chess 1868	3
83	90	—	— WILD! — Dee Dee Sharp, Cameo 274	2
84	86	94	— JENNY BROWN — Smothers Brothers, Mercury 72182	
85	95	—	— TOYS IN THE ATTIC — Joe Sherman, World Artists 1008	
★ 86	—	—	— YOUR TEEN-AGE DREAMS — Johnny Mathis, Mercury 72184	1
87	75	77	80 TEENAGE CLEOPATRA — Tracey Dey, Liberty 88604	5
88	88	98	— EVERYBODY GO HOME — Eydie Gorme, Columbia 42854	3
★ 89	—	—	— BETTER TO GIVE THAN RECEIVE — Joe Hinton, Back Beat 539	1
★ 90	—	—	— DETROIT CITY NO. 2 — Ben Colder, MGM 13167	1
91	99	—	— THAT'S THE WAY IT GOES — 4 Seasons, Vee Jay 562	2
92	—	—	— COME BACK — Johnny Mathis, Mercury 72184	1
93	—	—	— CUANDO CALIENTA EL SOL — Steve Allen, Dot 16507	1
94	—	—	— GOTTA TRAVEL ON — Timi Yuro, Liberty 88634	1
95	—	—	— COWBOY BOOTS — Dave Dudley, Golden Ring 3020	1
96	—	—	— SIGNED, SEALED AND DELIVERED — James Brown & the Famous Flames, King 5803	1
97	—	—	93 LONELY DRIFTER — O'Jays, Imperial 1976	2
98	—	—	— TWO-TEN, SIX-EIGHTEEN — Jimmie Rodgers, Dot 16527	1
99	—	—	— DON'T WAIT TOO LONG — Tony Bennett, Columbia 42886	1
100	—	—	— HEY LONELY ONE — Baby Washington, Sue 794	1

HOT 100—A TO Z—(Publisher-Licensee)

(alphabetical publisher-licensee index listing)

BUBBLING UNDER THE HOT 100

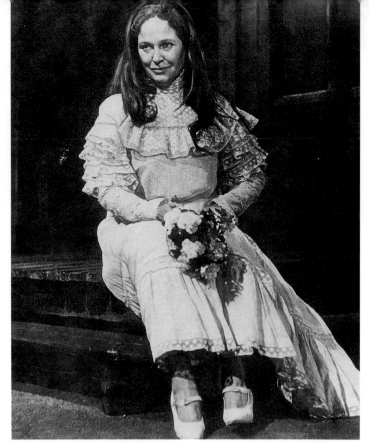

Colleen Dewhurst in *The Ballad of the Sad Café*, the Edward Albee play based on Carson McCullers' short novel, opened on October 30 at the Martin Beck Theater. Budgeted at only $120,000, the play was produced by Lewis Allen and Ben Edwards and directed by Alan Schneider (who also directed *Who's Afraid of Virginia Woolf?*).

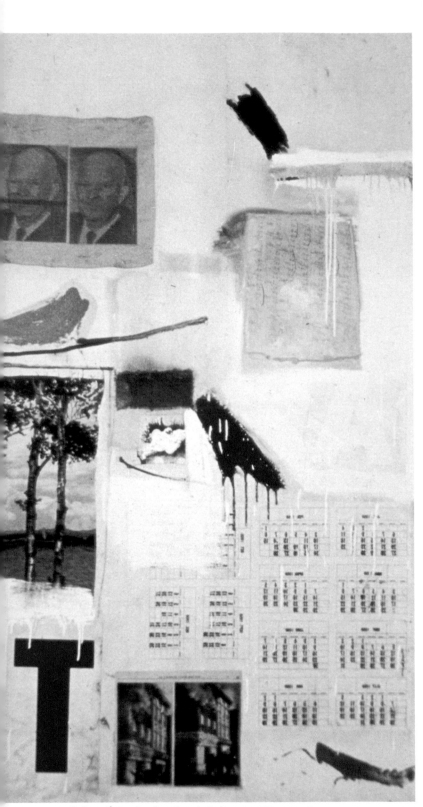

Robert Rauschenberg's painting entitled *Factum II*.

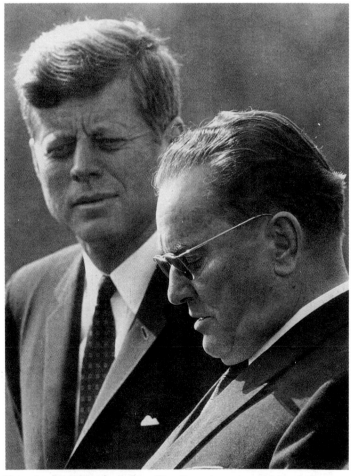

Yugoslav President Josip Broz Tito, the only communist head of state invited to the White House during the Kennedy administration. Tito had successfully kept Yugoslavia unaligned with either the Soviet or Western blocs.

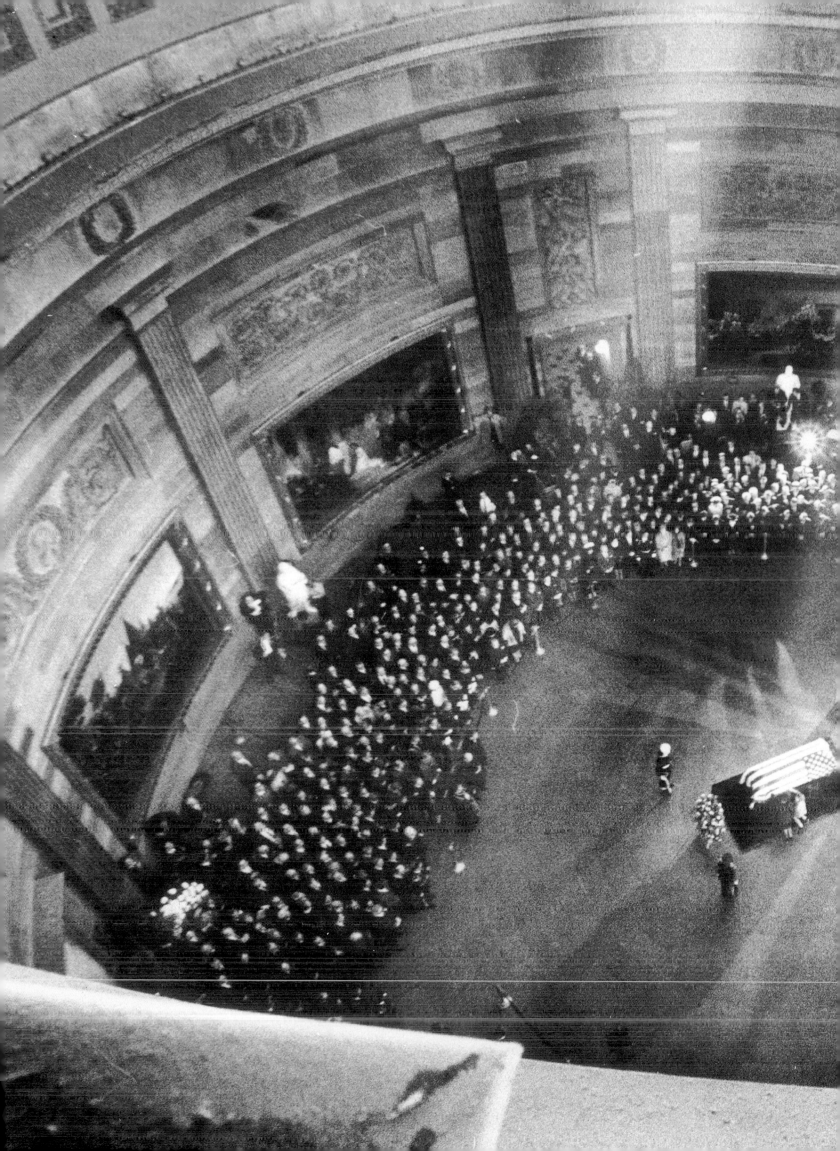

NOVEMBER

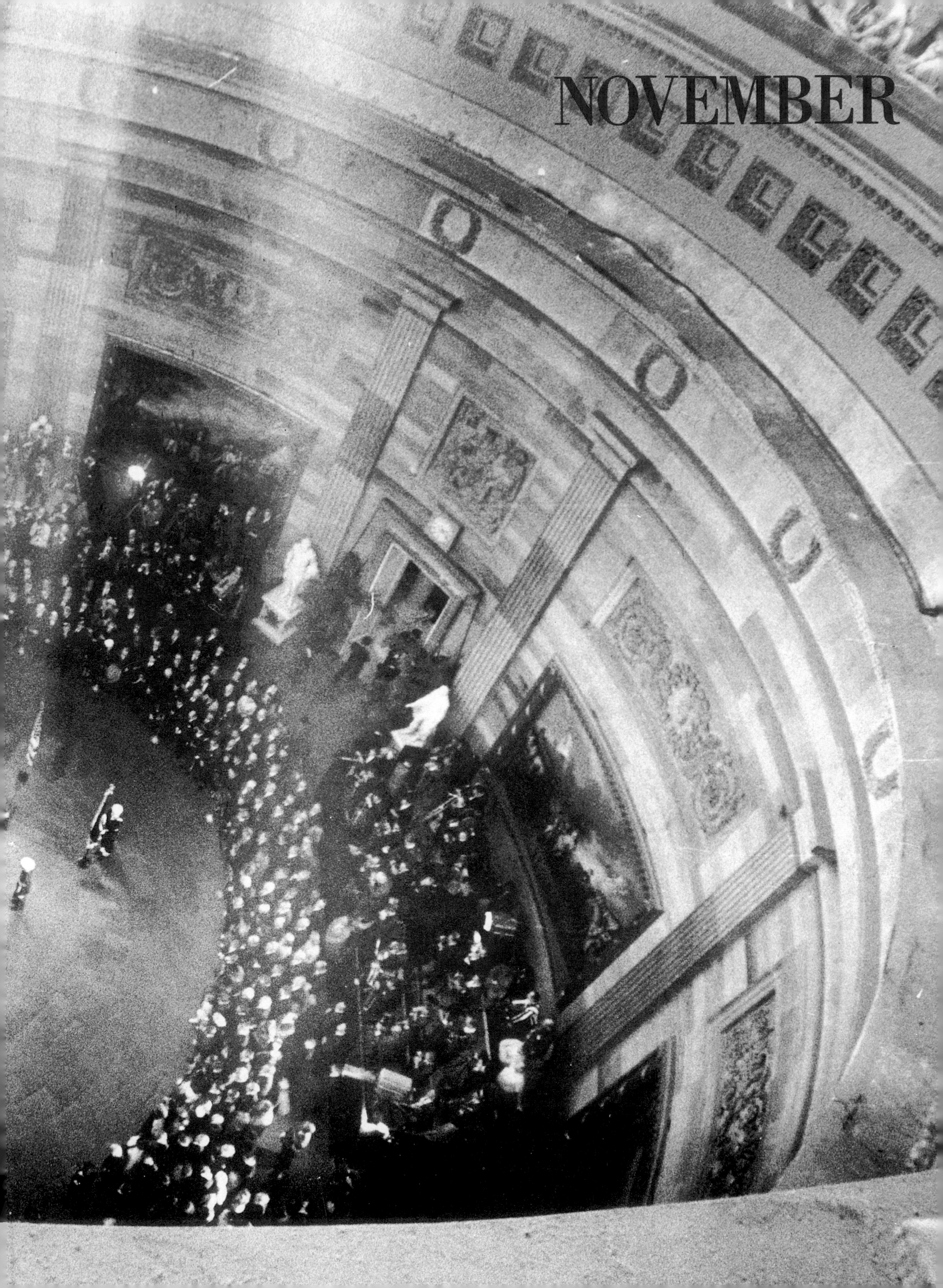

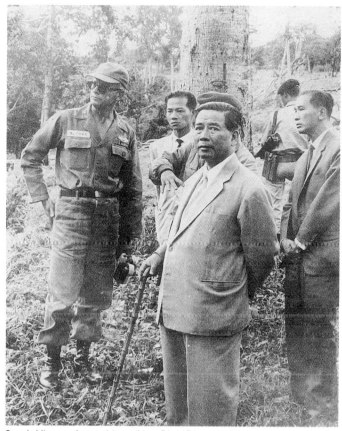

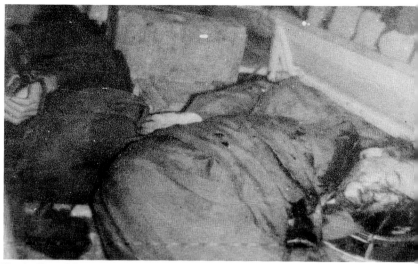

The bodies of South Vietnamese President Ngo Dinh Diem and his brother, Ngo Dinh Nhu, in disguise as priests, lay in an armored personnel carrier shortly after they were slain in the November 2 coup. After escaping to a church, Diem and Nhu had asked for safe conduct back to the palace, to make a graceful exit from power. But during their return they were murdered, on orders from General Duong Van Minh, one of the anti-Diem plotters.

South Vietnam's president, Ngo Dinh Diem, holding a cane and surrounded by advisers, is shown in this photo, taken the previous August.

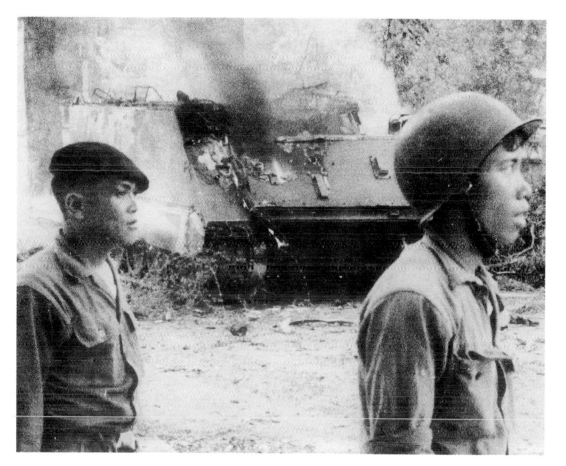

Rebel soldiers stood near an armored vehicle, wrecked in the November 2 attack on the presidential palace in Saigon which ousted the Diem regime. The concentration of power in the Diem family's hands, and the regime's repressive and corrupt policies, had alienated growing numbers of officials and citizens, paving the way for the takeover by generals of the South Vietnamese Army.

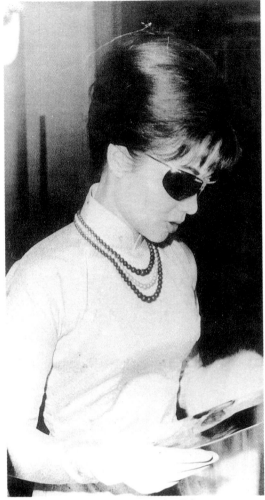

Madame Ngo Dinh Nhu was in the U.S. to promote backing for her brother-in-law, South Vietnam's Ngo Dinh Diem, when he was overthrown in a military coup.

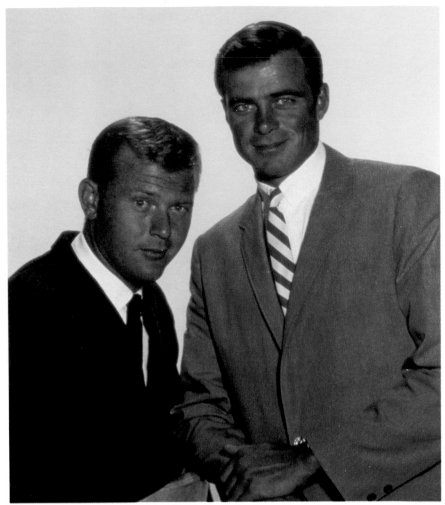

The TV series *Route 66* starred Glenn Corbett (left) and Martin Milner.

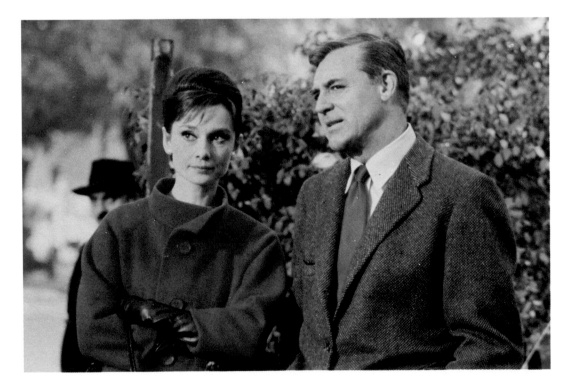

Charade opened at the close of the year. Sub-Hitchcock froth, it was effective largely because of the presence of Cary Grant, who lent the black romantic comedy his smooth, satisfying style. Able support came from Audrey Hepburn and Walter Matthau. Grant was sixty when the film was shot. He played a character who was supposed to be thirty-five. Stanley Donan performed the directorial duties, while Henry Mancini supplied the music.

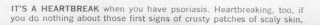
IT'S A HEARTBREAK when you have psoriasis. Heartbreaking, too, if you do nothing about those first signs of crusty patches of scaly skin.

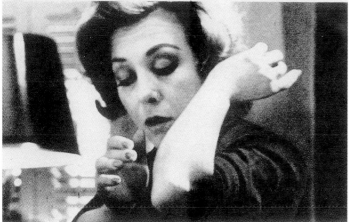

Now! Relief from the itching and scaling that cause the
HEARTBREAK of PSORIASIS
New fast-acting formula works 3 ways to relieve these symptoms of PSORIASIS

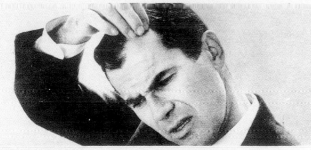

IT'S A HEARTBREAK when psoriasis leaves your skin rough and scaly. A heartbreak when medications fail to bring even temporary relief!

Guarantees relief or your money back. Today, for the first time, comes the promise of new relief for millions who suffer the heartbreak of the itching and scaling of psoriasis. It's a new formula called TEGRIN.™

Unique triple-action cream

TEGRIN is a fast-acting cream that can be used as often as needed, even on the scalp! It's pleasant, easy to use—no lingering medical smell or stain. It's extra effective because it works three ways:

1—Special soothing action speeds relief of that persistent and tormenting itch.

2—Special de-scaling action works fast to remove embarrassing scales, without harmful skin irritation.

3—Helps control recurrence of new scales with continued use on the affected area.

Dramatic relief reported

Tests prove TEGRIN's unique triple-action formula is so effective—brings such pronounced relief in so many cases—that we guarantee TEGRIN will leave your skin cleaner, clearer, smoother or we will refund every penny you paid. So why suffer from the itching and scaling that cause the heartbreak of psoriasis? Whenever these symptoms appear, get new TEGRIN!

Psoriasis symptoms —
13 common trouble spots:

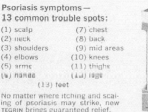

(1) scalp
(2) neck
(3) shoulders
(4) elbows
(5) arms
(6) hands
(7) chest
(8) back
(9) mid areas
(10) knees
(11) thighs
(12) legs
(13) feet

No matter where itching and scaling of psoriasis may strike, new TEGRIN brings guaranteed relief.

Tegrin did for psoriasis what Listerine did for "halitosis." It convinced millions that the only thing standing between themselves and public embarrassment was use of the product.

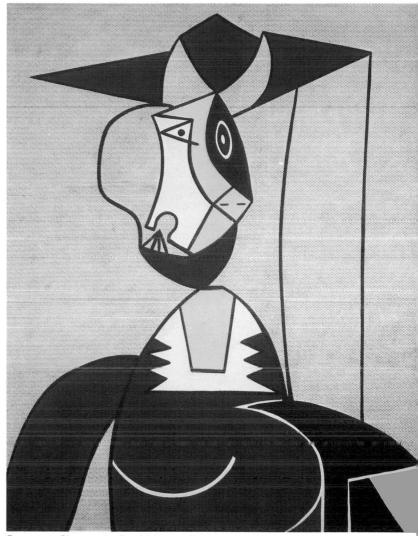
Femme au Chapeau by Roy Lichtenstein.

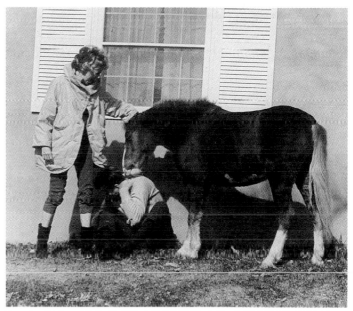
On a weekend retreat in Virginia, JFK encouraged the White House photographer to take this picture saying, "Keep shooting. You're about to see a president eaten by a horse."

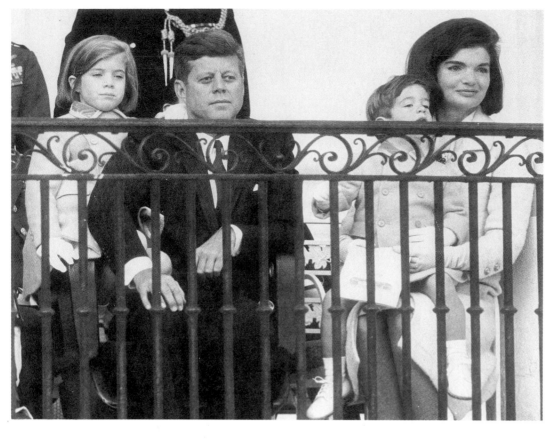

As the first family watched from the balcony on November 13, pipers, drummers, and dancers of Britain's Black Watch Royal Highland Regiment performed on the South Lawn. Some 1,700 children from child-care agencies were invited for the show.

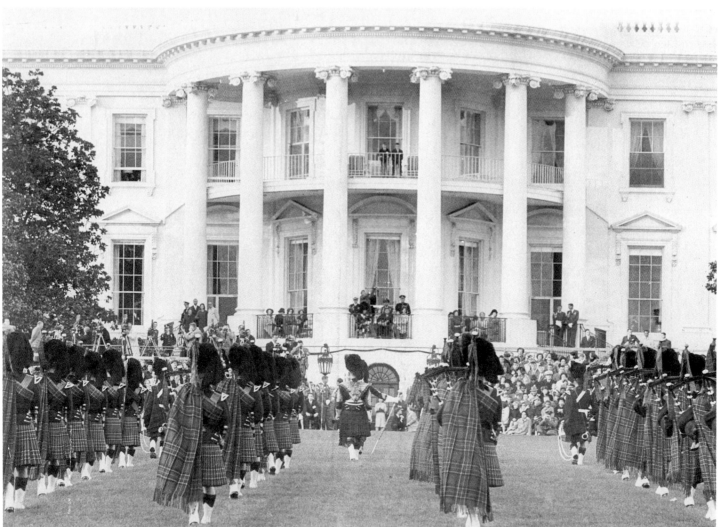

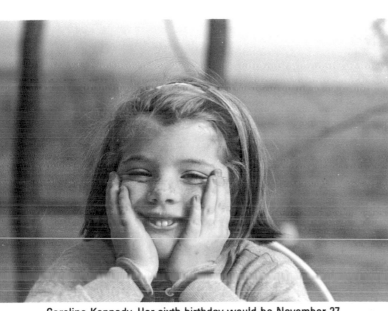

John-John displayed Kennedy vigor during a Veterans Day ceremony at Arlington National Cemetery.

Caroline Kennedy. Her sixth birthday would be November 27.

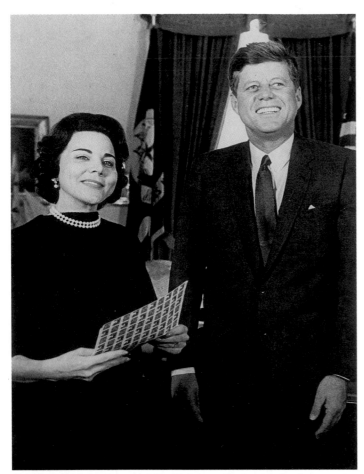

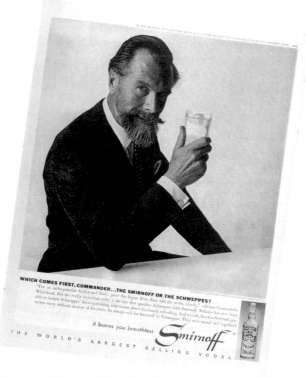

The key selling point for Smirnoff vodka was that it "leaves you breathless," from which you might infer that you could have two martinis at lunch and not return to the office stinking of gin.

President Kennedy launched the Christmas Seal campaign by accepting the first seals from advice columnist Ann Landers, honorary chairman of the campaign.

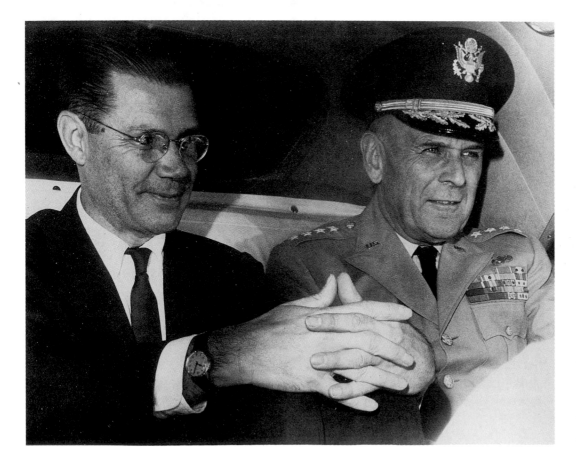

Secretary of Defense Robert McNamara (left) and General Maxwell D. Taylor, chairman of the Joint Chiefs of Staff, arrived in Honolulu on November 20 for a meeting with Secretary of State Dean Rusk and Ambassador Henry Cabot Lodge to discuss U.S. policy in Vietnam following Diem's death.

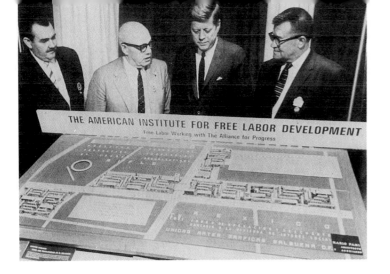

THE AMERICAN INSTITUTE FOR FREE LABOR DEVELOPMENT
Free Labor Working with The Alliance for Progress

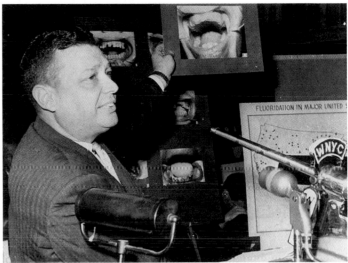

LEFT: The Kennedy administration's program to provide economic aid to Latin America was known as the Alliance for Progress. Here, the president with (left) AFL-CIO president George Meany, inspected the model of a union-funded housing project for Mexico City.

In November, New York City Health Commissioner George James displayed dental-decay photographs to support his case for fluoridating the city's water supply. The city approved the step the next month. In 1963, fluoridated water was available to some 45 million Americans.

H e recognized both the potential value and the potential danger inherent in our relations with Latin America. He would be sad that we seem to have given up on the value of aid and trade and diplomatic initiatives that were so important to him, and now reverted to an emphasis on military might in Latin America, and the revival of dictators like Noriega.

THEODORE SORENSEN

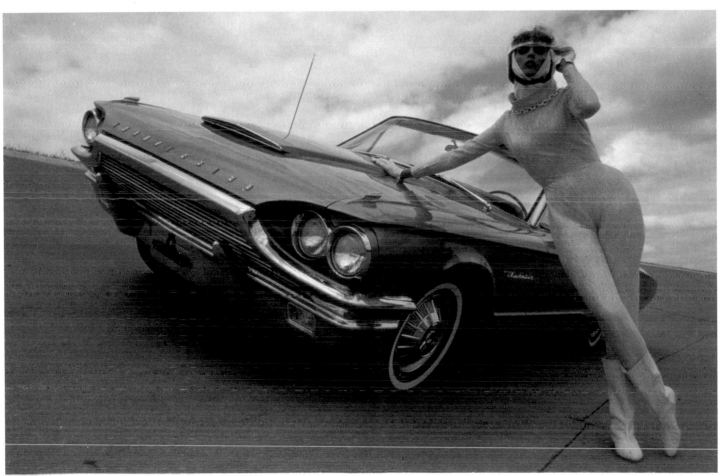

This *Vogue* model was meant to show off the aerodynamic possibilities of the costume rather than the car.

RIGHT: The Beatles were Britain's most popular band. A few of their records were released in the U.S. in 1963, but the group would not become the object of fan mania until their arrival on these shores and appearance on the *Ed Sullivan Show* in February 1964.

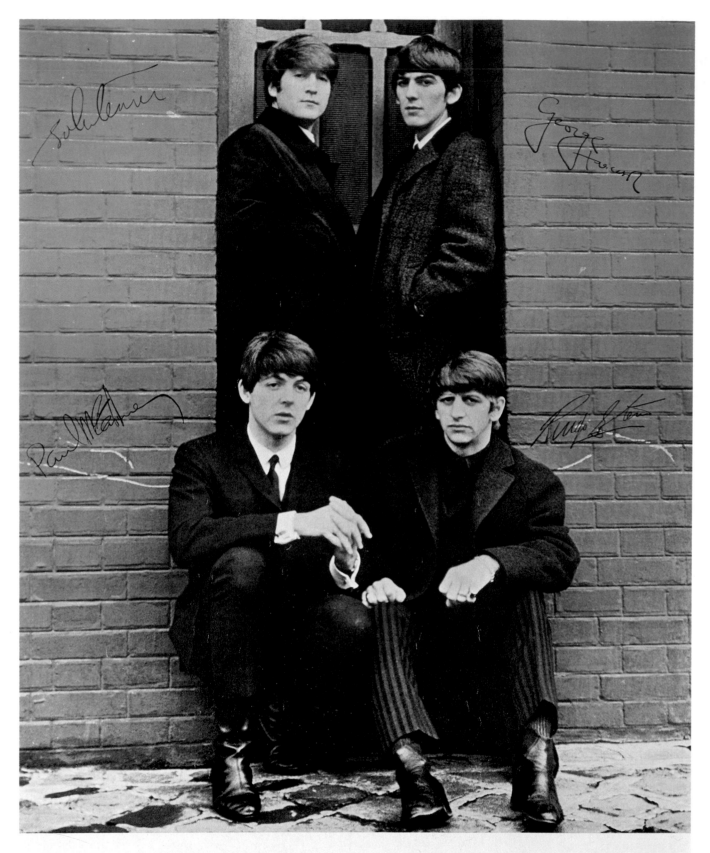

John Lennon
George Harrison
Paul McCartney
Ringo Starr

THE BEATLES.. LONDON PALLADIUM
ROYAL COMMAND PERFORMANCE.1963

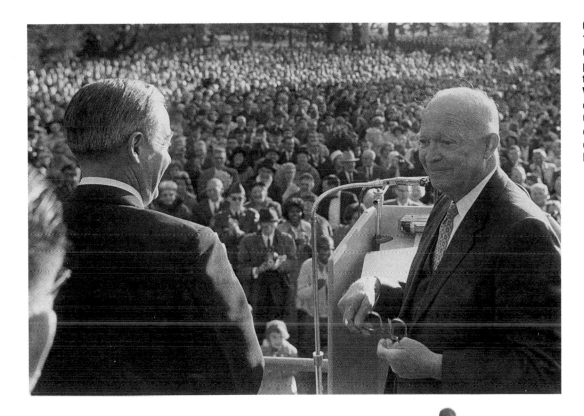

On November 19, marking the 100th anniversary of Lincoln's Gettysburg Address, former president Dwight Eisenhower turned to Pennsylvania Governor William Scranton before re-dedicating the Gettysburg Cemetery. Eisenhower, the oldest U.S. president to hold office, had been succeeded by Kennedy, the youngest.

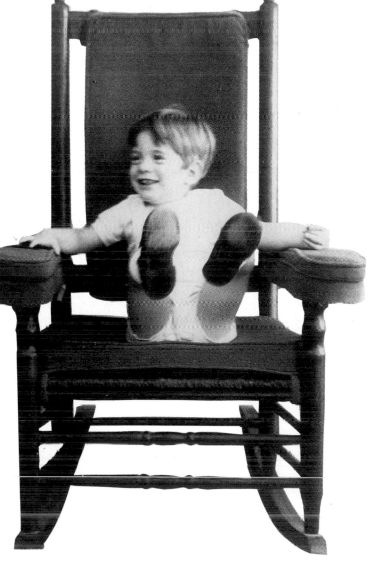

John [Kennedy Jr.] loved to ride up and down the elevator and loved to wear the policeman's hat. Miss Shaw [the governess] was expecting some guests one evening and had John, Jr. down in the main lobby with her, and the first thing John did was go over and get one of the policeman's hats—he put it on and wore it all over the lobby he even had to go look in that tremendous mirror in the lobby. He really enjoyed himself looking at himself in that.

NELSON PIERCE,
White House Usher

*S*pace is the new sea on which to sail, as Kennedy put it. One of the reasons he felt that we should sail that new sea was to prevent the militarization of space—to prevent the Soviet Union from having such a lead that space could be dominated for military purposes—as well as its use by the Soviet Union to show the Third World that the way to greatness was the Soviet way.

THEODORE C. SORENSEN

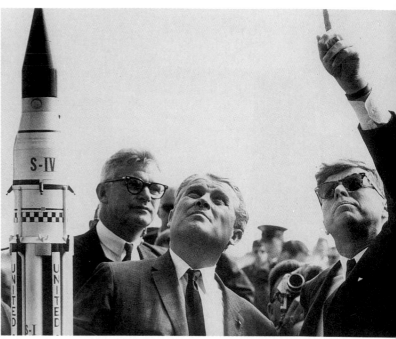

At Cape Canaveral, Werner von Braun explained the Saturn IV system to the president.

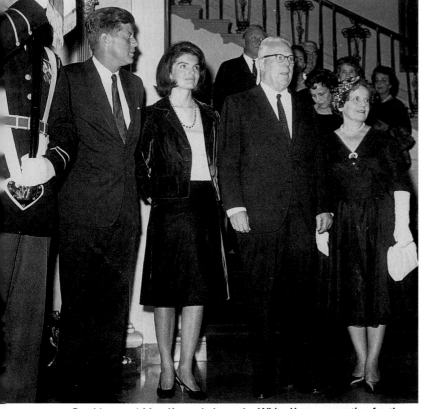

President and Mrs. Kennedy hosted a White House reception for the Supreme Court. The Kennedys posed for pictures with Chief Justice and Mrs. Earl Warren.

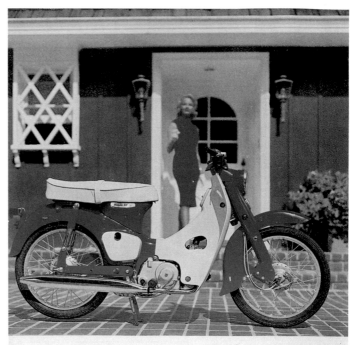

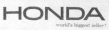
In 1963, Honda meant motor scooters—not cars, not motorcycles but motor scooters. This red job sold for $245, got 225 miles to a gallon of gas and could cruise at 45 m.p.h. If you wanted to find your local dealer you could write to the home office in Gardina, California.

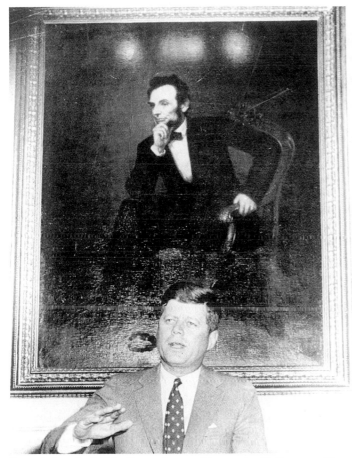

Hours before he left for Texas, the president met with the press. The selection of the site for the meeting, under a portrait of Lincoln, would turn out to be sadly prophetic.

I know [Jack] was warned not to go to Texas by Senator [J. William] Fulbright, by Adlai Stevenson, by Bobby, to whom they had given messages. I know he got really upset. Vice-President Johnson came to our hotel room in Houston the night before we went to Fort Worth. There was all of this about people not wanting to ride in the car with—I forget if John Connally wouldn't ride in the car or Senator [Ralph] Yarborough wouldn't. I remember we had dinner in our room alone, Jack and I. Then Vice-President Johnson came by, and they had a long talk. I know that was the point of the trip, to heal everything, to get everybody to ride in the same car. . . .

JACQUELINE KENNEDY,
First Lady

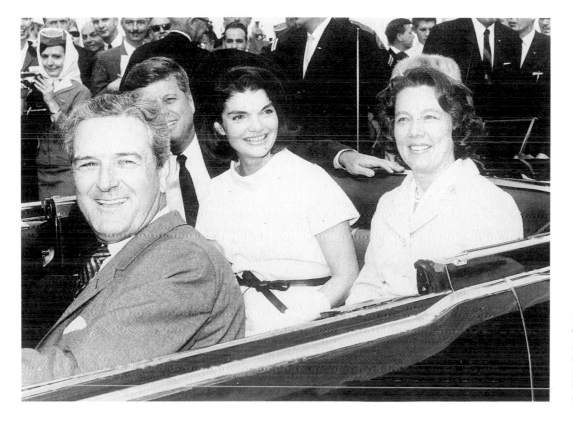

President and Mrs. Kennedy with Texas Governor John Connally and his wife Nellie, immediately after the presidential party arrived in San Antonio to begin the ill-fated three day tour of the state.

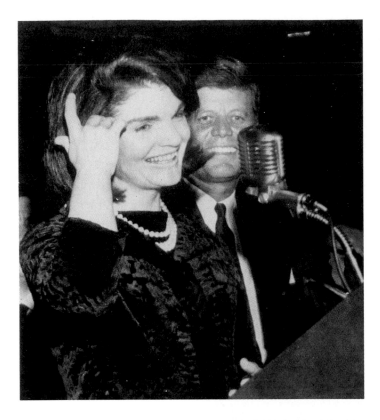

T his was the first political trip Jackie had made with him since . . . the primaries of '60, and . . . she was getting such . . . acclaim everywhere. People were asking, "Where's Jackie?" and there were as many yells for Jackie as there were for Jack. . . .

CHARLES ROBERTS,
Journalist, *Newsweek*

Jacqueline Kennedy received an enthusiastic reception in Houston from the League of Latin American Citizens because the First Lady spoke to them in Spanish.

Governor John Connally, Vice-President Lyndon Johnson and President Kennedy attended a prayer breakfast at the Fort Worth Chamber of Commerce the morning of November 22nd.

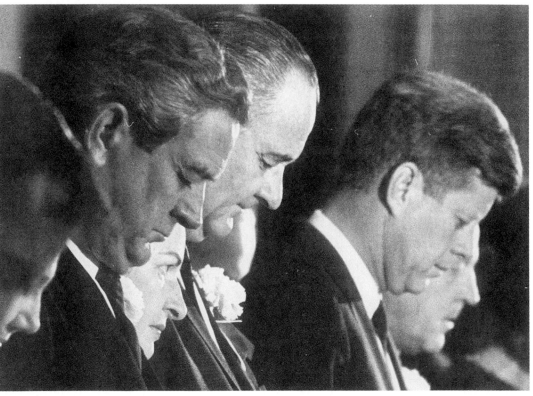

A s we talked in his hotel suite, Kennedy went to a window and looked down at the speaker's platform that had been erected for his appearance. He stared at it for a moment and shook his head.

"Just look at that platform," he said. "With all these buildings around it, the Secret Service couldn't stop someone who really wanted to get you."

LAWRENCE F. O'BRIEN, Assistant to the President

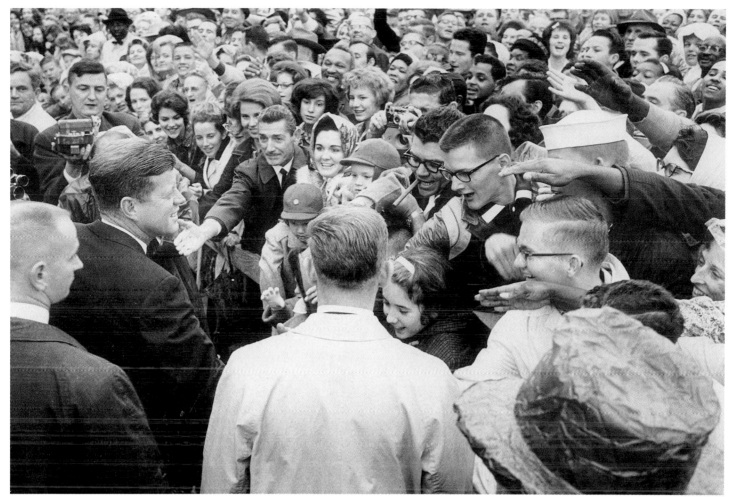

Kennedy's visit to Texas was planned for political purposes. The president's three-day tour was supposed to heal the growing factional rift in the Texas Democratic party and to thwart the growing popularity of the Republican party. The throngs who greeted JFK as he arrived in Ft. Worth on November 22 proved that this mission was succeeding.

And I remember the president going the whole length of a chain-link fence over at the airport with Jackie at his side. We had seen him do this many times before, but that morning I was particularly eager and walked most of the distance right behind him. When they . . . were turning to go back to get in the limousine, I asked Jackie how she liked campaigning. And she said, "It's wonderful, it's wonderful." This . . . would be about quarter of twelve . . . just about 45 minutes before the underpass.

CHARLES ROBERTS

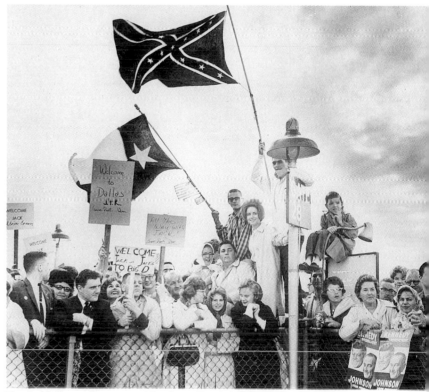

The Confederate flags waved by these Kennedy fans underscored the conservatism in the Texas Democratic Party that Kennedy had to confront.

WELCOME MR. KENNEDY

TO DALLAS...

...A CITY so disgraced by a recent Liberal smear attempt that its citizens have just elected two more Conservative Americans to public office.

...A CITY that is an economic "boom town," not because of Federal handouts, but through conservative economic and business practices.

...A CITY that will continue to grow and prosper despite efforts by you and your administration to penalize it for its non-conformity to "New Frontierism."

...A CITY that rejected your philosophy and policies in 1960 and will do so again in 1964 — even more emphatically than before.

MR. KENNEDY, despite contentions on the part of your administration, the State Department, the Mayor of Dallas, the Dallas City Council, and members of your party, we free-thinking and America-thinking citizens of Dallas still have, through a Constitution largely ignored by you, the right to address our grievances, to question you, to disagree with you, and to criticize you.

In asserting this constitutional right, we wish to ask you publicly the following questions—indeed, questions of paramount importance and interest to all free peoples everywhere—which we trust you will answer...in public, without sophistry. These questions are:

WHY is Latin America turning either anti-American or Communistic, or both, despite increased U.S. foreign aid, State Department policy, and your own Ivy-Tower pronouncements?

WHY do you say we have built a "wall of freedom" around Cuba when there is no freedom in Cuba today? Because of your policy, thousands of Cubans have been imprisoned, are starving and being persecuted—with thousands already murdered and thousands more awaiting execution and, in addition, the entire population of almost 7,000,000 Cubans are living in slavery.

WHY have you approved the sale of wheat and corn to our enemies when you know the Communist soldiers "travel on their stomachs" just as ours do? Communist soldiers are daily wounding and/or killing American soldiers in South Viet Nam.

WHY did you host, salute and entertain Tito — Moscow's Trojan Horse — just a short time after our sworn enemy, Khrushchev, embraced the Yugoslav dictator as a great hero and leader of Communism?

WHY have you urged greater aid, comfort, recognition, and understanding for Yugoslavia, Poland, Hungary, and other Communist countries, while turning your back on the pleas of Hungarian, East German, Cuban and other anti-Communist freedom fighters?

WHY did Cambodia kick the U.S. out of its country after we poured nearly 400 Million Dollars of aid into its ultra-leftist government?

WHY has Gus Hall, head of the U.S. Communist Party praised almost every one of your policies and announced that the party will endorse and support your re-election in 1964?

WHY have you banned the showing at U.S. military bases of the film "Operation Abolition"—the movie by the House Committee on Un-American Activities exposing Communism in America?

WHY have you ordered or permitted your brother Bobby, the Attorney General, to go soft on Communists, fellow-travelers, and ultra-leftists in America, while permitting him to persecute loyal Americans who criticize you, your administration, and your leadership?

WHY are you in favor of the U.S. continuing to give economic aid to Argentina, in spite of that fact that Argentina has just seized almost 400 Million Dollars of American private property?

WHY has the Foreign Policy of the United States degenerated to the point that the C.I.A. is arranging coups and having staunch Anti-Communist Allies of the U.S. bloodily exterminated.

WHY have you scrapped the Monroe Doctrine in favor of the "Spirit of Moscow"?

MR. KENNEDY, as citizens of these United States of America, we DEMAND answers to these questions and we want them NOW.

THE AMERICAN FACT-FINDING COMMITTEE

"An unaffiliated and non-partisan group of citizens who wish truth"

BERNARD WEISSMAN,
Chairman

Kennedy's political opponents in Texas weren't going to make his trip easy, as this November 22 *Dallas Morning Herald* advertisement shows.

I don't know whether hindsight makes me remember the next moments extra vividly, or whether—as I think was true—the image of the Kennedys framed in the doorway of the plane was thrust into my consciousness with more than usual force. As the sunlight hit Mrs. Kennedy's pink suit, it was like a blow between the eyes. As they descended the ramp, they seemed enveloped by an aura of extra light. At the foot of the stairs, someone gave Jackie a huge bunch of deep red roses and the effect of those, almost blood red against the pink suit, was electrifying. Her hair was glossy in the clear light. Her brown eyes gleamed luminously and I saw then clearly for the first time that what had looked like a dark blouse inside was the navy blue lining from her jacket, with the lapels turned out.

ROBERT MacNEIL,
Correspondent, NBC Television

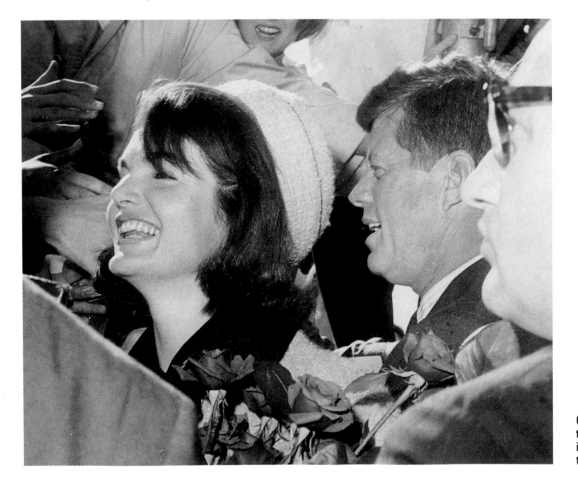

On the morning of November 22, the greeting at Dallas' Love Field included a bouquet of roses for the First Lady.

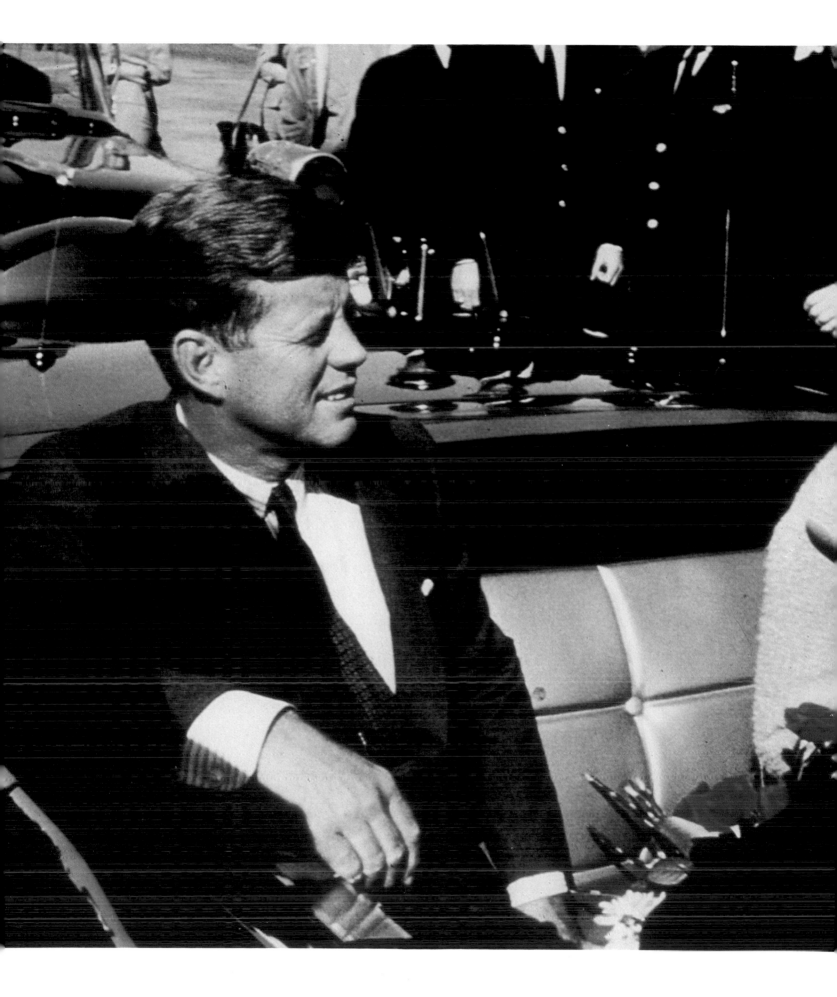

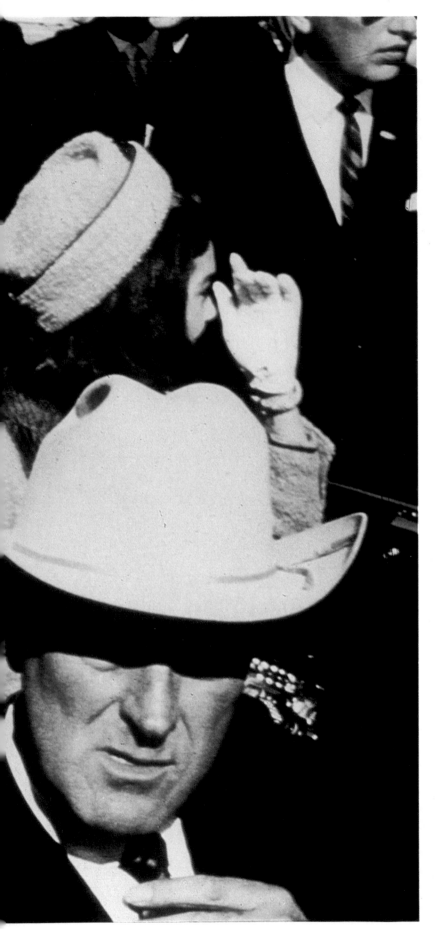

I wanted approval from the Secret Service and the people running the campaign in Dallas to publish the route of the motorcade. The Secret Service didn't want to, and the politicians of course wanted to. They wanted a crowd. It was a very easy decision to make—yes, publish the motorcade. I had made the decision the night before in Dallas. So that morning the Dallas News carried the map of the motorcade.

BILL MOYERS, Aide to
Vice-President Lyndon Baines Johnson

Then . . . the president got in his open car. . . . He had inquired about the weather that morning and decided that they would not have the top on it. They had a choice of three tops: a fabric top . . . [which] would have obscured him from the public; and the plastic top, which the Secret Service had told me would deflect a bullet but would not stop it; and then a metal top. But he didn't want any of those that morning, and so we started into downtown Dallas with him in an open car. There were, I think, 12 cars in the motorcade. And I was in the first press bus. . . .

CHARLES ROBERTS

The president's motorcade, which began at Love Field at 11:50 A.M., was scheduled to follow an eleven mile route through downtown Dallas. Kennedy's limousine had been flown in from Washington.

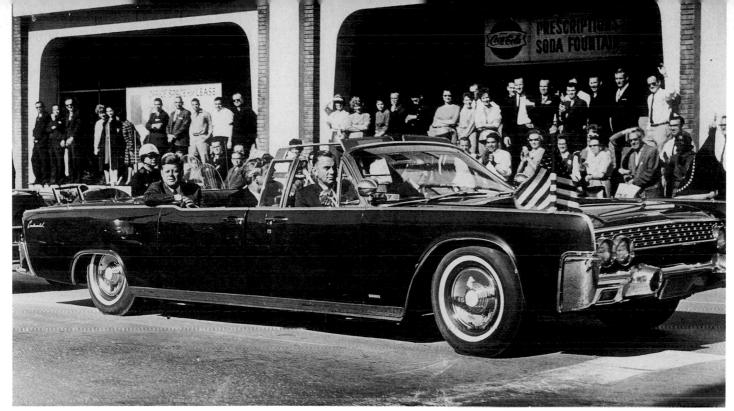

Kennedy must have been impressed by the crowds that lined Dallas streets as his limousine traveled en route to the Trade Mart where the president was scheduled to speak.

We turned off . . . Main Street and got over to Elm Street, and the last thing I remember . . . before the incident was looking up at the sign on the building as we came to a park and sort of turned to the right to go down this incline under the triple underpass. I saw the words "Texas School Book Depository" and thought it was a weird name for a building and wondered what it was. . . .

CHARLES ROBERTS

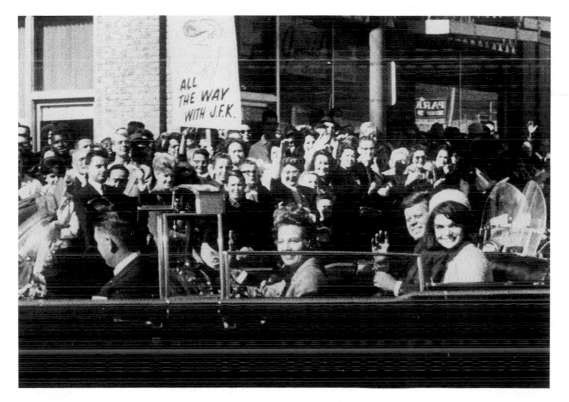

Moments before.

W hat were you doing when Kennedy was assassinated?" People can remember pictorially and vividly where they were. Roger Brown called them "flashbulb memories"; an indication of a critical moment, a moment so important that everything else stops. That vivid memory is something that survives, so that when everything else has faded you have a handle to retrieve the moment and the feelings that went with it and the despair and the whole set of social and personal reactions. You have a hook by which you can pull up those memories and that memory can survive.

ROBERT ABELSON,
**Professor of Psychology and
Political Science, Yale University**

We were rounding a curve, going down a hill, and suddenly there was a sharp, loud report. It sounded like a shot. The sound seemed to me to come from a building on the right above my shoulder. A moment passed, and then two more shots rang out in rapid succession. There had been such a gala air about the day that I thought the noise must come from firecrackers—part of the celebration. Then the Secret Service men were suddenly down in the lead car. Over the car radio system, I heard "Let's get out of here" and our Secret Service man, Rufus Youngblood, vaulted over the front seat on top of Lyndon, threw him to the floor, and said, "Get down." . . . The car accelerated terrifically—faster and faster.

LADY BIRD JOHNSON,
Wife of the Vice-President

Just seconds after that I heard what I thought was a backfire. . . . Bob Pierpoint [of CBS], who was sitting next to me, said, "That sounded like gunfire." And as he said it, I looked off to my left and saw a man sprawled over what I think was his daughter. . . . And I snapped back and said, "My God, it was gunfire!" because I realized that no parent would do this unless something terrible had happened. At the same second I saw a policeman running across the park to our left pulling his pistol out of a holster.

I heard a second shot . . . a split-second before—or after—seeing that policeman run across the park. . . . I then looked off to the right and saw a policeman drive a three-wheel motorcycle over the curb to the road off to the right of the president's car, pulling his pistol from his pocket and starting up an embankment there.

CHARLES ROBERTS

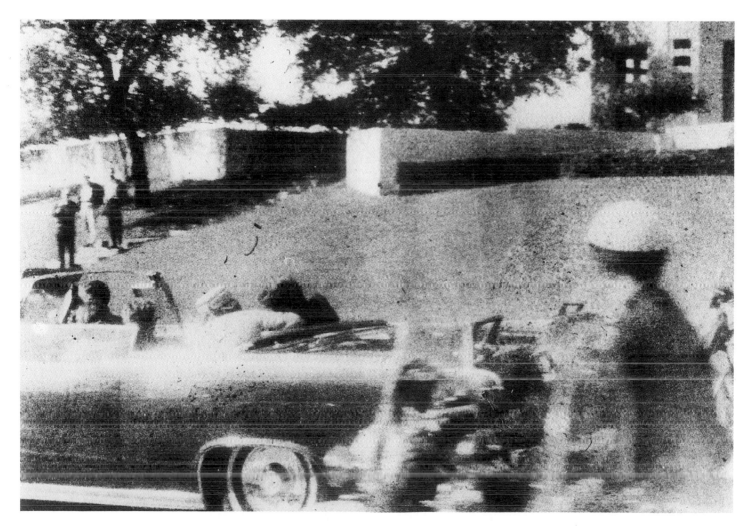

Everything happened in six seconds, the space of eight heartbeats: The president was shot in the neck and fell forward. His wife screamed: "Jack! Oh, no! No!" governor Connally, riding with the president, was struck by the second bullet and fell forward. The Governor's wife, Nellie, dropped unharmed to the floor of the limousine with her husband. A third bullet hit the president in the back of the head. As soon as he could react, the president's driver slammed on the brakes—after the third shot—and a police escort pulled up to the president's car. BELOW: Secret Service Agent Clint Hill leaped into the back of the presidential limousine, assisted by Mrs. Kennedy.

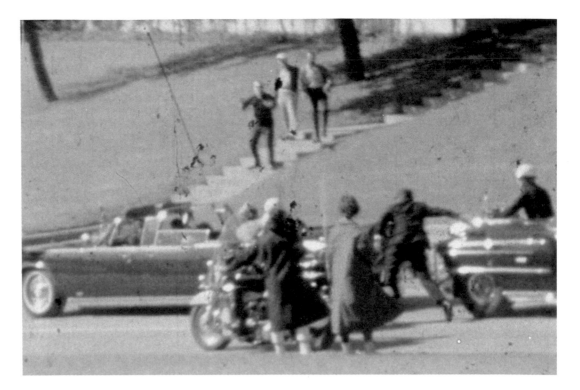

*S*uddenly there was an explosive noise—distinct, sharp, resounding. I could not be certain if it had been a firecracker, bullet, bomb. . . . I looked around quickly and saw nothing to indicate its source.

But the movements in the president's car were not normal. Kennedy seemed to be falling to his left . . . I turned instinctively in my seat and with my left hand I grasped Lyndon Johnson's right shoulder and with all the leverage I could exert from a sitting position I forced him downward.

"Get down!" I shouted. "Get down!"

The vice-president reacted immediately. Still not seeing the source of the explosion, I swung across the back seat and sat on top of him. There were two more explosions in rapid succession, only seconds after the first. . . . People along the sides of the street were scattering in panic.

RUFUS YOUNGBLOOD, Secret Service Agent

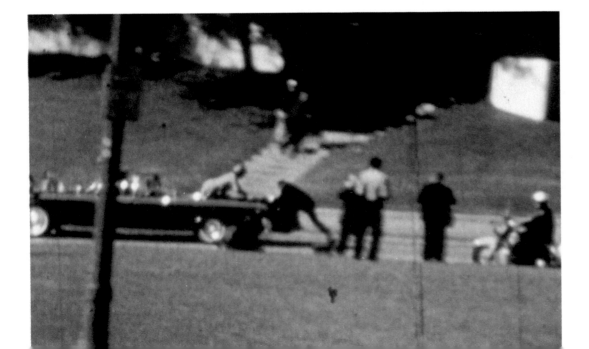

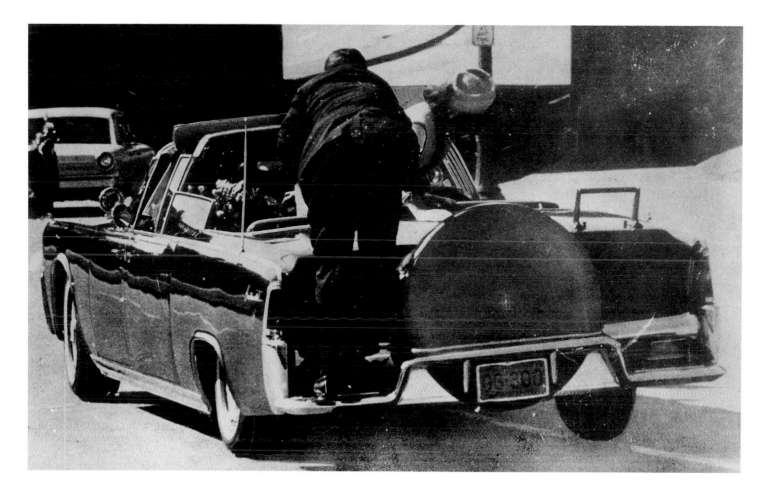

President Kennedy was rushed to Parkland Hospital. Machine-guns drawn, the Secret Service followed behind the presidential limousine.

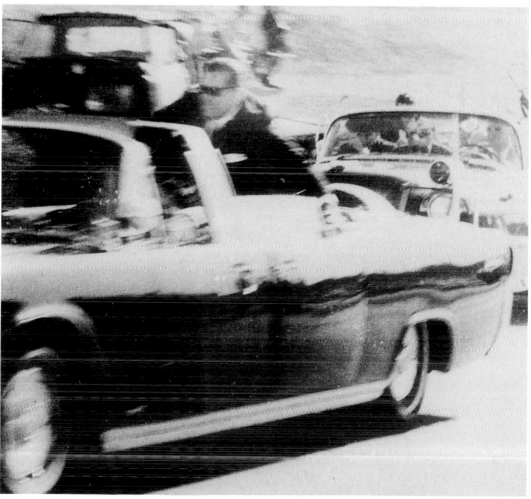

Spectators hugged the ground and newsreel cameramen filmed as the president was rushed to Parkland Hospital at 70 mph.

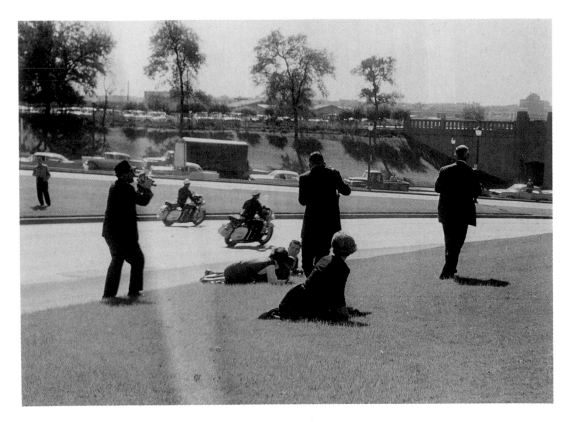

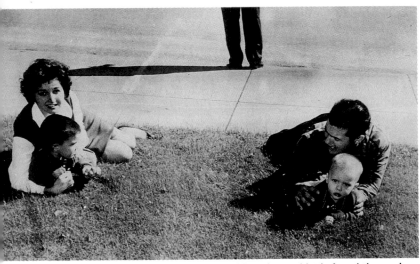

They just wanted to see the president, but suddenly found themselves protecting their children from bullets that might still be coming.
BELOW: A crowd, including reporters, converged on the grassy knoll believing it to be the direction from which the shots that struck the president were fired. NBC correspondent Robert MacNeil is fourth from the left.

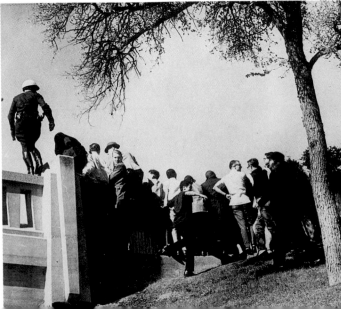

We heard what sounded like a shot. The bus was still on Houston Street.

I said, "Was that a shot?"

Several people said, "No, no," and others said, "I don't know."

That reaction took a few seconds, then there were two more explosions, very distinct to me. I jumped up and said, "They were shots! Stop the bus! Stop the bus!"

The driver opened the door and I jumped out, just as the bus was turning the corner of Elm Street. I couldn't see the president's car but I really started to believe there was shooting because on the grass on both sides of the roadway people were throwing themselves down and covering their children with their bodies. The air was filled with screaming, a high unison soprano wail. The sun was intensely bright. I saw several people running up the grassy hill beside the road. I thought they were chasing whoever had done the shooting and I ran after them. . . .

ROBERT MacNEIL

I ran to the right and into the first building I came to that looked as though it might have a phone. It was the Texas School Book Depository. As I ran up the steps and through the door, a young man in shirt sleeves was coming out. In great agitation I asked him where there was a phone. He pointed inside to an open space where another man was talking on a phone situated near a pillar and said, "Better ask him." I ran inside and asked the second man, who pointed to an office at one side. I found a telephone on the desk. Two of the four Lucite call buttons were lit up. I punched another, got long distance, and was through to the NBC Radio news desk in about ten seconds.

ROBERT MacNEIL

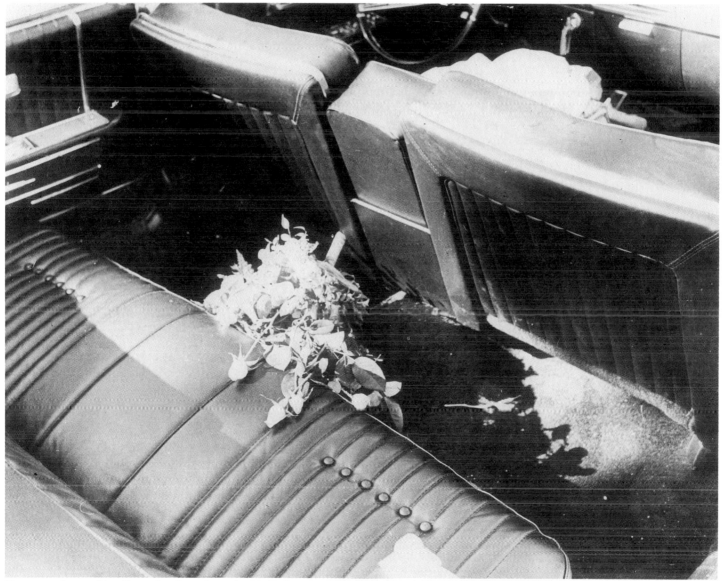

The roses given to Mrs. Kennedy when she arrived in Dallas were left on the seat of the limousine in which President Kennedy was shot.

Kennedy on the way to Parkland Hospital. The white arrow shows the president's foot protruding from the limousine, and the black arrow shows Mrs. Connally ducking bullets.

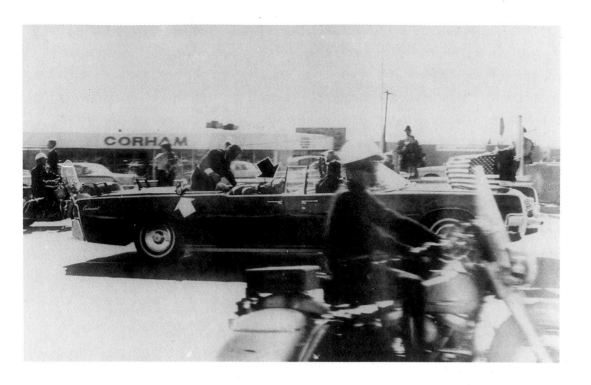

*T*he president's car was there, still at the point where it had pulled up, and they had taken the president out into that emergency entrance. . . . I remember that the Secret Service men were then starting to mop up the back seat of the big Lincoln the president was put in, and a few minutes later they started putting the fabric top on it. And when I went over to look at it a little closer, one of the agents waved me aside and said, "You can't look." Later, of course, it seemed to me ironic that this wall of protection went up when it of course could do no good. . . .

CHARLES ROBERTS

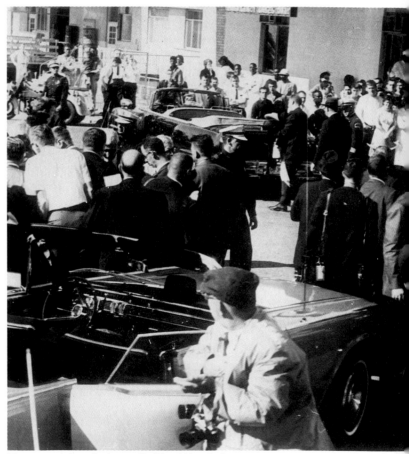

The scene of confusion at Parkland Hospital.

I got there just after the second part of the motorcade with the pool press and camera cars. The bus I had left was just arriving. . . . There was a cluster of reporters around Senator Yarborough, who said the president was "gravely wounded." I looked into the limousine. The roses from Mrs. Kennedy's bouquet were scattered in the bloody back seat. . . .

ROBERT MacNEIL

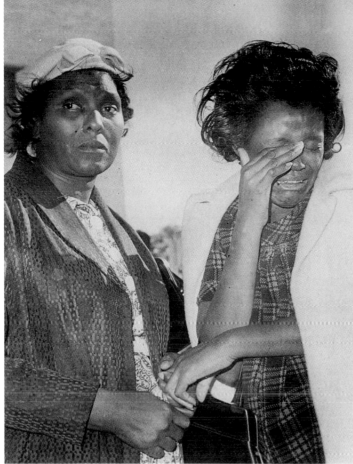

Outside the hospital, an unidentified woman cried as she learned of the president's death.

Suddenly I found myself face to face with Jackie in a small hallway. I believe it was right outside the operating room. You always think of someone like her as being insulated, protected. She was quite alone. I don't think I ever saw anyone so much alone in my life. I went up to her, put my arms around her, and said something to her. I'm sure it was something like "God, help us all," because my feelings for her were too tumultuous to put into words.

LADY BIRD JOHNSON

John F. Kennedy's burial transit certificate.

When the assassination occurred, I got to the hospital by securing a car through one of the Secret Service men. I was there probably within three to five minutes of the time the president arrived. I went immediately to the table on which he was being treated, and saw for all intents and purposes life did not exist.

I stood with Mrs. Kennedy, and one of the doctors came and said that they felt that the president was dead. I went over and pronounced him dead. . . . I came back to Mrs. Kennedy and said "The president is dead." And we went over to the president and we said prayers for the dead. . . .

GEORGE G. BURKLEY, the President's Physician

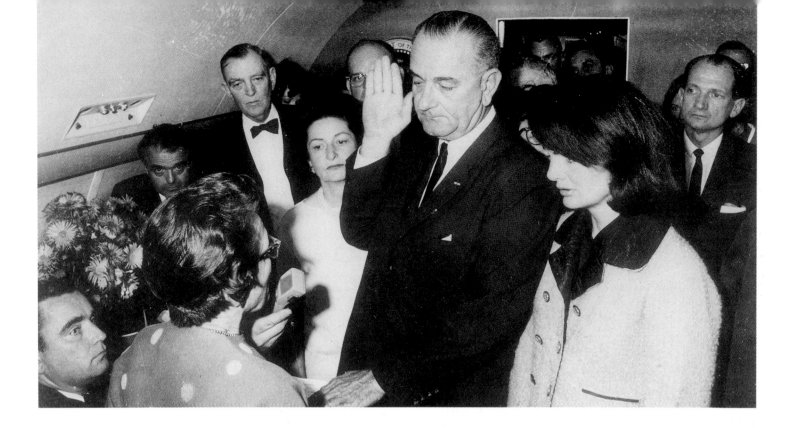

All the [plane's] curtains were drawn. They had gotten the president's casket aboard by removing some seats from the back of the airplane. . . . Jack Valenti had phoned Nick [Nicholas deB.] Katzenbach, the assistant attorney general . . . They had had the oath read to them over the phone from Washington. . . . The judge had that and the Bible. . . .

We waited quite a while for Mrs. Kennedy. And eventually she came forward from where they had placed the casket. She was in what appeared to me to be almost total shock—that strawberry wool suit, the skirt of it splattered with blood and her hose almost saturated with blood—and she took a position to the left of the president. Lady Bird stood on his right, and they faced the judge as she administered the oath. . . .

There was a minute or so of awkward silence, and the president turned and kissed Lady Bird. He embraced Jackie, holding her by the elbows. . . .

There was handshaking all around, but a very solemn sort of handshaking, of course. . . . And then Mrs. Kennedy did go aft, and then the president turned and said, "Now let's get airborne. . . ."

CHARLES ROBERTS

At 3:37 P.M., EST, the wheels of Air Force One cleared the runway. . . . When the president's plane reached operating altitude, Mrs. Kennedy left her bedchamber and walked to the rear compartment of the plane. . . . Kennedy's casket had been placed in this compartment, carried aboard by a group of Secret Service agents.

Mrs. Kennedy went into the rear lounge and took a chair beside the coffin. There she remained throughout the flight.

MERRIMAN SMITH,
Correspondent, UPI

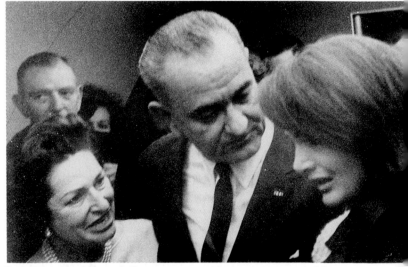

One of Lyndon Johnson's first acts as president was to console Mrs. Kennedy. To the left of the new president is Lady Bird Johnson.

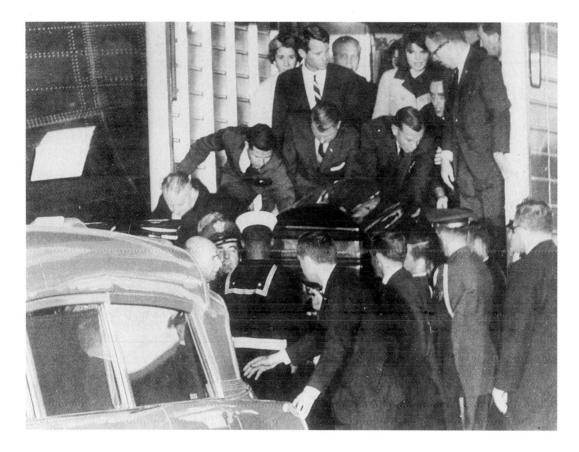

The casket that contained the body of the late John F. Kennedy was moved to a Navy ambulance from Air Force One after arriving at Andrews Air Force Base. Mrs. Kennedy is shown behind the ambulance on the elevator; Robert Kennedy is beside her; Lawrence O'Brien of the White House staff is at the right.

The plane landed, and as we stood there flattened against the walls of the plane, I suddenly was aware that pushing through us was Bobby Kennedy. He didn't look to the left or the right and his face looked streaked with tears and absolutely stricken. He said, "Where's Jackie? I want to be with Jackie." And he pushed through and we got him to her.

LIZ CARPENTER, Press Secretary to Lady Bird Johnson

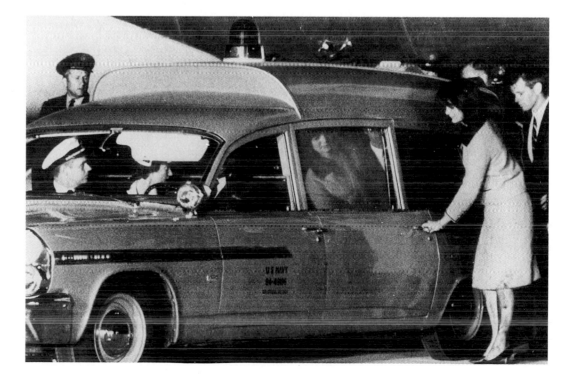

Mrs. John F. Kennedy—her stockings still blood stained—entered the ambulance carrying the body of her slain husband. Robert Kennedy stood behind her; Col. James Swindall, the pilot of Air Force One, is at the upper left.

*W*e landed at Andrews at about 6, and the whole top layer of government that was not on that plane on the way to Tokyo was there, of course. We stood by while the president's casket was removed by that lift truck. . . .

Then President Johnson, after this gray Navy ambulance had taken the casket, walked over to the battery of TV cameras and lights—by then it was dark, and things were a little eerie in that light—and read the statement he had prepared on the plane. . . .

CHARLES ROBERTS

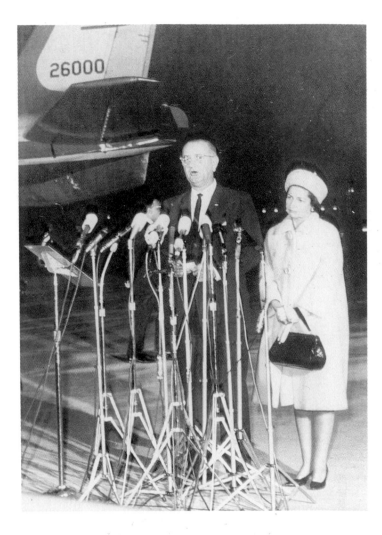

After landing at Andrews Air Force Base in Washington, D.C. the new president, Lyndon Baines Johnson, spoke to reporters: "This is a sad time for all people. We have suffered a loss that cannot be weighed. For me it is a deep personal tragedy. I know the world shares the sorrow that Mrs. Kennedy and her family bear. I will do my best. That is all I can do. I ask for your help—and God's." He was accompanied by Mrs. Johnson.

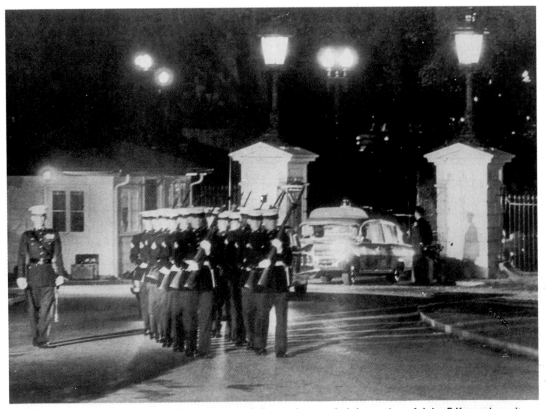

A military honor guard marched in front of the ambulance that carried the casket of John F. Kennedy as it was returned to the White House at 4:30 A.M. The casket was taken to the East Room of the Executive Mansion where Kennedy's body lay in repose.

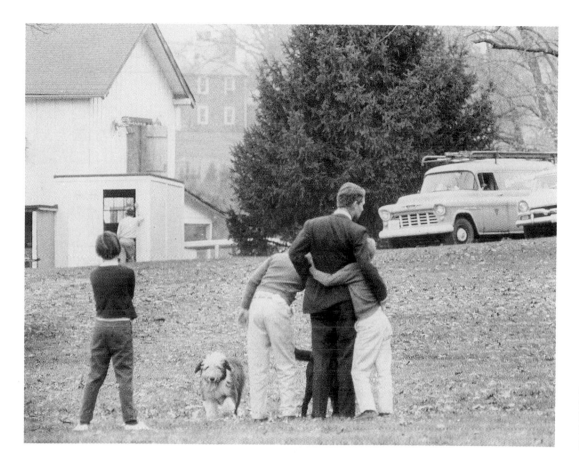

Attorney General Robert Kennedy being comforted by two of his children at their home in McLean, Virginia, after being told of the assassination.

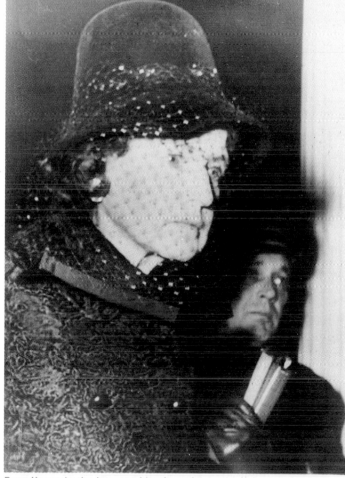

Rose Kennedy, the late president's mother, attended a memorial mass for her son at St. Francis Xavier Church in Hyannis, Massachusetts, the day after the assassination.

We got back to Ted's house. He was very distressed because all the phones were dead—his phone, the one next door . . . We decided to go right to the White House so he could get hold of a reliable means of communication. There was a crowd gathering around the White House as we drove in. The police, on seeing who it was, waved us right in [through] the entrance on East Executive Avenue.

No one had to tell Ted. Just from the look of the people's faces—the women sobbing—you could tell the president was dead. . . .

MILTON GWIRTZMAN,
White House Advisor

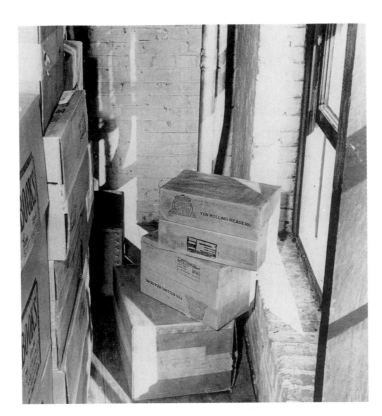

The spot on the sixth floor of the Texas School Book Depository from which Lee Harvey Oswald shot the president.

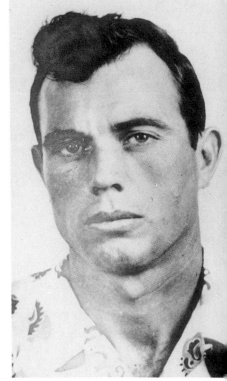

Dallas police officer J. D. Tippit, 39, was shot three times and killed by Lee Harvey Oswald. Oswald's description had been broadcast over police radios, and Tippit was the first to spot the suspected assassin. When Tippit got out of his police car to question Oswald, Oswald fatally shot him. A passer-by used Tippit's radio to summon help.

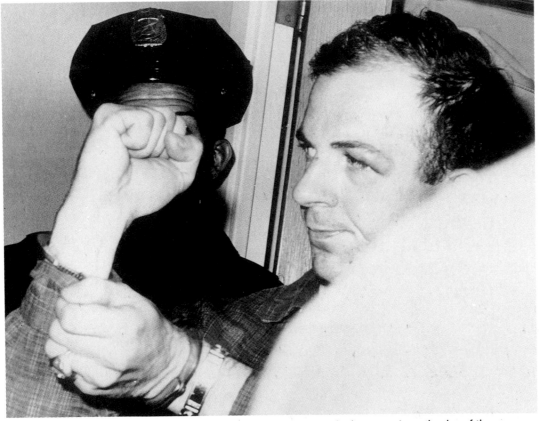

Lee Harvey Oswald, 24, was captured by the Dallas police at a movie theater at 1 P.M. the day of the assassination.

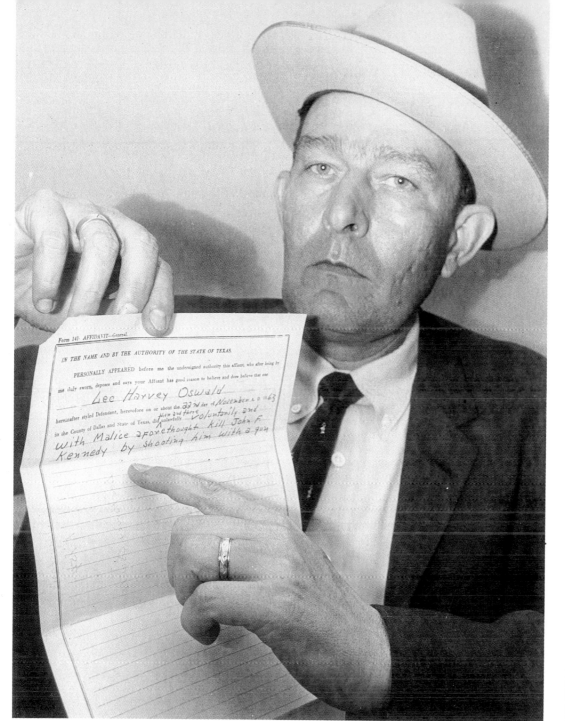

When word came that Lee Harvey Oswald had been captured, I immediately ordered his name checked in the [State] Department's files for any information that might cast light on his activities. Within minutes, word came back that he had spent 32 months in the Soviet Union as recently as June 1962. . . .

What was the connection? I called in Ambassadors Llewellyn Thompson and Averell Harriman—both of whom had served in Moscow. "Could this," I asked, "be a Soviet move to be followed up by a missile attack?" The answer was a resounding negative. The leaders of the Soviet Union, they insisted, would never sanction the assassination of other heads of state, as that might invite similar attacks on themselves.

GEORGE BALL, Undersecretary of State

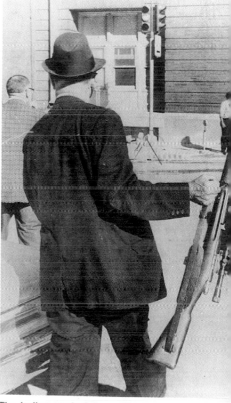

The Italian-made 6.5 mm Carcano carbine with which Oswald killed Kennedy.

Lee Harvey Oswald was born in 1939. The former Marine lived in the Soviet Union between 1959 and 1962. While in Moscow, he wrote John Connally, then Secretary of the Navy, protesting his "undesirable" discharge from the Marines. He was released from inactive reserve as an undesirable after he denounced his allegiance to the United States at the U.S. Embassy in Moscow and said he wanted to be a Soviet citizen. Oswald married a pharmacist from the Soviet city of Minsk. In 1962 he complained to Senator John Tower (D-Texas) that Soviet officials wouldn't let him leave. The State Department lent Oswald $435.71 for air fare so he, his wife and daughter could travel back to the United States. A self-described Marxist, Oswald became a part of the pro-Castro Fair Play for Cuba Committee in New Orleans. Two months before the assassination, Oswald sent his family to live with a friend in Irving, Texas, and soon after went to Dallas, where he got a job at the Texas School Book Depository building.

I t was about a year and a half later that I got a call in New York from William Manchester, who was writing The Death of a President. He said he had gone carefully over the ground to find out who had been in the Book Depository before and right after the shooting. He had seen a statement I had made to the FBI. He had traced my call through the telephone company to 12:34, four minutes after the shooting, and he was convinced that I had spoken to Lee Harvey Oswald. Could I tell him any more about it? I couldn't; it was possible, but I had no way of confirming that either of the young men I had spoken to was Oswald.

Then Manchester asked if I knew about the statement Oswald had made to the Secret Service. Oswald had told them that as he left the Book Depository, a young Secret Serviceman with a blond crewcut had rushed up the steps and asked him for a phone. Since no Secret Serviceman had entered the building, Manchester concluded that Oswald had mistaken me for one.

ROBERT MacNEIL

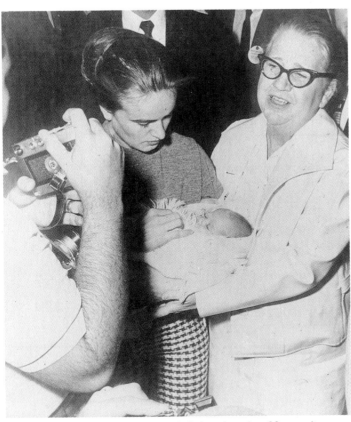

Oswald's wife, Marina (holding her baby), and mother, Marguerite Oswald, were interrogated by reporters at a Dallas police station on November 22, after being questioned by the police.

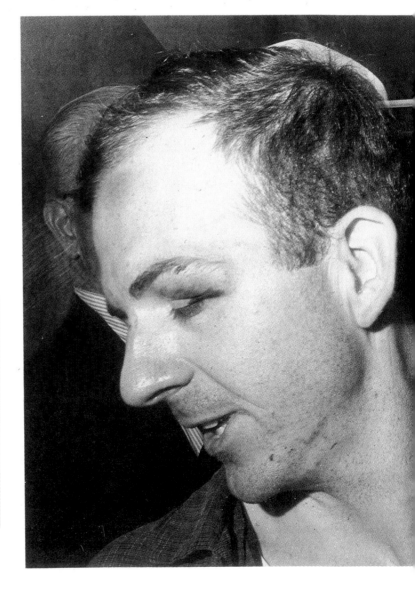

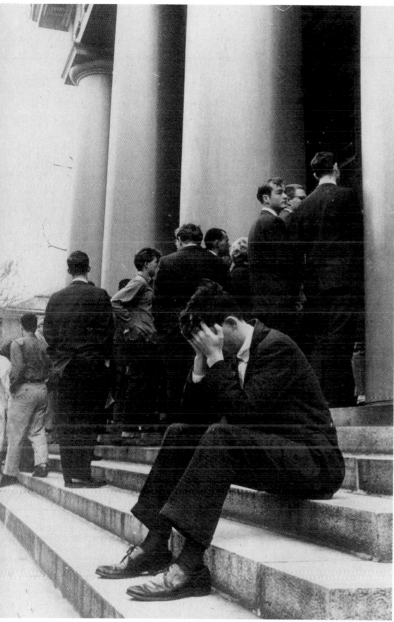

A Harvard student cried on the steps of Memorial Church in Harvard Yard during services for the late president, who graduated from Harvard in 1940.

There were a couple of students who worked for me as student photographers. They were active Democrats, and they knew I was an active Republican. Early in the afternoon, after Kennedy had died, one of them came up to me and said, "Well, you certainly ought to be happy today." I just stared at him. I couldn't believe that anybody would think that I would be happy about having the president shot. I was so angry that I wanted to hit him. I wanted to hit that guy more than I ever wanted to hit anybody in my life.

GIL MERRITT

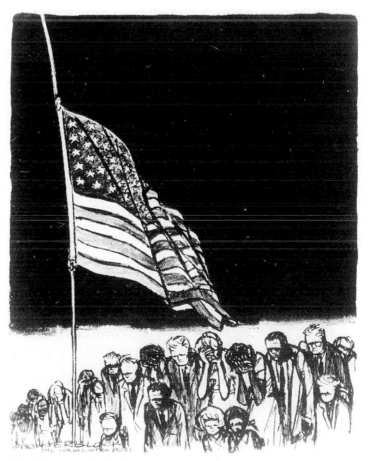

Editorial cartoonist Herblock expressed the nation's sadness and anger.

I was in shock. I called my father and said, "What will we do? What will happen?" It was not clear in my mind that anything would go on. I had the feeling that I think any child experiences when he or she contemplates his or her parents dying. There's that sense of "I can't live without my parents. I can't manage." And I felt that intense anxiety when John Kennedy died. A very real panic. I was thinking, "Oh my God, what will I do?"

LENI WILDFLOWER

I had just reported for active duty at the Philadelphia Naval Yard aboard a submarine that was in dry dock.

I was standing topside watch inside the guard shack outside the sub. After Kennedy was shot, someone ran in and said, "The president's been shot. Make sure the place is secure." They gave me a loaded .45. I looked at the gun and didn't know what to do with it.

The radio was on in the shack. Normally we listened to rock and roll. But after the president was shot, the station started playing Bach organ music. They just wanted something solemn. I think it must have been the only serious record they had. I remember hearing it over and over.

So this Bach organ music was booming out of the watch station, when I suddenly saw a senior enlisted man approaching. It was too late to turn the radio down.

He came up to me and asked me if I liked that kind of music. I didn't know what the right answer was. I wasn't sure I wanted to admit that I'd been a choirboy; I wasn't sure he'd think it was manly. But I finally said, "Yes sir, I do." As it turned out, he appreciated that sort of music.

MARCHANT WENTWORTH, Navy Recruit

In New York City and across the country, stores closed in remembrance of JFK.

The announcement came over the loudspeaker. I took the kids out for recess, because I didn't want to keep teaching. The kids were really too young to understand or to know how to react. I remember one little girl jumping rope, and in rhythm with the swinging rope she was saying, "Kennedy, Kennedy, Kennedy," over and over and over.

LOWELL KLOCK, Third-Grade Teacher, Niles, Mich.

My husband and I were eating lunch when our downstairs neighbor in the duplex called from the landing to ask if we'd heard that Kennedy was shot. We turned on the television. The end, of course, was near, and I remember vividly Walter Cronkite faltering. In numbness, the two of us watched, our arms around each other. I was 8½ months pregnant with our first child, wearing a maternity jumper and sweater, and I remember feeling as if the world had stopped. . . .

JUDITH A. HOOVER

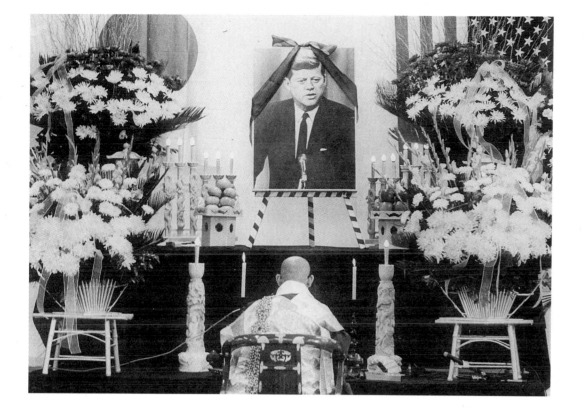

In Tokyo, the Japanese prayed for Kennedy.

My husband's birthday was November 22, and we left for a short vacation in the Western Ghats, where we stayed at a big Victorian-style resort hotel. We had a lovely birthday dinner, and the next morning when we got up and went into the dining room we sensed a vague uneasiness. The manager of the hotel was conferring with a small group of people and sort of looking at us. Finally, he came over and in great confusion sputtered: "I've come to offer you condolences." We must have looked blank, and he asked: "Can it be that you do not know?" Then he blurted out that John Kennedy had been shot and was dead. It was such a stunning statement that we simply couldn't believe it.

The Indians from the various tables around us started streaming over, some of them crying, giving us their sympathy and expressing their fear of what would happen without him. They told us how much they admired him, and how they felt as if a member of their own family had died, saying that they knew we must feel the same.

LUREE MILLER,
Foreign Service Wife, Bombay

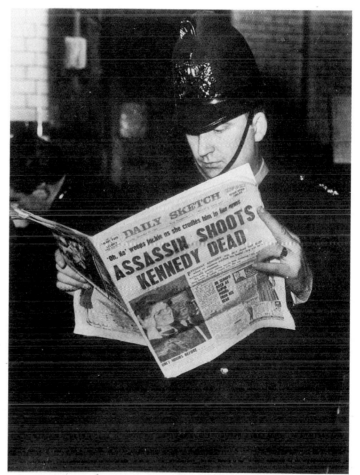

A London Bobby read about Kennedy's death in the London *Daily Sketch* on November 22.

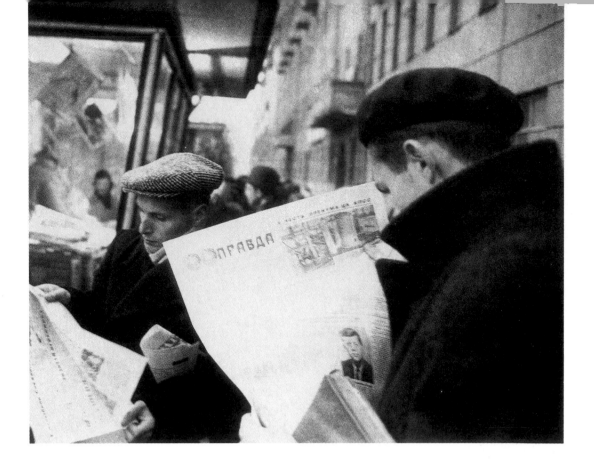

Russians read about Kennedy's assassination.

It was absolutely fantastic, the impact that this assassination had in the Soviet Union, the loss of Kennedy.

I had a long talk in Moscow with Ilya Ehrenburg, the writer, who was also deeply upset about the assassination in a very emotional way. He said to me—I remember it very clearly—he said to me, "Explain to me how a thing like this happens in a civilized country?"

HENRY BRANDON, Washington Correspondent,
London Sunday Times

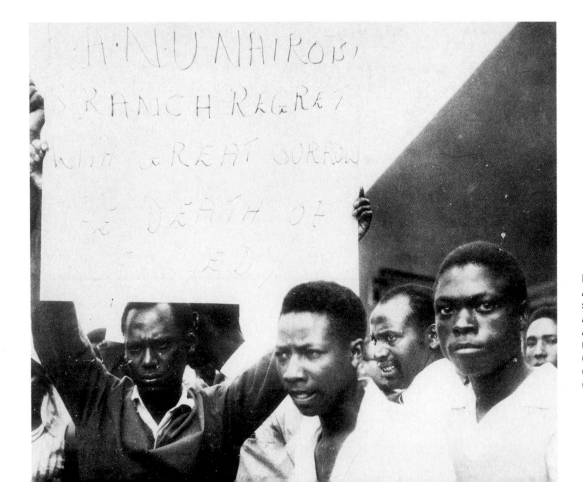

In Africa, members of the Kenya African National Union displayed signs of sympathy outside the American Consulate General. About 200 members of KANU marched to the Consul General's office to express their condolences over the president's death.

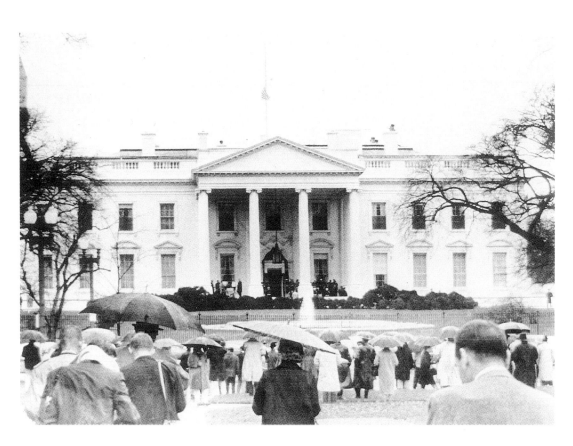

Mourners braved the rain outside the White House to pay tribute to President Kennedy. Inside the White House the president's body lay in state.

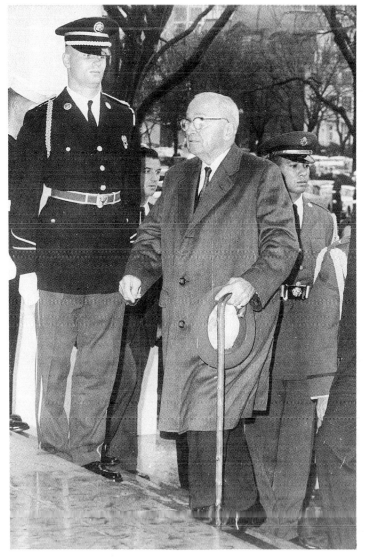

Paying their final respects at the White House were, among many others, former presidents Harry Truman (right) and Dwight Eisenhower (opposite page bottom), and Soviet ambassador Anatoly Dobrynin (opposite page top).

*W*itnessing the assassination on television probably had mixed impacts. Denial and disbelief are common reactions in the case of a sudden, unanticipated death. But the fact that the assassination was televised probably helped people accept the reality and finality of it. However, it was also shocking and traumatic to see this horror replayed again and again. It was hard to defend ourselves psychologically against that. Remember, this is before we became more calloused as a society, used to seeing that kind of violence on TV—this was before we began to see the killing in Vietnam. So it probably shook us more deeply. We couldn't shut it out.

THERESE A. RANDO,
Psychologist

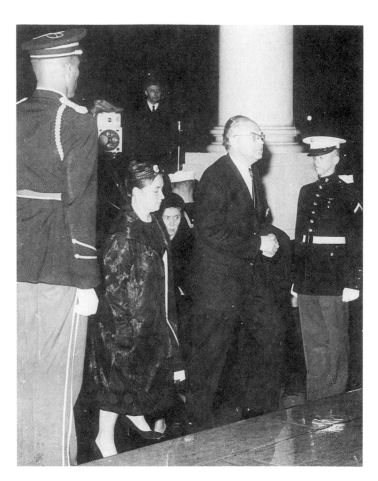

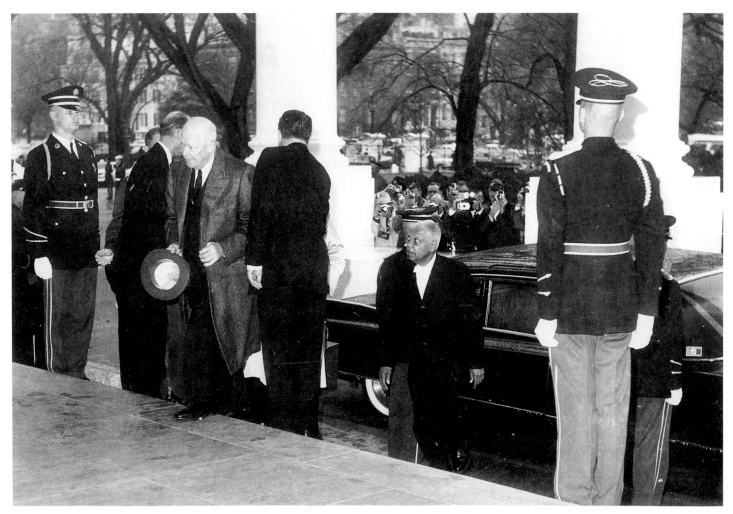

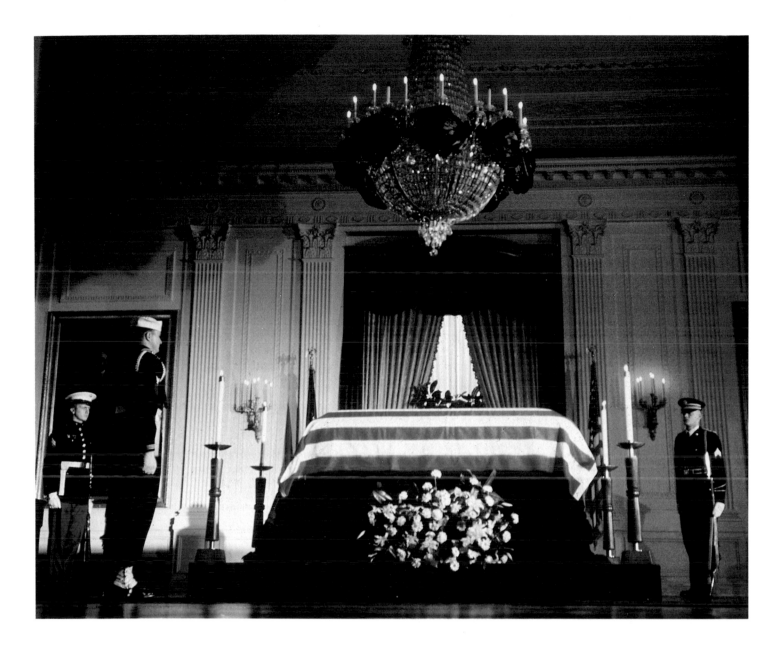

Mrs. Kennedy . . . radioed ahead from the plane to tell us exactly what she wanted. Of course, that afternoon was spent in finding the details, looking up the details of the Lincoln funeral so that we could have things as near as possible the way they were at the time Lincoln was assassinated. . . .

It was about 4:20 Saturday morning when Mrs. Kennedy came [back to the White House] with the president's body, and at 4:10 we had finished putting up the last pieces of crepe. . . .

I wondered what I would say to Mrs. Kennedy when I saw her. And as she came around the corner from the hall to the elevator, our eyes met and there was a rapport there just for an instant. She was crying very hard at the moment, but there was that rapport, and I knew no words were necessary.

NELSON PIERCE

John Fitzgerald Kennedy's body rested in the East Room of the White House as the nation mourned his loss. In the honor guard were four enlisted men of the Army, Navy, Marines, and Air Force.

I remember walking over to the president's doorway . . . and I looked in the [Oval] Office and I don't think I shall ever forget what I saw there at that moment. . . . The president's office had been substantially denuded of furniture—there was some redecorating being done—arranged as a surprise by Mrs. Kennedy. New draperies had been hung; the desk still remained in the office, but many of the other pieces of furniture had been moved into [his secretary] Evelyn Lincoln's office.

The memorabilia of which the president was so fond, which were such a common sight on his desk, had been moved, and the only activity in that office at that moment—probably within an hour of the president's death—was the quiet tapping of a carpet layer's hammer as he was laying a new crimson carpet in the president's Oval Office. . . .

EDWARD McDERMOTT, Director,
Office of Emergency Planning

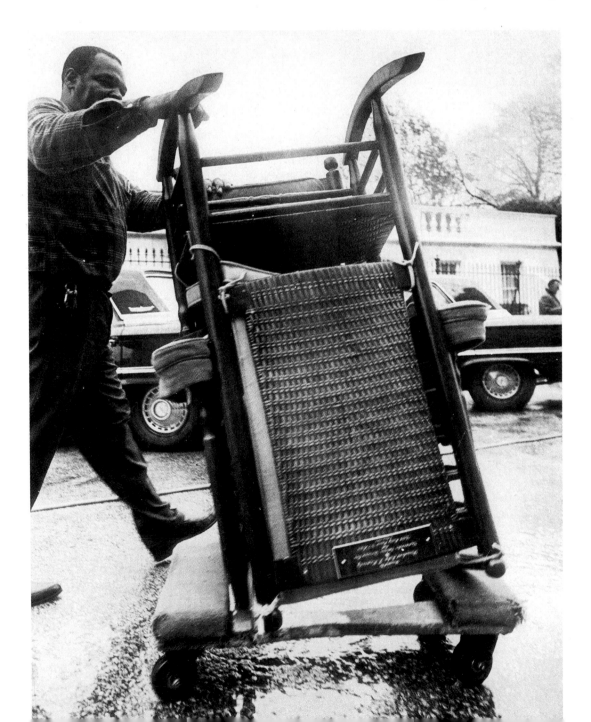

The late president's famous rocking chair being removed from the White House.

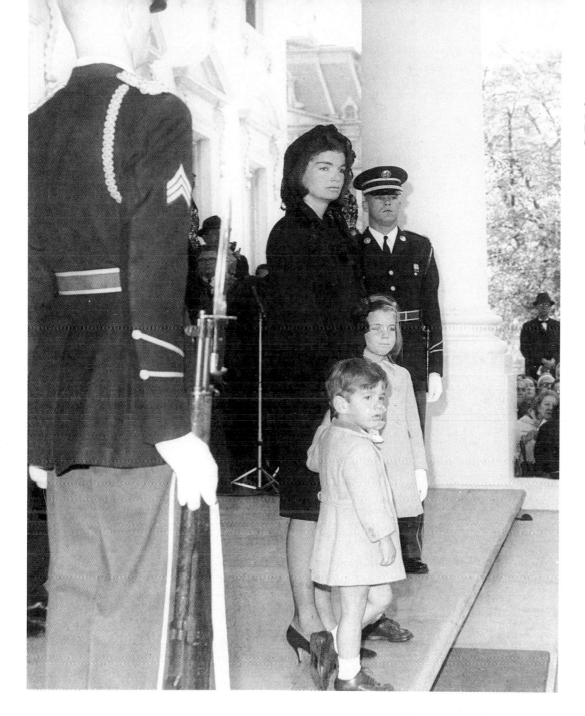

Jacqueline Kennedy and her children waited at the White House for the start of the procession to the Capitol.

I was in the joint service drum corps and marched in the cortege from the White House up Pennsylvania Avenue to the Capitol, where the body was brought to lie in state.

From the White House to the Capitol, the muffled drums were the only musical accompaniment. To create the effect of the muffled drum, we loosened the snare and cut up cymbal pads and positioned them between the snare and the head so that the snares could not respond. The effect is to enhance the solemnness of the occasion; it's a very dark sound.

Thousands and thousands lined the route, like they were attending a festive occasion. You know, a parade is normally a happy occasion. But you'd look up and all you'd see were handkerchiefs. I could actually hear people crying above the sound of the drums. There was nothing but the muffled drums and the tears.

CHARLES C. WELKER, Jr., Percussionist, U.S. Army Band

To the Capitol.

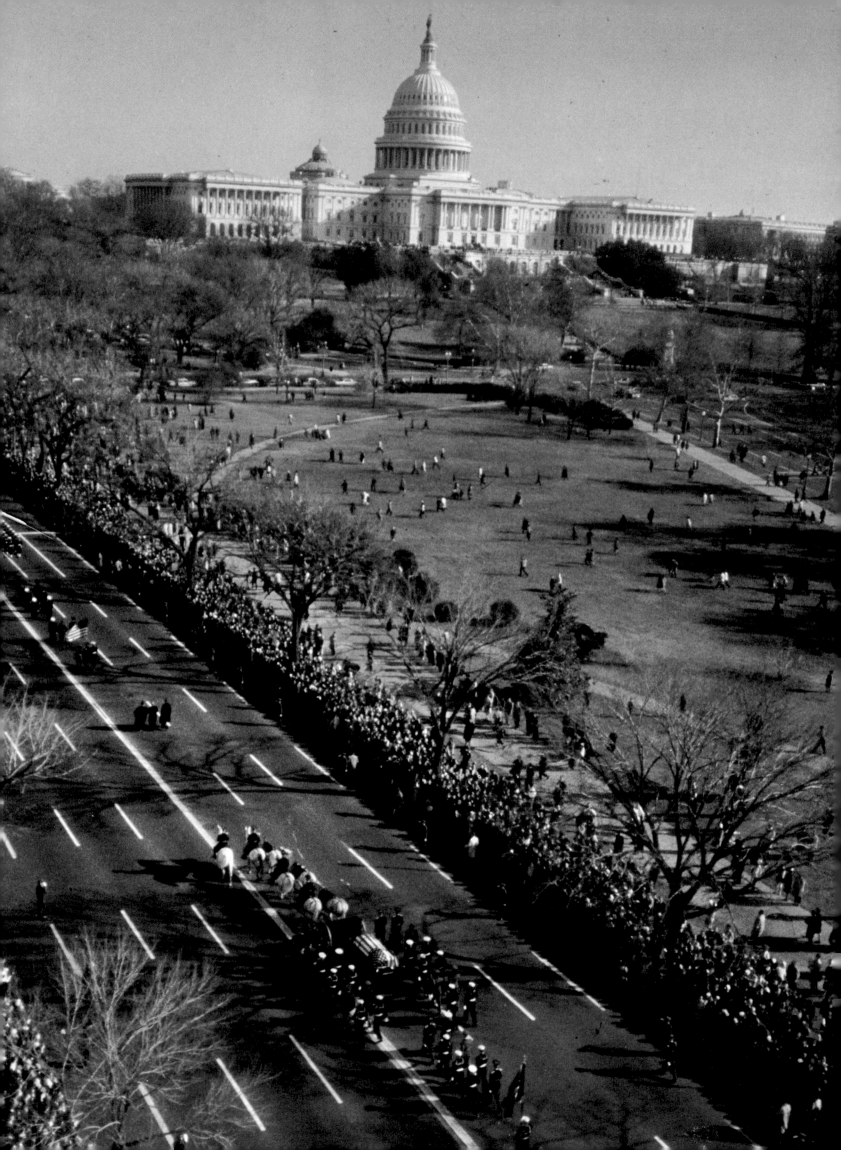

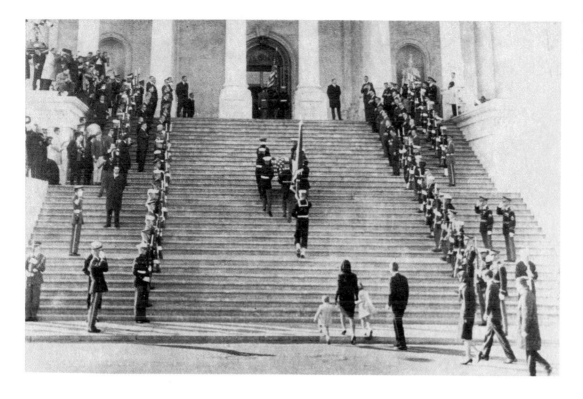

The Kennedy family followed the casket into the Capitol, where the president lay in state.

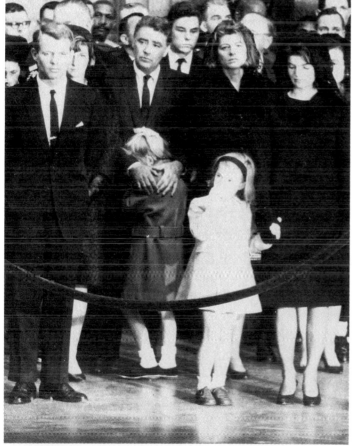

Senator Mike Mansfield, Chief Justice Earl Warren and House Speaker John McCormack gave eulogies at the Capitol Rotunda, while the late president's family listened in sorrow. "He had the bravery and a sense of personal duty," McCormack said, "which made him willing to face up to the great task of being president in these trying times. He had the warmth and the sense of humanity which made the burden of the task bearable for himself and his associates and which made all kinds of diverse peoples and races eager to be associated with him in his task."

I think you can make a strong case for the fact that as a nation we went through a grieving process quite similar to what an individual experiences when someone dies. I think it surprised people, because they did not believe the assassination would affect them at that level, but it did.

There were many reactions: fear and anxiety about what was going to happen; guilt and shame that we as a nation somehow allowed this to happen; and anger that we were robbed of a person we valued. In fact, it may be possible to look at some of the disturbances later in the sixties as one expression of society's anger. . . .

THERESE A. RANDO

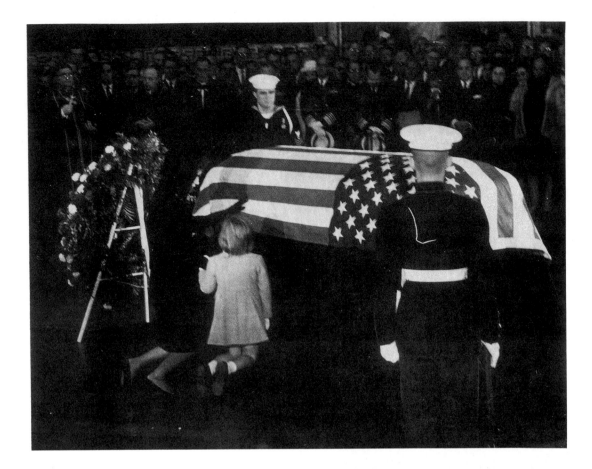

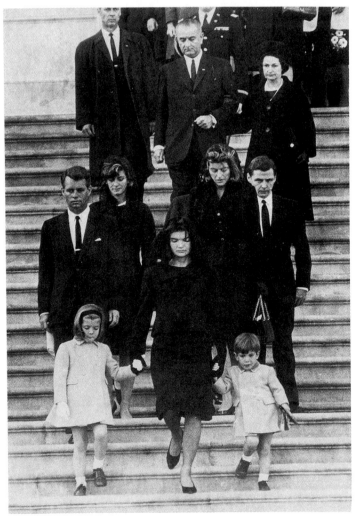

My birthday is November 24. I turned 12 that day, and was feeling upset and forgotten. I was wondering: "Is anybody going to remember my birthday?" I have memories of the TV flickering all day long, and grown-ups coming in and out of the house crying. It was as if somebody in the family had died. My parents did remember my birthday, and I was given some presents, but their heart wasn't in it. It was a halfhearted sort of gesture, because there was real mourning going on.

KATHY KELLY,
Elementary School Student, Buffalo, N.Y.

Jacqueline Kennedy held the hands of her children Caroline and John Junior, after ceremonies in the Capitol. Behind her were (left to right) Robert Kennedy, his sisters Mrs. Jean Smith and Mrs. Pat Lawford, and brother-in-law Steven Smith. President Lyndon Johnson and Mrs. Johnson followed.

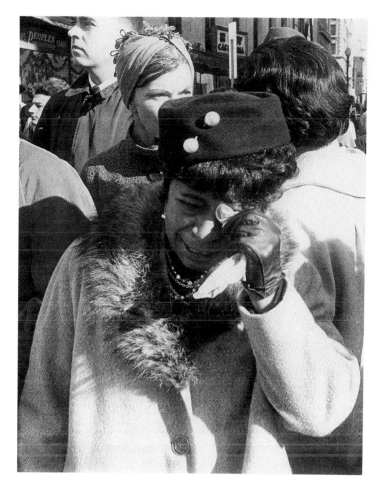

The family had [asked] me [as] one of the press to attend the funeral. . . . I was just almost amazed at the reaction of Negroes across the country at his death. It was just something that was unbelievable for me to see, when I went down to the Capitol, to see the people in line, Negroes coming in from distant places in America just to walk by the body. You could then see what the legacy of the Kennedys was on the Negro, how he had really reached them. . . . I think [Kennedy] . . . gave them a shot in the arm. And it wasn't through programs necessarily, but it was through a sense of new life, a hope, and he did it not only [for] our middle class, but he did it [for] people in the ghettos, slums.

SIMEON S. BOOKER, Journalist

Ted Kennedy said, "Let's go up." He meant up to the Capitol, where the president's body was lying on the Lincoln catafalque in the Rotunda. No other words were said.

As the car neared Capitol Hill, we began to see the enormous line of people waiting in the cold and the dark to pay their respects. The car dropped us off at the new East Front, and we went up to the Rotunda in an elevator. When the guards saw who it was, they quickly let him through the line; and when the people at the catafalque saw who it was, they stood aside. The slow, shuffling line halted for a few minutes, while Ted went right up to the casket, kneeled and prayed. Then we left. The entire incident, in the night light, the utter silence, and the atmosphere at the time, was eerie.

MILTON GWIRTZMAN

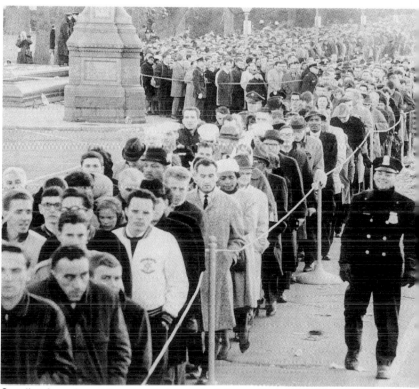

Standing four abreast in a line that stretched three miles, grieving citizens waited outside the Capitol to pay last respects to President Kennedy.

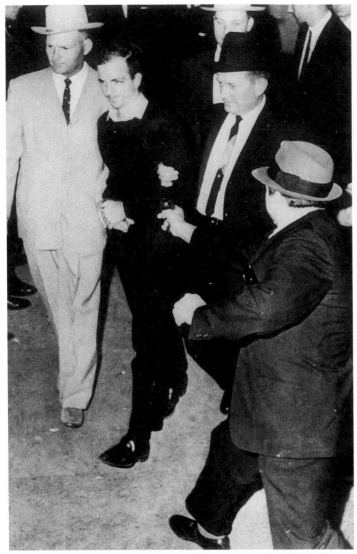

Dallas, November 24, 11:20 A.M.: The moment before Jack Ruby shot Lee Harvey Oswald in the stomach at the Dallas city jail. Millions of Americans were watching as Oswald was being transferred to the county jail. Ruby felled Oswald with a single shot from a .38 caliber pistol. Oswald was rushed to Parkland Hospital, where he died at 1:07 P.M. without regaining consciousness.

*O*n Sunday morning I was watching television. Eve [my wife] was upstairs. Suddenly, I yelled, "Jesus Christ, Eve, you won't believe this! Some son of a bitch just shot Oswald. Right on television."

The world was falling apart. It was mad.

ROGER WILKINS

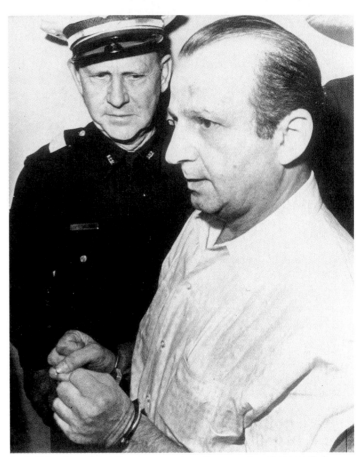

Jack Ruby, Oswald's killer, was arraigned on murder charges. Ruby was reported to be a great admirer of President Kennedy. Ruby's lawyer pleaded "temporary insanity" on behalf of his client.

*W*hen I saw Jack Ruby shoot Oswald I figured it had to be some kind of put-up job. I thought maybe the Mafia or organized crime was behind it. To see this gangster shoot Oswald right in front of the police made me think that those forces might be at work. Even though I don't have a conspiratorial mind-set, I didn't think it was a coincidence that this guy walked up and wiped Oswald out.

GIL MERRITT

*T*his [the shooting of Oswald], I must say, struck me in some ways as the most unforgivable thing of all. Perhaps it is impossible to prevent a madman from getting a rifle and striking down the president, but surely peace officers should be able to protect a prisoner in their own custody.

JOHN KENNETH GALBRAITH,
Ambassador to India

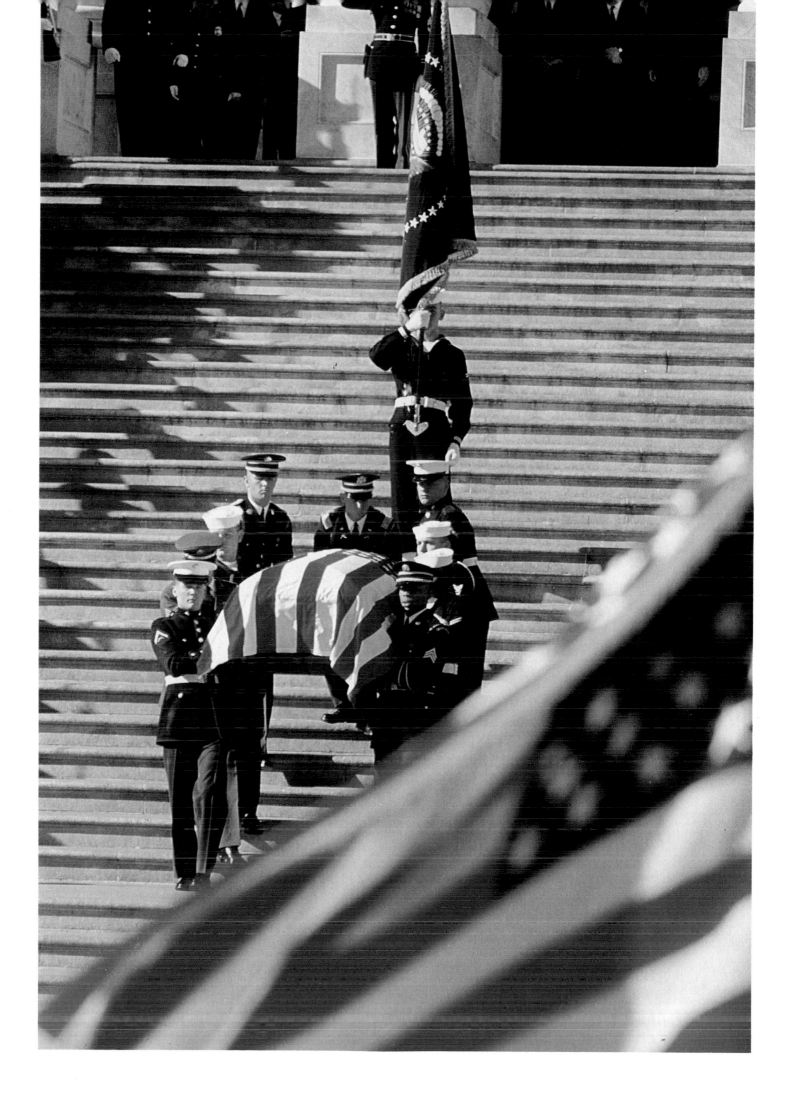

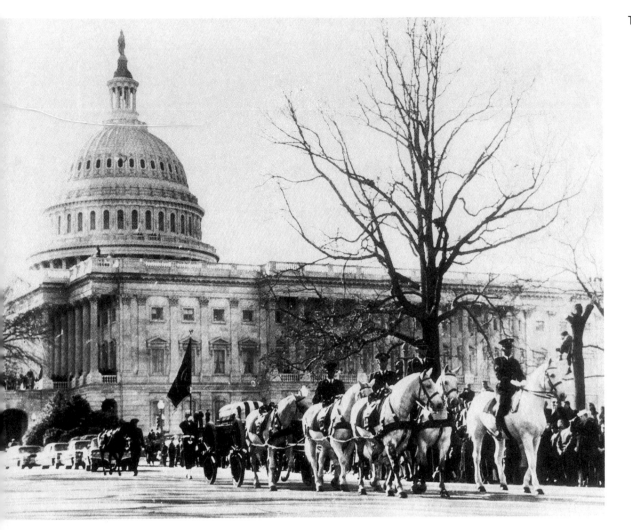

It was clear and cold that day. Eve and I went up to the corner of Constitution and 4th to see the cortege go by. The sky was sparkling blue. The riderless horse with the boots reversed in the stirrups went by. And then there was the coffin with a flag that seemed to have redder reds and whiter whites than I had ever seen.

ROGER WILKINS

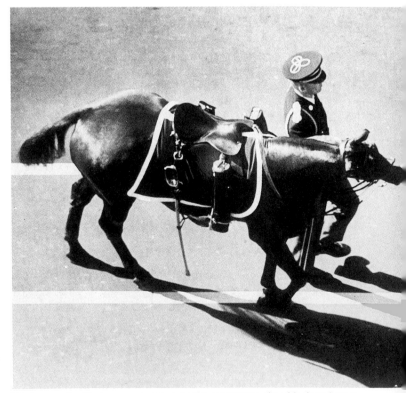

His hooves beating a nervous tap on the pavement, the riderless horse danced skittishly behind the casket along the procession route. Boots were reversed in the stirrups and a silver sword hung sheathed from the saddle, in an ancient tribute to a fallen leader.

LEFT: A military honor guard carried Kennedy's casket down the Capitol steps to begin the final procession on November 25.

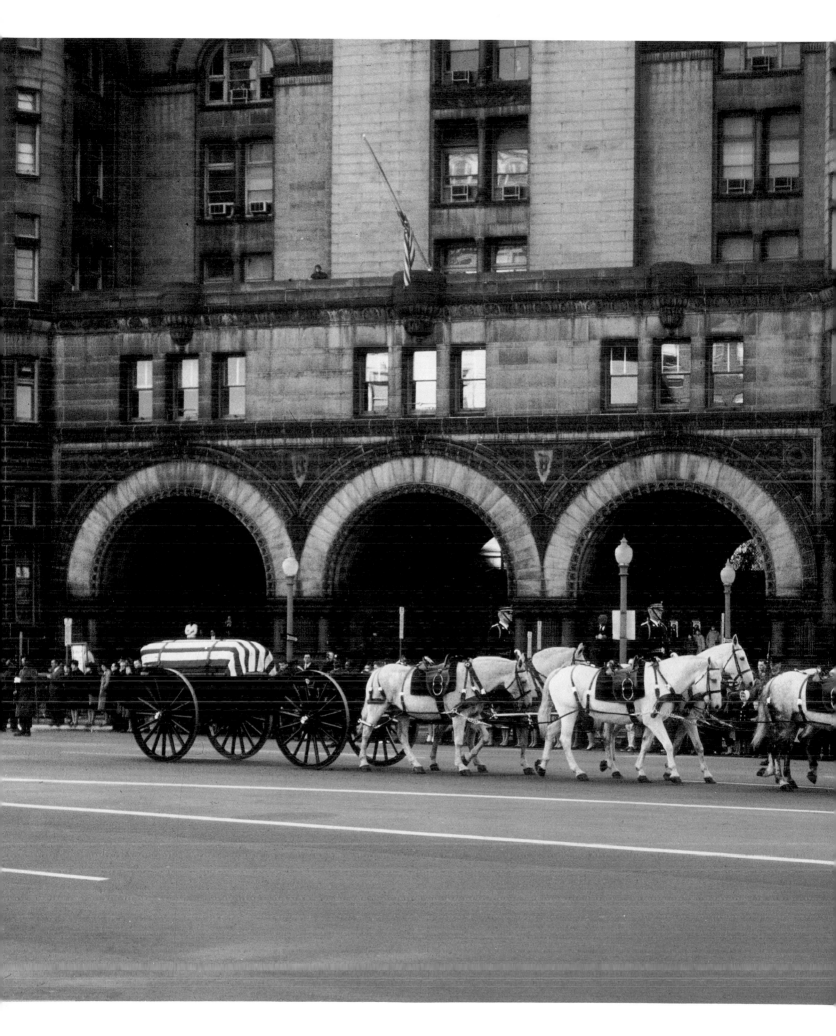

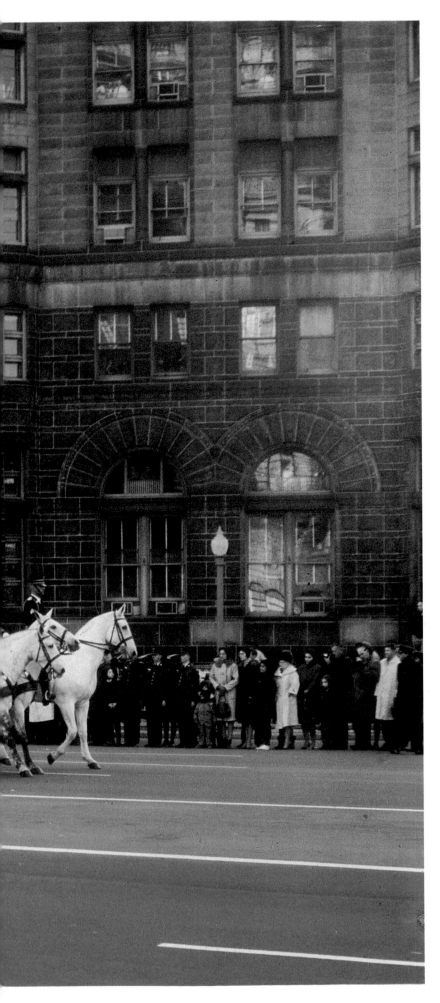

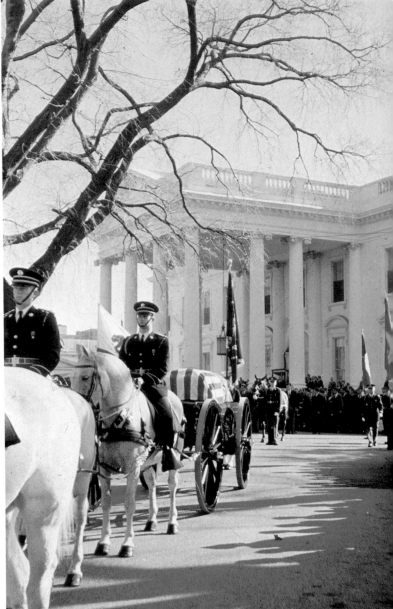

I didn't really realize what had happened until I saw the riderless horse in the televised funeral procession. It made me want to cry. But I couldn't cry in the middle of the barracks. I borrowed a friend's guitar and played it instead.

MARCHANT WENTWORTH

The caisson bearing the President's body traveled along Pennsylvania Avenue past the White House.

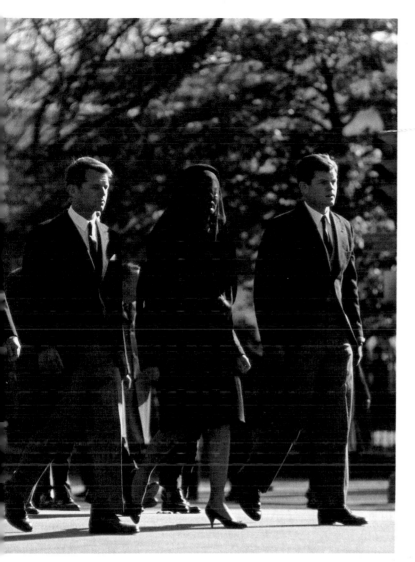

Almost immediately after the assassination, the decision was made to drop commercials and drop all regular programming. There was nothing on the air on the three network stations but the assassination coverage. The assassination happened on a Friday, so it left open a weekend for the coverage. And because a lot of other activities were canceled, essentially everyone was glued to the tube. It was the largest audience in the history of the medium; I don't know if it's ever been topped.

It was an incredible story. You had not only the assassination of this Camelot figure, but then you had the assassination of the assassin on live TV. You couldn't turn away. What the hell was going to happen next?

All those images we still remember—the coffin coming off the plane at night in those eerie lights, John Jr. saluting the coffin, de Gaulle walking down Pennsylvania Avenue—we saw them all live on TV. TV made that event indelible in the lives of anybody of any age. . . .

DON WEST

Jacqueline Kennedy, Robert Kennedy, and Edward Kennedy left the White House to walk behind the caisson bearing the coffin of the president.

Foreign dignitaries left the White House as the funeral procession continued to St. Matthew's Cathedral. Pictured here in the front row from left to right are: West German president Heinrich Luebke, French president Charles de Gaulle, Queen Frederika of Greece, King Baudouin of Belgium, Emperor Haile Selassie of Ethiopia, Philippine President Diosdado Macapagal, and German Chancellor Ludwig Erhard.

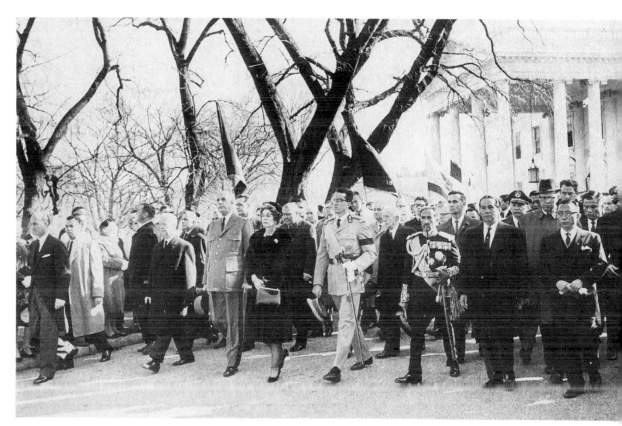

I remember being in the Peace Corps building in downtown Washington and standing on the upstairs floor and watching the funeral procession. I have a very vivid memory of that march—the riderless horse with the boots turned backwards, seeing de Gaulle, hearing the muffled drums. It was utterly silent except for the people walking and the muffled drums.

It affected me very strongly. I remember feeling that he was my leader, so I was really caught up in the whole thing. And I think it was later that I began to reflect on how a single individual gets elected to the presidency and establishes an organization like the Peace Corps that directly and indirectly has such a profound impact on individuals' lives.

ROGER LANDRUM

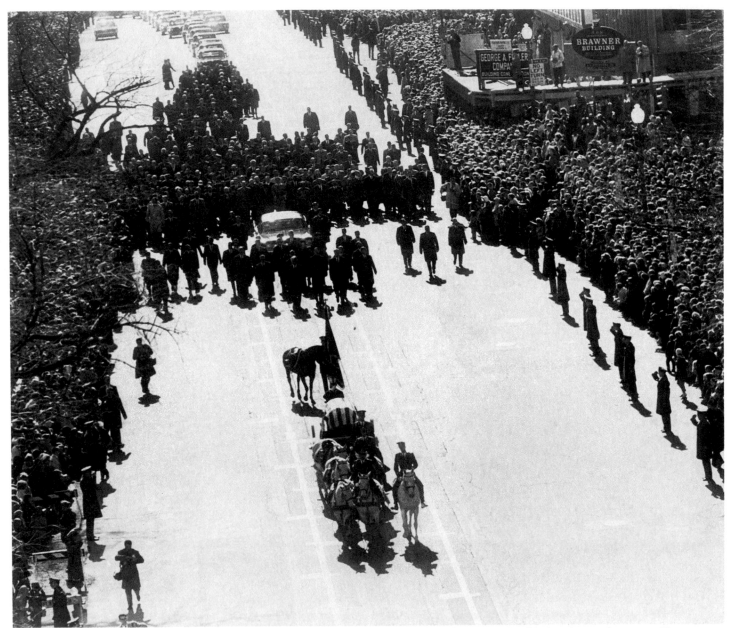

The funeral procession along Connecticut Avenue en route to the church. Following the caisson was the riderless horse; then came Mrs. Kennedy and other family members followed by leaders from around the world.

M onday morning, November 25, Dave [Powers] and Ken O'Donnell and I were in the upstairs living room of the White House, waiting to join the funeral cortege, which was then on its way from Capitol Hill. We were watching the cortege, and little John-John Kennedy came into the room and, suddenly, we saw him saluting the televised picture of the cortege.

One of the butlers came in and asked us if he could get us anything.

"Let's have a bottle of champagne," Dave said.

The butler brought the champagne and glasses, and we toasted Jack Kennedy.

"To the president."

"To the president."

"Good-by, Jack, good-by."

LAWRENCE O'BRIEN

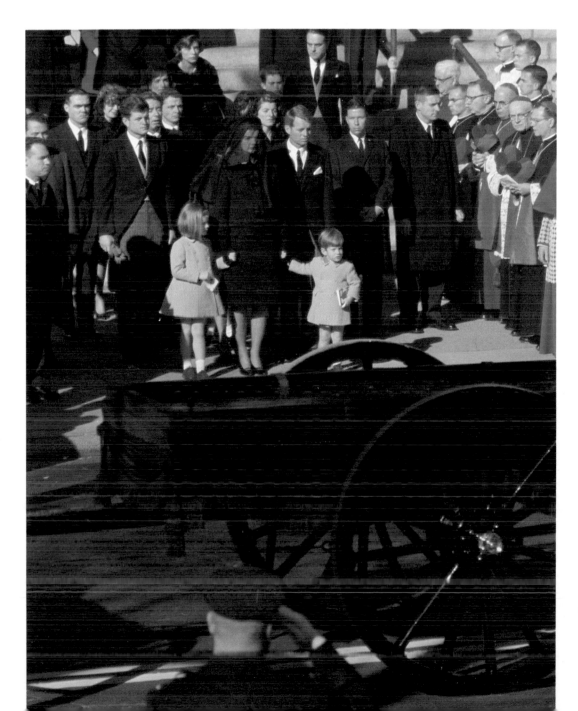

The casket leaving St. Matthew's.

John F. Kennedy, Jr. saluted his father.

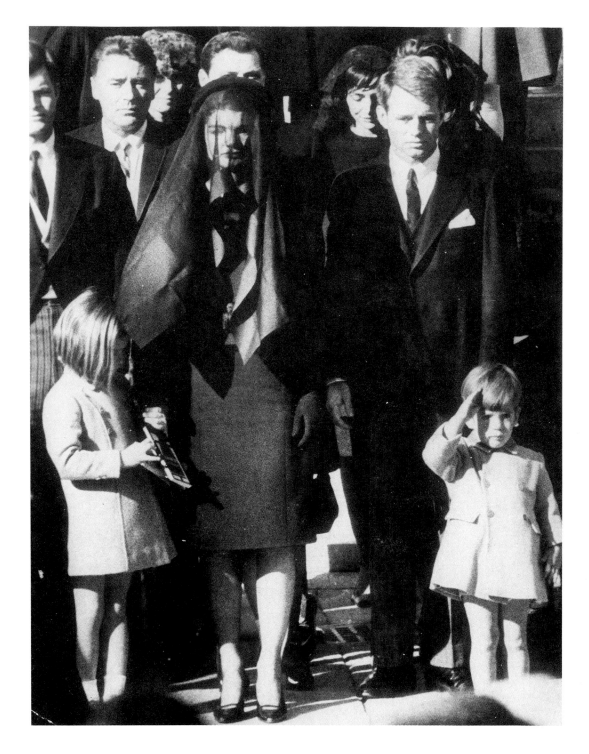

We stood outside during the mass. Then when the doors opened, the casket was brought back out and put on the caisson. And this is when little John came up and saluted the casket. It was gut-wrenching. It's not just that Kennedy was president of the United States, but you're talking about a very vibrant young man, his life snuffed out by an idiot, rendering these kids fatherless.

Throughout the whole thing, the crowd was very quiet, still stunned.

CHARLES C. WELKER, JR.

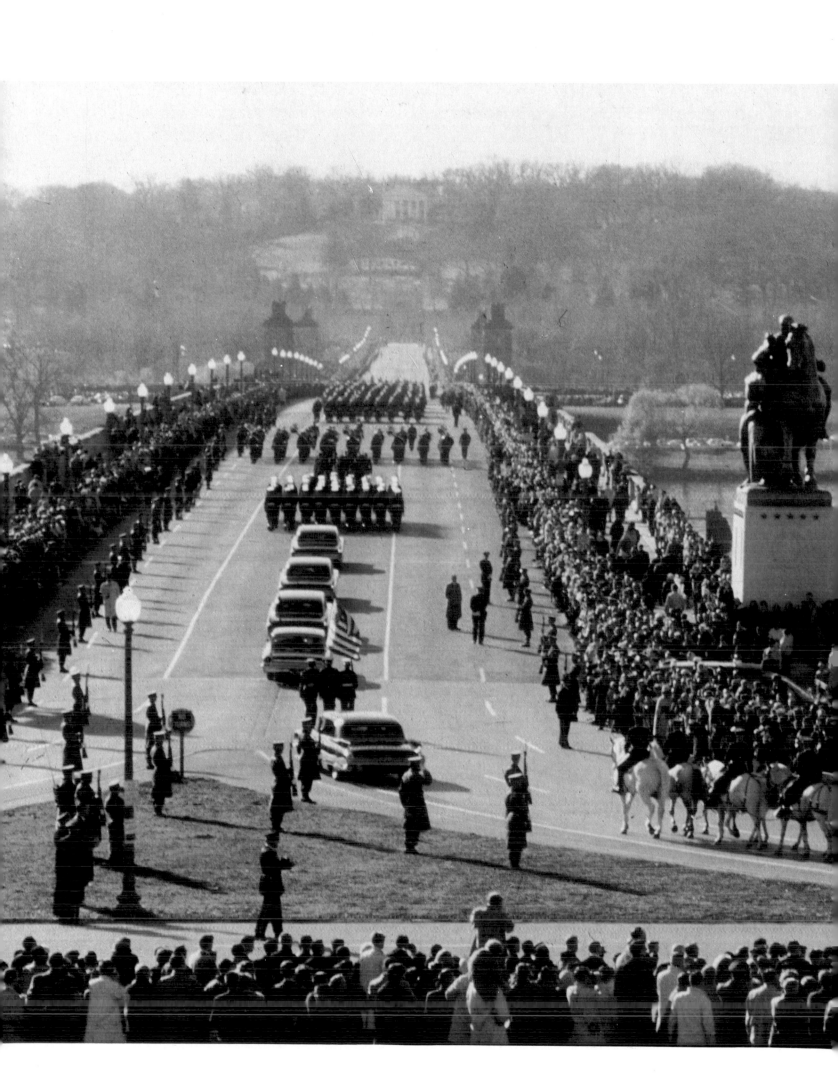

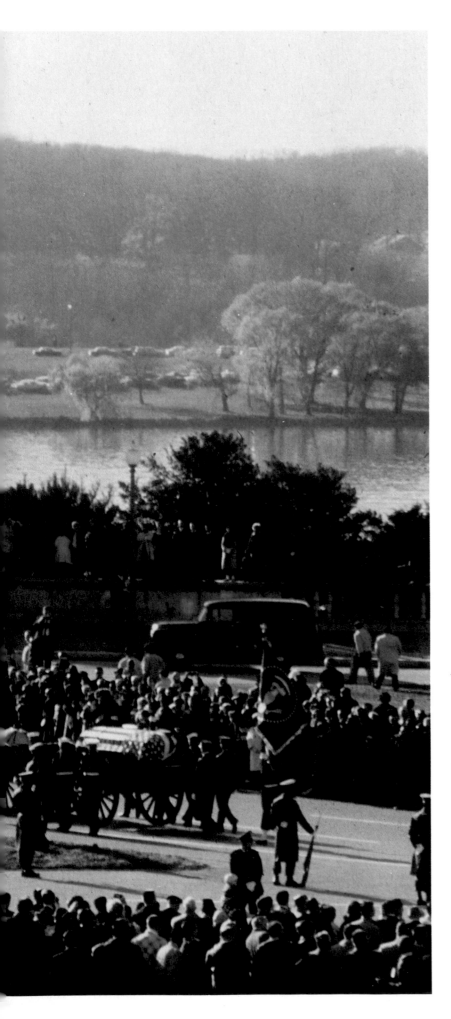

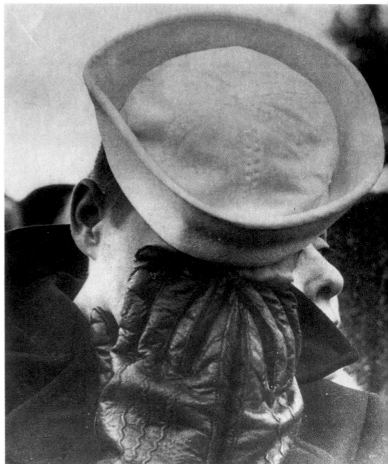

A sailor wept as the caisson bearing Kennedy's body passed him en route to Arlington Cemetery.

I remember the long, sad procession on Monday with the horse-drawn caisson bearing the flag-covered coffin, the black riderless horse, Mrs. Kennedy, followed by family, President Johnson, and dignitaries from the U.S. and all over the world. All marching on foot to the cadence of all-pervading drumbeats to the Cathedral—the service—the lighting of the flame at Arlington. Some details go, but many are left, especially that mournful and solemn drumbeat.

JOAN ROHAN, Librarian, Racine, Wis.

The horse-drawn caisson entered the last part of its journey as it crossed Arlington Memorial Bridge.

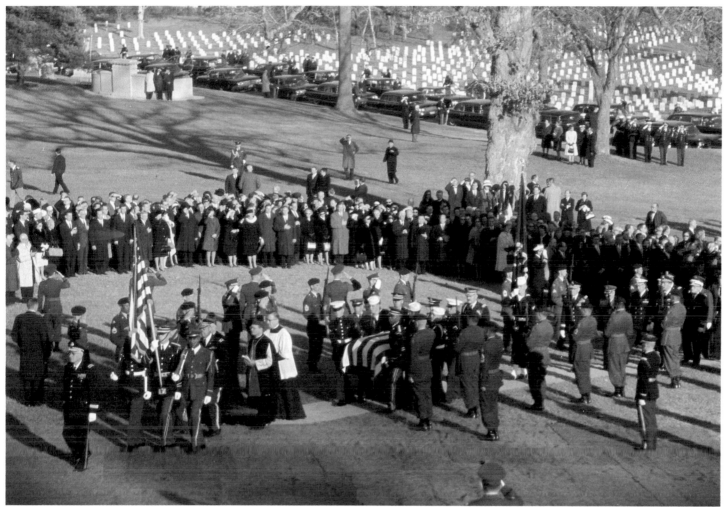

Military pallbearers lifted the late president's coffin from the caisson at the graveside.

I was up the hill on the mound, west from where the Kennedy flame is now. I could see Jacqueline Kennedy—the veil—and the brothers. I remember the flyover and the navy hymn. Wasn't there a Scottish group there with bagpipes? Then the firing squad took their position and fired three volleys. Then I stepped forward.

I pointed the bell toward Mrs. Kennedy. Then you take your breath and go at it. Taps runs about 47 seconds. There was a little flaw in the fourth note. I knew I had to put that behind me and go on. I tried not to think about anything, just the beauty of this sound.

Taps is a sorrowful thing. I'm a Christian, and I believe in the bible. When it says, "the trumpet shall sound, and the dead shall be raised," I can think of taps as being the promise of God's resurrection of the body—the hope of life after death. So I always think of that when I play taps.

KEITH CLARK, Principal Coronet, U.S. Army Band

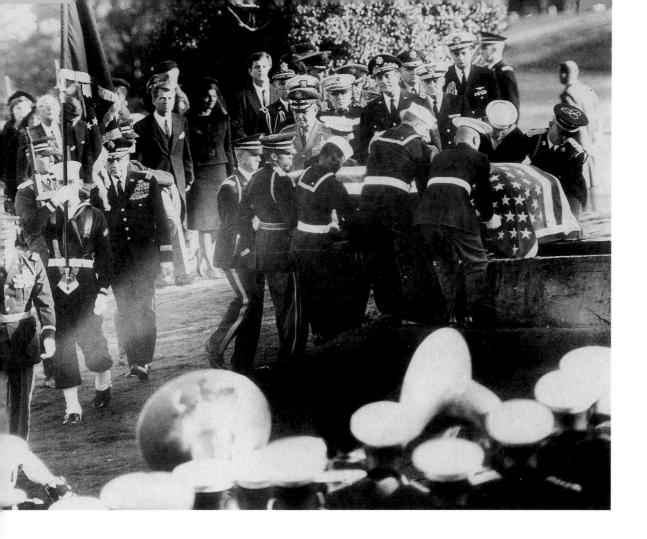

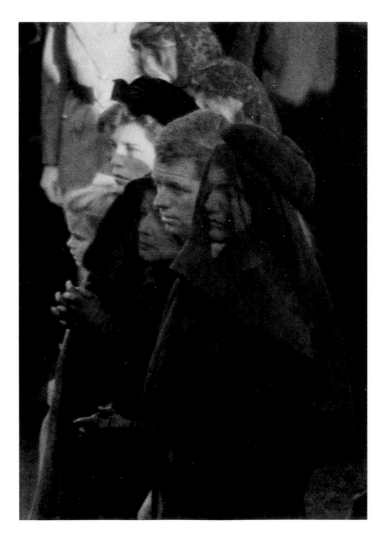

Majestic in her sorrow, Jacqueline Kennedy listened to the eulogies for her husband at Arlington Cemetery. With her were Rose and Robert Kennedy.

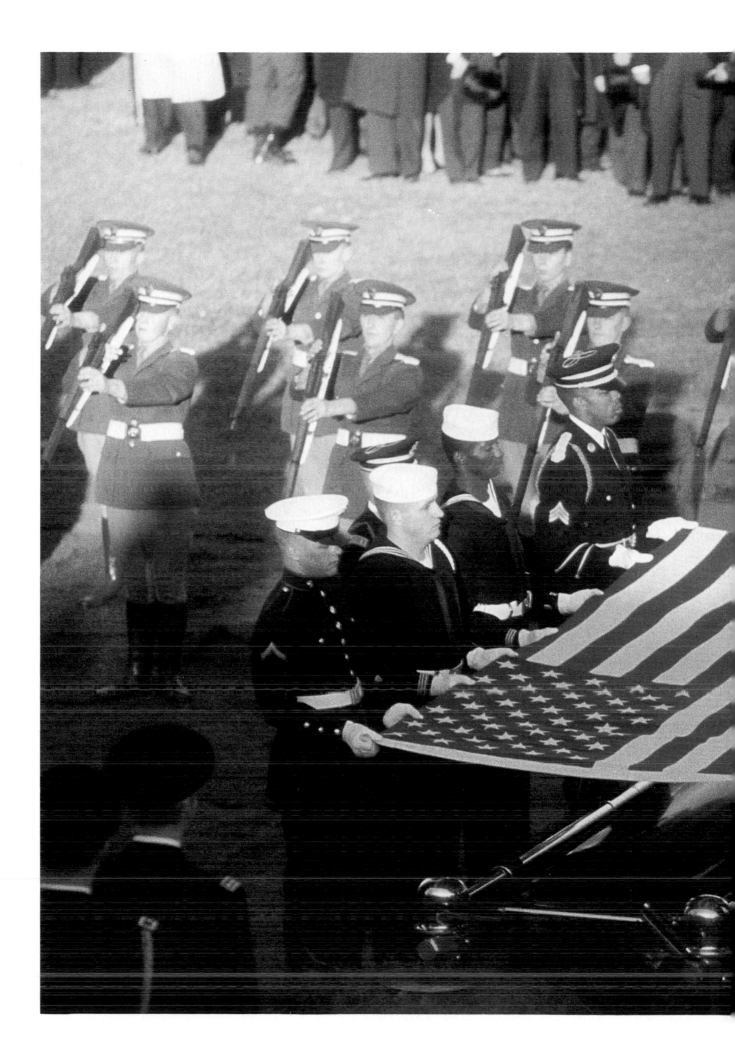

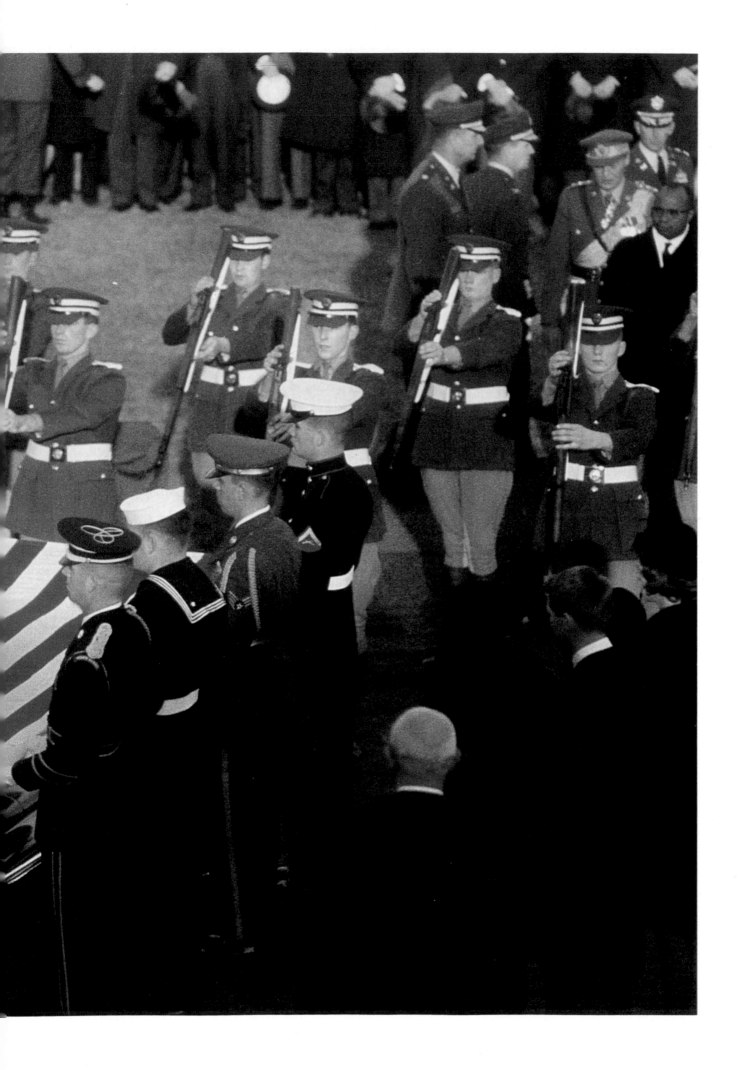

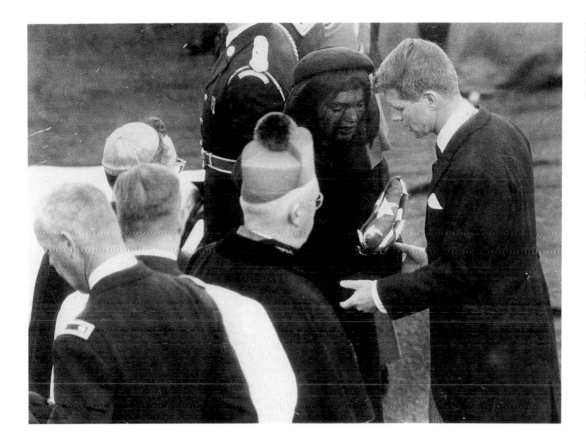

Turning from the graveside, Jacqueline Kennedy cradled the flag that draped her late husband's coffin. Cardinal Cushing and Robert Kennedy offered comfort.

Surrounded by branches of evergreen decorated with a rosary, the Eternal Flame, lit by Jacqueline Kennedy at the end of the funeral ceremony, burned in memory of the president.

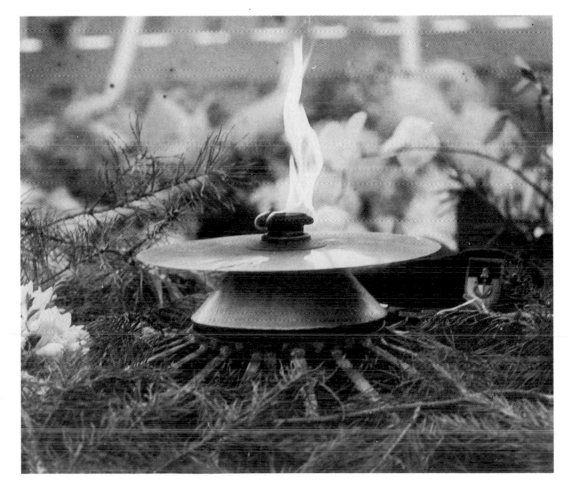

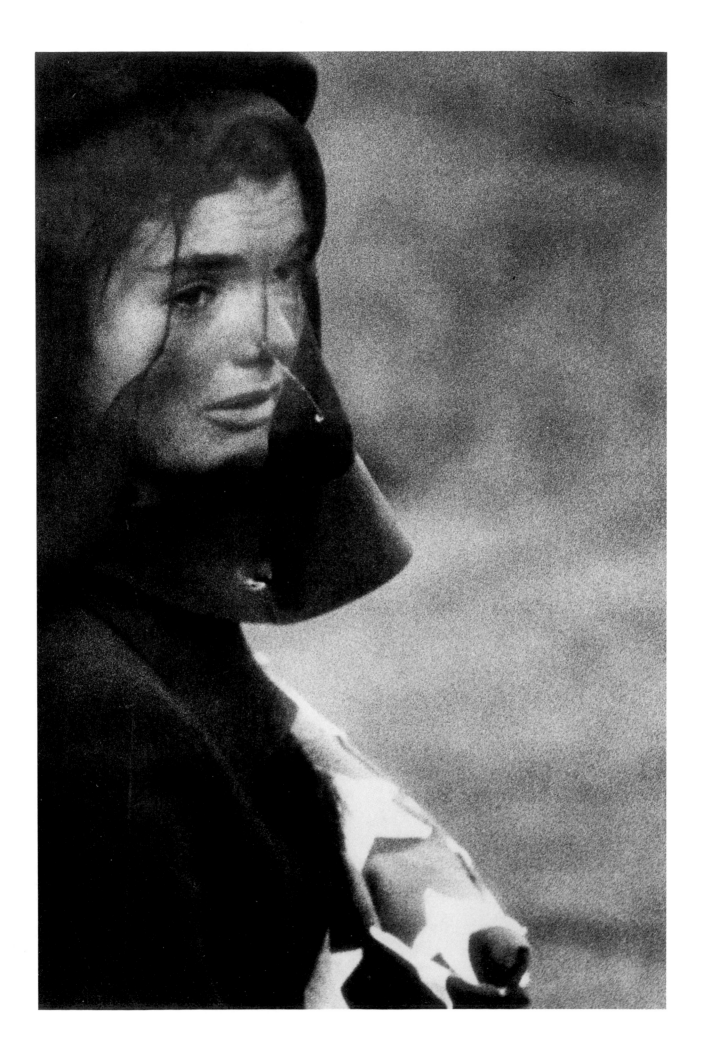

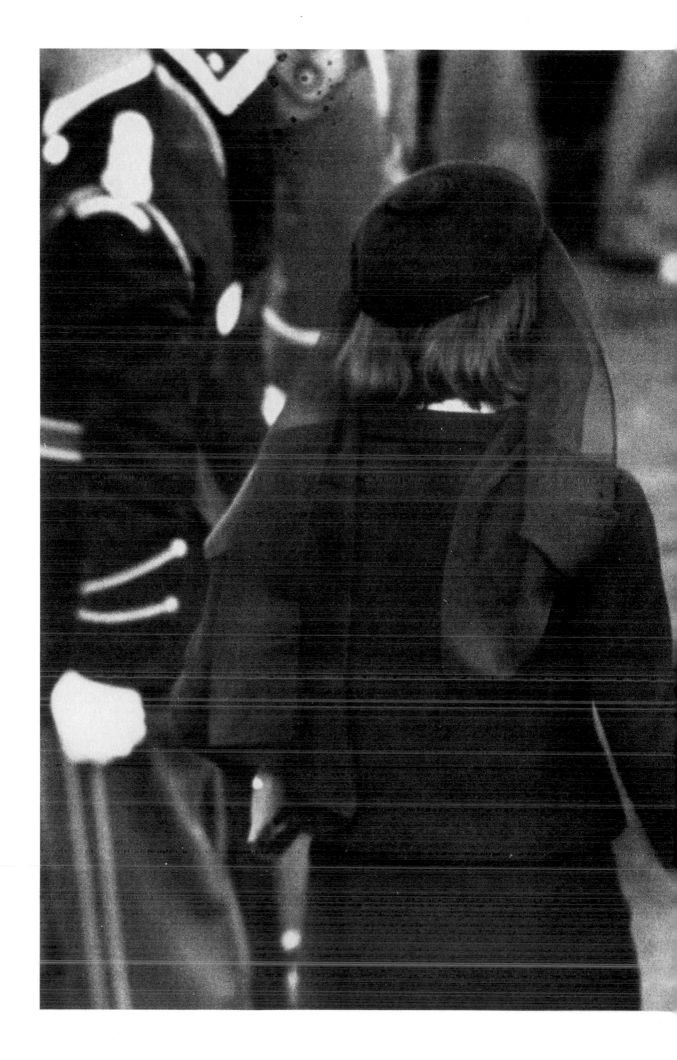

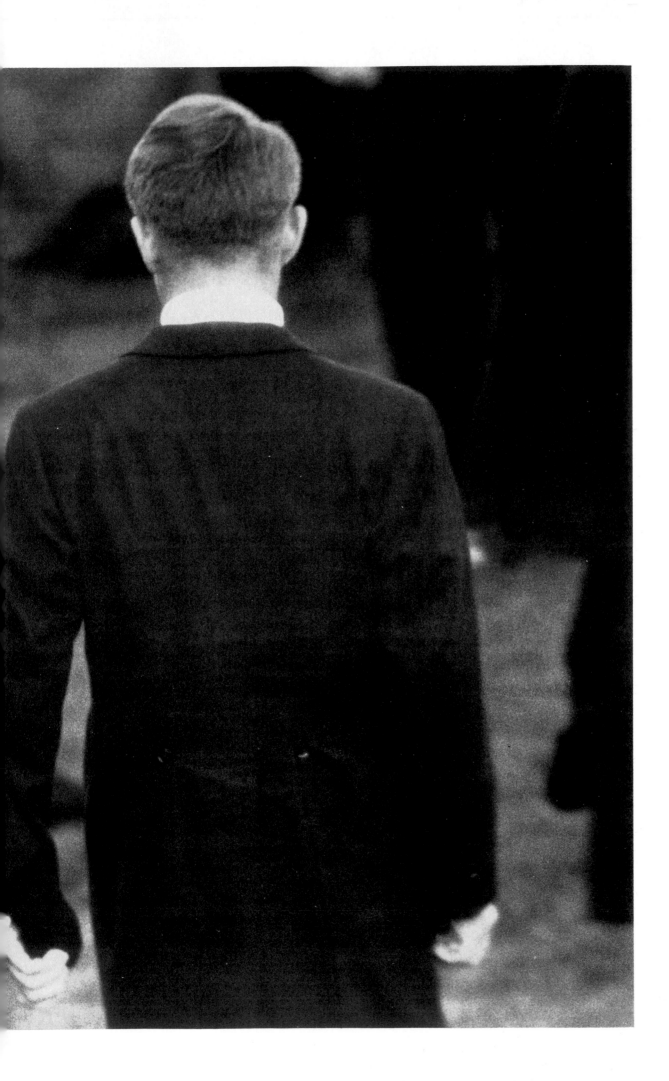

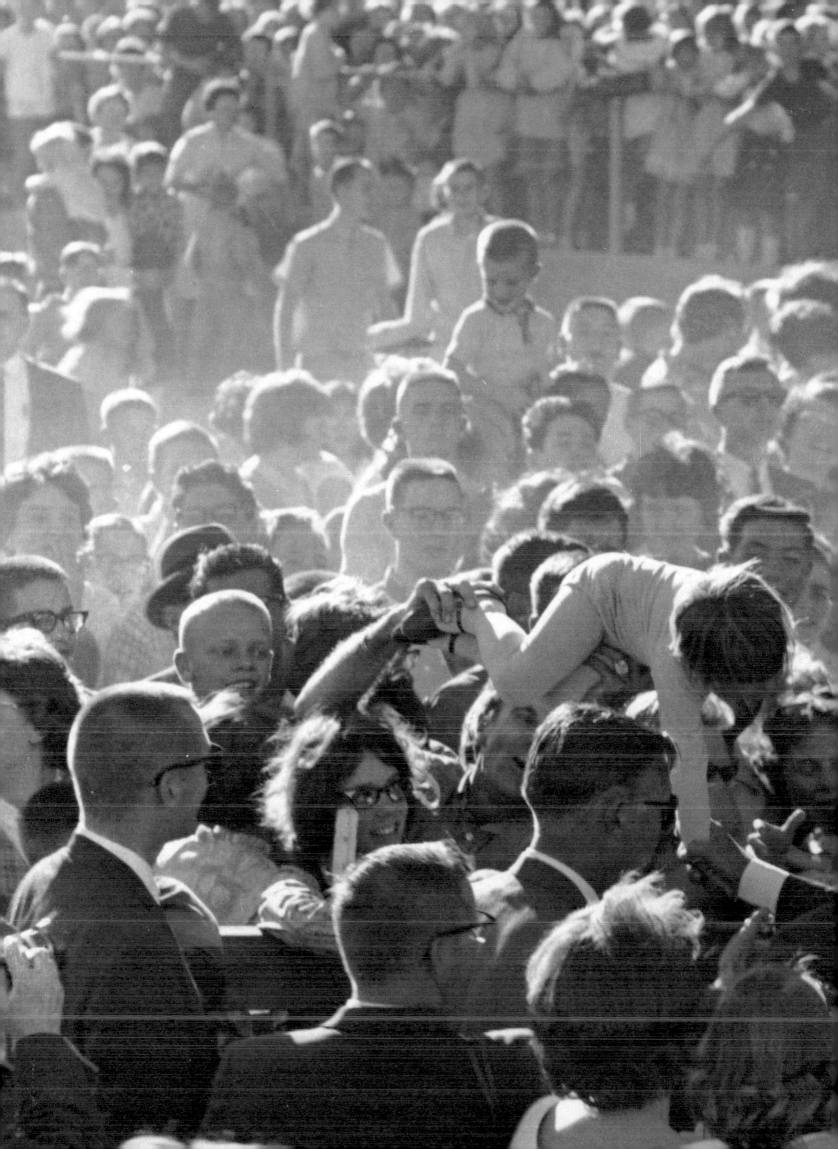

AFTERWORD

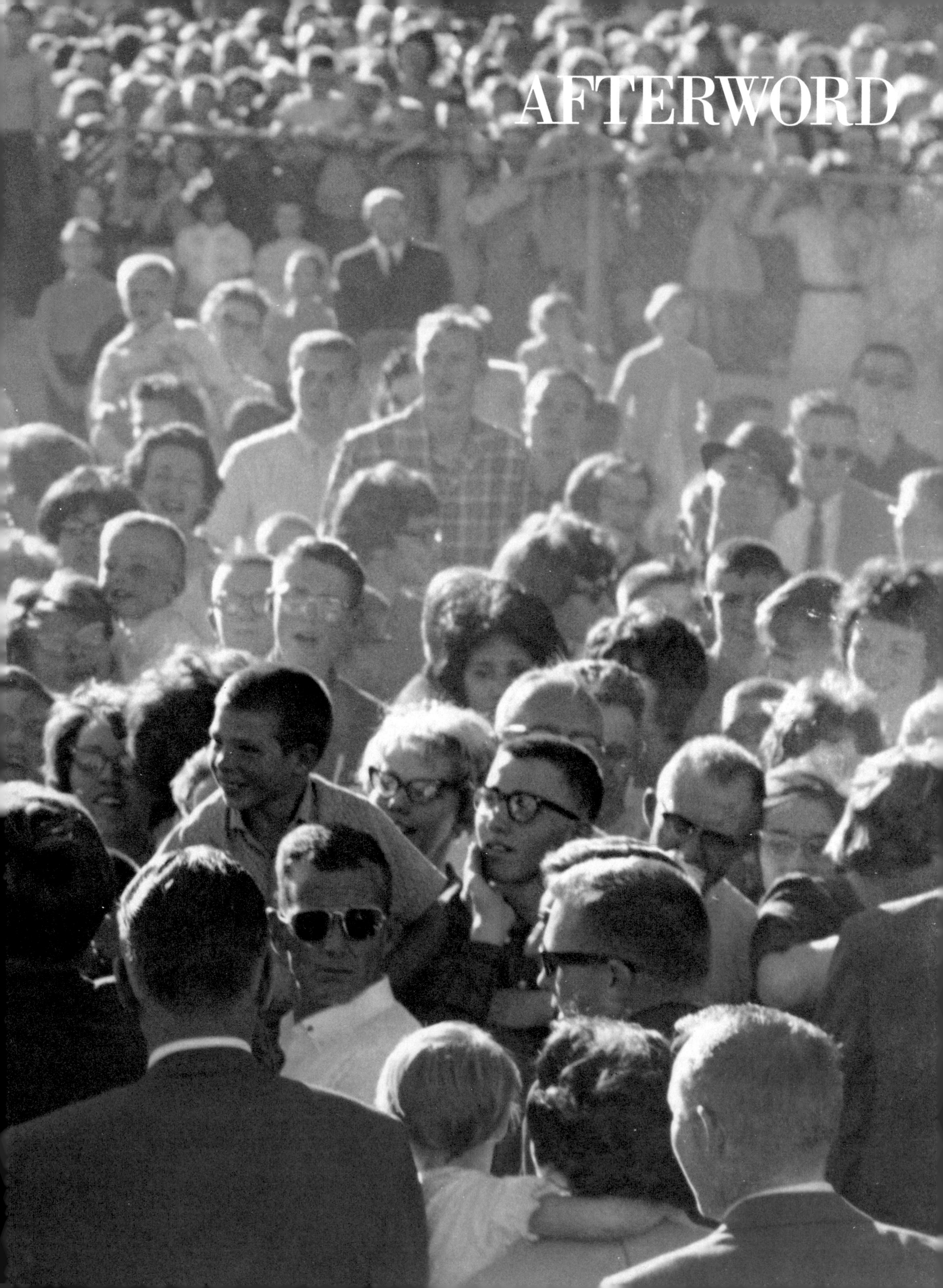

I think something died in all of us with the assassination of John F. Kennedy. Something died in the American spirit. I can remember during the 1960 campaign when he spoke at the University of Michigan, and he asked: "How many young people here tonight are willing to give of yourselves? How many of you are willing to give one or two years of your life to help people abroad?" Of course, that was the whole idea of the Peace Corps. And he could use an idea like that to challenge America. He challenged us to give of ourselves. I think during the years of his presidency we were on our way to becoming a nation with a sense of community, a nation with a sense of family.

JOHN LEWIS

We really never knew how different life was then until it was over. The murder in Dallas was, for me, the worst experience of my life. A personal experience. And I think for the artistic community, the whole American community, for that matter. But for thinking people and working artists, I had the feeling that at that moment, everybody became aware of how excited and happy they had been. There had been a good deal of talk about it during the administration when he was alive. The excitement of how different the White House was . . . the new steps that were being taken with the cultural center and the rest. But I don't think we all realized to what extent we were involved in it and to what an extent America had a new image and a new promise for the artist until he was killed. Then it dawned on us like a very bleak dawn. And I must say it's never been the same since.

LEONARD BERNSTEIN, Composer and Conductor

Again and again in the back streets of Calcutta, New Delhi, and other cities of India, and this [was] March 1965, I would run across stalls where there had been posted pictures . . . of Gandhi, Nehru, and of gods. And almost invariably along with those pictures was a picture of John F. Kennedy. Right along with Nehru and Gandhi and the gods. And I was walking up above Naples . . . and ran across a little shrine, a nativity scene set in the wall . . . and in the corner down there was a picture of John F. Kennedy in navy uniform. . . .

JAMES MacGREGOR BURNS, Educator and Kennedy Biographer

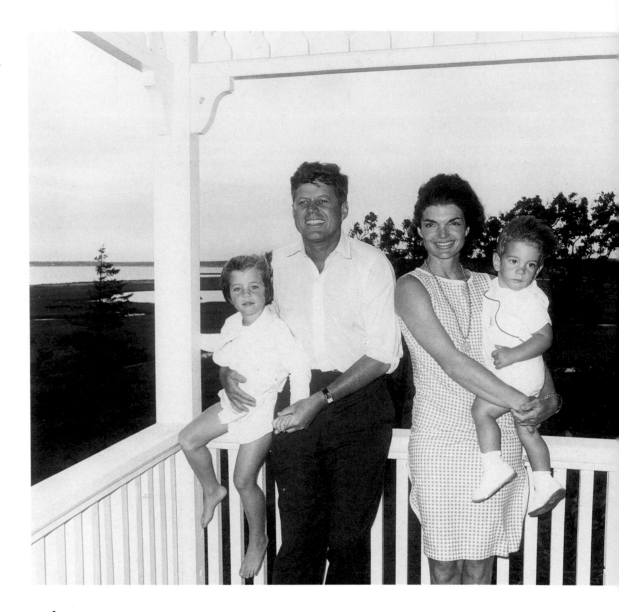

After the assassination, early in '64, I went with Sarge Shriver on a round-the-world trip. We were astounded by the affection for John Kennedy that we ran into everywhere. In Nepal, one young man said to me, "With the death of Kennedy, they have taken away our youth."
WALTER RIDDER, Chief, Washington Bureau, Ridder Newspapers

No one can say the turmoil of the sixties would not have happened if JFK had not been killed, or that it would not have happened had he been reelected president in 1964. But violence begets violence, and such a violent act begat the assassinations of two more leaders. The students at the universities began protesting, burning flags, setting fires, even blowing up buildings.

CHARLOTTE COTE

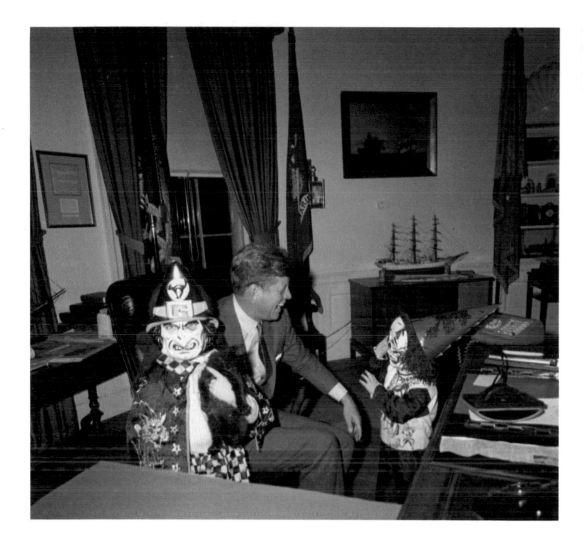

Kennedy's obvious affection and concern for his own children confirmed for people that he shared with them a common hope for the future.

The sudden death of a powerful figure can undermine people's sense of their personal safety. On one level, they're saying to themselves, "If this could happen to someone who's so powerful, and in control and protected, what could happen to me?" And, in fact, this helps explain people's desire to believe the assassination was part of a conspiracy. People were quite reluctant to believe that Lee Harvey Oswald acted alone. The notion that one guy could be crazy and could kill the most powerful man in the world was terrifying. The conspiracy theory gave some people more security, because they could then better understand the event.

THERESE A. RANDO

I don't think the assassination was the turning point that a lot of people do. Even though the country did feel something special about Kennedy, and even though it was the first of a number of assassinations and tragedies to come, I think that Kennedy has been mythologized and romanticized to an incredible degree in the last 25 years. At the time it was a terribly, terribly wrenching event, and I don't want to minimize that. But I think part of the mythologizing has been to make a turning point out of that assassination. But by 1963 the civil rights movement was already under way, and we were involved in Vietnam. We were already on the road to the chaos of the late sixties. Things were already in motion.

BARRY HOBERMAN

Lyndon Johnson was extraordinary; he did everything he could to be magnanimous, to be kind. It must have been very difficult for him. I don't know exactly how long [it was] before I could move. I moved out of the White House as quickly as I could, but it was a period of about [ten days or so]. . . . Now that I look back on it, I think I should have gotten out the next—I didn't have any place to go. . . .

I suppose one was in a state of shock, packing up. But President Johnson made you feel that you and your children [could stay], a great courtesy to a woman in distress.

It's funny what you do in a state of shock. I remember going over to the Oval Office to ask him for two things. They were two things I thought I would like to ask him as a favor.

One was to name the space center in Florida "Cape Kennedy." Now that I think back on it, that was so wrong, and if I'd known it [Cape Canaveral] was the name from the time of Columbus, it would be the last thing that Jack would have wanted. The reason I asked was, I can remember this first speech Jack made in Texas was that there would be a rocket one day that would go to the moon. I kept thinking, "That's going to be forgotten, and his dreams are going to be forgotten." I had this terrible fear then that he'd be forgotten, and I thought, "Well, maybe they'll remember someday that this man did dream that. . . ."

And the other one, which is so trivial, was: there were plans for the renovation of Washington, and there was this commission, and I thought it might come to an end. I asked President Johnson if he'd be nice enough to receive the commission and sort of give approval to the work they were doing, and he did. It was one of the first things he did. . . .

I almost felt sorry for him [President Johnson], because I knew he felt sorry for me. There wasn't anything anyone could do about it, but I think the situation gave him pain, and he tried to do the best he could. And he did, and I was really touched by that generosity of spirit. . . . I always felt that about him. . . .

JACQUELINE KENNEDY

Sure, I thought Lyndon Johnson would have trouble trying to fill John Kennedy's shoes. On a surface level, he wore brown suits and wide belts. He didn't have John Kennedy's sense of style. But he took care of civil rights in a hurry. Lyndon Johnson was a very smart man, and he knew the way to avoid being a southern senator in the White House was to be for civil rights. And he did that, and did it very effectively. The truth of the matter is that I don't believe John Kennedy would have ever passed that civil rights bill.

CHARLES WELTNER

If you look at both John and Robert Kennedy you sense that history was changing them. Both men moved to the left in their adult political lives, and their capacity to do so was unique. History and events were forcing them to move in that direction—the civil rights movement, and then later the antiwar movement for Robert. So I'm not sure the proper question is whether John Kennedy would have changed the course of history had he lived, but rather, how much history would have changed John Kennedy. To what degree would the unfolding of events in Vietnam have challenged his cold war mentality? Would the bad news have changed him enough to force him to make different decisions than Johnson made? That's something we'll never know.

LENI WILDFLOWER

I think it's a fair statement that it would have been extremely difficult for President Kennedy to have passed the kind of legislation that President Johnson got through. And again, you have to read it against the tragedy of President Kennedy's death that the nation moved a little more quickly on some of these things. That may have been a real part of it. I mean, martyrdom has a strong force on anybody's mentality and attitudes. . . . [As] someone said, after President Kennedy got shot, people thought a little bit harder about what the stakes were in America and what this kind of hatred led to, and it changed a lot of people's minds.

REVEREND THEODORE HESBURGH

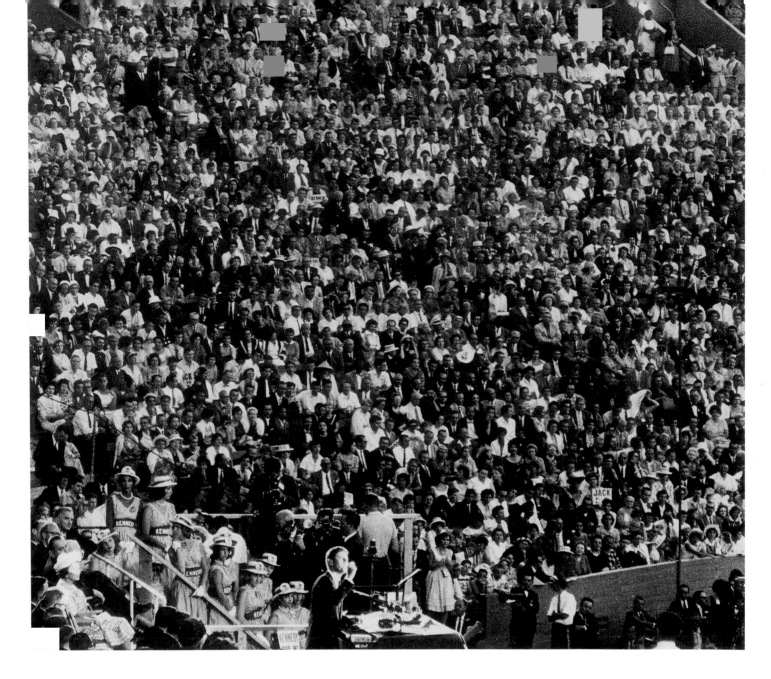

The rapt crowd that listened to the nominee's acceptance speech at the 1960 Democratic Convention in Los Angeles was an early witness to the merging of words and images that would find, in three brief years, an almost magical welcome from America and the world.

I was elected to Congress in 1962, a successful year for Republicans. Kennedy was considered to be neither strong nor popular, so Republicans did very well. In 1963, it looked as if all of his major programs were doomed.

The assassination changed the political complexion of the times. It put all of the Kennedy initiatives in a different perspective.

There was a big difference between the way Kennedy handled his job and the way LBJ handled his. I only met Kennedy once. He did not tend to invite Congressmen and their families to the White House. With LBJ, we, all of us—Republicans and Democrats alike—were frequent guests at the White House, meeting Lady Bird, Lucy, and Lynda. President Kennedy and his wife did not reach out in this fashion.

I served under six presidents. Kennedy was not one of the most effective of them. In the changed climate following the assassination, Lyndon Johnson made the Kennedy legacy a reality.

ROBERT McCLORY, Congressman from Illinois

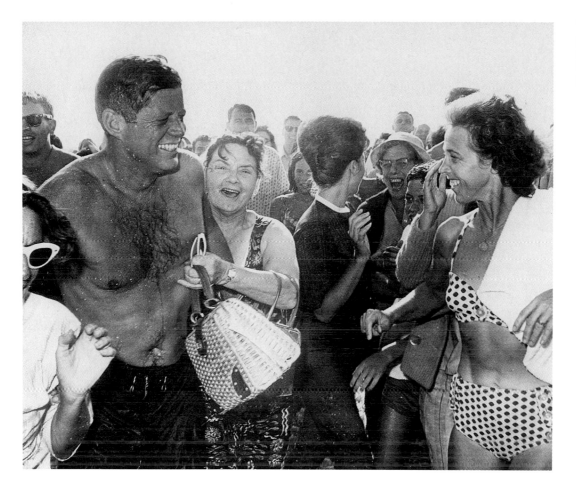

The president's physical appearance was for many the best evidence that the torch had indeed been passed to a new generation.

I think that President Kennedy had a capacity both to attract and [to] compel a certain kind of devotion . . . that would go beyond the ordinary. I think he had a way perhaps of reaching and leading the country, not the Congress maybe, but the country, that others have not had.

I think had he not been assassinated, we might not have had as much turmoil and dissension in this country, because of that capacity to . . . command the interest of the country and to get the majority of people to believe in the nation's leadership. I'm one who, for example, thinks President Kennedy . . . would not have gone into Vietnam, because I think he would have recognized the fact that there was a high degree of possibility that this would tear the country apart, and he was very sensitive to that in a way that I think President Johnson was not.

STEWART UDALL,
Secretary of the Interior

He seemed to reinvigorate us in our questing for meaning and beauty in the short passage of life. He seemed to understand the basic adventuring spirit of America, the eagerness to try and do things, and take risks to create a better and more meaningful life.

I think we need landmarks or benchmarks in our personal history. They are emotional and cognitive pegs on which we hang our memories: the birth of our children, the death of loved ones, certain school experiences, taking trips—and JFK's death, was certainly a peg on which we hung much of our memories of the time.

I think if you went to any generation they'd say, "Oh, I wish I were back in simpler times," and often it's the time they were growing up. So much of it is nostalgia and dream, but it capped the carefree fifties and moved us into serious issues we had to confront in this country. And after his death we seemed to fall from this grace to enter a period of self-doubt, national dissension, political ambiguity, sleazy leadership, with wars at home on our streets and campuses and wars abroad. His death itself brought us to confront the deepest divisions in the American psyche, that creative, positive, beautiful, and healthy side versus the violent and destructive side.

I'm not certain lots of people would cry now at the recollection. . . . I think people in their fifties might. Younger people still view him as a hero—he has entered a different level of history and—but I don't think they would feel the emotion; I think the emotion may be fading, or it's not translating down to younger generations. Now they see him more as someone who was a great hero, a person of courage and singularity and all of those things, but I think the moist eyes are going to be more and more restricted to those people who were there and saw it at the time.

FRANK FARLEY, Professor Psychology, University of Wisconsin

What he symbolized was the possibility that we could do anything. It was a time when we were optimistic, when we had control over our destiny. We used to think we could solve any problem, and now we don't think we can. We've lost that sense of control that he gave us. He was youthful and exhuberant, and witty, and wealthy, and he had it all. He was like a young prince in whom one could invest. I think his youth was important, because one could think that there was plenty of future ahead, but that was cut down so that the assassination in one blow quashed the future. There is a psychological reaction to catastrophe when people's whole neighborhood is burning and they lose their house in a fire, or when a village is wiped out in war. There's often a crumbling of the psyche, a feeling of listlessness and hopelessness after a sudden catastrophe that's overwhelming.

ROBERT ABELSON

The quiet humility with which [Kennedy] accepted victory in the Cuban missile crisis and went on to find the moment for the American University speech; his performance during the Bay of Pigs recovery; "Ich bin ein Berliner"; or the low-key grace with which he danced through Ireland. These were transcendent things. I don't know how to talk or write about this kind of transcendent quality. But it was there; and it was a kind of extra dimension.

Kennedy had become what everyone wanted for the president of the United States—the leader of the world—to be at this moment in history. That is why, quite aside from personal loss, there has remained in all of us the sense of a truly diminished world.

WALT W. ROSTOW

He lifted us up. That's the thing. He brought out the best in us. Some people diminish you. He brought out the best because he was so secure as a human being. He had such a sense of principles. He was always willing to do what was right.

ESTHER PETERSON

Kennedy used to think of Theodore Roosevelt, who accomplished much more in his second term than in his first. That gave him hope. The civil rights bill was making progress, and the tax cut, and he wanted to accompany the tax cut with the War on Poverty, which he had directed William Slayton [Commissioner of the Urban Renewal Administration] and Lyndon Johnson to carry forward.

Johnson was able to get the domestic program through because he picked up about 40 Democratic seats in the House, thereby creating for the first time since 1938 a working majority for progressive legislation. Kennedy would have beaten Goldwater by an even bigger margin than Johnson and would have picked up even more seats in the House of Representatives, and therefore would have had the votes to get the programs through.

I think that had he lived, we would have avoided a good deal of the turmoil of the 1960s. I think a lot of the sense of alienation that the young people had was due to the assassination.

ARTHUR SCHLESINGER, JR.

It was only about six weeks after Kennedy's death that the Beatle fervor hit in the United States. I think that there's a connection between those two events. America was really looking for something to be joyful about. Before Kennedy's assassination the Beatles had already been on the Jack Paar show—a tape of them. But it wasn't until the very end of December that you started hearing lots of Beatles' songs on the radio. My final memory of '63 would be that I was listening to Beatles songs. I think part of the joy and excitement and celebration that greeted the Beatles was part of the healing process—it was part of a post assassination catharsis for the whole country.

BARRY HOBERMAN

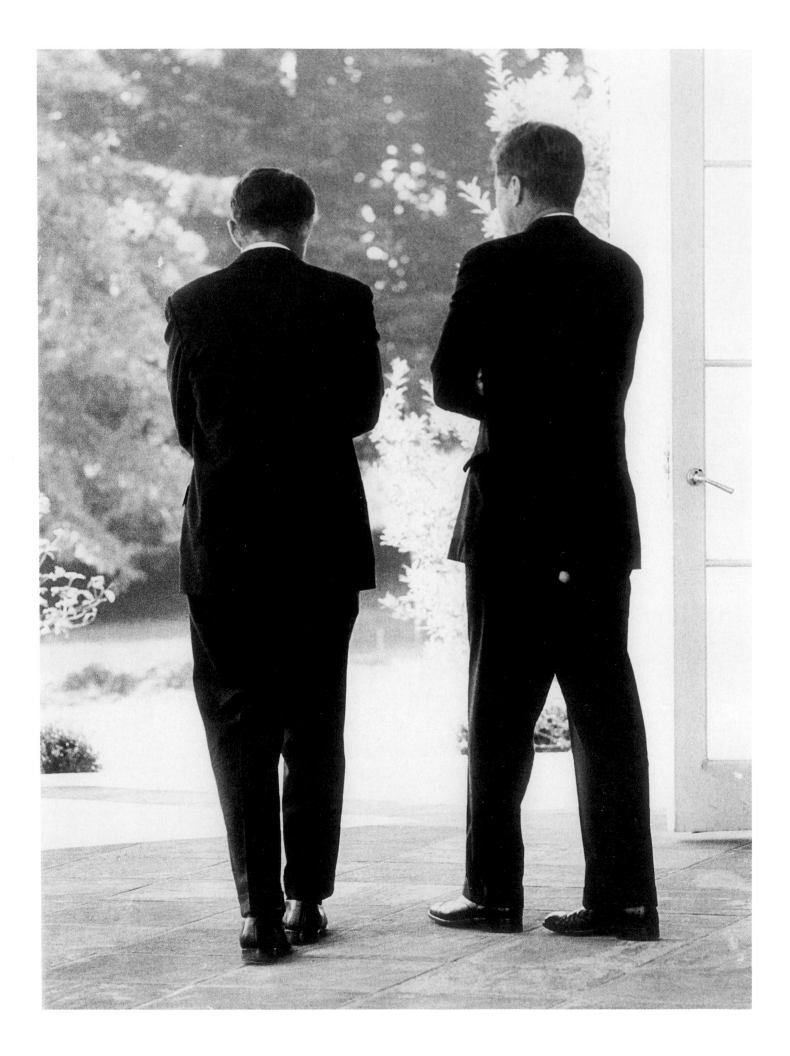

INDEX

ACKNOWLEDGMENTS

Most of the interviews appearing in the preceding pages were excerpted from original interviews conducted for this book or from oral histories conducted by the John F. Kennedy Library. We would like to thank Tim Wells for his valuable assistance in identifying interview subjects and conducting a number of the interviews. We would also like to express our thanks to the Kennedy Library, for use of excerpts from its oral history collection, and to the library staff, who provided expert and cordial assistance during the research process.

In addition, the publisher gratefully acknowledges use of excerpts from the following sources:

p. 30, **Joan Baez:** from Joan Baez, *And A Voice to Sing With* (New York: Summit Books, 1987); pp. 31, 219, 221, **Roger Wilkins:** from Roger Wilkins, *A Man's Life* (New York. Simon & Schuster, 1982); pp. 35, 128, **Glenn Seaborg:** from "Remarks by Glenn T. Seaborg at the International Scientific Symposium on a Nuclear Test Ban, Jan. 16, 1988"; p. 45, **Sidney Poitier:** from Sidney Poitier, *This Life* (New York: Knopf, 1980); p. 51, **Pete Rose:** from Pete Rose, *The Pete Rose Story: An Autobiography* (New York: World, 1970); p. 61, **Marilyn Bender Altschul:** from Marilyn Bender Altschul, *The Beautiful People* (New York: Coward-McCann, 1967); p. 85, 102, **Arthur Schlesinger Jr.** and p. 161, **William P. Bundy:** from *The Kennedy Presidency: Seventeen Intimate Perspectives of John F. Kennedy*, Kenneth W. Thompson, ed. (Lanham, Md.: University Press of America, 1985); pp.

66, 103, 135, 137, 147, **Dick Gregory:** from Dick Gregory, *Nigger: An Autobiography* (New York: Dutton, 1964); page 166, Dick Gregory: from Andrew J. Edelstein, *The Pop Sixties* (New York: World Almanac, 1985); p. 69, **Alistair Cooke:** from *Show* magazine, April 1963; p. 106, **Lillian Roxon:** from *Lillian Roxon's Rock Encyclopedia*, Ed Naha, ed. (New York: Grosset & Dunlap, 1978); p. 116, **J. Edward Day:** from J. Edward Day, *My Appointed Round* (New York: Holt, Rinehart & Winston, 1965); p. 123, **Peter Selz:** from Peter Selz, *Art in Our Times: A Pictorial History 1890–1980* (New York: Harcourt Brace Jovanovich, 1981); p. 127, **Gary Koerselman:** from Gary Koerselman, *The Lost Decade* (New York: Peter Lang, 1987); p. 134, **James Meredith:** from James Meredith, *Three Years In Mississippi* (Bloomington, Ind.: Indiana University Press, 1966); p. 136, **Emily Rock:** from William L.

Katz, *Eyewitness: The Negro in American History* (New York: Pitman, 1971); p. 187 et seq.: **Robert MacNeil:** from Robert MacNeil, *The Right Place at the Right Time* (Boston: Little Brown, 1982); p. 189, **Bill Moyers;** p. 193, **Rufus Youngblood;** p. 199, **Merriman Smith;** p. 200, **Liz Carpenter:** all from Merle Miller, *Lyndon: An Oral Biography* (New York: Putnam, 1980); p. 185 and 226: **Lawrence O'Brien:** from Lawrence F. O'Brien, *No Final Victories* (New York: Doubleday, 1974); pp. 192, 198, **Lady Bird Johnson:** from Lady Bird Johnson, *White House Diary* (New York: Holt, Rinehart & Winston, 1970); p. 204, **George Ball:** from George Ball, *The Past Has Another Pattern* (New York: Norton, 1982); p. 219, **John Kenneth Galbraith:** from John Kenneth Galbraith, *Ambassador's Journal* (New York. Houghton-Mifflin, 1969).

INDEX OF INTERVIEWEES

PHOTO CREDITS

The photographs and cartoons in this book were provided courtesy of the following:

BLACK-AND-WHITE PHOTO CREDITS

Bob Adelman: p. 80/81—© 1963. Photograph by Bob Adelman.

Associated Press/Wide World: pp. 14/15; 16; 17 (2); 23 (2); 25 (1); 30; 31; 34; 35 (1); 41 (1); 42 (1); 49 (1); 51 (1); 56; 59; 70 (1); 71 (1); 73 (1); 74 (1); 75 (1); 76 (1); 77 (1); 82 (1); 84/85; 92 (1); 93; 96/97; 99 (1); 101 (1); 103 (2); 105; 106; 114 (1); 119 (1); 120 (1); 123; 128 (1); 130 (1); 127 (1); 135 (1); 137 (1); 139; 142; 143; 146 (1); 147; 156 (2); 157; 160 (1); 162 (1); 161 (1); 166 (1); 179 (1); 182 (1); 184 (1); 196; 197 (1); 199 (1); 200; 201 (1); 202 (1); 203 (2); 204 (1); 205 (1); 206; 211 (1); 217 (1); 219; 221 (1); 229; 234 (1).

Billboard Publications, Inc.: p. 170; 72—"Hot 100" and Billboard are registered trademarks of Billboard Publications, Inc. Charts copyright © 1963 Billboard Publications, Inc. Reprinted by permission.

Black Star: p. 36—Photograph by Steve Shapiro.

Howard Frank: pp. 18 (1); 57; 76 (1); 119 (1).

Stanley P. Friedman Collection: pp. 112 (1); 176 (1).

Globe Photos: p. 246.

Jim Greene: Endpapers—*John F. Kennedy Cards.* Montage by Jim Greene. Courtesy of the collection of Howard Greenburg.

James H. Karales: p. 150—Photograph copyright © 1963 James H. Karales. pp. 154/155 Photograph copyright © 1963 James H. Karales.

John F. Kennedy Library: pp. 78 (1); 145; 153; 176 (1); 241.

James Kotsilibas Davis Collection: pp. 58; 64 (1); 91 (1); 122; 152.

Life Magazine: p. 44—© 1963 Time, Inc. Photograph by Jim Mahan.

Lincoln Center Library: pp. 24 (1); 38; 92 (1); 100; 130 (1); 164 (1); 171 (1).

Magnum Photos: p. 235—Copyright © 1964 Magnum Photos. Photography by Elliott Erwitt.

Museum of Modern Art: pp. 128 (1); 132 (1); 167.

National Aeronautics and Space Administration: p. 183.

The New Yorker Magazine, Inc.: p. 24—Drawing by Chon Day, © 1963; p. 43—Drawing by Alan Dunn, © 1963; p. 55—Drawing by Whitney Darrow, Jr., © 1963; p. 78—Drawing by Lorenz, © 1963; p. 91—Drawing by O'Brian, © 1963; p. 107—Drawing by Robt. Day, © 1963; p. 117—Drawing by Weber, © 1963; p. 159—Drawing by Alan Dunn, © 1963.

New York Racing Association, Inc.: p. 64 (1).

Reuters/Bettmann: p. 114 (1).

United Press International/Bettmann: pp. 2/3; 6; 18 (2); 19 (1); 21; 22; 25 (1); 28; 29; 35; 39; 41 (1); 40 (1); 41 (1); 42 (1); 43 (2); 44 (1); 46/47; 48; 49 (1); 50; 51 (1); 55 (1); 60; 61; 64 (1); 65; 66; 67; 69; 70 (1); 71 (1); 73 (1); 74 (1); 75 (1); 77 (1); 79; 82 (2); 83; 86; 87; 88; 89; 90; 95; 98; 99 (1); 101 (1); 102; 103 (1); 104; 107 (1); 108; 109; 112 (2); 113; 116; 117 (2); 120 (1); 122; 126; 127 (1); 131; 132 (1); 133; 134; 136; 137 (1); 138; 146 (2); 148; 150 (2); 156 (1); 158; 159 (2); 160 (1); 161; 162 (1); 163; 164 (2); 166 (1); 172/173; 174; 175; 177; 178; 179 (1); 180; 182 (1); 183 (1); 184 (1); 185; 186; 187; 190; 192; 194; 195; 197 (1); 198; 199 (1); 201 (1); 202 (1); 203 (1); 204 (1); 205 (1); 207; 208; 209; 210; 211 (1); 213; 214; 216; 217 (1); 218 (2); 221 (1); 224 (1); 225; 227; 231; 234 (1); 236/237; 245; 249.

United States Information Agency: p. 19.

WGBH Educational Foundation: p. 40 (1).

COLOR PHOTO CREDITS

Hanna Barbera: pp. 32–33

Leo Castelli Gallery, New York City: p. 54—*Flatten Sand Fleas:* painting by Roy Lichtenstein. (1962); p. 55—*Marilyn Monroe:* silkscreen by Andy Warhol. (1962); p. 73—*Three Flags:* painting by Jaspar Johns. (1958). Collection of the

Whitney Museum of American Art. 50th Anniversary Gift of the Gilman Foundation, Inc., The Lauder Foundation, A. Alfred Taubman, an anonymous donor and purchase.; p. 130—*False Start:* painting by Jaspar Johns. (1959); p. 171—*Factum II:* painting by Robert Rauschenberg. (1957); p. 176—*Femme au Chapeau:* painting by Roy Lichtenstein. (1957).

Ford Motor Company: pp. 62/63; 92

Howard Frank: pp. 20; 34; 100; 113; 133; 148; 158; 175 (1).

Gaslight: pp. 16; 36; 56; 58; 93; 99; 115; 118 (1); 121; 131 (1); 144; 152; 167; 188.

Globe Photos: p. 175 (1).

Jim Greene: pp. 165.

Jay Hirsch: pp. 21; 116; 135; 156.

John F. Kennedy Library: pp. 26/27; 110/111; 127 (2); 140/141; 144 (1); 153; 163; 169; 178; 238/239; 242.

James Kotsilibas Davis Collection: pp. 45; 104.

J.R. MacDonald International Corporation: pp. 52/53.

Magnum Photos: pp. 118 (1); 124/125; 136; 151.

Memory Shop: p. 151.

Museum of Modern Art, New York City: p. 123.

National Cash Register: p. 106. Courtesy of NCR Corporation.

Marvin Newman: pp. 69; 79; 109; 220; 224; 226; 230; 232/233.

Publisher's Collection: pp. 24; 61; 91; 107; 122; 145; 179.

Silver Screen: p. 18.

United Press International/Bettmann: pp. 94; 149 (2); 157; 188/189; 193 (2); 212; 215; 222/223; 228/229.

Vogue: p. 38—Copyright © 1963 by the Conde Nast Publications. Photograph by Louis Faurer; p. 131—Copyright © 1963 by the Conde Nast Publications. Photograph by Horst; p. 141—Copyright © 1963 by the Conde Nast Publications. Cover photo by Burt Stern; p. 180—Copyright © 1963 by the Conde Nast Publications. Photographs by Gene Laurents.

Henry Wolf: p. 68

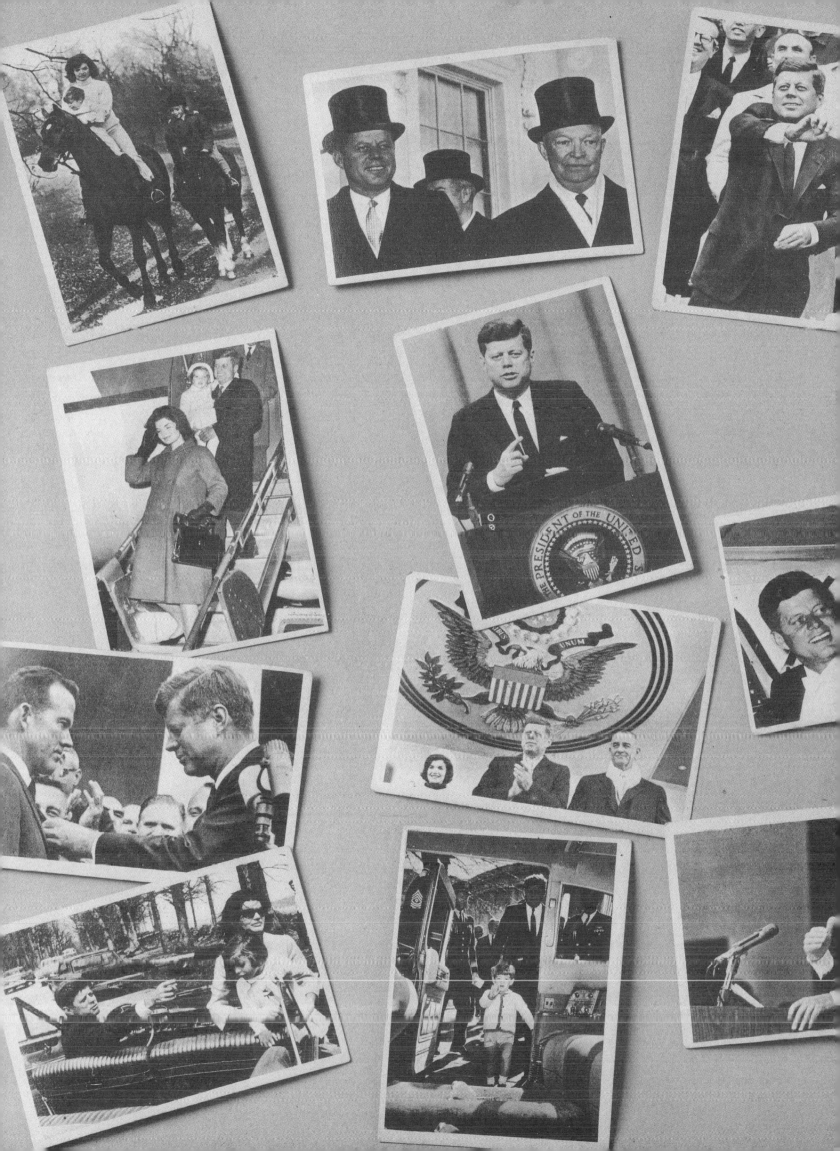